STATE AUTHORITY,
INDIGENOUS AUTONOMY

STATE AUTHORITY, INDIGENOUS AUTONOMY

CROWN–MAORI RELATIONS IN NEW ZEALAND/AOTEAROA 1900–1950

RICHARD S HILL

VICTORIA UNIVERSITY PRESS

VICTORIA UNIVERSITY PRESS
Victoria University of Wellington
PO Box 600, Wellington

ISBN 0 86473 477 8

First published 2004

Published wih the assistance of a grant from the
History Group of the Ministry for Culture and Heritage

National Library of New Zealand Cataloguing-in-Publication Data
Hill, Richard S.
State authority, indigenous autonomy : Crown-Maori relations in
New Zealand/Aotearoa 1900-1950 / Richard S. Hill.
Includes bibliographical references and index.
ISBN 0-86473-477-8
1. Self-determination, National—New Zealand. 2. Maori (New
Zealand people)—Ethnic identity. 3. Maori (New Zealand
people)—Government relations—History. 4. Maori (New Zealand
people)—Politics and government—20th century. 5. New
Zealand—History. I. Title.
323.1199442—dc 22

Printed by PrintLink, Wellington

CONTENTS

for
Aaron, Rosa and Emma

PREFACE

This interpretation of Crown–Maori relations in the first half of the twentieth century was first generally expressed in a report for the Treaty of Waitangi resolution processes.[1] The report, commissioned by a Treaty claims funding agency, the Crown Forestry Rental Trust, provided an overview of Maori quests for rangatiratanga/autonomy in the twentieth century and the Crown's responses to them. A number of readers suggested wider dissemination of its arguments. Undertaking this required extensive reworking and expansion of the original text, which had been limited by considerations of time and terms of reference. The Marsden Fund kindly provided support for the revising process, and this book – a greatly expanded and fundamental rewriting of the first half of the report – is one result. While the thrust of the report's arguments remains intact, the book is a quite different product and should be seen as completely superseding it. I thank the Trust and the Fund for their support in assisting me to fulfil long-held research plans, and the History Group of the Ministry of Culture and Heritage for supporting publication.

The work examines Crown–Maori relations at a macro level throughout half a century, the Crown being the seamless lego-constitutional controlling authority in New Zealand history since 1840, including executive government and its officials. It does not pretend to offer any analysis of – in the words of a scholar who chooses to 'privilege' the 'vantage point of the colonized' – Maori 'ways of knowing, our imagery, the things we create and produce'. Nor does the book set out to advocate for one side or the other in the Crown–Maori relationship. Its analyses of why the Crown acted as it did are intended to explain – not to explain away – those actions. Equally the book is not a pakeha (white/'European'/non-Maori) equivalent of writings by Maori scholars who have been inspired by, as well as their own people's struggles, works such as Brazilian educator Paulo Freire's *Pedagogy of the Oppressed* – which is dedicated to 'the oppressed, and to those who suffer with them and fight at their side' – or Frantz Fanon's *The Wretched of the Earth*. It avoids judgments such as that of a 1940 assessment that the 'history of the State's dealing in Maori lands is a sad story that makes the heart sick'.[2]

I leave it to readers to decide whether their heart is sick at the events about which they read, or whether the book can or should be used as 'an instrument of liberation'. I simply note here that in recent years scholars, both pakeha and Maori, have been emphasising Maori agency in the struggle against Crown expropriationist and other policies; and that, as a result, Maori have gained extra knowledge and tools in their ongoing attempts to fight assimilationist tendencies and regain rangatiratanga. But it is not, in the historiographical tradition to which I adhere, the task of the scholar to attempt to proselytise or guide. While 'objectivity' is most certainly a problematic and now (correctly) much-interrogated concept, this book *strives* to be objective; if it were consciously a 'subjective' account, it might be a very different work. Moreover, although believing it essential to examine critically many of what have long been regarded as historical 'truths', I do not subscribe to an extreme postmodernist position that denies the existence of *any* facts or truths (and therefore the ability of scholars to find or relate them). If I did, I would not have taken the trouble to write the book.

To help make its scope containable, the work omits significant dimensions, particularly the class relations which are so integral to structured inequality. On the surface it might seem to perpetuate something for which a North American observer has recently criticised modern New Zealand scholarship: an oversimplification whereby society 'is seen to be organised bi-culturally'. However, while I am very conscious of the primal importance of class relations in a capitalist society, and the significance of subjects (including other cultures and ethnicities) that do not fit within a binary model, this book is about something else: politico-cultural relations between Maori and state leaderships, in the context of the ongoing Maori assertion of rangatiratanga and the Crown's various responses to this. Moreover, while I have some sympathy with a Maori historian's call for a 'reconceptualisation of bicultural politics in Aotearoa/ New Zealand', I note that this assertion was made in the context of a conscious 'project of a counter-hegemonic cultural politics'. This gives me occasion to repeat that this book is not intended as a contribution to 'activist history', although it may provide evidence for those seeking change. Suffice it to say here that the institutions it covers are often sites of both *control of* and *opportunity for* Maori, and that knowledge of how this has occurred in the past may guide actions in the future.[3]

The text is based on a large corpus of research material, secondary and primary. In an attempt to avoid excessive numbers of endnotes and with a general readership in mind, I have omitted citing most archival sources and secondary references not readily accessible to the public. The endnotes reflect the nature of the work as an interpretive survey. Each endnote is a composite covering the text following the previous endnote. The references have several purposes: indications of key works which have informed the text of the preceding passages, sources of specific pieces of information or citation, pointers to areas of focus for further or related reading, and (in the case of multiple citings) a means of assisting the reader to follow through themes. I have avoided personalised engagement with fellow historians, in order not to distract from the focus and flow of the work. But I do sketch broad historiographical agreements and disagreements, and reference to the endnotes will assist further pursuit of such issues.

Some of the coverage of Crown–Maori negotiations reflects government-held archival evidence viewed during my experiences of working in the resolution of historical Treaty of Waitangi grievances from 1989, the year the Crown took new policy directions, including exploring the concept of direct negotiations with tribal groupings. Other coverage reflects material I have had access to as Director of the Treaty of Waitangi Research Unit at Victoria University of Wellington. Some small portions of the book incorporate oral testimony from Maori who have preferred to remain unreferenced, and general guidance on this and other cultural matters was kindly provided, right up to his death in 2003, by the Research Unit's greatly missed Kaumatua, Tamihana Te Winitana.

I have had many discussions with friends and colleagues both on the issues canvassed in the text and on history and scholarship in general, most frequently with Professor James Belich and Drs David Pearson and Brigitte Bönisch-Brednich. As with my previous projects, I have been warmly supported and encouraged by my now-adult children, and – as with my very first publication – I dedicate this book to them.

I have benefited from lively discussions with various people at and associated with Victoria University's Stout Research Centre for New Zealand Studies (in which the Treaty of Waitangi Research Unit is located) over the years. Maureen West of the Research Unit has provided valuable back-up assistance, and Stout Research Centre directors Professor Vincent O'Sullivan and Associate Professor Lydia Wevers have given ongoing support. I thank Andrew Mason for his careful and thoughtful editing, and Fergus Barrowman and Sue Brown at Victoria University Press for their encouragement and support.

As well as the above, I owe a debt to others (such as the participants in the 'informal seminars' in various hostelries in Wellington on Friday nights, at which academic subjects are often pursued, at least early in the evening) for discussions which have helped shape the text. However, the responsibility for this preliminary and interpretive general survey, which is intended to promote debate, lies solely with myself. It will be followed by a successor work covering the second half of the twentieth century.

Richard Hill
Victoria University of Wellington

INTRODUCTION

Colonisation was essentially concerned with exploitation of territories and their human and physical resources. Indigenous peoples worldwide have never fully accepted the subsuming of their cultures and polities by those of the imperialist powers and their successor regimes. In the face of colonisation by a coercively superior power, indigenes have struggled to retain as much of their own value systems, resources and socio-political organisation as possible. Some colonising powers, after coming to realise this, believed from time to time that extreme coercion, even up to genocide, was the only way of eliminating politico-cultural resistance. This was both expensive and technologically difficult, as the German state, for example, found in its efforts to physically exterminate the Herero of South-West Africa in the early years of the twentieth century. Thus it was used sparingly. Given the strength and persistence of resistance by subjugated peoples – however powerful the tools involved in their subjection – the colonising powers normally came to appreciate the need for accommodation with them.[4]

The nature of such accommodation frequently allowed indigenes initially to continue their everyday lives much as before under pre-existing social control systems, albeit subject to certain overarching codes of behaviour. This situation was intended to be temporary, pending full 'civilisation' of the indigenous people. But it showed a great propensity to survive, to a greater or lesser degree, albeit in changing forms through history. At times such accommodation, and the ongoing negotiations associated with it, allowed the existence of political, cultural or other types of resurgence among some or all of the indigenous population. These renaissances differed greatly in their degree of support, their focus,

11

their structuring, their frequency and their success. Some indigenous peoples had to wait a very long time for their first significant revival – Australian Aborigines experienced theirs well into the post-colonial period, for example. New Zealand has witnessed many indigenous resurgences in its relatively short colonial and post-colonial history, with the Treaty of Waitangi between chiefs and the Crown in 1840 constituting a major Maori point of reference.[5]

But New Zealand's origins as a 'settler colony' in which immigrants soon outnumbered indigenes (called tangata whenua/'people of the land' as well as Maori) have ensured that the state's accommodations with Maori have always been within strict limits. It is apparent that, all along, 'Maori had never ceased to resist and protest against the spoliation' visited upon them by the pakeha colonisers, an assessment (by a leading scholar) which encapsulates the consensus in the modern historiography of 'race relations' in New Zealand. Much of the evidence lies in relatively inaccessible reports generated by the Treaty of Waitangi claims settlement processes. In reading some such findings, to be sure, one might be forgiven for thinking that Maori had seldom succumbed to the hegemonic behaviours and beliefs desired, encouraged and imposed by the state. Yet it is clear that, through time, the coercive and ideological might of the state has been powerful and effective. That caveat noted, in general terms the paradigm of ongoing protest or resistance in relatively recent historical writing has overturned the ethnocentric 'received wisdom' of previous generations of pakeha historians. Such work can move outside the past comfort zones of pakeha history, showing for example how Maori social structure is endemically adaptive in its responsiveness to internal and external pressures and challenges.[6]

Indigenous peoples have not only persistently resisted the colonising powers' coercive or accommodatory attempts to expropriate their resources and suppress their cultures, but also actively striven to re-establish their own political or other types of autonomy. While such aspirations usually remain relatively fruitless for very long periods, because of the physical and/or hegemonic might of the imperial (or post-colonial) state, they persist nevertheless. The quest to re-establish some of the independence which prevailed before colonisation has been as strong with the indigenes of Aotearoa/New Zealand as elsewhere in colonies and post-colonies. It has generally been fought for in terms of the rangatiratanga promised Maori in the second article of the Treaty of Waitangi. Following the physical suppression of Maori during war (from 1860) and its aftermath, the Crown's assessment in 1886 was that Maori were so defeated and even hegemonised that 'peace and good order' (or, in a term used at the time, a society of 'tranquillised' citizenry) had been achieved. But ever since then Maori have striven for autonomy in the various ways open to them within the parameters of the newly disciplined, and increasingly 'self-disciplining', society. Apparent Maori quiescence for much of the following hundred years was strategic rather than actual – a strategy framed to relate to (even if to undermine or subvert) the ascendant Crown's coercive and hegemonic indigenous policies, with their insistence on the indivisibility of sovereignty.[7]

Rangatiratanga has been interpreted in many ways – chieftainship, tribal control of internal affairs, self-determination, mana Maori motuhake, Maori sovereignty, governance, independence, devolved control by the state, self-management, Maori nationalism, tribal or pan-tribal self-government, and so forth. But for the purposes of this work it is encapsulated in the word 'autonomy'. Its core is the aspiration of a Maori collectivity to 'manage its own affairs, members and possessions'. In the literature it has generally been assumed to refer to the aspirations of tribal or subtribal collectivities, but the struggle to attain rangatiratanga can also reflect the strivings of any descent grouping, from small tribally based units (eg, whanau/extended family), through larger tribal (especially hapu/subtribe and iwi/tribe) and pan-tribal groupings, and ultimately to te iwi Maori (all people identifying as Maori). It can also embody the organisation and aspiration of Maori 'assent groups', ranging from local to national in scope, that have voluntarily come together in non-tribal ways for cultural, social, political, religious, economic or other purposes.

There is considerable evidence to suggest that Maori have frequently regarded the Treaty's endorsement of rangatiratanga as a guarantee to Maori of the type of sovereignty that the Crown saw itself as holding. It seems, at the very least, that for Maori Article Two was in effect an affirmation that two sets of sovereignties could co-exist in some kind of partnership arrangement, a 'declaration of interdependence'. The aptly named book *The Maori Magna Carta* notes with regard to the Treaty that the 'indications are that the chiefs thought they were retaining their own authority over their people according to their customary law'. An implicit, and sometimes explicit, debate over the meanings and balance of rangatiratanga and kawanatanga (a transliteration of 'governorship', conceded by Maori to the Crown in Article One; 'sovereignty' in the English version) has continued intermittently from 1840 to this day. In the last quarter-century or so, this has led to polarisations in society (and scholarship); one infamous Maori manifesto in 1984, for example, pronounced that the 'white way and the Maori way have always been incompatible' and concluded that there could be 'no justice where Maori sovereignty is not acknowledged'.[8]

It is now a commonplace in scholarship that the Treaty's two basic versions embodied such incompatibilities of 'translation' that they meant different things to Maori and Crown – that there were in effect two treaties, the Treaty and Te Tiriti. But whatever the Treaty articles meant to each party, the second article in either language clearly implied at the very least Maori control over affairs Maori, or a significant degree of autonomy. Unifying all such developments is the Maori understanding of the Treaty as (in the words of a prominent Maori jurist) 'nothing like a treaty of surrender'. Rather, it was an agreement for Crown and Maori 'to respect the integrity and authority of the other'. As one historian has put it, it is clear that 'Maori had never considered that the price of Pakeha knowledge was loss of autonomy'. Another concludes that in the Treaty 'the Maori, who first colonized this land and considered it to be theirs, agreed to share power for mutual benefit'. But the promise to respect rangatiratanga (in any of its definitions) has been violated endemically by the Crown: 'almost all land purchases after 1865 were under laws and processes which breached the rangatiratanga' promised in the Treaty, for example. By then, Crown actions or omissions had led a number of tribal groupings to assert their rangatiratanga by taking up arms against the imperial and colonial governments.[9]

While being quick to adopt the new technologies and other 'western' innovations which enhanced their lives, Maori sought at the same time to minimise the damage to their political economy and culture. Not wanting to leave behind completely their own manners, customs and ways of life, even those Maori who were exceedingly adaptive would join the struggle to retain or regain autonomy. As well as groups and communities that had fought the Crown in the Anglo-Maori wars in the 1840s and 1860s, some which had reached accommodation with it also held out for periods in *de facto* or would-be independent states. Even kupapa, broadly defined as Maori who had fought for the Crown, became disillusioned when their tribes suffered similar (or even worse) land and other alienations to those of the 'rebel' or 'neutral' tribes. In 1880 former kupapa leader Major R Keepa/Kemp, for example, established a land trust along the Whanganui River to try to retain tribal land and regional control by chiefs rather than the Crown. He set up carved posts to mark the extent of the area. Most pakeha were banned from going upriver from a point not far from Wanganui, the town which had almost fallen to Titokowaru in the wars.

'No-go' zones, however, became increasingly anachronistic or unviable as the state's coercive machinery gradually but inexorably turned nominal sovereignty into substantive sovereignty. Even the biggest independent area, the King Country, was 'opened up' in the 1880s; even the most 'rebellious' of tribes had then to seek more accommodative ways of retaining key aspects of their own organisational culture. All of the various 'rival sovereignties' eventually came to recognise the massive power imbalance between Crown and Maori. Thus, along with the other groupings, they searched for ways to adapt which retained key elements of Maori culture, sometimes hiding the latter from the imperial gaze. But their ultimate goal was always clear, as exemplified in the 1870s Repudiation Movement in Hawke's Bay: separate institutions to run things that properly belonged, in their eyes, to Maori.

Despite Crown and pakeha assessments to the contrary, then, the struggle for rangatiratanga was never abandoned. In fact, the Crown suppression of Maori autonomy, and Maori resistance to this, became the most fundamental and ongoing relational nexus between state and indigenous people in New Zealand. The Waitangi Tribunal, in its account of the relationship between the state and the Taranaki people, has in effect summed up the thrust of modern historiography on Crown–Maori dynamics as follows: the 'single thread that most illuminates the historical fabric of Maori and Pakeha contact has been the Maori determination to maintain Maori autonomy and the Government's desire to destroy it'.[10]

In one sense it does a disservice to both major historical 'races'/ ethnicities in New Zealand to portray a long and complex relationship so sweepingly and starkly, and this book attempts to avoid a tendency among scholars and others to oversimplify and exaggerate in an effort (however laudable) to 'seek to decolonise their writings'. Yet the bold depiction of endemic friction between Crown and Maori that has emerged in relatively recent historiography was a necessary (and overdue) corrective. It was needed in order to address the ethnocentrism (and at times racism) underpinning historical work in the past in which Maori were first seen as 'troublesome' and then later allowed to fade from view during much of the rest of New Zealand's history. The Tribunal's emphasis on what is in essence the Maori quest for rangatiratanga, and the Crown's negative response to it, reflects this core result of modern historical enquiry. It is central to the story of New Zealand to a degree unrealised by western scholarship only two decades or so ago. But such literature focuses mostly on the nineteenth century. This book's overview of the quest for autonomy, and the state's reactions to it, during the first half of the twentieth century sets out to provide some introductory balance of coverage.[11]

A distinguished head of the Waitangi Tribunal has noted that Treaty matters are, in the final analysis, about possession of *authority*; and that, throughout post-Treaty time, the essence of Maori history reflects 'dogged determination' to assert collective 'identity and autonomy against every obstacle'. In this struggle, which began almost before the ink on the Treaty was dry, the Crown's access to the mighty resources of the British Empire meant that Maori strategies and tactics needed great subtlety if they were to have even partial success. They needed to be adaptive (especially by incorporating aspects of 'western systems' of actions and belief) as well as resistant, especially after the late 1850s when the pakeha population surpassed that of the tangata whenua and armed resistance was soon to be crushed.

Adaptation thereafter came in a multitude of structural combinations and recombinations, micro and macro, a continual seeking of ways of ensuring that the fundamentals of Maori beliefs, institutions and customs were not totally swamped. The nineteenth-century quest for rangatiratanga, then, entailed exploring many and varied possibilities relating to a separate role for Maori within settler society and under the overarching power of the state. This search underwrote the great majority of all Maori political movements from the middle to the end of the century. The 'politics of autonomy' at that time generally combined traditional tribal organisation with adaptive action, aiming to preserve as much of Maori lifestyles, customs and culture as was possible within the 'parameters of control' of the settler state.

This book, examining the same struggle after 1900, takes into account the complications and contradictions of the interrelationship between the Crown and Maori. While this was a mostly 'post-colonial' century, insofar as New Zealand ceased to be a colony in 1907, Maori still largely regarded themselves – with good reason – as a colonised and subjugated people within the Dominion of New Zealand and its independent successor. Some tribes were speaking of continuing raupatu (confiscation) well over a century after the Crown had stopped seizing lands confiscated from them under 1860s legislation. Many Maori groupings, in fact, see 'ongoing colonisation' and raupatu occurring up to the present time, as the 2003–4 debate over ownership and control of the foreshore and seabed once again emphasised.

One reason for the relative historiographical neglect of Crown–Maori and (more broadly) race relations in the twentieth century is the general absence of dramatic events of armed conflict between Maori and pakeha. Maori marginalisation through the century was underpinned by modes of state control less overtly coercive, more subtle, than those of the early years of the colony. In response, methods of resistance to the Crown's plans for a subsumed Maoridom became more benign and disparate. Changing demographic and socio-economic circumstances added further subtleties and varieties to the mix. Unmistakably, however, all through the century the state attempted to defuse Maori organisings and proposals which involved or seemed to involve any meaningful degree of self-determination: 'any indication of a separatist trend in Maori society has been strongly resented and opposed'.

With the rapid widening of intellectual horizons in the western world from the 1960s, historians tended to turn their attention away from traditional history's focus on 'great men' (especially politicians and statesman) and their deeds. Refreshingly, the trend was instead towards investigating the lives of people (or 'the people') and their social and economic environments. This helped ensure a much higher profile for the ongoing Maori effort to resist subjugation and build alternatives to it. Eventually, however, so much attention was being paid to restoring 'agency' to people marginalised or oppressed by power structures or dominant cultures that the machinery and methods which controlled and contained them tended to be overlooked or dismissed as irrelevant.

More recently, while rightly retaining an emphasis on people's life experiences, there has been some scholarly effort to 'put the state back in'. Much more is needed on this subject. In studies of empire, resistance in colonised societies has come to the fore and redressed an imbalance (or even hiatus) in traditional historiography. But the fact that tribal societies were colonised and exploited by various means that were essentially based on the coercive force of the state is seldom explored in any significant way. Scholarly attention is needed to unravel the complexity of the relationship between, on the one hand, subjugated people or peoples and, on the other, the imperial state, its devolved colonial forms and its post-colonial structures.[12]

In the settler colony of New Zealand an ultimate state goal was to assimilate the indigenous inhabitants to pakeha 'habits and ways'. In fact, political decision makers and settlers alike 'simply assumed that British values and institutions were the most advanced in human history' and naturally *expected* that Maori would 'automatically accept their superior way of life'. With the arrival of George Grey as Governor in 1845, a policy of 'quick and complete' assimilation was adopted. Traditional New Zealand mythology, still perpetuated by many historians in some respects, has it that the state's paramount 'urge to assimilate' was part of a 'great and novel experiment' in 'humanitarian' treatment of 'savages'; that New Zealand was unique in having been colonised peacefully and with the very best of intentions towards the indigenes; that the annexation of New Zealand marked 'a new and a noble beginning in British colonial policy'. Revisionist historiography has shown, however, that pakeha and Crown aversion in the nineteenth century to the preconditions for a true assimilation meant that only 'a show of justice', nominal rather than genuine equality, was offered to Maori.[13]

Maori, too, saw things differently at the time. For them, cultural homogenisation, which involved gaining control of minds (and therefore behaviours), was a complement to the violence inherent in the state's subsuming of the Maori political economy and acquisition of the resources of Aotearoa. Maori soon assumed that the state's strategy involved the 'inexorable devaluation of every social, economic, religious, cultural or political institution' that did not meet the authorities' approval. In the 'social Darwinist' nineteenth century, indeed, the ultimate (and desired) end of the assimilation process was that the 'Maori race' would 'die out', although there were different schools of thought as to what that meant and how it would happen. Thus a Maori scholar has referred to 'that ancient Pakeha myth that the Maori people and their culture represent a sort of temporary disease. With time and suitable Pakeha medicine, they will pass away and never be seen again.'[14]

The Crown, most pakeha and some Maori believed that assimilation was indeed working towards some kind of 'demise of the race' because of the dramatic decline in Maori population after contact and colonisation. Towards the end of the nineteenth century the number of recorded Maori had fallen to a nadir of just over 40,000. This, generally now viewed as an underestimate but certainly reflective of a trend, seemed to confirm for the settlers that the superimposition of a 'superior culture' on an allegedly inferior one would create a 'fatal impact'. However, Maori demographic revival from the turn of the century, although officialdom took a long time to recognise it, led to alteration of the assimilationist policy agenda. The previous aim of actual or virtual disappearance of Maoridom changed into an endeavour to 'make good Europeans out of Maoris'.

The concept of the 'dying Maori', then, was replaced with that of the 'whitening Maori'. While they were expected to retain aspects of their

Maoridom into the foreseeable future, 'brown Europeans' would resile from the 'beastly communism' of the tribal collectivity. They were expected to embrace individualism fervently, maximise their profits by selling the land to those with the superior technology to use it efficiently (whites), and behave in such a fashion as not to disrupt 'the natural order of things'. Antipodean life should as far as possible replicate that of the Home Counties of England. Maori were deemed to have a head start over other indigenous peoples. As the Minister of Defence said in 1914, they were 'the chief of the dark races'.[15]

Thus they would easily learn from 'the Englishman', the ideal imperialist who 'loves order and justice'. Because he had secured 'orderly government at Home', the coloniser 'knows how to establish it in new lands'. The English nation and its auxiliaries had, in short, a 'civilising mission' in the British Empire. While this was clearly based on exploitation of colonial peoples and extraction of their resources, it was rationalised by a mixture of altruism and scientism. Maori were assessed to be 'advanced' enough to be invited to learn to become (ultimately, full) participants in the superior political economy and culture. Such an intellectual paradigm has now largely disappeared, at least in raw form, but vestiges remain that still have an impact on historiography – and, by extension, on national mythology.

Many historians have believed that the assimilation policy encapsulated a benignly attractive (or, at the very least, less unattractive) form of imperialism, which has made New Zealand distinctive among colonies and post-colonies. Even some who are in tune with recent revisionisms that interrogate pro-imperialist assumptions have been inclined to underplay the fundamental intent of the assimilation policy, which essentially implied a strategic transfer of resources from Maori to colonisers in a way that minimalised resistance. Such 'soft' or 'wishful thinking' approaches have manifested themselves in, for example, analyses which find that the Crown from time to time 'missed out' on a chance to forge a 'true partnership' with tribes or to hand autonomy over to them.

Thus officially franchised runanga (councils) in the 1860s are generally seen (if noticed at all) as a 'progressive' development in working with Maori that failed because of lack of nerve or resources or wisdom. In reality, however, they were socio-racial control devices that used Maori political structures for state purposes. It was never intended to hand any meaningful power over to indigenous structures. The official runanga were mechanisms which, in view of the imperial prescription for settler colonies (as opposed to that for vast tracts of the world which fell under 'indirect rule' regimes), could not conceivably have been created or allowed to evolve as parallel (if lesser) sovereignties inside the colonial state imposed by the metropolis. The Anglo-Maori wars of the 1860s – during which time the 'new institutions' of official runanga were established – can in fact be viewed best as a clash of rival bidders for sovereignty, contributing to the ongoing Crown imperative to institute a fully substantive sovereignty underpinned by a total capacity to control.[16]

Military might, and the socio-organisational appropriation represented by the official runanga, were both components of a continuum in modes of control and subjugation. This continuum ran from overt coercion at one pole (including invasion and killing) through to the much more favoured, cheaper and less disruptive pole of control of mind and behaviour. Some New Zealand historians have come to appreciate that the realities of imperial control applied as much to their own country as elsewhere – that in this key respect it was not an exceptional colony and post-colony. But even most of these tend to miss the point that the fundamentals of colonisation and settlement *precluded genuine power sharing*. An autonomous indigenous political economy within a settler colony or its successor state would, in British eyes, have been tantamount to tolerating the intolerable – a potential or actual sovereign threat to the politico-capitalist order on the imperial periphery, and by extension to the 'metropolitan centre' and its diverse global interests.

The historians who have come to understand some of the coercive realities underpinning imperialism, but who cling to a wishful thinking approach, continue to be susceptible to the myth of a benevolent founding and development of New Zealand. So a new historical paradigm has been created as a result of the historiographical search for situations in which the Crown might have wanted or been able to implement forms of Maori political or cultural autonomy that were meaningful devolution or power sharing. This perspective, which sees the Crown as forever 'missing opportunities' to share power or behave better, originates in a perfectly praiseworthy empathy with the plight of the marginalised and dispossessed. But its 'presentism' has led to major conceptual tangles.

One variant of the syndrome, for example, presents a past that had no option but to produce the present, while simultaneously rebuking those who shepherded this along. Other presentists working in Treaty of Waitangi claims, and reinterpreting the past within the politico-legal parameters of the 'principles of the Treaty of Waitangi', do accord the Crown a sizeable degree of agency. Not surprisingly, they find the institution wanting through most or all of its history, while deploring apparently missed chances at various times for creating a bicultural Aotearoa/New Zealand. Many revisionist writings, it has been argued, reflect a biculturalist 'fiction of harmony' that was belied by the very events the authors were examining. Seeing the Crown as possessing 'good intentions' but forever missing opportunities to bring Maori into partnership, revisionist historians can in fact be portrayed as retrospectively stripping agency from Maori – a depiction which then re-emerges in 'popular history', gelling as it does with previous historiographical paradigms.

The 'lost opportunity' school is flourishing (and some Maori scholars are members). The most important reason of all for fundamental Maori grievances by the end of the nineteenth century, for example, has been depicted as 'the fact that the chiefs had been excluded from the political life of New Zealand. The government might have conciliated them by offering them positions of responsibility, such as judgeships in the Native Land Courts or posts as tribal dignitaries in their tribal areas. As the opportunity was not taken, the chiefs spearheaded the movement for a separate Maori constitution.' The author of those words has searched for 'a sympathetic overture' from the government, even just 'discussion and co-operation'. But at a time of post-conquest hegemonic euphoria, chiefly inclusion was not on the Crown agenda.[17]

A handful of scholars, though appearing at least as sympathetic to Maori as the lost opportunity school with regard to Crown violations of the Treaty, have been more hard-headed. Such an approach is neither new nor confined to academic commentators. Six decades ago the Senior

Inspector of Native Schools noted in relation to the state's 'native policy' that, in 'desiring to change the mental and social patterns of a people, assimilation is ruthless in its repudiation of the indigenous culture'. In recent times the hard-headed approach has been making some headway against wishful thinking, 'Treaty principles', counterfactual and older scholarly paradigms. This book reflects a 'hard approach' insofar as it perceives the state to be, in the final analysis, a mechanism for defining and implementing 'peace and good order', and therefore for imposing and preserving certain rhythms of life (behaviours, activities, internalised disciplines, thoughts, etc) in the most efficient ways it can in light of the circumstances at any given time. The state (including the lego-constitutional concept of 'the Crown') does not have 'humanitarian' instincts and propensities, even though some of its (even key) personnel may well possess these, and even though some of its tactics and strategies might seem to be 'humanitarian'.

Ever since 1840 Maori have demanded that the Crown honour its promise, in the Treaty of Waitangi's second article, to respect te tino rangatiratanga, or full autonomy; all the while, the Crown has resisted this, or interpreted the term in anodyne fashion. What is meant by autonomy in terms of concrete Maori aspirations has differed according to circumstances. There are 'many degrees of autonomy and independence short of complete political independence'. The Crown, however, which initially used the word 'chieftainship' as synonymous with rangatiratanga, has invariably seen any 'concession' based on Article Two as being subject to its full authority. In other words, the kawanatanga/sovereignty conceded to the Crown in Article One has been defined by the state (initially backed by the might of the world's biggest empire) to mean not just an overarching sovereignty but *indivisible* Crown sovereignty. Thus, in the eyes of the Crown and of the general pakeha population, the tribes had placed themselves fully under the 'protection of the Crown': Article Two merely ensured continuation of 'chieftainship'. Whatever the state's definition, Maori have believed that their own authority structures could co-exist with Crown sovereignty.

Such matters constitute far more than niceties of lego-constitutional interpretation, given that all facets of Maori politico-cultural life have been deeply affected by the practical operation of the Crown's definition. This, with its emphasis on indivisibility, does not preclude devolution. But the Crown has seldom conceded any significant power to Maori, however determined their struggle. They have fought long and hard for the kinds of rights that indigenous people in colonies and post-colonies the world over have fought for – which they perceive to be embedded in the Treaty of Waitangi. Their weapons have been many and varied, ranging from disseminating information and ideas (through creating Maori newspapers, for example, or contributing to other print media) through to armed force.[18]

At times in history the Crown has appeared to make significant concessions to the Maori struggle for rangatiratanga. This has led some of the wishful thinking 'Treaty studies' scholars to interpret *apparent* devolutions of power to Maori as actual developments, or minor devolutions as well-intentioned, non-temporary actions that heralded the possibility of greater and permanent concessions of autonomy. Some historians display palpable disappointment when the state falls short, as it invariably does, in their well-motivated but ahistorical scenarios. Such analyses are concerned, in effect, with examining the past against the measuring rod of the Crown's propensity to ignore or counteract the (still evolving) modern construct of the 'principles' of the Treaty. The literature remains pervaded with the Crown 'missing' (for reasons such as inadvertence or lack of courage) yet another grand opportunity to implement, to some degree or other, the promise of rangatiratanga that for Maori lies at the heart of the Treaty of Waitangi.[19]

In reality, the state's policies – whatever the fine words uttered from time to time in policy statements and the like – have focused on definitions of 'public good' that suited the interests and predispositions of the authorities. This remains the case. Maori self-determination has never, from 1840 to the present, been a state goal. It does not fit ruling definitions of public good, peace and good order, or appropriate modes of thought and behaviour. At best, devolutions of power have been temporary and anodyne expedients. Even the government focus since the 1980s on the Treaty has been driven primarily not by a search for justice and equity but by the need to remove a major perceived problem in the body politic, the so-called 'Maori problem' (although it has given the 'struggle without end' for Crown recognition of rangatiratanga some hopes of success).

Until relatively recent times the Crown's stated aim remained that of assimilation of Maori (and all other non-dominant culture groups) into the mainstream or state-desired culture and social behaviour of the New Zealand polity. This becomes clear when historians immerse themselves in the mores of the past and contextualise historical happenings within the terms of reference of the decision makers and participants. Some historians have shied away from this altogether, because it is too difficult or involves too much research and reading, or in the belief that to understand and relate the motives and thought patterns of past times is to become somehow complicit in them. More commonly, historians who belong to the wishful thinking school attempt to write humanitarian, Maori autonomy and other 'attractive' factors into the state agenda whenever they can.

In contrast, this book patterns the past to reflect the state's fundamental motivations for its actions through time. It does not, for example, examine the past within a whiggish macro-paradigm of steady 'onwards and upwards' progress by the general citizenry, a perspective subliminally pervading many Treaty studies. Its line is 'hard' because dispassionate analysis points clearly to the inadequacy of wishful thinking and other 'benign state' and 'advancing society' perspectives. In the political field, for example, 'Treatyists' (as right-wing commentators call them) often locate themselves within a post-war historiographical convention that focuses on a move away from the apron strings of the metropolitan 'Home' towards the emergence of a 'national identity', and on the theory and practice of 'raising' Maori to the 'civilised' socio-economic and behavioural standards of pakeha. Some 'Treaty historians' have become positively proactive within such paradigms, creating, for example, 'spaces of resistance and hope' within the broader 'spaces of marginalization'.[20]

Such interpretations often accommodate ethnocentric perspectives. At first tangata whenua are seen as blocking progress, and they more or less disappear from the historians' gaze when they are perceived to have been mainstreamed (that is, until 'urban problems', and the 'Maori Renaissance' from the 1970s, mean that they cannot be entirely overlooked). The overarching paradigm of 'progress' reinterprets the Maori experience as socio-economic advancement via assimilation. Even those who add to this an account of progress towards some form of self-determination tend to see it as a means of 'closing the social indicator gaps' between Maori and pakeha. Many developments along the way are judged against *how far* – not *if* – they contribute to this supposed grand patterning. The state is presumed to be at least sometimes an empathetic player in relation to, even if often or always falling short of, Maori requests and aspirations.

Such wishful thinking historiography is an advance on that of narrative or would-be postmodern historians who do not perceive, or actually deny the worth of discovering, patterns in history. Moreover, it does acknowledge that Maori did continue their nineteenth-century fight for autonomy throughout the twentieth. But this is an advance that leaves us far short of understanding Crown–Maori dynamics. For the real question is not how far the Crown went towards meeting Maori aspirations for rangatiratanga in the twentieth century, but whether it was *ever* really concerned with doing so. This book argues emphatically that it was not.

State authorities are always concerned to impose or maintain sufficient peace and good order in the country to enable, with minimal impediment, the 'regular pursuits' of civil society – matters posited firmly within the requirements of a capitalist political economy. Classical political and historiographical assumptions that certain types of 'progress' benefit society both reflected and reinforced the processes of hegemony, the state's quest for control of minds once control of bodies had been attained. The fact that even historians empathetic to Maori struggles have been complicit in such processes, generally unaware of their own 'internal colonisation' by the official or dominant ideology, itself reflects successes within the hegemonic agenda.

That being said, such revisionists produced historical writing that, in overturning past paradigms, is seen by many as truly subversive in its effect. While all scholarly discussions are shaped by or resonate with politico-ideological assumptions, Treaty revisionist scholarship has become overtly intertwined with politics. A scholar, for example, is reportedly 'disgusted' by an argument that sovereignty was seized as an act of state in 1840 and thereafter regularised by the conventions of international law. Although such an analysis is perfectly arguable in an academic arena, a minister's support for the 'act of state' argument is seen as 'finally admitting that the Treaty was a sham document'. Instead of the Treaty representing the 'basis of the Crown's sovereignty – rather it was taken by military force. And they say that over time that becomes legal!'[21]

On these issues emotions are high because the stakes are high. The Treaty debate addresses issues at the core of the nation's past, present and future, and the discussions are therefore vigorous. Some believe that, if the Treaty of Waitangi is assessed as fraudulent in terms of the Crown's motivations in 1840, the modern Crown might well renege on its (reluctantly conceded) obligations to Maori. Others (and the author is among them) note that, whatever the motivations of the imperial state of 1840, promises to Maori should be, like other promises, honoured to the fullest extent possible and (in this case) reparations negotiated for breaches. Scholars are needed in the processes of advocacy and negotiation. But scholarship and advocacy should not be conflated, and this book strives to avoid doing so. Its attempt to get to the heart of the matter of the twentieth-century relationship between Crown and Maori thus eschews moralising. It argues that Crown–Maori relations after 1900 continued the pattern of the nineteenth century, centring on a quest for autonomy by the tangata whenua and the state's various efforts to repel, contain, defuse or use this.

Given the enormous discrepancy in physical and ideological power between the state and the tribes, Maori inevitably succumbed to the forces of might and hegemony. In other words, they internalised many of the mores and behaviours which the Crown desired to impose on all of its citizenry. At one extreme, some Maori had become positively jingoistic products of this process by the beginning of the twentieth century. Henare Kohere, a member of the Maori Coronation Contingent to London in 1902, extolled the virtues of 'places where the English flag is flying'. Maori like him felt 'fortunate' to be able to be 'civilised' by supposedly the most progressive and enviable 'race' of all, the British. Most Maori, however, while using practical and conceptual facets of 'Britishness' which advanced their prospects or enhanced their lifestyles, were not prepared to give up many fundamentals of their culture, of their 'Maoriness'. Maori social and cultural life would certainly evolve, but not into something completely different.

After the Anglo-Maori wars, Maori had withdrawn into 'reservation-like areas and villages' to preserve their identity. By the end of the nineteenth century, then, while they necessarily had to engage with the politico-economic world of the pakeha, 'Maori cultural autonomy and identity [had] survived the impact of Europe'. At the same time, Maori had been determined to preserve or claw back as much political self-determination as was possible under the relentless onslaught of colonisation and capitalism. It is 'now recognised by most New Zealand historians that throughout the nineteenth century, tribes and hapu all over New Zealand sought to defend and sustain their independence of identity, and the independence of their activity'.

To secure a distinctively Maori place in the new colonial order against the prevailing European desire to destroy tribal and ethnic identity, komiti/committees and similar institutions developed out of the older institution of runanga. These, with acute awareness of the realities of the new order, attempted to regain sufficient autonomy to administer their own lands and communal affairs. While welcoming the new opportunities brought by western culture and technology, Maori continuously adjusted, but never accepted the state's goal of full assimilation. From the time of the arrival of imperialism in the South Pacific, in fact, they attempted to preserve or develop as much as possible of their own culture, customs and way of life.[22]

Historians have covered such phenomena for the nineteenth century. One scholar has made a hostile assessment that 'autonomy [has become] the organising principle of the analysis of nineteenth-century Maori experience'. Whatever the merits or otherwise of opposition to this development, such a portrayal of modern historiography is correct enough. This book argues that ongoing Maori structural and conceptual reorganisation, reflecting Maori aspirations to become as autonomous from the state and the institutions of the dominant culture as possible, have been central to the post-nineteenth-century story of New Zealand. In a tribal context Maori aspirations tended to remain organised through the hapu, 'the effective, independent political unit of pre-contact Maori society', with pan-tribal and Crown–tribal interactions often occurring (but not necessarily so, in the dynamic and evolving world of Maori) at iwi level. In overviewing the assertion of rangatiratanga in the first half of the twentieth century, this work explores the resilience of indigenous people in the face of an enormous power imbalance, and the Crown's adversarial and inclusionist responses. It concurs with the view that decision makers on both sides, through time, 'understood the other very well indeed in the direct conflict of interest over the land and its resources, and over the control of state power'.[23]

The problem for Maori was to build on this understanding and organise in a way that would lead to concrete results. Against the odds, they made many attempts to embody rangatiratanga. The book explores the strategic and tactical complexities involved in this. It covers, for example, not only hegemonic imposing of ideas on Maori, but also their use of some of those ideas for their own purposes. It does not go into every byway, however, such as the intricacies and impacts on people of a 'hybrid' existence, that which combines Maoriness with the culture of the pakeha (or other ethnicities). The quest for a rangatiratanga that the Crown would recognise is seen as a process of searching out matches between ideas (from various sources, traditional and 'new') and organisation (Maori, non-Maori and mixed), but the book necessarily focuses on attempts to maximise the Maori position and the Crown's responses thereto.

The process continues, amid both old and newer difficulties. The Crown's preference is often, for example, to deal (if at all) with groupings and configurations that might not be the preference of Maori. This has usually meant engagement with as large a 'tribal' or other grouping as possible, especially at iwi, confederation of iwi or national level, rather than with a more primary unit of Maori society. But there are many versions of the appropriate vehicles for expressing rangatiratanga within Maoridom, from non-tribal to pan-tribal, from iwi to hapu to whanau, and others besides. This book does not prescribe an 'ideal' form, now or in the past; nor does it pretend to depict an 'insider' Maori perspective on the events it relates and analyses through a half century of politico-cultural interaction.[24]

Rather, it examines how Maori responded to the implications of colonisation and post-colonisation in a conceptual and organisational way, and how the Crown, in turn, handled this. While some readers might see it as negative in its implications, such a response would no doubt reflect its exploration of the difficulties inherent in the relationship between Crown and Maori. This is, after all, a work of history, not of social prescription. Suffice it to note here that the author has recorded elsewhere his optimism, at least in global comparative terms, that 'race' and Crown–Maori relations in New Zealand now hold out some prospects of accommodating rangatiratanga within kawanatanga – of fitting Aotearoa into New Zealand. It is difficult, however, to see how this can occur without an informed understanding of the past. But comprehension is complicated by the biases and imperfections of western historiography, as well as by the fact that '[t]here have been two remembered histories of New Zealand since 1840: that of the colonizers and that of the colonized'. This work aims to assist greater understanding.[25]

CHAPTER ONE

THE QUEST FOR AUTONOMY IN THE NINETEENTH CENTURY

While this book focuses on the first half of the twentieth century, to begin at 1900 would be misleading. First of all, then, it sketches out themes from the previous century which are relevant to the quest for rangatiratanga. In their counterfactual quest for ways in which imperialism might have been more accommodating to indigenes, 'wishful thinking' historians have highlighted British acquiescence in the continued existence of certain indigenous customs and institutions, suggesting that such tolerance could have been greatly expanded. This is to miss the point that has already been stressed, that such concessions were expedients *designed* to be no more than temporary. The goal remained that of fully 'civilising savages'.

Institutions of indirect control

The imperial reality was generally that the Crown could only *gradually* extend its sway over the territory over which it held nominal sovereignty, and New Zealand was no exception. Until it gained first physical and then full hegemonic control over all the colony's inhabitants, the Crown had little choice but to allow chiefly institutions and Maori customs to continue. These needed, however, to be subject to controls, including the franchising of chiefs to keep a degree of 'law and order' on its behalf in buffer or even outer zones. Both within the areas under direct state control and in liminal regions where it had temporarily devolved authority to chiefs, the state would establish control institutions based on, derived from or equivalent to indigenous structures. These were not, despite the retrospective optimism of some historians, either designed to be or operated as concessionary organs of self-determination.

The official runanga institutions of the 1860s, for example, were quickly abandoned by the Crown when they proved to be no longer useful as institutions of socio-racial control of Maori. While the state presented a unified stance at any given time, within it such matters as enfranchising indigenous institutions as modes of state control were contestable. In settler colonies, in particular, indirect control methods were far from universally popular among colonisers and their political representatives. When Native Minister Donald McLean proposed in the 1870s that 'Native Councils' could manage Maori areas, this was rejected by Parliament as too concessionary, even though they were to be headed and directed by pakeha officials. All the same, proposals for indirect control continued to be floated, partly in response to Maori organisational initiatives, which in turn partly addressed government intentions and actions.

Also in the 1870s, for example, Maori developed their own komiti/ committees, reviving the old runanga institution in a new form which constituted one of the post-war strategies of resistance to the Crown. In some regions a komiti-based government and policing system arose beside that of the state – in Rotorua, Wanganui and the Far North, for example. The Crown could temporarily tolerate such developments, so long as they met state requirements. Komiti could not, for example, enforce their local or regional laws on pakeha, even when tikanga/customs or livelihoods were adversely affected by such matters as desecration of taonga (treasured items or places); this had happened at the internationally renowned Pink and White Terraces, for instance. Moreover, while some komiti remained resistant to the Crown and to colonisation, many came to grips with the inevitability of settlement. They calculated that by helping regulate it they would retain at least some tribal influence over events. Some groupings helped open up regions to settlement, including areas from which Crown personnel and settlers had been forcibly excluded.

The Maori MPs (themselves representing a supposedly temporary measure, pending assimilation) were often in the forefront of collaborative efforts aimed at ameliorating the effects of settlement. In 1883, for example, they secured the Native Committees Act to enable establishment of officially constituted komiti, believing this would benefit Maori as well as the Crown. But the compromises involved in procuring the legislation were great. The Crown's aim was to ward off separatism by encompassing it. The final product, which was therefore far from their original idea, typified appropriative attempts by establishing a system that was toothless for Maori.

In the twelve large areas of the North Island designated under the legislation, the committees had few meaningful powers. They were denied, for example, the right to issue summonses. The committees were, moreover, to be used to promote government policies for investigating and individualising communal Maori land tenure. Yet even co-operation for limited objectives, such as providing advice to the Native Land Court, proved to be of little value, for the court would often ignore their deliberations. Maori soon found that their own informal komiti remained far more useful to them than those franchised by the Crown. A series of hui (meetings or assemblies) that called for real powers to be given to the official committees was ignored, and the system thereafter languished.

Such dashed hopes did not deflect Maori from their struggle to find an independent place within the pakeha-dominated polity. Their spokespeople, official and unofficial, consistently stressed that 'autonomy was fundamental', expressing this in many ways through time. Mihipeka Edwards, for example, has noted the struggle of Maori to establish that they were a 'people with our own dignity, pride and mana'. Even towards the end of the nineteenth century, when most pakeha believed Maori to be a 'dying race' which had lost its social control mechanisms, tribal control structures were still very much alive and new politico-cultural preservation techniques were being developed.[26]

Kingitanga

Many Maori came to believe that the chances of even partial success against the might of British imperialism required a mass organisational assertion, one assisted and shaped by insistence that the Crown be held to account over its promise in the Treaty to respect rangatiratanga. While representing a significant experiment in the search for 'realistic' methods of pushing for self-determination within state parameters, the komiti had proved to be too small in scale against a colonial government of marked centralising tendencies. Among the other sites and modes of resistance, some institutions were on a much grander scale.

Kingitanga/Kingism structures were particularly powerful, based on a pan-tribal unity movement centred on the Tainui iwi. Headed by a king, this movement had arisen in the 1850s as an effort to pre-empt the ongoing encroachment of the Crown on the Maori polity. 'Mana motuhake', often translated as separate government, was emblazoned on King Tawhiao's coat of arms. Kingitanga, viewed by the Crown as an attempt to establish a rival sovereignty to that of the state, had been militarily suppressed. After wartime defeat, confiscation of land and forced retreat from the Waikato into the Rohe Potae/King Country, the movement fought on for autonomy in ways other than military.

At first the Kingite leaders experimented with a unilaterally declared 'state within a state' in the King Country. When this proved unviable, they sought to open up their region to economic opportunity, but under their own control. For some time they believed that they had reached a 'compact' with the Crown to achieve at least some measure of this. The arrangement included retention of tribal ownership of lands, with leasing rather than selling to pakeha. But in the 1890s the Crown began divide-and-rule purchasing, while at the same time prohibiting private purchasing (under which sellers might at least have obtained better prices). By 1900 a third of the land had left Maori ownership, and large state inroads had been made into governance of the tribally owned areas.[27]

Meanwhile, the Kingite leadership had concluded that the Crown's strength lay partly in its centralised unity of purpose: regional unities were insufficient. The movement came to aim for, and in some interpretations had always in essence worked towards, a form of autonomy involving a unified Maoridom that operated alongside the British Crown for some purposes and under its umbrella for others. King Tawhiao told the Secretary of State for the Colonies that 'I am called a king, not for the purpose of separation, but in order that the natives might be united under one race, ever acknowledging the supremacy of the Queen, and claiming her protection'. The Maori MPs asserted in 1883 that Tawhiao was 'the head of our race' and sought 'an elective body of Maoris' to 'get control of our lands', while also affirming that they did not want to 'obstruct the progress of colonisation'. The Kingitanga leaders pursued several possibilities for parallel government, hoping that the Maori people would throw their unified weight behind them and that this would lead to significant government concessions.

While many tribes declined to accommodate a movement which had ambitions to unite all tribes under its own leaders, Kingitanga pressed on nevertheless. After his reconciliation with the government, for example, King Tawhiao tried to get official endorsement for a 'Council of Chiefs' which would both share power with the Crown and attempt to secure 'all the rights and lands confirmed by the Treaty of Waitangi'. Kingitanga remained the most unified movement in the quest for autonomy, eventually establishing at Maungakawa in 1892 a Kauhanganui/Great Council headed by a Tumuaki/Premier and a cabinet. But its laws went unrecognised by the Crown.[28]

Kotahitanga

Unity under a king was only one sort of unity, and a number of tribes were working on solutions based on Maori unity through intertribal co-operation. Such efforts underpinned Maori efforts in the 1880s and 1890s to get real powers for their representative committees. These 'federal' Maori unification movements have generically, and sometimes specifically, been known as kotahitanga. Some sought to emulate and complement the Crown's parliamentary system, an aim mostly associated with tribes which had a history of co-operation with the Crown. It was partly because collaboration had less value for the Crown once the wars were over that such tribes sought to enhance their influence by increasing their pan-tribal critical mass. In 1879 Te Arawa tribes established a 'Great Committee' with the potential to expand beyond their region. That year too a meeting to discuss the establishment of a Maori parliament (based on komiti) was hosted by Ngati Whatua at Orakei. In 1881 'Te Komiti o Te Tiriti o Waitangi' was set up at Waitangi, with its own parallel authorities and annual meetings.

In 1886, the year Tawhiao asked the government to agree to a 'Council of Chiefs', the Crown had deemed the colony's inhabitants – Maori and pakeha – to have finally been 'pacified'. State-desired modes of social behaviour were assessed as having been generally accepted by most citizens. The state authorities, therefore, saw no need to alter existing constitutional arrangements. Maori pressure increased, especially after intertribal hui in 1888–9 began preparations for a 'Maori union at Waitangi' that could make decisions on matters relevant to all Maori. Progress was co-ordinated from 1890 by northern iwi regarded as guardians of the Treaty, to which kotahitanga looked for its mandate. At the beginning of the new decade, various large pan-tribal meetings indicated that the demand for a separate Maori authority had spread out far beyond Kingitanga. Such instincts for unity resulted partly from Maori alarm at the demographic data which had caused pakeha to believe they were a dying race. Even those many Maori who did not believe their race would physically disappear were aware that united action was needed if the Crown and settler goal of full cultural assimilation was to be resisted.

In 1892 a hui at Te Tiriti o Waitangi marae in the Bay of Islands agreed to build on many precursor meetings and networks and formally establish the unity movement Te Kotahitanga o Te Tiriti o Waitangi/ The Unity of the Treaty of Waitangi, to be headed by a parliament. Its main purpose was to procure the honouring of the Treaty promise of rangatiratanga, tying this especially to retention of the remaining land-base. One of its platforms, for example, was abolition of the Native Land Court in favour of 'native committees' more sensitive to Maori needs and wants. But its bid was essentially for parallel state institutions within the New Zealand colonial nation-state. The main Kotahitanga method for achieving this, as the parliament's first Speaker was to say, would be strength through unity of the tribes from 'the four winds'. Without unity of the tribes, Maori aspirations would be treated as 'the murmuring of the wind'.[29]

In response to such strengthened politico-racial assertion, in the last decade of the century the state became more averse than ever to Maori unification. This it saw not only as a threat to its plans to alienate the bulk of remaining Maori-owned land, but also to its sovereign authority.

Both land and sovereignty were key factors in a refrigeration-based technological drive to 'recolonise' New Zealand as an essential supplier of the Mother Country's meat and dairy products. What had only half a century before been nominally independent 'Aotearoa' would now become the most loyal, if most distant, outpost of empire. In this 'Better Britain', in effect, assimilation was deemed to have occurred almost by definition. In 1892 it was announced that the Native Department was to be abolished; in the following year 'Maori became amenable to the ordinary legal machinery of the land'.

With Maori now placed under the same jurisdiction as pakeha, the Native Land Court and related state bodies remained the sole agencies dealing specifically with Maori matters. A royal commission later noted that, in terms of legal issues, by the end of the nineteenth century the question of separate institutions for Maori 'had been settled, if not resolved. Except in respect of Maori land and certain related matters, the Maori people were to be governed almost completely by the English derived law.' In terms of Crown actions, then, the very opposite to endorsing rangatiratanga had occurred.[30]

At the time, both state and settler pronouncements remained full of optimism about the full assimilation of Maori. This merged into an opinion in even the most 'progressive' of pakeha thinkers that, in the 1901 words of the President of the National Council of Women, 'Maori and pakeha have become one people'. At the very least there was a firm belief that the disappearance of Maori separatism, if not of Maori culture or 'bloodlines', was nigh. One of the Native Department's last statements, in the colony's 1892 *Official Handbook*, predicted that the 'so-called Maori King' had been tamed as a result of his acceptance of a government pension. 'This is looked upon as an auspicious event, and it is hoped that it will lead to the end of the "King movement", which, although it has lost much of its former power, has, nevertheless by its existence, tended to maintain an isolation injurious to both races.'

But it was in this very year, alongside Kingitanga's revivalist strategising, that kotahitanga tribes with a history of support for (or at least non-opposition to) the Crown finally established a Maori Parliament. The new institution provided another forum for pan-tribal Maori opinion and action aimed at holding the remaining Maori land, among other matters. But in this and the various regrouping and fight-back efforts to resist assimilation, the push for a form of authorised parallel government was the key feature. Unity-based organisational assertion has persisted to the present. But unity has not usually been the *ultimate* aim. In a tribally rooted society, the push for unity generally represented a way of achieving a goal rather than itself constituting the goal. The Maori aim was always Crown recognition of their right to run 'their own' affairs without state interference.[31]

While Maori were deemed sufficiently subject by 1886 to hegemonic norms for the Crown to be generally satisfied with the state of social order, the fact remained that almost all Maori had resisted *full* assimilation. But Maori had still to grapple with the fact that, assuming the official 'best case' scenario did not eventuate – that Maori did not fade away altogether as a physically present 'race' – total assimilation remained the Crown and pakeha aspiration. A Member of Parliament would put the matter succinctly: 'The objective of a good Native policy should be the Europeanising of the Maori.' Even indigenous bids for 'loyal self-determination' had been perceived as too much of a threat to the sanctity of the Crown and the settler capitalism it represented. Indeed, in the 1890s Kotahitanga was in the Crown's eyes a bigger problem than Kingitanga, even though it tended to be based in tribes which had been considered allies or neutrals.

Such hostility to a relatively 'friendly' grouping indicated the depth of the problem from a Maori perspective, and the firmness of purpose Maori needed. The numbers backing the unity method rose. The movement was particularly spurred on by increasing awareness of the Liberal government's determination to get pakeha 'small farmers' onto the land. The implication from the beginning was that this would be at least partly at the expense of what was left of the tribal patrimony, despite much rhetoric about 'bursting up' the big pakeha estates; as events turned out, it was mostly at Maori expense.

The Kotahitanga movement would centre on the deliberations of its annual Maori Parliament/Paremata Maori. At its first meeting at Waipatu in June 1892, with typical Maori capacity for adaptation it took on the contours and procedures of the 'pakeha parliament'. An elaborate structure of (tribally based) electorates, prime minister and ministerial portfolios was created at central level. Organisational networks would report or relate to it – a network of marae-based women's committees (Nga Komiti Wahine), for example, was responsible for 'overseeing and attending to general health and well-being'.

During a decade-long attempt to gain official recognition as a complement, or at the very least a supplement, to the 'Wellington Parliament', the Maori Parliament sought legislative autonomy on the basis of the Treaty's second article. It also cited section 71 of the 1852 Constitution Act, whose provisions for discrete (and intended to be temporary) 'Native Districts' had never been taken up. While it had a loyalist base, Kotahitanga embodied an unprecedented degree of Maori unity, and it worked diligently to 'show how parallel institutions might work in New Zealand'. Because of such success it even gained the co-operation of (though not merging with) the Kingitanga.[32]

The Urewera experiment

The settler state could not have contemplated any kind of parallel power at national level. But had it been serious about addressing at least some Maori aspirations at a regional level it could have done so under the 1852 legislation. This enabled some form of regional or tribal self-government in areas that remained remote from pakeha settlement. The Crown's concessions to a Maori autonomy movement independent of the unity organisation were greatest for the isolated Urewera people, whose attempts to preserve their independence were long-standing and determined. At a Tuhoe tribal gathering in 1894, Chief Numia Kereru confirmed to Premier R J Seddon that his tribe did not want the 'temporary prosperity' that came with the selling of land that was inevitable after the individualising of tenure. Instead, it wanted to continue to manage its tribal land and political affairs collectively through its own structures. In gauging how genuine the Crown's concessions were, the Premier's reply is instructive. It repeated the long-standing state policy on autonomy: if Tuhoe was asking that tribal committees could have law-making powers, they could not.

But regular police and military expeditions to the Urewera to deter ongoing tribal disruption to surveys were too expensive for an area that could produce no short-term economic gains. And so the imposition of substantive sovereignty needed to be suspended. This created a problem for Crown-defined 'order and regularity' in a rugged area where, within living memory, the 'infamous rebel chief' Te Kooti Arikirangi had operated. State–iwi negotiations resulted in 1895 in a *modus vivendi* that partially reflected ideas generated by an earlier commission. Local land block committees with specified powers would be established, and would elect an umbrella organisation, the Komiti Nui o Tuhoe/General Committee, to handle region-wide matters. The Crown agreed that the government would survey only with the concurrence of the tribes and the Native Land Court would be excluded from the region. Instead, seven 'Commissioners' (five of them tribespeople) would deal with land ownership matters under customary law and certificates of ownership, and the general committee alone would be able to alienate land (and then only to the Crown).

The resulting Urewera District Native Reserve Act of 1896, establishing some 650,000 acres of the Urewera as a reserve under Maori 'local government', seemed to be a significant precedent for the concession of rangatiratanga. But, as noted by the leading politician of mixed-race descent, James Carroll, this development could occur only because no significant state or settler interests were involved at that time. In return, moreover, the government gained Tuhoe's recognition of the mana of the British Queen and all tribal powers under the Act were devolved and constrained by the Crown. The state intended that in due course it would impose on the Urewera all the 'responsibilities and liabilities' of the other citizens of New Zealand. As the parliamentary opposition noted, the legislation was designed to be the thin end of the wedge for settlement and exploitation of timber and other resources, and for the 'civilising' of Maori that would follow. From the very point when Tuhoe consented to have their lands surveyed as part of the agreement, the tribe began to lose its authority *vis a vis* the Crown.[33]

The trend towards unification

Meanwhile, with the Crown refusing to give the Paremata Maori any official recognition, the unity movement tended to operate as an unofficial state within a state. While different from the King Country and Urewera territory-based unofficial states, it nevertheless carried out state-like functions, including the capacity to coerce. Like the Ringatu Church (founded by Te Kooti), Kingitanga and other pan-tribal and tribal organisations before it, the Kotahitanga district committees produced their own laws and attempted to enforce them through pirihimanatanga/policing regimes. These were runanga-based organisations, some with professional police paid from tribally imposed fines.

From one perspective the Crown appreciated their minimising of disorder, with their control of liquor consumption, patrolling functions and tasks such as keeping order at marae. But it was not prepared to contemplate the existence of local governance regimes that were loyal primarily to a 'national' organisation unsanctioned by the colony's political executive and implicitly posing a threat to indivisible sovereign power. Yet the Maori Parliament movement could not be ignored, especially when almost half of Maoridom signed a petition in support of its aims. The Crown became still more concerned when the loose alliance between the Maori Parliament and King movements began to form.

Both had begun to experiment with securing a voice in the colonial Parliament with the election of Hone Heke (1893) and Henare Kaihau (1896) as MPs. This had, if nothing else, considerable publicity value. The former, for example, introduced draft legislation to devolve power to the Maori Parliament, and the latter promoted a Bill aimed at removing the Native Land Court and establishing a 'Maori Council' under the auspices of the Maori King. These measures were acceptable neither to many tribes nor to the Crown, but through such devices Kotahitanga and Kingitanga procured political discussions and negotiations. The Crown responded to the unity movements' potentially potent strategy of combining 'protest and co-operation' by seeking accommodation with them. The state's aim had always been encapsulated in the words of the colony's first leader, Lieutenant-Governor William Hobson, that 'we are now one people'. It now saw, in effect, that full realisation of its assimilationist 'dream' would have to be further deferred. In seeking meanwhile to maximise its own interests, the Crown searched for a solution that would not only deflect Maori aspirations into something anodyne, but would actually advance the assimilationist agenda. It believed it had found this in 1900.[34]

CHAPTER TWO

SEEKING POLITICAL AUTONOMY IN THE EARLY TWENTIETH CENTURY

Just as the search for autonomy by Maori had been fundamental to Maoridom in the nineteenth century, it remained at the heart of Maori aspirations throughout the twentieth. For decade after decade 'Maori people in each district constantly endeavoured to find ways to control their own affairs, proclaim their group identity whether as tribe or hapu, and enrich their lives; they aimed at enhancing the mana of the hapu in their inner affairs, and sometimes that of the tribe as they looked outward, striving to control their land and membership and take their affairs out of the hands of government.' But the Urewera example soon revealed that the Crown would not contemplate any meaningful tribally based autonomy, even in areas of minimal interest for settlement at that time. The best chance of major concessions, then, seemed to lie with the powerful unity movements.

The Young Maori Party

Meanwhile, a new generation of Maori leaders, educated the pakeha way, believed that full tribally based autonomy was not only unviable but undesirable. They became mediators between the Crown and the powerful unity movements, proving instrumental in procuring 'compromises' that were deemed to be measures of self-government. In 1900 the Crown made what seemed to be significant colony-wide concessions to autonomy – legislating for land management and 'local government' organisations for Maori.

Since most pakeha continued to believe the tangata whenua were a dying race, a perception that persisted for another two decades or so (until the Maori demographic revival recorded in the statistics from the turn of the century could no longer be regarded as temporary), the timing of this initiative might seem surprising. But the state needed to put in place a new set of 'new institutions', whether or not Maoridom was dying, to divert pressure from Kotahitanga and its semi-ally Kingitanga – pressure that had intensified among Maori concerned about the 'survival of the race'. Throughout empires it was typical that, after initial resistance to colonisation from 'traditional leaders' attempting to preserve customary authority, younger 'modernisers' schooled in compromise rose to leadership positions. New Zealand was no exception. The main mediators between the Crown and Maori were highly educated young men loosely associated under a succession of names. After precursor groupings, the movement found firm footing in the Te Aute College Students' Association (TACSA), established in 1897. But at the time and afterwards it was generally called after an early nickname given to it by Apirana Ngata – the Young Maori Party. This reflected his political interests, and the group eventually became officially known by that name.[35]

Often depicted as total converts to western ways and proselytisers for assimilation, in fact the Young Maori Party members generally sought to *combine* the technological, cultural and other benefits of European civilisation with preserving 'the best' of Maori culture. Only in this way could Maori 'save the race'. The grouping was following in the footsteps of elders who, since the 1880s, had sought western knowledge 'to do the things that the Pakeha did for his material welfare, without, however, unduly straining the fundamentals of our community life or our tribal organisation'. Ngata put it this way in his proverb 'The Challenge':

E tipu e rea, mo nga ra o tou ao,
To ringa ki nga rakau a te Pakeha
Hei ara mo to tinana.
To ngakau ki nga taonga a o tipuna Maori
Hei tikitiki mo to mahuna.
[Grow up o tender youth, in the time of your generation,
Your hand reaching for the Pakeha tools
For your physical well being.
Your heart dedicated to the treasures of your ancestors
As a plume upon your head.]

Young Maori Party members understood that, even had they been so inclined, total or overt resistance to the state and settlement would have been counter-productive. They were well aware of the overwhelming might of the Crown, its command of the forces of coercion and its control of the apparatus of hegemony. 'Insurrection and agitation are in no way constructive, and the weight of the state opposes them', as one sympathiser later put it. They had, then, to work within existing state structures and imperatives. They saw that they needed to work within existing Maori structures too, and so sought to work with both traditional chiefs (on many of whom they bestowed honorary membership) and newer constructs such as Kingitanga.[36]

The obstacles were great. Despite the 'kind of equality' that existed under colonial law, 'no real participation in the European order – economically, socially, or even politically' had eventuated for Maori. A combination of state and pakeha attitudes and Maori refusal to assimilate had manifested itself in tangata whenua 'withdrawal'. The Young Maori Party proclaimed the need for change within Maoridom to counteract the 'dangerous hopelessness' of retreat to 'primitive' tribalism, which seemingly led to racial extinction. Instead, a constructive engagement was needed that might protect the best components of Maoridom. From this would come 'fusion' of the two peoples on the *highest* of planes, a state that would induce in Maori 'pride of race', in pakeha respect for the tangata whenua, and 'the practical salvation of the Maori race' from marginalisation or even extinction.

The Young Maori Party leaders were, like those of Kotahitanga, principally from tribes which had histories of past co-operation with the Crown: Ngati Porou, Arawa and Te Atiawa, for example. Some degree of collaborative endeavour between indigenous people and colonial state is one of several possible forms of adjustment to colonisation. Some scholars of empire in fact argue that it was the most subtle and (at least at times) effective form of resistance to full subjugation by the imperial power. Even had they been interested in mobilising tribal or other structures in the pursuit of a *separatist* self-determination, the Young Maori Party knew that any such efforts would be negated by suppressive, appropriative or hegemonic reaction by the Crown. Rather than acting against or attempting to operate in parallel with the state and settlers, then, Maori should work together with them. By accepting in effect that they had been overwhelmed by a stronger polity, Maori could utilise western science, medicine, communications and other aspects of European culture for their own well-being. Preservation and renewal of those facets of their own culture which they *did* see as highly desirable was possible only within the paradigm of British ideas, policies and culture.[37]

The Young Maori Party members were therefore prepared to pay a high cultural price to secure socio-economic progress. But, whatever many history books have said, this did not mean 'progress at any price'. 'Typical' Young Maori Party statements such as 'Communism has been the death trap of the Maori race' or arguments that there was for Maori 'no alternative but to become a pakeha' have been taken out of context, obscuring the fact that it was *because* they wanted to protect their own people and culture from subsumption or annihilation that the Young Maori Party met, formulated and acted.

Maui Pomare, the most assimilationist of the Young Maori Party leaders, had listened to the plea of his dying father to 'seek the wisdom of the white man' and warned his people against separatist thought: 'We have one king, one country, and we should have one law.' But even the adaptation to the pakeha world that he preached was in order that Maoridom survived as a discernible entity. To this effect the Young Maori Party aim included stopping 'inappropriate' customs (especially those that had 'degenerated' as a result of colonisation) as well as retaining those that were deemed to be appropriate, salvageable and commensurate with absorbing the skills of the pakeha. The 'accumulation of *Pakeha* knowledge', in short, while necessary, was far from sufficient. The Young Maori Party, then, represented a *response* to state aspirations to incorporate Maori into economic, legal, socio-cultural and political life entirely on its own terms – a response that sought to combine 'the best of both worlds' in producing a 'blended culture'. The man who would become its most influential leader, Apirana Ngata, would even sometimes come to expound a form of separate development, albeit within the parameters of settler capitalism.

To effect its aims, the Young Maori Party joined the many other

Maori at the end of the nineteenth century who saw the need for united action. This was a prerequisite if they were to avoid being swamped by the western civilisation they otherwise welcomed. Through united action, Maoridom could preserve appropriate elements of its own culture while taking up the many desirable ideas, technologies and lifestyles of the pakeha. Young Maori Party views in a sense codified adjustment strategies by different Maori groupings, including those of kupapa in the war years. Maori would learn from and, in Te Rangihiroa/Peter Buck's words (the dual name is significant), bring 'his equal contribution to the partnership with the Pakeha'.

The Young Maori Party and the unity movements spoke to one another with some understanding on such matters, although the party's strident denouncing of tribalist 'negative isolation' and 'disillusioned fatalism' caused severe tensions. While tribalism made Maori in Young Maori Party eyes 'the conscious or unconscious players in the final scene of the tragedy of decadence', the unity movements wanted federal, tribally based action. However, unity/kotahitanga perspectives sat well with the Young Maori Party's call for a 'new race-pride and race-consciousness' through 'self-respect' and 'self-reorganisation'.

The views of Ngata, Buck, Pomare and their co-thinkers became highly significant for all Maoridom towards the turn of the century when, no longer able to ignore the clamour of the unity movements, the government turned principally to the Young Maori Party for advice and mediation with Kotahitanga and Kingitanga. The result was two sets of what were depicted then, and have often been interpreted since, as large concessions to the Maori demand for self-government.[38]

Mediation and legislation

The Crown, while refusing official recognition of the Kotahitanga Parliament, tolerated it so long as it did not explicitly claim to impinge on British sovereign rights. But even Kotahitanga's mildest request, for a Maori subsidiary of the 'pakeha parliament', was considered an implicit challenge to sovereign indivisibility. While by 1899 attendance at the Paremata Maori was declining because of its lack of practical successes, the Crown remained perturbed at mass Maori acceptance of the Kotahitanga demands. Ministers sought a safety valve. It was through the services of Carroll, who rejected autonomy but saw the need to retain some Maori customs and land, that they turned to 'moderate' Maori reformists for ideas and advice.

For some time Ngata, Heke, Tureiti Te Heuheu Tukino and others had taken heed of the Crown's attempts (however desultory) to sanction and make use of 'native committees'. While some influential Maori such as Kaihau continued to press to officialise the Maori Parliament, they had been seeking a more attainable solution, legal status for the committees. Many ideas for this were in the air. In 1896, for example, Ngati Porou advocated 'Maori Committees' with the power to 'keep the peace, observe the law and determine those activities which they feel necessary for their well being'. While from its beginning the Young Maori Party had noted the need to meld Maori and pakeha ways, it had quickly seen an opportunity in many existing Maori demands and in the Urewera experiment. It was soon campaigning, along with some tribes, for local Maori self-government through statutory recognition of the komiti system, and for representative Maori involvement in deciding the future of tribal land. It sought the support of traditional leaders and elders, and organised meetings in Maori pa/villages.[39]

Given so many past rejections of their aspirations, and the Liberal government's policy of wholesale acquisition of Maori land, large numbers of Maori were suspicious of any watering-down of goals. With persistence, however, the Young Maori Party and their co-thinkers persuaded many Kotahitanga activists that adapting the committee system to the machinery of state was the only demand then viable. In a sense, both Kotahitanga and a newer, younger kotahitanga were beginning to converge over ways of working together for the common Maori good. At the same time, influenced by Carroll and the Young Maori Party, the government was coming to believe that conceding limited self-government and land management might be a controllable and economic way of meeting Maori demands.

This process would not be easy, given European attitudes to indigenous power and the government's resonance with a pakeha electorate that was at best ethnocentric and at worst racist. An Auckland newspaper's reference to 'that inherent detestation of the white races, and especially of British peoples, towards anything which savours of rule by coloured or native races' indicates the depth of the problem. But by 1898 Seddon was willing, on expedient grounds, to consider universalising the principles underpinning the Urewera legislation. While full assimilation was still the aim, the pace – especially on land and political matters – would be in effect slowed or even suspended by such a system. Yet it was also hoped that it would enable acceleration of other facets of assimilation and detribalisation, such as the introduction of western health services, something stressed by Carroll and the Young Maori Party.

While the party acted as mediator with Kotahitanga and other Maori movements, it was Carroll who in turn mediated between it and the Crown. He liaised particularly with Seddon and with Ngata, who was made 'travelling secretary' of TACSA in 1899. While Maori remained generally suspicious of the government, even though (and also because) its overtures were headed by the Premier, the Young Maori Party and its co-thinkers assisted the growing acceptance of a form of devolved local power. Their persuasion was such that at the March 1900 Maori Parliament at Ohinemutu in Rotorua, a subcommittee was selected to draft a Bill for the proposed new institutions. Chaired by Heke with Ngata's assistance, this body reached a unanimous conclusion which was then endorsed by the Paremata Maori. In effect, Kotahitanga had rescinded its minimal demand for official endorsement of a standing national Maori representative body.

The suggested institutions were to be based partly on previous experiments: the 'official runanga' of the 1860s, the Maori Committees of the 1880s, and Crown-tolerated de facto iwi and hapu social control mechanisms among tribes such as Ngati Porou. Since the draft plans provided for state supervision, and in the final analysis state control, of the proposed committees, the government accepted them in principle. Seddon himself introduced into the House of Representatives two Bills, drafted by Carroll and Heke (assisted by Ngata), which embodied the ideas which had emerged within the Kotahitanga fold. One was to do with land (discussed in Chapter Three), and the other politics. During their fine-tuning and passage through the chambers of Parliament the government sought advice from TACSA, and the Bills passed without difficulty and became law in October 1900.[40]

Maori Councils established

The political legislation, the Maori Councils Act, provided for elected, self-governing bodies in the rural areas where most Maori lived. In particular, the Maori Councils were authorised to control the 'health and welfare and moral well-being' of Maori. They would operate at regional level, laying down rules of social control through bylaws valid within their own boundaries, which were designed to reflect meaningful tribal clusters. Beneath them, elected village committees/komiti marae would supervise and enforce their rules in the small communities in which most Maori lived. These worked with non-official flax-roots organisations such as Kotahitanga's Komiti Wahine, which became commonly known as 'Ladies Committees'.

On the surface, the legislation provided for devolved local government powers which approached those of boroughs and town boards. The operation of the Maori Councils (nineteen were initially established) was to be heavily constrained and guided by the state, as one might expect from the Crown–Young Maori Party collaboration in their emergence. But they were designed to draw their energies from the rhythms of everyday tribal life. Thus the unity movements, as collaborations of tribally based bodies, had backed the ideas behind the legislation. They appreciated that the Councils marked a break from the effective exclusion of Maori from New Zealand political processes, and that the Crown accepted that they would broadly reflect tribal configurations and operate accordingly.

For its part, the Crown's short-term aim was to indicate that nationwide tribal unity of organisation and action was unnecessary. More generally, it sought to appropriate tribally based vitality and steer it in a 'safe' direction that would ultimately contribute to assimilation. Sections of the legislation which allowed Maori custom were thus qualified by others which worked in the opposite direction, such as suppression of

Maori notions of compensatory punishment for offenders. While the Crown had not abandoned its view that (in C W Richmond's words) the desired virtues of '[c]hastity, decency and thrift cannot exist amidst the waste, filth and moral contamination of the Pahs', it believed the Maori Councils could be used to lay the groundwork for removal of the 'communistic' way of life that allegedly perpetuated this state of affairs.

The official village committees were often easy to establish, as many were based on pre-existing komiti. For such matters of communal and state interest as sanitation, they had coercive powers over their people. Their tasks of enforcing Maori Council bylaws and local regulations and of carrying out specified devolved state duties were often assisted by the appointment of their own policemen. Ever since the founding of the colony the Crown had used the services of Maori to help control, and if necessary coerce, Maori and sometimes pakeha citizens. This function had been carried out continuously in many Maori communities whether or not there was official sanction for it. The various pan-tribal, religious and other Maori movements had their own systems for imposing and maintaining order – Kingitanga's watene and Ringatu's pirihimana, for example, controlled their own adherents. Maori and state interests often coincided in large areas of rule enforcement.[41]

Where there were actual or perceived discrepancies between the needs of the state and those of Maori, however, the Crown was always proactive to ensure that its requirements prevailed. There were incentives for the Maori Council system to promote social control measures that met the Crown's wishes; its structures, for example, were to be funded partly from fines levied under approved bylaws. With Council and komiti representatives, assisted by their own policemen (often working in arrangement with regular constables), controlling 'suppression of injurious customs such as drinking and gambling' and other behaviours considered undesirable, the Crown gained an extra enforcement regime at no cost to itself.

Moreover, some Maori Council activities that had been devolved by Parliament removed sources of strife between Crown and tribespeople, placing the onus on Maori authorities. In the past, for example, collecting the dog tax had been a matter of contention and tension. For the state, dog-tax enforcement was partly a way of reducing the number of dogs and thereby minimising danger to settlers' farm stock. Quite apart from their incapacity to pay, given a semi-subsistence lifestyle, Maori viewed the tax as an assault on their way of life. The issue had been the catalyst for the last armed rebellion against the Crown in the nineteenth century, the 'Hokianga Dog Tax Rebellion' of 1898.

The Maori communities themselves were now given the task of collecting the tax. As it was to be one of the Maori Councils' main sources of revenue, there was a great deal of incentive to collect. If they were to make full use of the Maori self-management system set up by the Crown, then, the komiti marae had to work actively to extract what was seen as an unjust tax. Some Maori argued from the beginning that, rather than being organisations to empower Maori, the Maori Councils and their committees were nothing more than agencies of the state. The whole structure was characterised in some quarters, in fact, as the Ture Kuri or Dog Law.

The Young Maori Party had been invited to draft model bylaws to guide the Maori Councils. It had done so, with Crown requirements firmly in mind, at its annual conference in December 1900. This was held in association with Kotahitanga's hui in Wanganui and so the Crown agenda, mediated by the party, was furthered in the heart of the major unity movement. The model bylaws emphasised such matters as the suppression of what were seen as 'pernicious customs', and some Maori observers were distinctly uneasy about what such phrases really meant.

There were also suspicions of the Crown's intentions from Kingitanga, which (correctly) believed that the state's primary aim with the new institutions was to head off kotahitanga. From the beginning, the government had explored various ways of gaining sufficiently widespread acceptance of the Maori Council system to supersede Kotahitanga and Kingitanga. It had decided that a colony-wide pan-tribal body placed above the local and district structures was necessary. But this could not be allowed to be too powerful. Thus the shapers of the system found a relatively anodyne solution, with the Act allowing for general conferences of Maori Council representatives.

In the event, this was not sufficient to head off Kingitanga, which within a year had rejected the new institutions and set about establishing its own local committees. However, the main perceived threat to the Crown's indivisible sovereignty doctrine had been Kotahitanga, and here it had success. From the time of the legisation it attempted to persuade the Maori Parliament movement to disband, on the ground that it had been made redundant by the Maori Council structures. Despite Ngata's reservations about the Councils' potential effectiveness, he and Carroll had accepted the government's desire to dissolve the main unity movement. As a result of their hard-argued persuasion at a joint Kotahitanga–Maori Councils meeting at Waiomatatini in 1902, it was decided to disband Te Kotahitanga o Te Tiriti o Waitangi and merge it with Maori Council general conferences. Some groupings retained an independent 'Kotahitanga' identity, but the unity movement never again reconvened under the Paremata Maori umbrella. The main perceived threat to indivisible Crown sovereignty, an authentic major Maori political movement, had quickly been subsumed and then removed. In return, the Crown was obliged to hold some general conferences. While these did provide an occasional pan-tribal forum of some value, they did not represent any significant advance for autonomy.[42]

Maori Councils in operation

At first the political institutions set up under the 1900 legislation did reflect and give effect to some of the aspirations of iwi, hapu and whanau. They tended to comprise 'chiefs and notables not invariably the most amenable to the new influences resulting from the crusade of the Young Maori Party' and some of their activities did not therefore entirely please the Crown. The representatives, in fact, generally shared the long-standing Maori vision of retrieving meaningful communal control over the Maori way of life. While the Councils and their committees were designed to appropriate Maori collective energies for state-desired purposes, then, many communities did attempt to use them as a state-provided device to promote their aspirations for autonomy. Moreover, the various levels of the Maori Council system, along with other Maori organisations, shared several significant aims with the Crown. The model regulations, for example, covered hygiene, a ban on liquor in pa/villages at hui, and the exclusion of animals in specified Maori spaces. These were adopted or adapted by the Councils, and many village committees enthusiastically accepted delegation of Maori Council powers of enforcement.

As Kotahitanga and Kingitanga made clear, the system fell far short of meeting their collective wish. But its implementation provides an example of the Maori propensity to experiment with whatever could be extracted from the Crown, however inadequate, rather than to boycott it. Such expedient use of the Council and komiti system, insofar as it has been noticed at all, has been generally seen as reflecting a genuine Crown–Maori 'compromise' over the quest for recognition of rangatiratanga. The state has been seen as providing a real chance for Maori to control their own destinies in at least some aspects of life. This is another example of the prevalence in modern scholarship of wishful thinking on Crown–Maori issues. There has been a tendency to extrapolate from the Liberal government's incipient pakeha 'welfare state' and find a genuine desire to give effect to Maori political aspirations. But once again the Crown is depicted as perennially falling short in the execution, because of failures of will, courage, personality or whatever, and there is regret at the lost chances of meaningful partnership.

This regret co-exists with modern scholarly appreciation that the Liberals' 1890s Maori land policies were essentially about completing the colonisation process over Maori and their communal lifestyle by parting them from the bulk of their remaining lands. Lack of interrogation of the state's ultimate intentions and goals, however, has allowed a government geared to depriving Maori of their land and ways of life to be depicted as having had the *will* and *potential* to meet at least some key Maori aspirations. While Maori have been contextualised as major losers in the Liberal 'social laboratory', there is still much comment along the lines that Seddon's government 'widened the fracture in the New Zealand dream' because it had 'lost an opportunity for the development of a truly bicultural society'. This, of course, implies that the state had an enlightened vision of a bicultural New Zealand in the first place. The history of Maori politico-cultural interaction with the Crown and settlers suggests clearly that the dream of a 'bicultural society', especially one which included autonomy or partnership, lay mostly on the Maori side alone (albeit in different forms according to period, politics and place).

The supposed Crown quest for 'progressive measures' for Maori, paralleling progress for settlers, holds understandably strong allure. Even the 1984 Maori sovereignty manifesto declared that, after 1900, 'the destiny of the Maori people turned away from the determined uncompromising desire for the return of Maori sovereignty' because such aspirations had been partially met by the Maori Council institutions. It is clear that the komiti marae often ran their own affairs successfully, but this the villages had already been doing. Moreover, the government's response to accusations that the Maori Councils would delay assimilation was to stress that their powers would be slight; they were 'something to occupy [Maori] attention'.

The modern (subliminal) search to find evidence of state willingness to endorse Maori aspirations can be viewed as reflecting a residual adherence to the former national myth that 'New Zealand had the best race relations in the world'. As part of the sales pitch for the Maori Councils, indeed, Maori were 'reminded' that indigenous people were better treated in New Zealand than anywhere else on the colonised globe. Yet even Ngata, who as one of the architects of the Councils had attempted to get more out of the Crown, felt at the outset that they were too underpowered in resources and authority. While backing the scheme as the only way of obtaining *any* devolved power during this period, he was one of many who saw that by its very nature it 'doomed Maori self-government'.

This was indeed what had been intended. The history of early colonial New Zealand can be conceptualised as the interaction of two sets of autonomous zones. When this ended with Maori autonomy being physically crushed after the conflicts of the 1860s, it thereafter sought new forms of expression and the Crown found new ways of countering it. In the state's eyes, the process *away* from autonomy needed encouragement. In 1900 it saw appropriation of Maori desire for organisational autonomy as a means not just of diverting that desire but also of marshalling it in the ultimate quest for full assimilation.

Interpretations which see the 1900 experiment as having been initially motivated by an urge to meet Maori aspirations, and then as having fallen short in the execution of policy, miss this key dynamic of history. In so doing they inadvertently denigrate the strength of indigenous resistance to what remained a policy goal of full assimilation. The interesting story is how the Crown, with all its coercive and appropriative power, and with the help of sites of collaboration, failed to crush aspirations for rangatiratanga. Maori actions to achieve autonomy have, in fact, persisted to this day, often *sotto voce* to the pakeha and therefore to historians who work from pakeha documentation and world-views. What the 1900 experiment reveals is both the pressure for autonomy which Maori placed on the Crown at the end of the nineteenth century, and the government's determination to ensure that, whatever it seemed to be doing, it always had the ultimate aim of full assimilation in mind. At the very least, it was anxious to neutralise dangerous opposition to its hegemony – as can similarly be seen in its diversion of trade union activity away from strikes into the more tranquil world of industrial conciliation and arbitration.[43]

However, as with unions, those who were to be controlled engaged with the state to maximise their own positions, and became increasingly strident as they came to appreciate just how far the system had been designed to counteract rather than endorse their aspirations. With the Maori Councils, this had initially been disguised not only beneath accommodatory rhetoric but also by the exigencies of the situation. Even the most pro-western of Maori involved in operating the new structures realised that their success would depend partly on mobilising elements of pre-existing Maori authority structures. Moreover, close association of rangatira/chiefs and kaumatua/elders with the process of establishing and running the system helped give it mana/prestige. On such issues, despite its ultimate assimilationist goal, the Crown once again proved to be flexibly realistic in the 'public good'. This in turn had benefits for Maori: the Councils which operated vigorously on behalf of their people were usually those in which tribal and chiefly power was prominent.

This did not mean that the Crown in any way faltered in its efforts to maximise its influence on the Maori Council system, especially through Ngata and his Young Maori Party colleagues. Not content with model bylaws reflecting its own requirements, it set out to ensure co-ordination, inspection and (in effect) control of the movement from the centre. With royalty visiting Rotorua in 1901, the government arranged through the Council system for a large hui that doubled as a village operating under the hygiene and coercive rules of the model bylaws. The Councils and their committees were urged to take the methods demonstrated there back into their communities.

A small office was established in the Justice Department to run the Maori Council system. Ngata was appointed as 'Organising Inspector' in 1902 and Gilbert Mair, a pakeha former leader of kupapa forces, was appointed 'Superintendent' the following year. Through the head office mechanism the Crown sought tighter monitoring and control of the system. Ngata's first notice to Council chairs included a request for detailed reports on their districts. The Maori Council system's part-time police personnel were generally under the guidance of the New Zealand Police Force and were used at times by the regular police as auxiliaries (the only occasion on which they were allowed to coerce Europeans). Some Councils even came to be dominated by pakeha with official links.

When Seddon proclaimed at Putiki in late 1902 that the Maori Council experiment had proved that Maori could be trusted with local body powers, he was hoping that the system, while initially using the tribal milieu, would eventually speed up detribalisation and assimilation. If it performed satisfactorily, he opined, from time to time its powers might be extended. While most of its participants sought the empowering of communal lifestyles and tribal decision making, the Crown was increasingly instrumental in effecting a different agenda. This had been implicit from the beginning, of course. In the related area of health reform, for example, when Maui Pomare was appointed the first Native Health Officer in 1900 (in the new Department of Public Health), it was later reported, '[e]very step he took cut across customs and traditions'.

One of the reasons the Young Maori Party was so favoured was that some party policies sought to phase out customs and activities, such as certain tangihanga/funeral rituals and types of hui, which were deemed to be damaging. While Maoridom's strong desire to control its own destiny did not preclude an evolution in lifestyles, the state's programming of its own imperatives into the structural and policy reforms led to reactions, even within the Maori Council system, which looked to the past. Other of the new institutions preferred a 'modernising' line. Some Councils took the Crown at its word in terms of self-management and unilaterally attempted to take greater powers than allowed by law – exercising controls over pakeha, for example, or over Maori from 'outside' areas. They found out the state's limitations in tolerance when such practices were proscribed.[44]

In view of such differing agendas, the Maori Council system was soon increasingly abandoned as a vehicle that could be used by Maori leaders to fulfil their aspirations for autonomy. Some remained with it because the mechanisms and associated Crown activities were providing at least some benefits for their people. These benefits, however, came at the price of continued tightening of the Crown's general surveillance and control of Maori. At the first general conference of Maori Councils in Rotorua in 1903, Pomare procured a motion for Maori villages to come under sanitation surveillance. When he followed this up the following year by establishing a network of 'Native Sanitary Inspectors' reporting to him in his official capacity, there was far from universal welcome for their activities – inspecting villages and monitoring komiti marae programmes, among other things. And yet they were carrying out reforms that undoubtedly led to considerable improvements in Maori health, so much so that they contributed to the demographic revival among Maori.

From the beginning, Pomare had seen that working through the Maori Councils, rather than through a separate Maori-oriented health workforce, was a way of marshalling collective endeavour both to effect health reforms and to undermine some of the bases of that collectivism. After his appointment as Assistant Native Health Officer, Te Rangihiroa reflected the views of his circle in urging a vigorous attack, through the community-based institutions, on customs detrimental to health. He explicitly linked the concept of communal life and organisation to anachronistic health practices. 'The communism of the past meant industry, training in arms, good physique, the keeping of the law, the sharing of the tribal burden, and the preservation of life . . . The communism of today means indolence, sloth, decay of racial vigour, the crushing of individual effort, the spreading of introduced infectious disease, and the many evils that are petrifying the Maori and preventing his advance.'

One of the inspectors' targets was the institution of tohunga, often at the time translated pejoratively as 'witch-doctor'. In traditional Maori society tohunga combined religious, medical and other services and social control functions. The Crown had long seen the presence of tohunga as an implicit challenge to the European mores which underscored the state and its doings. Its allies in the Young Maori Party believed that colonisation's impact had destroyed genuine tohungaism, leaving charlatans to ply the trade, and they passed resolutions accordingly. But the profession retained much power in the majority world of Maori who wished to regain control over their own affairs and customs.

Thus the Crown needed the inspectorate, operating under the umbrella of the Maori Council structure, to build up a dossier that equated tohungaism with fake faith-healers playing on people's fears. This became ammunition for the eventual passing of the Tohunga Suppression Act in 1907, although the legislation was intended specifically for potential use against resistance leader Rua Kenana. While the Act was supported on public health grounds by some important Maori leaders, many others observed that, while it might have the good effect of suppressing fraudulent tohunga who had thriven in the liminality which followed tribal breakdown, it also constituted parliamentary interference in their customary law and tribal office-holders.

The measure was a high-profile example of actions and institutions associated with the 1900 structure which had the ambitious aim of helping state and private institutions to undermine the Maori communal political economy and way of life. Temporary drafting into service of the communalist structures on which such lifestyles had been based in the first place was as common a phenomenon in New Zealand as in the history of empire generally. When a Maori Council was established in 1902 in the remotest inhabited area of New Zealand, the Chatham Islands (Rekohu/Wharekauri), for example, it was linked to enlisting 'loyal' Taranaki tribal elements. Here the Crown had previously paid little attention to indigenous matters, such as the enslavement and then marginalisation of the Moriori (a people conquered by Taranaki tribes prior to British colonisation), so long as an acceptable degree of order prevailed. But from time to time the actions of followers of the prophet Te Whiti o Rongomai had been seen as a threat to order in the islands, and this was again the case. The new structure was intended to help undermine their resistance to the Crown.

The Young Maori Party members appreciated that those who followed

Whatever the Crown's motivations and actions, however, in many areas covered by active Maori Council committees the people *did* gain positive benefits from the new institutions. At the 6000-strong 'model' hui/village at Rotorua there was no sickness, disorder or drunkenness over a two-week period, and this prompted attempts at emulation. Collaborating or co-operating with the state, and even helping direct its 'native' policies and structures, was considered in many quarters as contributing to 'raising up' rather than to disappearing. In the Chathams, as elsewhere, children entered school, sanitary reforms began, drunkenness and other forms of disruption to village life fell off. In the Waikato, where Kingitanga hostility prevented the institution being established, living conditions remained reportedly most unhealthy.[45]

The Young Maori Party members appreciated that those who followed resistance leaders such as Te Whiti were engaged in the same general project as themselves, working to better the prospects of their people *as a people* within a settler-dominated society. But they believed that the opportunities offered by Maori Councils could lead to concrete improvement in the short term that would provide a basis for longer-term developments. Moreover, they argued, the Maori Councils system, together with recent legislation conferring legal equality, ensured that Maori had a greater degree of actual or potential control over their own destinies.

Concomitantly, however, under the new processes the state had increased its capacity for socio-racial surveillance of Maori, their aim being similar to that of the official runanga system of the 1860s upon which, via the komiti, they were conceptually modelled. The system's boosting of chiefly authority, therefore, was intended to be only temporary, part of the Crown's broader 'civilising mission'. The bylaws of the (eventually 25) Maori Councils reflected the Young Maori Party-generated prototypes, whose aims were to assist the resuscitation of Maoridom through westernisation. They and the Council enforcement arms complemented the state's instruments of coercive and hegemonic control over the whole population.

But the Maori Councils and allied bodies did not act entirely as creatures of the Crown, and failed in several ways to effect its wishes. Many of their members believed that to 'suppress the tohunga was to strike at the roots of Maori value systems', and so declined to promulgate prohibitive bylaws. That is why the Tohunga Suppression Act was needed – to give regular police the power to move against millennial prophets, religio-medical healers and others who were deemed to be socially corrupting. As a prominent detective said, after the failure of the 1900 institutions to move over an issue of such significance for the state, '[g]aol seems to be the only way to break down the prestige of a recognized tohunga'.

Even if the only achievement of the Maori Council system had been to get the Maori Parliament disbanded, the strategy would have been deemed successful as a return on a very small Crown investment. The key state strategy, however, remained the hegemonic winning of Maori adherence to western ways of thinking and doing. But its results were jeopardised by the state's fear of devolving too much power to Maori authorities. The first general conference of Maori Councils asked for greater powers. They wanted to regulate Europeans living in Maori villages, deal with such offences as assaults and thefts, and have full delegated local government powers in wholly Maori areas.

Carroll sought to gain such extra authority, but during the passage of amending legislation in 1903 (following a 1901 amendment which provided some enforcement powers) he managed to obtain only minor accretions in powers and resources. The Councils were, therefore, denied the means to achieve the results that both they and the Crown wanted. Occasionally, state and/or Maori institutions would have to intervene when Councils or komiti marae exceeded their statutory powers – in disciplining pakeha, for example, or taking modernising zeal too far by 'oppressing' tribal members who had clung to the old ways.

The waning of the Maori Councils

Enthusiasm among Maoridom for the Maori Councils waned, and in the event only six general conferences were ever held. Even Ngata resigned from the system in 1904, in despair at the lack of state support, and after Mair left in 1907 the central administration languished. The Maori Council system, now run from the Native Department (which had been reinstated in 1906), was on a downward spiral. Denied meaningful rangatiratanga, the Councils declined; they therefore became of decreasing significance as agencies of government instrumentalism, and were even further starved of funding and authority.

While some continued to operate, others became defunct or continued only in name. In some Council districts, officially endorsed komiti marae flourished regardless of the health or otherwise of the regional bodies. In others, Maori reverted to customary structures 'untainted' by Crown authority. In particular, Maori would shun the system in areas where pakeha 'excesses' – liquor selling, stock trespass, wahi tapu violations and the like – which the Councils were generally powerless to stop, were rife.

Within a few years of their establishment the resource-starved Maori Councils were manifestly unable to address the concerns of either Maori or state. Attempted revivals by the minister in charge, Ngata, especially by convening a general conference in 1911, did not succeed. After that hui, indeed, no further general gatherings occurred. Nevertheless, activities under Council auspices continued in many areas. When smallpox broke out in the Auckland region in 1913, for example, Maori Councils and their komiti actively aided the police, health and other authorities in restricting travel, vaccinating and monitoring social distress.

All in all, it would be a mistake to echo some modern reassessments that depict the Councils as no more than a typical and successful state ploy to suppress Maori. It should be remembered that they were in fact initially an experiment forced on the Crown by exigencies, that prominent Maori had felt this could bring benefits to their own people in different ways as well as assisting the Crown's agendas, and that there were achievements which benefited Maori. Historians who have tended to blame the Crown's lack of resourcing for the gradual demise of the Maori Councils have equally downplayed Maori agency, ignoring the fact that many Maori organisations not funded by the state had been (and were to be) highly successful. In essence the Councils languished because their primary purpose was not to effect but to contain, even to restrain, rangatiratanga. Maori who had sought to make use of them in pursuit of autonomy found the state's parameters too constraining to do so effectively. But meanwhile they had produced results that both Maori and the Crown had wanted, such as 'play[ing] an important role in the cultural adaptation of tribes to modernity in isolated rural areas'. In fact, because Maori in some areas saw some *residual* use for the Councils and their sub-institutions, and that suited the Crown too, the latter continued to see some leverage in keeping the system alive.

In the suspicious atmosphere of the home front during the First World War, however, the wielding of Maori Council powers by elected persons was seen as potentially dangerous. In 1916, therefore, by legislative amendment the Councils became Crown-appointed entities. After the war, following enormous Maori casualties in the great influenza pandemic, the government decided for several reasons to concentrate its official Maori energies on health matters. The new 'Health Officer for Natives', Te Rangihiroa/Buck, recommended that the most convenient way to do so was to locate the new programmes in the pre-existing community-based structures of the 1900 system, especially since health had tended to be the main work of the functioning Councils that remained. Such ideas had been mooted since the early years of the Maori Council system, and the politicians now accepted the argument.

In 1919, then, Maori Councils were required to work in close co-operation with the Department of Public Health. Reform went much further in 1920, when the Department of Public Health was restructured. Te Rangihiroa was appointed director of the specialist Division of Maori Hygiene, and in specified 'Maori Health Districts' the Councils were to be defined as Maori Health Councils. The Councils' main official function became raising the health and well-being of Maori, given that they were no longer seen as a dying race.

In terms of either fundamental state purposes or substantive Maori autonomy, neither the Crown nor Maori gained a great deal out of the 1900 institutions and their successors. Many observers, including historians and other scholars who have interpreted both the Maori Councils and the superimposed Maori Health Councils as a genuinely motivated 'compromise' by the Crown, have pronounced the experiment a failure. But by creating the Maori Council system the Crown had considerably defused a late-nineteenth-century build-up of Maori protest. Moreover, the Councils and their committees had played some part in the relative quiescence of Maori as a political force in the first decades of the twentieth.

On the Maori side, a degree of autonomy had been carved out considerably beyond that which the Crown had intended, and even traditional cultural and organisational arrangements had secured a degree of clandestine protection – including even the tohungaism so detested by officials and Maori modernisers. Undoubtedly, the Councils' work – especially in health – brought considerable benefits to Maori communities. Some revived sufficiently to continue on through the 1920s and beyond; when the system was superseded in 1945, six remained. In an official chronology of the Department of Maori Affairs, compiled six decades after their founding, the original Maori Councils and their health-oriented successors had disappeared from sight altogether. They deserve greater recognition.[46]

CHAPTER THREE

SEEKING LANDED AUTONOMY IN THE EARLY TWENTIETH CENTURY

Land and people

'The problem of the Maori and his land are one', noted a leading Young Maori Party member concerned about ongoing land loss. This theme has been a commonplace in scholarship: 'Land was the cornerstone of society upon which the Maori political, economic, and social system depended.' 'To Maori, the land was paramount. It was the foundation of social and economic life, and it also provided a cultural stability essential to survival. Every aspect of life for Maori could be anchored into the land'. That the land was and is integral to Maori has become a truism. Its incantation in literature and elsewhere tends, indeed, to *underplay* the overwhelming significance of the land and its resources in the Maori cosmos, which can be expressed in the saying:

People have come and gone
But the land remains steadfast
Bindings of people, and the land
Is our history.

Modern scholars, especially Maori writers, have stressed the integral link between land and rangatiratanga. A direct linkage is often made between the results of the three major modes of land alienation in the nineteenth century – Crown purchases, state confiscations and Native Land Court operations – and the ongoing loss of autonomy for Maori: 'With their land base gone, the chiefs were totally disempowered . . . Land is the very basis of Maori, of mana Maori motuhake, of tribal sovereignty. So once the land goes, the mana of the chief goes with it.'

Land is also used as the crucial interpretive device to explain the endurance of politico-cultural loss through to the present, as a recent comment by a Maori scholar on the centrality of land in the Maori world-view indicates: 'The key symbol between past and future in the present context is land.' Another writer assesses that '[t]raditional Maori society was based on the land. Once this basis was removed, only chaos could follow'.

An overwhelming focus on land, however, can obscure the agency of people. It is clear that the various movements for Maori autonomy in the early twentieth century were underpinned by a yearning for a rangatiratanga that was rooted in the land and its resources. Most of these movements sought at the very least to retain all land still remaining in Maori hands. Most Maori land, including almost all of the *fertile* land, had disappeared by 1900, however. And thereafter, despite initial hopes for retention, an almost inexorable loss of land – through taking for 'public purposes' as well as further purchases – continued, with very limited chances of getting even some of it back in any conceivable future. Yet Maori continued to maintain great pressure for autonomy. However significant the autonomy–land nexus, then, the quest for rangatiratanga was pursued from a state of relative (or even total, for some smaller tribal groupings) landlessness, with little prospect of altering this situation in the lifetimes of those involved. It is hard to escape the conclusion that for Maori, as with indigenous people throughout empires and within post-colonies, the quest to regain autonomy took total precedence over all else, including reacquisition of land. But a significant landed base always remained one ultimate goal of rangatiratanga.[47]

Alienation versus retention

In effecting the alienation of the bulk of the land from Maori, as indeed in the colonising project in general, the Crown had contributed to the disruption of traditional social and economic structures, including the power base of chiefs. It seems that, given the relative disempowerment of traditional chieftainship after the land alienations, Maori increasingly reinforced a pre-existing capacity to turn to leaders recognised for their *achievements*, as opposed to their hereditary status, in order to reforge self-determination. This does not imply any faltering in the collective desire to retain and regain land and control. The ambition to retain land was in fact encouraged at the turn of the century by the government's review of its alienation policies, a reflection of concern that tangata whenua might become a strain on the state as a result of total landlessness. Realisation among officials and politicians that a slow-down in the alienation rate might benefit state aims had, in fact, already featured in the Crown's negotiations with Maori bodies in the later 1890s.

Any possibility of resiling from alienation had been pegged to a *quid pro quo*: productive use by Maori of the soil for the 'public good'. The involvement of Maori in Crown-approved ways to 'improve' non-alienated land had been explored in the past – in the 1883 experiment of committees which could investigate title to land, for example, and some shortlived legislation three years later which allowed owners of a Maori block to act as a single legal entity. But the advent of the Liberal government in 1890 had meant that a concerted push for closer pakeha settlement at the expense of Maori land ownership was inevitable, a key electoral base of the party being the actual and would-be European 'small farmer'. The best Maori could hope for was that their views would be *partially* taken into account.

This had seemed to be happening when W L Rees and James Carroll, constituting a commission of inquiry on Maori land law established soon after the Liberal victory, endorsed an 1885 idea (from the head of the Native Department) for, essentially, tribal determination of title. They proposed, moreover, state-authorised, Maori-based management regimes to lease out Maori lands and sell those not needed or which required 'unlocking' by pakeha investment. But settler pressure had ensured, instead, an escalation of aggressive Crown purchasing under the Native Land Court system. The government accepted only those Rees–Carroll Commission's recommendations which facilitated its land buying, such as the reintroduction of the Crown's purchasing monopoly. Over the five years from 1894, well over 1.5 million acres of Maori land were alienated. As we have noted, in fact, the Liberal government was a key regime in the history of the relentless parting of Maori from most of their land. Its aim was bald and bold: to remove 'uneconomic' (Maori) owners from fertile and accessible land in order to replace them with 'productive' and 'scientific' (pakeha) farmers.

Everyone involved in examining the politico-organisational future of Maori needed to address the question of land. Within the ranks of the Young Maori Party, the lack of full agreement on the exact extent or type of adaptation, partnership or autonomy that should be sought partly reflected differences over land. Pomare and Ngata, for example, were at opposite poles over how land fitted into 'the rehabilitation of their people'. Ngata's solutions were much more popular, and were (in the words of a later commentator) 'in the direction of communistic management': by collectively occupying and developing the land, it could be saved from loss by Crown action. Assimilatory tendencies, then, should have very strict limits when it came to what was left of the landed base of the indigenous political economy. Until Maori could obtain capital and know-how for development, the land could be made productive by leasing it to pakeha. Pomare, however, felt that collective tribal land tenure was outdated, given the requirements of farming in a capitalist economy and the Native Land Court's operations to individualise interests in land. If farming by Maori proved not to be viable, as would often be the case, selling their interests and seeking wage work instead (perhaps on the same land, with a new pakeha 'settler') was the answer. For him, leasing was not an acceptable alternative, as living off rents from the land created idleness and degeneracy rather than the regeneration he sought.[48]

But not even the government thought it could implement such a regime, at least not at that stage. Under enormous Maori pressure, Premier Seddon had succumbed to the view that the tangata whenua could retain much of their remaining land, so long as they agreed to a new land administration system. In 1898 the Maori Parliament debated his proposal, which watered down the Rees–Carroll recommendations for state-sanctioned, Maori-run committees to manage indigenous land matters. Kotahitanga's eventual draft Bill on Maori land issues was influenced by these processes and the Urewera legislation. It sought to replace the Native Land Court with local Maori committees operating under six district land boards, block committees to bring land into production, and an appeal board. It was envisaged that sales would cease and, once ownership was established, block committees would lease out some land and use the capital from there and elsewhere to finance development of the rest.

The Crown was not prepared to go so far as to abolish the Native Land Court, or give farming powers to committees, but negotiators on both sides were feeling their way towards a deal. There seemed to be general acceptance in Maoridom that the government's proposals marked progress, but only so long as all purchasing initiatives ceased. The government was in fact increasingly realising that, if land alienation escalated, indigenes might become so economically marginalised as to be a major burden on the state. Quite apart from the 'law and order' ramifications of such a scenario, Liberal philosophy saw the state as taking some safety-net responsibility for the poor: it would be difficult to escape such an obligation to an impoverished Maoridom. Maori MPs passed the qualified support of Maori on the Crown proposals to the Native Affairs Committee, and the government incorporated them into draft legislation in 1899. Pending further action, new purchasing was suspended (although current transactions were to be completed). This became known as the taihoa/slow-down policy.

The Crown had been influenced by its 'mediation' discussions with the Young Maori Party, which generally favoured leasing out quantities of land as a way of meeting both pakeha demand and the Crown's desire to put all lands to maximal productive use. Such arrangements would enable tribes to retain the mana of underlying title and gain the land back at the end of the leasehold period. In December 1899 James Carroll (known as 'Jimmy Taihoa' for his delaying tactics on land purchasing) became the first Maori appointed to the position of Minister of Native Affairs. This assisted further progress on Maori land issues. By the end of the century, then, land policy negotiations facilitated by Carroll and Young Maori Party and allied leaders were coming to fruition, in tandem with the negotiations which had led to the establishment of the Maori Councils.

Carroll and the Crown then built on the various draft land Bills, as well as on the results of consultations, when preparing sister legislation to that setting up the Maori Councils. The main factor for Maori was retention of ownership, which would require a great deal of leasing out.

A revised administration system as sought by the Crown was an acceptable 'compromise' for the main Maori groupings, so long as it simplified and expedited leasing arrangements and protected owners' rights. This the Maori Lands Administration Bill, introduced in 1900, seemingly did.[49]

Maori Land Councils

There was therefore little Maori opposition to the passage of the Bill, despite its various shortfalls from a tangata whenua perspective. It proposed establishing councils to superintend Maori land matters, having the capacity, for example, to assume in certain circumstances Native Land Court powers to determine ownership of customary lands. In supporting its introduction as the best deal they could get from the Crown, Maori MPs noted that preservation and control of the remaining Maori land could only come about at this late point through state action. That the Bill was the best they could hope for was a point Seddon reiterated. Ngata argued to the 1900 TACSA conference that, while the 'compromise' was far from ideal, it was a good enough start. Few Maori saw it as a panacea for controlling their remaining landed patrimony, but when placed alongside what seemed to be the exciting 'home rule' development of the Maori Councils, it was deemed to be progress along a route towards rangatiratanga. The Maori Lands Administration Act, by which Maori gained at least 'a small degree of local say in land matters', together with the suspension of purchasing, constituted a significant development at the end of a century that had been marked by contact, colonisation and conflict.[50]

Maori hoped that this could become the platform for other developments central to their collective future, goals summed up by Ngata as 'the retention of Maori culture while adapting to the dominating Pakeha society, and the improvement of the Maori race spiritually, economically, and socially'. The new land administration system, then, would not just help prevent politico-cultural disaster, but positively assist in a revival of Maori fortunes. The Act's preamble, in stating that Maori should not be left landless, seemed to confirm that the Crown appreciated Maori wishes on this fundamental issue. The Maori Land Councils it set up were to ensure that sufficient area was left for 'maintenance and support' of Maori communities. They could also set aside inalienable reserves for other purposes, such as burial, fishing and birding.

The legislation, too, seemed to meet some Maori requirements for self-management of the remaining communally owned lands. Block committees, for example, could investigate ownership of papatupu/customary land in line with tribal rules, draw up hapu boundaries and lists of owners, and make recommendations to the Maori Land Councils. The latter could ascertain ownership, except where there was contention, in which case the supreme power of the Native Land Court would come into operation.

Most significant of all, the legislation embodied the triumph of the Maori negotiators who had, while agreeing with the Crown that development was necessary, influenced it into accepting that this could generally come through leaseholding rather than through alienation of freehold. The idea was to complement Maori-farmed and -inhabited lands with retention of a broader turangawaewae/'place to stand', albeit comprising lands often leased out for the time being. Pakeha know-how and capital would develop the latter while preparing them for ultimate handing back to Maori. The Act confirmed, in short, that land development need not be posited on pakeha *ownership*: tribal lands could be voluntarily vested in the Maori Land Councils, which would guarantee title and thereby facilitate leasing out.

It was envisaged, indeed, that leases could become the *main* means by which Europeans and their capital gained access to and worked the land, and that the Maori Land Councils' main function would be to administer the leases of lands vested in them. The monies could be used to develop those blocks that stayed in Maori hands to meet the immediate needs of the tribespeople. When the leases expired, Carroll argued, a new generation of Maori would have developed the skills and finances to farm the lands themselves, and thus benefit their families, their sub-tribes and their tribes, and all New Zealanders. This was the philosophy behind the taihoa on initiating new sales of Maori land.[51]

There was provision for one Maori Land Council for each Maori Land District in the North Island, and over time seven were set up, with five to seven members each. An indigenous majority on a Council was possible, as two to three members were to be elected by Maori landowners of the district and another Maori member would be appointed by the Governor. A sizeable proportion of Maori members, the mediators believed, would help effect rangatiratanga in matters such as management of leased-out lands.

The Act was presented to Maori principally as a measure to conserve land in collective ownership, with Hone Heke and other MPs stressing the importance of tangata whenua taking advantage of the lease provisions. Such endorsements have led many historians, even those generally disinclined to take the Crown's explanations at face value, to interpret the Maori Lands Administration Act as a 'creative and constructive' attempt to preserve a patrimony for Maori. The legislation's fundamental aim has been depicted as giving tangata whenua 'control over land management and alienation' and enabling them to 'restrain the rate of alienation'. Some say it went 'a long way' towards meeting Maori aspirations to keep and develop their land, or even that the Maori Land Council system provided 'real autonomy'.

In shepherding the measure through Parliament, however, Seddon and Carroll openly admitted the government's major motivation: making accessible more land to settlers for grazing and cultivating, in the 'public good'. As even an autonomist interpretation has acknowledged, 'legal control and governmental supervision' prevailed within the Maori Land Council system. Moreover, the Native Land Court could 'wrest the ultimate *mana*' from a block committee by 'handing down an irrevocable decision' of contrary nature. While Maori operated the 'processes of investigation and decision-making', these could be overridden by the Crown and its agencies.[52]

On paper a 'feasible compromise' had been achieved. The Crown had ceased initiating the buying of land, in return for arrangements for Maori to lease to pakeha and play a prominent role in the institutions handling such arrangements. In reality, however, the sole criterion of success in state eyes would be the proportion of 'idle lands' brought quickly into settler production, and the system's future hinged on this. Such intentions, and the Crown's pressure to give effect to them, contributed to the results. Whatever the arguments about the Maori Land Councils' independence and consultation, through this system Maori were to be 'deprived of all authority and management of their ancestral lands' for the foreseeable future. This seemed to be 'simply another means of the State taking their lands' rather than any acknowledgement of their rangatiratanga. And so there was, initially, considerable reluctance to place tribal patrimony under the control of a government organisation.

When appointments to Maori Land Councils were finalised towards the end of 1902, moreover, tribes could see that Crown-appointed Maori had 'loyalist' backgrounds. One key member, for example, had served a long apprenticeship on official 'native committees'. The pakeha head of his Council was, equally typically, a former Crown land purchase officer. He and the other chairs knew which purchase transactions the Crown wished to complete or (if policy changed) initiate, and their organisations prioritised accordingly. Other factors, too, militated against the Maori Land Councils being self-determinationist mechanisms. While they held many of the powers of the Native Land Court, for example, they could never become an alternative to it. Even had they been inclined to meet local and regional wishes for autonomist preservation and control of patrimonial lands, they held insufficient authority to satisfy tribespeople who might put their faith in them.

When word spread in Maoridom about such ineffectiveness, some tribes began to boycott the Maori Land Councils or disrupt their work. Only two districts co-operated quickly with the government's plans to 'open up' sizeable lands to pakeha through leasing. In turn, the Councils could do little to fast-track the government's prime aim of pakeha settlement and development. Hopefully, wrote a Poverty Bay commentator in 1902, 'the district should reap the benefit of this fine bush country being speedily settled' as a result of the Council's work. If land could be readily developed in this way, it would be a process of 'great simplicity as compared with the tortuous methods of the Native Land Court'. But once the Maori Land Councils were fully operating in 1903, such hopes were generally dashed. This was partly because of the ponderousness of the system the Crown had set up. Even in an area where the committees were supposedly 'working well' for the Crown, a royal commission investigation revealed that only 28,315 out of 175,393 acres had been uncontested in a way that would facilitate development.

Maori who used the system tended to do so in their own interests rather than adhering to the Crown's agenda. Papatupu block committees, for example, might expedite determination of titles for customary land with an eye to ongoing occupancy rather than temporary loss through leasehold. With title investigations completed, pakeha expected the new system to 'test the feeling of the owners as to placing the properties in the hands of the Council, for administration' and leasing. When early results showed that often this did not occur, there was chagrin among officialdom and settlers. Block committee investigations, in other words, tended to subvert Crown intentions by focusing on or assisting community aspirations.

Through using the committees Maori could both avoid Native Land Court costs and create the conditions for raising their own farming productivity. Indications are that they tried to operate fairly within Maoridom. One committee, for example, declined to assess that an historical conquest had occurred, even though some of its members 'would have benefited to a large extent' from such a finding. The 70 committees in Taitokerau worked hard to reconcile differing viewpoints, attempting to create stability within their communities. Commenting on general criticism that the block committees had 'ignobly failed', a royal commission would praise some of them for advancing Maori interests in an 'astonishing' fashion. Moreover, many Maori considered that, compared with what had existed before the legislation, even the Maori Land Councils represented progress towards their aspirations. Some groupings which initially opposed or resisted working through them realised, after close observation of their operations, that they could be used for their own collective benefit. Such opting-in began to move some Council procedures in the direction of autonomy.[53]

Other tribes bypassed the new machinery altogether, especially if Maori representatives on the Councils were from rival iwi or were deemed to be too compromised by association with the Crown. Such iwi sometimes attempted to minimise the impact of irreversible alienation or to meet Crown pressure to 'free up' lands by establishing leasing regimes independent of the Maori Land Councils. In some places such as the Rohe Potae, indeed, tribes had long preferred to lease rather than sell. The increase in Maori interest in direct leasing arrangements after the 1900 legislation, while not seen as ideal, was nevertheless welcomed by the Crown. 'Temporary alienation' through leasing under any arrangement was now accepted as an appropriate Maori response to national needs, legitimating the (relative) taihoa on Crown purchasing.

For Maori, the taihoa policy and the leasing option gave them a chance to regroup collective interests, working such land as they could while receiving rentals from the remaining tribal patrimony. Once the leases had finished, they would be able themselves to develop the bulk of the land remaining in Maori ownership. This seemed a suitable statement of rangatiratanga in difficult circumstances. But the 'leasing solution' was problematic from the outset. Pakeha generally preferred freehold tenure, distrusting the very concept of Maori landlords, and so Maori wanting to lease did not necessarily find viable takers. Moreover, the brake on Crown purchasing had been justified, in terms of public good, partly by the prospect of Maori farming portions of their tribal land. This they would do using development monies not only from pakeha rents, but also from loans. Despite Carroll's and others' efforts at persuasion, however, neither Crown nor private enterprises were generally willing to provide tribes with credit (although loans were provided to pakeha farmers to develop their land).

Whatever the difficulties, the Young Maori Party's and others' concerns to prevent 'disintegration' of their people 'as a race' *had* resulted in a system in which Maori could retain *some* measure of control over the land. Numerous tribes had determined to make the best of it. Papatupu block committees did a great amount of work and the Maori Land Councils were used to seek better prices for leases. Yet the initial positive Maori responses to the 'leasing solution' were too few in the eyes of both Crown and settlers. The moratorium on new state purchasing would, therefore, constitute no more than a *brief* holding operation in the inexorable settler push for land. Some pakeha MPs and others had said from the beginning that, since Maori did not view the system as anything other than an *imposed* 'compromise', they were scarcely likely to make great use of the block committees or Councils – at least not in a way the Crown wished. Such views appeared to be vindicated when the system did not result in releasing land for pakeha farming anywhere near fast enough to satisfy settler demand.[54]

From a Maori perspective, however much some tribes used it, the system could not provide many opportunities greatly to advance autonomy. The increasing numbers who decided to explore it did so in an attempt to take advantage of whatever the Crown was willing to proffer. The Crown came to share the view many Maori had had in the first place. It eventually decided that the 1900 Act held no great prospect for bringing undeveloped land into production, by Maori or pakeha, or for a satisfactory land control regime. It therefore reverted to its old policies, including promoting land purchasing for white settlement.

With taihoa gone almost as soon as it had been put into place, tribal authorities had to continue to watch land and resources slip away, often as a result of the impoverishment of Maori in a cash-oriented economy at a time of demographic revival. This was a far cry from that which so many had sought, a land base (with, at the very least, Maori managerial input) from which, ultimately, to reclaim their collective local and regional autonomy. The 1894 reintroduction of Crown monopoly on purchase meant that the state 'bought on its own terms' when it resumed purchasing, and this resulted in low prices. Those who saw autonomy in terms of the ability to do what they wished with their ancestral lands, including selling them, were particularly vigorous in criticising the absence of a free market. The situation constituted a double blow for those compelled reluctantly by marginalised circumstances to sell.

The resumption of permanent land alienation helped revive fears that tangata whenua would become 'idle' and therefore a call on the state coffers. In the past, 'idleness' had been seen as a reflection of collectivism. 'As long as we have communism so long shall we have non-employed Natives, and so long shall we have idleness', Pomare had thundered, reflecting general pakeha sentiments. In 1900 Seddon opined that communal life on the land meant 'idleness, carelessness, and neglect'. But removal of all links with the land, in a situation where there were few suitable waged jobs, would – policy makers feared – lead to destitution, which would be potentially costly to the Crown, rather than to assimilation.

This led to some exploration of new ways of developing the 'leasing solution'. One government response to Maori reluctance to voluntarily lease their land was to move towards *compulsory* vesting of lands for leasing. This concept emerged as early as 1902, with legislation allowing compulsory vesting of land in Maori Land Councils for 'native townships'. In 1904, with increasing pressure on the Crown to make more land available to pakeha, the principle was considerably expanded. Properties on which rates were owed could be compulsorily vested in the Maori Land Councils for leasing out and other purposes.

This has been seen as the beginning of the process of 'transforming the Councils into coercive and interventionist institutions rather than expressions of Maori self-government'. But such coercion had been implicit in the system from its inception – one of the reasons many Maori had been initially reluctant to co-operate with it. Ngata supported the 1904 measure on the ground that compulsion via Maori Land Councils would retain the land for future generations, there being no alternative other than to lose it altogether, but he was soon acknowledging that the 'Maori ideal is opposed to the whole of the legislation from 1900 down to the present time'.

From the beginning, Crown 'concessions' to Maori in the Maori Lands Administration Act, especially its restrictions on full land alienation, had been seen by some pakeha and their political representatives as impeding the job of settlement. Now, given the slowness of the new machinery, many Maori-owned lands were seen to remain 'unused', and settler pressure grew even stronger. Extension of compulsory leasing provisions was seen as a possible compromise solution. Ever since the Rees–Carroll Commission's findings in 1891, James Carroll had been arguing that compulsory vesting of all 'idle' Maori-owned land would address both Maori and pakeha problems. In 1905, as Minister of Native Affairs, he proposed that the time for this had come: pakeha farmers would contribute to the national economy on the leased-out acres, while Maori would both benefit from rents and retain underlying title to their remaining patrimony. But the Crown was, by this time, disinclined to undertake any more 'half measures'. New legislation would not only embrace compulsory vesting, but also facilitate full alienation.[55]

Maori Land Boards

Under the Maori Land Settlement Act passed in 1905, the Maori Land Councils were replaced by Maori Land Boards. The new legislation acknowledged, in effect, that the voluntary leasing policy had not met Crown objectives. Replacement measures included the Maori Land Boards' overseeing the renewal of large-scale Crown purchasing of Maori land in four Maori Land Districts. The other two, Taitokerau and Tairawhiti, hosted very strong tribal sentiments against selling land, and to avoid conflict the Act spared them from Crown purchase attempts. In return, however, the Minister of Native Affairs could compulsorily vest in the Maori Land Boards, for leasing out, any Maori lands which he deemed to be 'not required or not suitable for occupation by the Maori owners'. The Act also greatly expanded potential use of compulsory vesting in the boards of Maori-owned land in the other districts, following Native Land Court investigation of its title. The Maori Land Boards were to administer vested land for the 'benefit' of the owners, but this included leasing it out for as long as 50 years. Some Maori called the legislation, therefore, the 'Land Alienation Law'.

The new boards were portrayed as another 'compromise' between the Crown's imperatives and Maori concerns to preserve land-based rangatiratanga. 'Safeguards' to 'ensure' adequate remaining landed endowment for the groupings relinquishing the land were stressed, for example. Carroll, continuing to mediate between the two ethnicities whose heritage he shared, pronounced the measure an acceptable balance between pakeha land hunger and Maori interests.

However, as three Maori MPs and many other people protested, the new machinery had a negative impact on rangatiratanga. Quite apart from its compulsion and purchase clauses, the Act also removed the Maori Land Councils' elected Maori component from the replacement bodies. Not only had the element of democracy disappeared, there could no longer be Maori majorities. Two of the three Maori Land Board members were to be pakeha, usually the regional Native Land Court judge and his registrar. The third member was to be a Maori appointed by the Crown – not necessarily someone who would represent the interests of the iwi concerned. The boards, moreover, had lost most of the Maori Land Councils' judicial powers, such as examining recommendations on and determining title to papatupu lands, reducing the amount of Maori input. Clearly, the new appointment, membership and jurisdictional arrangements represented a move towards disempowerment of Maori authority in controlling and administering land.

From this time on, pretences that the Crown's Maori land mechanisms were intended to provide a degree of self-government were gradually abandoned. This message was reinforced by the new Act's greater coercive strength in several areas, not just compulsory vesting. Once land had been vested in a Maori Land Board, for example, the owners might well lose management and control of it for often very long periods. The reasons for vesting, moreover, continued to widen under further policy and legislative moves. From 1906, to cite one instance, land covered with noxious weeds could be taken. When the Tangoio South block was vested in the Ikaroa District Maori Land Board because of such an infestation, the owners were to have no say in its management for two decades. When they received it back, it was in a worse state than originally. Although they had retained title, preserving their land-based rangatiratanga at a formal level, over a long period their turangawaewae could not form an effective base for politico-cultural autonomy – or for their tribal economic development. While land had remained the base for most of the autonomy aspirations at the turn of the century, even the small degree of jurisdiction granted in 1900 to Maori to control its rate and mode of disposition had quickly disappeared. The Maori Land Boards were, more openly than the Councils, conduits for the transfer of ownership and control to Europeans. Maori protests were to no avail.[56]

State encroachments into the interrelated issues of turangawaewae and politico-cultural power went beyond the Maori Land Boards. Alienation mechanisms soon expanded. The abolition of the Native Department by Liberal ministers had been an expression of the prevailing 'dying race' belief and faith in the speed of assimilation. Its re-establishment acknowledged that such an assessment had been far too 'optimistic'. Not only were Maori not disappearing, but also, at least for the foreseeable future, their affairs needed some specialised state attention. But departmental duties now related mostly to land alienation. Where they were protective, this reflected the need to ensure that Maori had sufficient land remaining to prevent them from becoming a burden on the state. The department's operations shifted decision making even further from the Maori Land Boards, even though the latter gained extra administrative and other functions as time went by.

Those aspects of Maori Land Board work which, it was said, would benefit Maori were seldom implemented. This was due in part to the lack of resourcing available for anything but the mainstream function of transferring control of land from Maori to pakeha. The boards had no capital to assist Maori development, for example. Therefore owners' or lessees' attempts to make vested land fully productive frequently failed. As lease periods fell due, the land was often allowed to revert to an underdeveloped condition, burdening its owners on its return rather than enhancing their prospects of rangatiratanga and prosperity. Successive amendments to the legislation, from 1906's extension of compulsory vesting powers on, made the fundamental premises of the Maori Land Settlement Act all the more clear to Maori.

In any case, purchasing rather than leasing remained at the forefront of the Crown's intentions. State bureaucratic methods were often devoid of niceties. A 'laudable provision' in the 1905 Act, whereby the price offered could not be below capital value (as assessed by government valuers), was in practice 'emasculated by Crown pre-emption'. The value was assessed as that of the land alone, even though much Maori land was covered by rich resources such as millable forests. Conversely, land retained by Maori was habitually overvalued, raising its land tax and rates liabilities, as the Valuer-General himself acknowledged in 1913. Meanwhile, a great deal of pressure to sell had been placed on Maori who were unable to meet the state's monetary demands. In these and many other ways, land alienation rates picked up again, despite alleged safeguards to ensure the continuance of Maori mana over the remaining tribal estates. Maori came to give the 1905 legislation a new nickname, the 'Ture Kohuru Tangata', which had connotations of confiscation, treachery and destruction.[57]

The Stout–Ngata investigations of 1907–8

The 1906 extension of compulsion embodied government acceptance of a policy that people should not be able to 'own land without using it'. It also reflected Native Minister Carroll's view that leasing out Maori land under Maori Land Board control remained a better alternative to purchase. But it seemed insufficient to save many remaining tribal patrimonies, and so the minister needed other policies if a vestige of land-based rangatiratanga was to remain. Again, paradoxically, these hinged on compulsion. He called for a systematic appraisal of the status of Maori-owned lands, a prerequisite for implementing a plan that would enable Maori to maintain direct control of land they 'needed' and to have the rest in effect compulsorily managed on their behalf or, if really necessary, sold. As a result, in January 1907 the government appointed a commission of inquiry into the best ways to use the remnants of the Maori-owned estate. Lands definitely required and fully used by the tribes would be identified. The rest would be vested with Maori Land Boards for sale or leasing, whichever was deemed appropriate.

This was Carroll's way of meeting the growing tide of both Maori and pakeha disaffection with the government's land policies. The intention was that Maori would negotiate with the commission over the productive land they needed for their own immediate future, but the exercise clearly had ramifications for Maori autonomous control and retention of their land. To help persuade them to co-operate, Ngata was selected as a royal commissioner, along with a veteran Liberal politician, Chief Justice Sir Robert Stout. This was a highly important 'mediating role between the Pakeha government and the Maori tribes'. The pair would investigate all Maori lands in an attempt, in consultation with the owners, to identify those that were 'idle' or not 'profitably occupied'. They were then to recommend to the government how the various lands could best be 'utilised and settled in the interests of the Native owners'.

Despite the degree of consultation involved, the commission's tasks were far from unproblematic, given a fundamental Crown agenda that sat uneasily with rangatiratanga. As Maori leaders were well aware, the commissioners were to conduct their inquiries and frame their recommendations firmly within the parameters of 'the public good'. This meant that which best suited the capitalist political economy and the pakeha settlers on which it primarily rested. To place optimistic faith in the official reassurances of the time, as many commentators have done, is to obscure the ultimate motivations for the exercise. These were clearly not to restore or protect remaining turangawaewae, but to secure its use in approved ways by (usually pakeha) approved persons.

Nevertheless, many Maori took advantage of the commissioners' willingness to travel and listen to their views. Many hoped not only to influence the recommendations, but also to send strong messages to the state. Some submissions, for example, called for an end to the Maori Land Boards. As it turned out, the commission was as sympathetic to Maori aspirations as it could be within its own terms of reference. Its reports during sittings in 1907–8 stressed that Maori desires for land retention needed addressing (so long as they were compatible with 'the national interest') and generally accepted owners' views. It also criticised aspects of state land acquisition, such as the Crown's overriding the interests of minorities of 'non-selling' collective owners when purchasing. It proposed that all alienations go through the Maori Land Boards, to provide some measure of protection.

The commission believed that, while permanent alienation would inevitably continue, it should be limited to less than a fifth of the remaining Maori lands. Ngata, moreover, was especially sympathetic when reporting that '[t]he Maori ideal is that he should be left alone'. The best way to achieve this, and to assist Maori to hold onto their land, the commissioners (and Carroll and the Young Maori Party) believed, was by *using* the land. This Maori could not do unassisted, and so the state needed to help. Stout and Ngata thus argued that greater powers be given the boards to assist Maori landowners by, for example, raising money on the security of land for their farming developments.

More fundamentally, development required addressing the fractionation of interests in land that had resulted from Native Land Court judgments. The commissioners proposed two ways to remedy this: incorporation and consolidation. In the first, the multiple owners of a block of land would 'incorporate' their fragmented shares in holdings to keep them in collective ownership, vesting control of the incorporation in a committee of management that represented and worked on behalf of the owners. This seemed to fit one definition of rangatiratanga over land that had passed through the Native Land Court's allocation procedures. In the second method, 'uneconomic' holdings in lands would be, through exchanges of shares, 'consolidated' into economic units for farming and development by individuals or small groups, along lines pioneered in Ngata's own Ngati Porou territory.

Provision for land exchanges for consolidation had, indeed, been enshrined in legislation since the establishment of judicial devices to detribalise land ownership in the 1860s. With the reintroduction in 1894 of Crown 'pre-emption' over Maori land purchase, too, the state had encouraged incorporation, hoping this would lead to leasing. The Crown was now particularly receptive to these aspects of the Stout–Ngata recommendations, for increasingly fragmented share ownership had meant that Maori holdings had been more difficult to acquire, and less productive if not so acquired. It envisaged purchase as the main solution to the 'public good' issues surrounding Maori land; both development methods highlighted by the commission ideally enabled easier purchase and hence quicker pakeha settlement.

At the very least they facilitated greater Maori production, and tribal spokesmen stressed this as well as ownership and control. They noted that, if several recommendations were taken together, consolidations and incorporations would enable them to develop the land themselves. Whatever the ravages of the past, some land-based rangatiratanga might be retrieved. Incorporation could certainly be seen from a Maori perspective as (in Ngata's words) 'in effect an adaptation of the tribal system, the hierarchy of chiefs being represented by the Committee of Management'. Consolidation, too, was often an affirmation of collective autonomy over land, especially via whanau-based ownership and production.[58]

Continuing setbacks for Maori

While the Stout–Ngata recommendations fell short of ideal from a Maori perspective, being encompassed within a directive Crown system, they seemed to hold out prospects for significant retention of Maori ownership and control of land. A mix of leasing out and Maori-run development could lead to increased production in the 'public interest', and the Crown might well have been expected in turn to ameliorate its compulsion and purchasing regimes. But a government increasingly pressured by settlers for freehold access to land believed that the commission had been too protective of Maori interests. The Native Land Settlement Act, passed in 1907 against considerable Maori opposition, reflected few of its interim recommendations. Instead, the legislation embodied many of the Crown's preoccupations with 'opening up' the countryside.

Section 4, for example, allowed Maori land deemed 'surplus' in *any* Maori Land District to be compulsorily vested in the Maori Land Boards, for both sale and lease. Moreover, the Act overturned the 1900 principle that lands which had been voluntarily vested could not be permanently alienated. Additionally, from a Maori point of view the success of the Stout–Ngata recommendations on incorporation and consolidation depended on state assistance for procedures already available, and the Act did not provide for this. The Western Maori MP depicted it as a 'trampling-upon the mana' supposedly assured to Maori by the Treaty of Waitangi. If that document meant anything, he stated, it was surely that the tangata whenua had the capacity to control their own lands.

While the Act reflected some Stout–Ngata recommendations, then, its spirit was generally against that of the commission – which itself had fallen short of Maori aspirations. Ngata joined fellow politicians and other Maori leaders in coming out very publicly against the thrust of the legislation (although he voted for it when some concessions were gained). But the interests of the settlers were steadily gaining powerful momentum. The Native Land Settlement Act was followed by other legislation which also went against the grain of Stout–Ngata recommendations in particular and Maori aspirations in general. The Maori Land Boards became ever more central to land alienation processes. One historian has bluntly dismissed the Maori Land Councils and their successors as 'bodies that wholly served European interests', and it is hard to modify this with reference to the boards. For decades to come, the Maori Land Boards were to control and decide the fate of Maori lands.[59]

Yet the negotiations and legislation at the turn of the century had enabled Maori to force themselves further into the political and land-use discourses and processes, complementing (and to a degree feeding into) their demographic revival. In that sense the land policies which gave them some initial benefits, however constrained and short-lived, provided a concrete illustration that it was possible to make some gains for rangatiratanga in the most adverse of circumstances. This strengthened Maori resolve. Reactions to the inexorable whittling away of the limited degrees of collective autonomy that had been granted were increasingly forthright.

This could be seen in the follow-up to a 1906 Crown 'settlement' with Ngai Tahu, after decades-long protests over their landed and political marginalisation. The South Island Landless Natives Act, which embodied the settlement, had provided for shares in reserves to be awarded to 'landless' tribal members, and this appeared to endorse Ngai Tahu's rangatiratanga. But, among the resulting problems, the areas eventually selected for the reserves turned out usually to be not only economically poor or 'useless', but also far from their tribal lands. The awards therefore provided 'an almost totally unsatisfactory resolution to the problem' experienced by the tribe in the first place. From 1907 Ngai Tahu began to formulate claims which amounted to a quest to regain Crown acknowledgement of its rangatiratanga. The iwi persisted with Te Kereme/The Claim throughout the century, in a complex and changing relationship, finally settling over the Crown's breaches of the Treaty of Waitangi in 1998.

Other tribes had equally long and troubled relationships with the Crown, all shaped to some degree by the developments of the early years of the twentieth century. The Crown's propensity to examine grievances when under great Maori pressure held out hopes of progress that in turn fed Maori resolve. There were various parliamentary and other inquiries into such matters as Taranaki kupapa claims to land, the terms of leases on Maori-owned timberlands and the Crown's non-fulfilment of obligations on properties gifted for educational purposes. Overall, however, very little progress was made in satisfying Maori aspirations. At this time some Maori leaders came to realise that hopes for significant land-based rangatiratanga might well be unrealistic.[60]

Land and autonomy

The politico-economic subsuming of Maori could be challenged and partly resisted. But in the early twentieth century the accompanying alienation of most tribal lands seemed largely irreversible. Accepted wisdom would have it that large-scale possession of ancestral land was absolutely crucial for exercise of rangatiratanga. But, when many Maori came to realise that their demographic up-swing would not be accompanied by victories on the question of land, the struggle for self-determination was far from abandoned. Even when it became clear that much of the remaining Maori land would continue to be lost to bureaucratic and (pakeha) farmer control for decades of leasehold, or disappear altogether from tribal patrimony through Crown purchasing of shares from individuals, the quest for the maximal ways of exercising rangatiratanga proceeded unabated.

This discussion has, then, contextualised and corrected a tendency in the New Zealand literature to conflate land-holding and collective indigenous agency and identity. Here, as throughout empire, despite the undoubtedly fundamental nexus between the political culture of indigenous people and the land, collective ethno-cultural identity was the crucial defining factor. The politics of socio-cultural agency prevailed, in spite of land loss and the everyday pressures to subsume indigenous culture.

It is true that struggles for self-determination often centred on the question of land retention or restoration as an immediate tactic, a longer-term strategy or an ultimate goal. But it is equally true that only total assimilation (or genocide), not land loss, could obliterate indigenes *as* indigenes. The land question, however crucial, was – in the final analysis – subordinate to people. A whakatauki/proverb asks what is the most important thing in life, and the answer is: 'He tangata, He tangata, He tangata'/'It is people, it is people, it is people.' With much of their land base irretrievably lost, and the rest subjected to whittling away of ownership or control (however hard their resistance), Maori increasingly saw the need to focus for the foreseeable future on attaining politico-cultural autonomy. The tribal or pan-tribal regimes embodying this struggle were not geared to prospects of regaining a sizeable landed base within a short or even medium timeframe, or even necessarily of retaining all the land that was left.

To sum up, the integral connection between tangata and whenua – the fact that even the most alienated patch of land was 'still there' and could retain 'spiritual' or other significance and be regarded as potentially repossessable – and the ultimate goals of rangatiratanga gave a profound importance to the role of ancestral land. Yet it was the collectivity of a tribal or other grouping that continued to make an impact, whether or not most pakeha appreciated it, on the social landscapes of New Zealand. When Maori hopes for exercising rangatiratanga through retention and development of the remaining patrimony were, whatever the official line, dashed by Crown actions in the early years of the twentieth century, their focus switched to the quest for politico-cultural autonomy.[61]

CHAPTER FOUR

DIVERSIFYING WAYS OF SEEKING AUTONOMY

Pursuing tribally based autonomy in the Urewera

Maori had before them a model other than that of the local government
and land institutions: the one-off tribal deal between the Crown and the
Urewera people. But its statute-based 'self-government' regime, within
a revealingly titled 'reserve', was firmly and increasingly under Crown
tutelage. While title of tribal lands could be divided up hapu by hapu
(rather than be awarded to individuals), this was only after investigation
by a government-appointed commission. The latter's Native Land Court-
style operations would feed into a pre-existing system of strategic land
purchases by the state, with land-sellers' awards becoming beach-heads
for Crown purchases of desirable adjoining lands, for example. Yet there
were advantages for the iwi. Tuhoe and other regional groupings were
not only free from armed Crown incursion aimed at suppressing their
autonomist aspirations, but also had gained a new, state-implemented
institutional means of resisting some of the Crown's more draconian
aims. A new site of engagement for their struggle for autonomy had
been opened up.

This site never constituted the actual autonomy depicted by 'wishful
thinking' and other scholars. The state, moreover, broke its own rules as
soon as the tribes were seen to be too assertive. It has been assessed, in
fact, that even the degree of autonomy embedded in the Urewera District
Native Reserve Act of 1896 was 'honoured more in the breach' than
otherwise. When appeals against the decisions of the 'First Urewera
Commission' (1899–1902) were heard by the second commission
between 1906 and 1914, Tuhoe representation had been dropped. It
had been intended that the general committee provided for under the

1896 Act would approve all land sales. When that body was finally established in 1909 (a development spurred by the Stout–Ngata Commission), the Crown was able to undermine it through new legislation by which the Native Land Court regained jurisdiction in the Urewera. The agreement of 1896 already meant little. As in so many other areas, any faith Maori had put in legal processes was very quickly countered by the harsh realities of power dynamics.

From 1910 the Crown began buying interests in Urewera land. Eventually the purchases would often be from individuals, many of them induced to sell by poverty, rather than through any process of collective decision making by combinations of owners. An equivalent of the imperial 'divide and rule' strategy, a feature of land acquisition throughout much of the colony, was being applied to an allegedly autonomous zone. The Crown had delayed establishing the general committee in the knowledge that it would scarcely be willing to endorse widespread purchasing, a correct surmise given its concerns to safeguard the tribal patrimony. But its very functions ensured that it came to play virtually a facilitating role in extensive sales. It was given the task of identifying areas that should be set aside for collective purposes, for example. Although the committee complied in order to ensure retention of crucial areas of turangawaewae, in so doing it implicitly sanctioned Crown purchasings elsewhere within its tribal boundaries. This was important in the Crown's plans to impose productivity on all usable 'idle' Maori land nationwide: with the 'the last frontier' making 'use' of hitherto non-producing land, a powerful symbolic message would be sent to Maori and pakeha alike. This was intimately connected with the colonising enterprise – as late as 1919 an observer stated that 'even today the Urewera Country is foreign territory'. Because of such perceptions, in the final analysis, the state was determined to 'tame' it as quickly as possible, including through settlement of cultivable lands within the region.

This process took precedence over the 'autonomy agreement', from which the Crown continued to depart. Acquisition of interests in land from individuals was eased by general 1913 legislation which further marginalised the general committee, and from late 1914 the land purchase authorities set about buying land direct from individual owners in the

Urewera without reference to it. When the first sale sanctioned by the general committee was finalised in 1912, it had been sought by the generally anti-selling prophet Rua Kenana. His purpose was to gain capital to promote his own self-sufficiency enterprise, itself a quest for autonomy that lay outside the Crown-imposed parameters of the Urewera arrangement. By 1916, the year of a bloody invasion by armed police of the prophet's stronghold at Maungapohatu, the state had so violated its own rules that retrospective legislative amendment was needed. This legalised past Urewera Reserve transactions, and also regularised the status quo by allowing the Crown to purchase any interests without reference to the general committee.

By the following year the general committee was so moribund that the Native Minister, William H Herries, did not know if it still technically existed. When considering a request that it be effectively re-established, he opined that its 'criteria' might be a 'hindrance to purchasing'. The Crown was determined to remove all impediments to 'taming' the Urewera. Since 'cutting out' its existing interests in blocks would lead to unwieldy 'patchworking', it would push on with purchasing until it had a greater number. It would then secure partitioning out of interests, setting the scene for a Ngataist 'consolidation' under the 1909 Act. Ngata had been urging this 'solution' since 1916. While consolidation would potentially benefit non-sellers as well as sellers, meanwhile those non-sellers who held interests in areas desired for pakeha settlement faced considerable Crown pressure to sell.

By late 1919 the Crown's land interests in the Urewera Reserve were sufficient for it to begin planning the consolidation, and by 1921 it had purchased two-thirds of the interests, even though most owners' meetings had rejected selling. Without reference to the general committee, in that year the Crown convened a hui at Ruatoki where Herries' successor, Gordon Coates, presented the case for consolidation. The nature of the occasion can be seen in the fact that government representative Ngata was selected to look after the interests of non-selling Maori. Shortly afterwards, an Act repealed all legislation governing the operation of the Urewera Reserve. 'Ordinary law' was to prevail in the area, and Tuhoe were obliged to help finance consolidation by paying roading costs. The consolidation commissioners paid little heed to the wishes of non-sellers to be awarded the lands of their sacred places and ancestral ties. Coates, moreover, rejoiced that 'tribal holdings are gone', for after non-sellers' exchanges with Crown interests 'family allotments' replaced hapu-based communal holdings. The consolidation, together with an ongoing alienation that would eventually lead to three-quarters of the Urewera passing to the Crown, removed any lingering illusions of a 'state within a state' based on ancestral landholdings. Substantive 'colonisation of Tuhoe' had been achieved.

Some tribes drew specific conclusions from the Urewera experiment. One was that, as Tuhoe memory has put it, the setting up of Crown-endorsed structures had acted to inhibit 'tribal administration'. It was noted that the subsequent processes had led to a faster and more cost-effective system for the Crown's alienation of land for settlement, saving it the costs of court procedures and coercive control. They had also resulted in some decommunalisation of lifestyle. Another conclusion related to the fact that Tuhoe and associated tribes had pursued their autonomy aspirations, whether sanctioned by the state or resistant to it (in the case of Rua's 'rival sovereignty' movement), without reference to Maoridom in general. The route Tuhoe had taken in conjunction with the Crown, therefore, meant that it did not link up with pan-tribal movements. Lacking outside support, a stand-alone tribal effort at self-determination had in practice been overwhelmed by the imperatives of a vastly more powerful government. Conversely, the Crown's dealings with Tuhoe at iwi level helped marginalise Urewera groupings which asserted their rights to be regarded as separate, primary entities with their own rangatiratanga.[62]

The Crown, regarding itself as possessing supreme sovereignty in domestic and international law, felt able to act in any fashion it wished to pursue what it saw as the public good. Its perspective on indigenous issues remained influenced by the 'dying Maori' belief. While 'the race' might not be physically disappearing, prevalent 'Social Darwinist' views required that, as a socio-cultural phenomenon, Maori were (as an archdeacon wrote in a work on 'The Passing of the Maori' in 1907) 'already potentially dead'. The remnants would assimilate, gaining all the benefits of 'civilisation', albeit in a marginalised position. In the Urewera, this process required political detribalisation and 'scientific farming'. The latter was preferably to be carried out by pakeha, for even post-consolidation Maori family plots were not expected to match European results. Figuratively, in the words of a contemporary official, the aim was to 'Kick the Maoris out'.

Realising the relentlessness of the Crown agenda, many Urewera Maori abandoned any attachment to their increasingly irrelevant 'self-governing' machinery. Rua's 'kingdom on earth' ideas attracted some of them, boosting the Crown's willingness to initiate its only armed encounter with Maori during the First World War, the 1916 invasion of his rival sovereignty base. Even after this last battle in the 'wars of sovereignty' between Crown and autonomy-seeking Maori, and Rua's imprisonment, the prophet gained new followers in the Urewera. In effect arguing that autonomy did not in the end depend on retaining a significant land base, other tribespeople campaigned to be allowed to sell their land to private purchasers. This way, market prices could be gained. In one interpretation, unfettered selling capacity would have constituted a greater exercise of autonomy than the structures provided for by the Crown, although many countered with the argument that selling, however much forced by economic plight, amounted to acceding to state pressure or propaganda.

The Crown's interests in such a remote region at this time were primarily to assert its substantive sovereignty; this was a prerequisite for ultimately harnessing the region for the 'public good'. If there were to be a degree of Maori autonomy, it would be firmly under the auspices of the state. The Crown and the interests it represented would need, in other words, to have potential benefit from it. In the event, a great deal of the Urewera was to remain of little use to pakeha farming or other interests, Maori-owned land often continued to be unproductive even after the consolidations, and leadership problems were rife within a tribe divided by the Crown's actions. Much of the territory secured by the state would be used not for 'national production' but rather within a broader definition of the public good, including 'climatic and water conservation' services and the Urewera National Park. Meanwhile, a long quest for compensation for concrete losses from the Crown's breaches of its promises had begun. Other tribes took note of the fate of the Urewera experiment.[63]

Political movements

Many of the iwi which had attempted to work with the Crown-provided machinery pursued their interests through the land-oriented institutions. Enthusiasm waned rapidly, particularly as land alienation picked up speed. Large numbers of Maori had appreciated early on that working through Crown bodies, while apparently enabling self-determination, did little to advance rangatiratanga. Most iwi soon generally disengaged from 'collaboration' as a strategy, concentrating their flax-roots energies on their own rather than on the official komiti. In particular, they came to emphasise the politico-cultural interests of the collectivity. But there was a myriad of opinions on the appropriate way forward.

As early as 1904, some Maori organisations were discernibly turning from the idea of 'special legislation', which already seemed to be expediting their dispossession, to a demand for equal rights with pakeha. Once they had achieved these, their intention was to use them to maximise tribal advantage. Some sought Maori unity in their search for equality between the races, such as the well-supported 'Maori Association', founded at Wanganui in 1908. Others continued to campaign to be free to sell (or lease) land to whomever they wished, in the belief that market prices would provide them with resources to achieve their goals. Some, including senior chiefs, saw solidarity with pakeha workers as a way forward, and among other things supported the 1913 'great strike' against the state.[64]

A more immediate challenge to pursuit of rangatiratanga through a special relationship with the state, however, came from those who felt that preservation of their 'race' lay in going some way towards accommodating Crown policies aimed at assimilation. On the fringes of the Young Maori Party there remained people who even supported almost total assimilation. Pomare was convinced that Taranaki Maori were 'reactionary' to continue seeking restoration of confiscated lands, urged collaborative endeavour, and campaigned against the 'separatist' goals of the regional prophets Te Whiti and Tohu Kakahi. While the prophets' grand pan-tribal dreams had been physically suppressed by the New Zealand Constabulary Force at Parihaka in 1881, their movement had quickly revived (including, as previously noted, in the Chathams).

Contemporary pakeha commentators believed that the deaths of these two politico-spiritual leaders in 1907 symbolised the end of significant Maori protest and heralded total assimilation to the pakeha political economy: 'The rapid absorption of the native race is inevitable.' But even Pomare, whose own interpretation was close to this, took the opportunity to organise a Maori-only body as a means of achieving assimilationist 'progress'. His 'Maori Union' sought a base for concrete gains by working towards the return of leased land for use by its Maori owners. Along with the Maori Association, it became the dominant Maori movement for a short time. But it foundered when people appreciated the full extent of Pomare's collaborative agenda. When he sought to enter Parliament to further such aims, the vehicle he used was Reform, the most conservative of the parties.

After 1905, however, with a revival of political protest and other developments in the quest for autonomy, the proponents of self-determination were to discover that most Young Maori Party leaders and cadres were not antagonistic to them. Indeed, the Young Maori Party/Ngataist milieu was positively favourable to some of their aims, especially the preservation of Maori culture. As will be seen, it would come to support a number of methods and goals mooted and attempted, from time to time, at local, regional and national levels.

The quest for rangatiratanga was both complex and continuous. This has generally been downplayed, even in 'sympathetic' literature. When a chronicler of kotahitanga, after covering the failure of the 1900 experiments to produce autonomy, leaps straight to the Second World War era, this has the effect of cloaking the determination and resourcefulness of the iwi in the decades between. Kingitanga leaders had early tested the Crown's intentions. Their tribes had engaged with 1900's new institutions, Henare Kaihau had taken up a Maori Land Council seat, and from 1903 King Mahuta had accepted positions on the Executive and Legislative Councils. But they had quickly reverted to pursuing a non-statised rangatiratanga, united in the belief that the future lay in their own hands rather than with the Crown's bureaucracy. The permanent head of the Native Department would later note that for decades 'the Waikato people were averse to anything and everything connected with the Government', including even state assistance for health and unemployment. The 'Kingmaker' grouping, indeed, continued to pursue the full Kingitanga programme for the first three decades of the century. In response to the initial decision to experiment with the new institutions, Kingmaker Tupu Taingakawa had organised a Kingite sector which demanded immediate return of confiscated lands and untrammelled self-government. At a hui at Waahi in 1907, moreover, a new movement inside Kingitanga, Te Kotahitanga Maori Motuhake, was launched. It was depicted as a revival of Kotahitanga and legitimated by citing Kingism's forging of links with the rival unity movement in the 1890s.

Mainstream Kingism, despite its general 'withdrawal' from participation in Crown activities, continued to deal with the government in pursuit of its struggle. Mahuta and others formed the Maori Rights Conservation Association in 1906 and, after considerable representation, land distribution was discussed with the Crown and some land was eventually regained as a base for tribal rebuilding. Believing that such dealings were locking Kingitanga into the state, rather than liberating it, the new Kotahitanga movement distanced itself and continued to promote rangatiratanga uncompromisingly.

Its subsequent creation of the 'Federation of the Maori People of the North and South Islands of New Zealand' indicates the grandness of its plans. The movement demanded full autonomy under the Treaty of Waitangi. It garnered the support of some traditional Kingite elements, and even Te Rata, crowned king after Mahuta's death in 1912, was sympathetic. Owing to differing views on what was achievable in the foreseeable future, however, organisational unity proved a chimera. After long deliberations on how best to fill the gap left by the Paremata Maori's self-immolation, Kingism reconstituted the Kauhanganui in 1919 at Ngaruawahia. Its meetings focused on attaining a distinct identity for Maori, with a view to strengthened advocacy before the New Zealand

Parliament. But its base remained essentially within the Tainui confederation and it could not gain unified Maori support for its strategies to achieve autonomy.

In any case, formal unity had been tried and failed. For the moment, iwi, hapu and other groupings would concentrate on maximising their own tribal independence within a context of *informal* pan-tribal activities, links and consultations. They would, for example, get together from time to time through intertribal hui. These could be hosted by remnants of formal unity organisations, or be a one-off invitation by a tribe; they could occur *ad hoc* at an important ceremonial or other gathering, or be convened under the umbrella of Maori Council general conferences – using, for example, the Kotahitanga facilities that had been centralised at Papawai in the Wairarapa.[65]

The 'retreat' to seeking a tribally based autonomy in the context of loose intertribal association and interaction was designed to avoid the factors which had led to, at best, a very temporary and partial success for previous 'go it alone' attempts – be they in association with the Crown (as with the Urewera experiment) or aloof from it. The King Country was a key example of the latter. In effect Kingism had continued to run a 'state within a state' there even after it ceased to be a no-go zone for Crown and pakeha in the 1880s. But this could not be sustained either formally or informally, and interaction with Crown and settlers had practical ramifications.

As part of an agreement with the state to 'open up' the King Country for settlement, for example, tribal leaders had signed a 'sacred pact' with the Crown. It included a liquor regulation regime, under which, with state endorsement, the chiefs would act to prevent the ravages of alcohol on their people. But the Crown transformed this into a prohibitionist 'dry' zone in pursuit of its own view of appropriate 'law and order' in Maori regions. While there was some opposition to the fact that the state decreed and policed the region's liquor regime, the majority of chiefs decided to collaborate in defining and enforcing it. Over time they came to regard what was originally a second-best option as 'their own'. The Licensing Amendment Act passed in 1910 reaffirmed the general embargo on liquor in the King Country and it remained a 'dry' district for decades.

This and other tribally based liquor-control regimes have been seen as an example of the exercise of rangatiratanga. Were they to take a form antithetical to Crown interests, however, they would be disallowed and if necessary physically suppressed. Where they were acceptable to the Crown, they were often contested within the tribe. In the East Coast tribal region, a prohibitionist liquor regime had been established after Ngata's strictures against excessive alcohol consumption. The Horouta Maori Council was the vehicle, and opponents could thus depict the regime (imposed after a narrow regional polling majority) as an attack on their autonomy. In the name of indigenous rights, they campaigned to abolish prohibition, seeing its implementers as lackeys of the Crown in applying a definition of 'order and regularity' in Maori regions that differed from that in settler regions. An opposition haka denounced the various impositions of the state but focused on liquor regulation. Ngata was depicted as 'the man/Who keeps coming from Wellington'. This was followed by an aggressive: 'Ahaha!/Show me your laws!/Show me your laws!/Ahaha!/Rating laws!/Council laws!/The Prohibition!/I want whisky/But it's been sold to the dead!/Bloody bugger!/Slave!'

Frequent petitions and other East Coast initiatives argued that allowing Ngati Porou communities to regulate their own liquor consumption was preferable to its prohibition by the state. But the Crown did not provide the tribe with an opportunity to revisit its decision until 1922, following which the regime was dismantled. Meanwhile, an apparently autonomist tribal structure reflecting the wishes of the leadership had been taken under the wing of the state – and turned into a lifestyle strait-jacket for many of the tribe. While the Maori liquor regimes appeared to be fully autonomist, the fact remained that they were state-franchised. And, it might be added, such franchises could be withdrawn even against the wishes of the tribal leadership, as would later happen in the King Country.[66]

The 1909 Native Land Act

By 1908, Maori land administration had diverged widely from the system implemented in 1900. Many lands controlled by Maori Land Boards had been compulsorily vested, and since 1907 the boards had been able to sell some of the property in their charge. Groupings struggling for autonomy, while increasingly less confident about retaining a significant land base and focusing instead on their collective identity, continued to stress the ultimate nexus between land and people. In 1909 a major Kingite petition demanded both full Maori political autonomy and land rights. But that year became infamous for Maori as yet another signpost on the long route to losing their land. Legislation was passed that was to sharpen their need to work on a form of autonomy that would not necessarily be based on any substantive turangawaewae. This was the Native Land Act, which grew out of the Stout–Ngata highlighting of the confused state of Maori land legislation. Among its many rationalisations, clarifications and consolidations, the Act further simplified and accelerated procedures for the alienation of land from Maori. Once again the Young Maori Party aided the Crown's endeavours, hoping to secure compromises along the way. Ngata himself had been appointed Parliamentary Under-Secretary to Carroll in 1908 to assist the Counsel to the Office of Law Drafting, John Salmond, prepare the Act. Soon Ngata took over many functions within Carroll's portfolio, including that of land legislation.

Various measures (most recently the 1907 Native Land Settlement Act) had ostensibly protected chiefly mana over the land, but contained overriding provisions which minimised such protection. Although it contained some protective devices, the Native Land Act removed others. Among many things, it abolished Crown pre-emption again, ostensibly giving comfort to those Maori who had argued that participation in the free market embodied their rangatiratanga. But even the permanent head of the Native Department, Judge T W Fisher, acknowledged that the 'main feature of the present law is the widening of the avenue and facilitating the alienation and settlement of Native lands'. The rationalisation of Maori land legislation, in short, was used to contribute to ongoing alienation. There was no longer even any *talk* of taihoa.[67]

Scholars have tended to see the 1909 Native Land Act as a turning point in the processes of land alienation. Even a defence of the Act as a 'major concession to Maori', arguing that it was 'carefully studded with safeguards to protect long-term Maori interests', agrees that it greatly facilitated alienation. A cautious analysis concludes that 'due consideration of Maori interests failed to carry the political weight it perhaps should' in Parliament, the desire to free up more land for pakeha settlement having taken precedence over supposed good intentions. More commonly, the Act is baldly depicted as a 'complete reversal of the sentiments expressed in the Act of 1900': it 'opened up the trading and alienation of Maori land and it allowed for removal of all previous restrictions on the sale of Maori land'.

But the Act was little more than another (albeit significant) milestone along a well-established road towards alienation, although in preparing it Ngata and Carroll undoubtedly attempted to make the best of a bad situation for Maori. Settler pressure on the Liberals (from both 'radical leaseholders' and right-wing 'freeholders') ensured that its primary thrust could be in no other direction than that already firmly established. The name of the new Native Land Purchase Board was evocative enough of the Crown's aspirations to gain most of the rest of Maori land for pakeha settlement. The 1909 legislation, moreover, cemented in place a long-lasting regulatory regime, creating 'an integrated system for the control and alienation' of Maori land that gave potential purchasers a variety of strategies. Under its principles, which remained in place over the next half-century, transfer of control of land 'between races' was the focus of Maori Land Board activities.

Some of the Native Land Act's provisions, however, especially those inserted under pressure from the Maori MPs, could be used by Maori communities to further their own purposes. A depiction of them as a 'significant recognition of rangatiratanga' is highly debatable, but does remind us that Maori agency continued to operate in even the bleakest of circumstances. From the corridors of state to the humblest villages, Maori people attempted to maximise their communal gains within the range of possibilities available. One such device had been included in the legislation in response to the Stout–Ngata Commission's criticisms of bulk Crown purchasing of individual interests in Maori-held land. This was the provision that, generally, owners needed to be assembled in order to approve the disposition of land. The 'resolution of assembled owners' became a key element of the sales method for decades. The meetings enabled leaders to speak out against improvident sales of land, in many cases encouraging leasing out in preference to irreversible loss. In the eyes of the official historians of the Native Department, this provision 'gave rangatiratanga a legal recognition in a crucially important area'.

Ngata had fought hard for this. His motives in helping prepare the Act included, as always, the desire to preserve as much Maori culture as was compatible with the benefits and inevitabilities of 'western civilisation'. Acutely aware of the culture–land nexus, he felt that the only way for his people to successfully farm, and therefore retain, a sizeable number of their remaining estates was to secure pakeha capital and 'scientific' know-how. The Native Land Act, therefore, included procedures for boosting Maori agricultural and pastoral production. Consolidation procedures, for example, were streamlined and incorporated blocks were given a firmer legal footing. Once incorporation had been approved by assembled owners, management committees could be established. These had the ability to borrow money without the involvement of officials. The Act also gave Maori Land Boards powers to invest Maori clients' money through the Public Trustee, holding out the possibility of finance for collective ventures. More important still, it was in this Act that Ngata had secured for the first time (citing his own commission's findings, which reflected a number of Maori submissions) specific legislative provision for Crown-aided land consolidation.[68]

But none of these altered the fact that the legislation as a whole was essentially another measure to effect rapid land alienation. Concomitantly, it sought to encourage breakdown of a communal way of life and operation. It abolished the papatupu block committees, which had made many successful title recommendations, and once again the Native Land Court possessed sole jurisdiction to investigate customary title. Hui of assembled owners were obliged to work through Maori Land Boards, and this was seen as compromising their independence. People soon learned that the overriding purpose of the boards had now become that of the prime 'facilitators and promoters of the alienation of Maori land'. Even though they were formally charged with preventing Maori landlessness, for example, they rarely refused to confirm alienation when vetting land transactions. The Waikato–Maniapoto Maori Land Board is said, baldly, to have 'operated as an agent of the Crown'. The removal of the Crown's monopoly on buying Maori land, moreover, often interpreted as Ngata's concession to frustrations over low prices and hence a way of meeting Maori demands for self-determination, was no more than a supplementary means of speeding up alienation.

The main aim of the Liberal government had always been pakeha land settlement, even through the taihoa period. Alienation of land from Maori was integral to it, particularly given New Zealand's increasing role as 'the farm of Britain', based on sheep but reinforced by the rise of dairying. State-imposed 'compromises' of various sorts were intended to disempower Maori, marginalising their land and (related) political aspirations. Even the Native Land Act's consolidation measures were to be made available to Maori only at the Crown's discretion, a state-defined public good constituting the main criterion. The Act was 'the juggernaut of legislation relating to the purchase of Maori land', *designed* to force the pace on sales.

Between 1911, when it began producing results, and 1920, the total sales of Maori land almost surpassed those of the massive alienations of the 1890s. Within two decades of the legislation, over 2.3 million acres had been sold. The Maori Land Boards were, in other words, very efficient at the major job expected of them. Government expectations had, in fact, risen with the coming to office of the conservative Reform Party in 1912. To meet the wishes of would-be and actual 'small farmer' constituents, it escalated land purchases through the Native Land Act machinery. Ngata believed that Native Minister Herries, who had long advocated (along with Pomare, the Member of the Executive Council Representing the Native Race) rapid individualisation of customary tenure, 'will poison by aiming at the foundation of our strength . . . the proprietorship of the land'.[69]

Herries had an extreme 'use it or lose it' approach to Maori land. In proclaiming a policy that was overtly the opposite of taihoa, that of 'hustle', he was impatient with the 'safeguards' which the Young Maori Party had secured in Maori land legislation. Believing that the Native

Land Act needed amending to facilitate purchase, his 1913 Native Land Amendment Act was designed to enable quicker alienation. The only significant amendment to the 1909 legislation before 1931, it further boosted state powers to vest land for leasing in the Maori Land Boards. At the same time, it facilitated the transfer of vested Maori leasehold lands to the (generally pakeha) tenants. The 'protection' afforded by vesting land in the boards, then, turned out to be 'only marginally better than none at all', and a third of the leasehold acreage was permanently alienated well within two decades. Other patrimonial 'safeguards' were also removed. In particular, the necessity for the Crown to purchase through 'resolution of assembled owners' and Maori Land Boards was rescinded. Although on the surface such moves gave greater autonomy to collectives, it was also easier for Crown agents to buy interests in land from individuals, often clandestinely, following this up by securing Native Land Court intervention to gain usable and saleable blocks.

Moreover, the 1913 amending legislation merged the Native Land Court and the Maori Land Boards. Carroll and others had suggested that Maori representatives on the boards were a 'check . . . against unfair dealing' in alienation and management of the lands vested in them. But now the boards not only covered the same districts as those of the court, but comprised only two people, the Native Land Court judge and his registrar. Even the minister acknowledged that in effect 'the Native Land Board will be the Judge himself'. With no Maori input into the institutions that were supposedly buffers between Maori and the Crown, there were many ramifications for rangatiratanga. Owners of blocks which had been vested in Maori Land Councils or their successor boards, for example, 'no longer had any vestige of direct involvement in decision-making with respect to these lands'.

Ngata and Carroll had wanted to give a culture 'steeped in Communism' time to adjust, seeing leasehold as the way of retaining vestigial Maori land in Maori hands while improving their socio-economic circumstances. When the leases expired, the Maori patrimony would be ready for further development via newly acquired farming skills and the accumulated proceeds from ground rents. For Herries and his co-thinkers, however, for Maori to be 'hustled' into the 'civilisation' of the twentieth century meant that they were to be parted from most of the rest of their land. Learning quickly to be 'European', speaking only English, living in western ways, behaving like the British through observing and copying such exemplars of society as policemen – all involved leaving the land or, at most, working for the pakeha farmer on it. Herries had, in fact, sponsored legislation enabling qualified Maori to be legally declared European, one intended effect of which was that their interests in land could be purchased without any inconvenient restrictions at all (not that many took the bait, and some who did were actually attempting thereby to facilitate their management of collective lands). Under the Native Land Amendment Act, land alienation became more than ever the dominant activity of the Native Department, the agency in charge of the assimilation agenda as well as the Crown's land purchasing.[70]

The Young Maori Party, then, had failed to persuade Reform in its early years in government to continue policies which played for time, on both land and lifestyle issues, until tribal mana could be re-established in a way that fitted contemporary developments. Despite consistently attempting to get greater Maori collective input into the administration and disposition of their lands, often invoking the Treaty of Waitangi in the process, Ngataism was fighting a losing battle. In its very attempts to ameliorate the consequences of the pressures for alienation, it became complicit in them. The imperatives of the hegemonist paradigm within which it operated, and the power of the state with which it co-operated, had led inexorably to government machinery that was increasingly geared to disempowering Maori as collectively organised and resourced groups. After 1913, with the organised pakeha working-class crushed after coercive suppression of the great strike, the final Crown push for Maori land alienation accelerated.

First World War

With the advent of the First World War, the Dominion focused its energies on the 'patriotic' war effort. All elements of society were expected to 'pull together' in the common good of defence of empire. This precluded any chances of progress towards either resource- or people-based autonomy for Maori, or even any realistic possibility of ameliorating assimilationist pressures. Wartime was a particularly intensified episode in a long period, beginning in the late nineteenth century, of 're-colonisation'. Nationalist historiography, in its constant search for an emergent sense of New Zealand 'identity', has overlooked this 'tightening of links with the metropolis'. But the ideological onflow from the emphasis on massive farm-based production for England was to inform race relations policy in New Zealand for decades.

On the outbreak of war, Maori MPs and leading Ngataists quickly concluded that a loyalist Maori response would pay dividends in pakeha and British perceptions of their people. They secured agreement that New Zealand request of the Mother Country a departure from the imperial practice that indigenous soldiers not be used in European theatres of war. This was granted, and a Maori Recruitment (or Maori Contingent) Committee (chaired by Pomare and comprising the Maori MPs and Carroll) was established in September 1914 to run the Maori war effort. Its network of local committees procured Maori troops for the New Zealand Expeditionary Force. After agitation from the men in camp, followed by some political manoeuvring, this was allowed to be organised along tribal lines. The Recruitment Committee allocated troop quotas whose make-up reflected tribal affiliations, and was permitted to select some of the officers and NCOs.

There were difficulties, generally reflecting European perceptions that Maori were unable to contribute to the war effort without guidance. The military, for example, insisted on an element of pakeha leadership of Maori troops. It was not at ease with elders being sent to camps to ensure that tribal customs were respected, nor with tribal rivalry within camps, nor with a strong (and successful) Maori lobby that their troops not be sent to Samoa. Moreover, despite the wishes of the Maori MP lobby, imperial policy had moved only a certain distance in the deployment of indigenous soldiers. Maori troops could be raised only for garrison protection duty (in Egypt and Malta) rather than for a front-line combat role. But the response of many tribes to the recruiting call, especially those that were traditionally 'loyalist', heightened pakeha awareness of Maori and their aspirations, especially after the 500 troops of the First

Maori Contingent sailed in February 1915.

Yet the fact remained that they were to be a 'pioneer' group which provided skilled labour for the New Zealand Expeditionary Force but was 'not considered good enough to fight'. Maori leaders at home and abroad urged that their men be allowed a combat role in order fully to prove their skill and commitment. When pakeha fighting casualties proved to be high, the imperial command agreed that Maori troops could be assigned to front-line duties. In July 1915, Maori soldiers were sent to Gallipoli. Here they technically remained 'pioneers', but were quickly engaged in battle. Deeds of heroism, and their many casualties, were much reported and discussed within the Dominion. This undoubtedly contributed to changing pakeha attitudes, and helped lay the foundations for more positive Crown policies towards Maori aspirations in the post-war world.

Many Maori, for various reasons (hegemonic, opportunistic and tribal among them), showed willingness, even enthusiasm, for the overseas fighting effort. Rua Kenana himself, on release from imprisonment, urged his followers to sign up. Some tribes therefore fulfilled the aim of Ngataist leaders by demonstrating their value to the Dominion in a way – the shedding of blood – that could never be forgotten. The overseas service contribution was complemented by a high profile on the home front. Maori played a part in many voluntary war effort groups, with Maori women, for example, working in such bodies as 'Lady Liverpool's and Mrs Pomare's Maori Soldiers' Fund'.[71]

During the war, however, Maori discovered that the Crown and its agents continued to fear the consequences of even partial empowerment for Maori. The New Zealand Expeditionary Force commander, Major-General Alexander Godley, found the Maori attitude to the chain of command particularly difficult to cope with. Allegations that Maori officers were incompetent, together with high casualties and a fall-off in Maori recruiting, provided him with a reason to disband the Maori Contingent as a discrete entity within the force. His dividing the Maori platoons among the battalions of the New Zealand Infantry Brigade led to much Maori anger. There was a general belief among the tribes and their soldiers that Maori wishes were once again being overturned, in a way which amounted to suppression of rangatiratanga for race-based reasons. Elders threatened to stop recruiting.

In response, the military tried generally to keep men from similar tribal backgrounds together in the same units. This satisfied neither the Maori Recruitment Committee nor other Maori leaders, who kept up pressure, and meanwhile morale in the field suffered. When Godley reorganised the Expeditionary Force into the New Zealand Division in February 1916, he took the opportunity to reunite most Maori troops within a 'New Zealand Pioneer Battalion'. The new unit was half pakeha in membership, but designed eventually to become fully Maori. The development met many rangatiratanga-based criticisms.

But what the military gave with one hand it took with the other. For the battalion was established – as with the original Maori Contingent – to provide labour back-up to the front-line forces, rather than to be a fighting unit. Men who saw themselves as warriors were soon building roads, digging trenches and laying railways in France. This met the criticisms of some tribal leaders who called for fewer casualties in the interests of 'the preservation of our race', but it was generally interpreted as dismissing mana Maori. So too was a low priority for tribal organisation within what was seen by the military as essentially a pan-Maori grouping. And the leadership remained mostly pakeha, although the second-in-command was Te Rangihiroa.

In the event, Pioneer Battalion troops became inexorably involved in fighting on the western front. As casualties rose, so did pakeha gratitude. Moreover, Maori recruiting picked up again, assisting the general image of Maoridom. By October 1917 almost all of the battalion's company commanders were Maori. But its designation as a non-fighting body meant that a perceived race-based slight continued, contributing to temporary difficulties in attracting Maori volunteers for military service (with Pacific Islanders recruited to fill the gaps). But the fact remained that a definable, high-profile Maori presence had returned to the war effort abroad, and this was highly significant in the eyes of Maori and pakeha alike.[72]

Meanwhile, from the beginning of the war some tribal and regional groupings had protested against the state's past and present 'native policies' by declining to co-operate with the war effort. The Kingitanga tribes, in particular, while having long since abandoned overt resistance, had remained intensely dissatisfied with the loss of their ancestral lands in the confiscations (raupatu) of the nineteenth century. This loss had caused them to make tighter connections between their land and political aspirations than most tribes. Well versed in applying organised pressure on the state, Kingitanga declined to encourage its young men to enlist in the armed forces pending the addressing of tribal grievances. This official line, the Crown knew, was merely for the sake of avoiding prosecution. Privately, the leadership was proactive in discouraging any of its young men who might be inclined to assist the 'pakeha war effort'.

Princess Te Puea, leading a revival of the Waikato tribes, consolidated her power base by refusing to disguise her opinion. It was clear that she was adamantly against any form of service; and that, whatever the circumstances, her people would struggle fiercely for the independence of their political culture within the New Zealand polity. No Waikato volunteered, a lesson for the Crown in the power of Maori control mechanisms. The Kingitanga was considered to be potentially, even (in some interpretations) actually, subversive of the state. While its stance did focus minds on grievances held across numerous tribes, many Maori leaders feared that this would detract from their efforts to convince pakeha of a new place for Maori in society. When conscription was introduced in 1916, the Crown proposed exempting Maori, partly in order to avoid a showdown with oppositional tribes, but the Maori MPs and other Maori leaders remained hostile to exemption.

In the event, Maori were excluded from compulsory military service, as there was too much at stake for the Crown in presenting a harmonious domestic face to the world. But the mainstream Maori leadership continued the fight for compulsion, fully aware of a general pakeha feeling that all sectors of society should be pulling their weight (although workers noted that, while their labour and lives were conscripted, capital was not). In June 1917 the Maori Recruitment Committee was instrumental in persuading the Crown to extend conscription, in theory, to all Maori. But it did not want to provoke tribes which had voiced mild opposition but were in other respects co-operative. In practice, therefore, attempts were made to extend it only to the tribes which had fully resisted, Tainui's Maniapoto and Waikato. When the young men of Kingitanga continued to reject forced participation in the conflict, the iwi was subjected to coercive scrutiny. By the end of the war 111 of its members were in gaol, with another hundred awaiting service of warrants.

Despite this, and indeed aided by the fact that only one tribal movement remained fully resistant, widespread appreciation of the Maori war effort continued. On 1 September 1917 Maori troops were finally granted their own battalion, with the formation of the New Zealand (Maori) Pioneer Battalion, and by the end of the year it had 928 members. The battalion was the only one in the Expeditionary Force to return as a complete unit and the welcome was tumultuous. A total of 2227 Maori and 458 Pacific Islanders had served with the unit and its predecessors; 336 of them had died and 734 were wounded.[73]

Politics and land

Such sacrifice did not, however, lead to immediate Crown concessions. Indeed, the acquisition of Maori land went on apace. Herries' push for speedy alienation actually increased under pressure from land speculators as the war was drawing to a close. Extra land was needed for the rehabilitation of soldiers, as well as for general post-war reconstruction. But, in the long run, the indigenous war contribution did help lead to the state's addressing Maori causes. This was not from any sentiment of 'gratitude', as historians have been wont to suggest. Had policy been driven by *grateful* politicians, one might have expected (at the very least) that the state would have assisted rehabilitation for Maori ex-soldiers to the same extent as it did for pakeha returnees. This was not the case. To take the crucial matter of livelihood, while in theory the allocation of farms through balloting was equal among all returned servicemen, in reality few Maori were assisted in this way.

Ngataist legislation of 1916 had provided for Maoridom to assist its returned servicemen in land-based rehabilitation. This was a new means of keeping Maori land in indigenous ownership, and therefore of promoting land-based rangatiratanga. But it had been introduced in a context of Maori appreciation that their interests were unlikely to prevail within the state, and that the best they could do was to procure legislative assistance for taking on the major burden themselves. In fact, by 1917 Maori leaders so doubted the government's intentions that they set up the Maori Patriotic Committee to raise funds among their people for their ex-servicemen. In the event, this organisation had to abandon the plan to help returnees gain farms, opting instead for purchasing a handful of stations whose income could be used for relief purposes. This was another blow to the possibility of enhancing the land base of Maoridom. The perceived disloyalty to 'New Zealand' among some elements of Maoridom, moreover, had served to reinforce stereotypes about the danger to the socio-political fabric of the state from collective expressions of indigenousness. The difficulties caused to the Crown by Maunga-pohatu's rival sovereignty and Kingitanga's political stance, in particular, reinforced its determination to not to alter its attitude to political autonomy.

But some state concessions to Maori were to emerge in due course in the context of greater pakeha public acceptance of Maori following their war effort. These related, however, to 'national goals'. Maori had proved to be of use in 'defending' the scientifically farmed, pakeha-governed New Zealand in which they were ultimately destined to become absorbed as 'brown-skinned Europeans'. The Maori fighting effort had reminded the authorities, at a time when the international and domestic ramifications of war had widened the horizons of possibility for Maori, that it was preferable to have the tangata whenua as satisfied as possible, or at least not too dissatisfied. The social, financial and other costs of the invasion of Rua's headquarters had been a chastening example of the difficulties of subduing even the core of a movement comprising only a thousand followers. There was a feeling that, while autonomist developments would be encouraged if any concessions to self-determination were made, they might be circumvented by addressing rangatiratanga in a lower-key way.

After the war, then, the state reconsidered its generally hard line against Maori aspirations for better access to and use of resources. Expedience assisted its decision making. The Crown could, for example, cease to concentrate its Maori policy energies on alienating land, as more or less sufficient had now been acquired – enough, even, for resettling pakeha returned servicemen. The head of the Native Department summed this up in declaring that it would be reasonable for Maori 'to retain the small area remaining to them', so long as they did not become 'a charge on the State'. In 1920 the official calculation was that Maori retained title to well under a million acres 'that may be considered suitable for settlement' (at a time when 62 million acres had been 'acquired' by pakeha). This amounted to an average of 19 acres per Maori, barely enough for self-sustenance let alone for other purposes.

Much of the land which had remained only two decades before, then, had by this time disappeared, despite the Crown's ostensible commitment to preservation in 1900. The official analysis, tellingly, assumed that the more than three million acres leased to Europeans would 'never return to the occupation of the Native owners'. A land-purchase scenario that risked escalating Maori landlessness or marginalisation, which were seen as potential drains on state resources, was not in the national interest. While purchasing did not totally stop, the state now interpreted the public good as requiring improved Maori productivity on their remaining land, especially through title reform that would put Maori in a better position to farm.[74]

But the question of how best to preserve and use the land that was left in Maori hands would increasingly tax both Maori and the state. Ngata and other 'modernising' Maori leaders had long sought ways of providing their people with the means to develop their lands for 'scientific' farming. They appreciated several imperatives. The most important, and the truism of the time, can be seen in the Young Maori Party acknowledgement that '[o]nly those lands which the Maoris themselves will *usefully* occupy will remain or be allowed to remain to them'. But they also emphasised the significance of retaining communal initiative and organisation in relation to the land. In this way, not only could productivity rise through the skills of those individuals engaged in farming, but Maori culture would be encouraged to survive and evolve.

Ngata had set out long before to promote economic and social revival on the East Coast. He intended to demonstrate that this was viable through collective endeavour. After his election to Parliament, he had urged Ngati

Porou farmers to create incorporations to develop large areas of multiply owned land. The incorporation was (in the words of an official inquiry) 'a private company the fractions of ownership in which correspond to the shares in the block or blocks of Maori freehold land' concerned. Its management 'block committees', elected by the shareholders, had the legal right to 'act for all the owners in farming, selling or leasing blocks of Maori land'. Ngata advised incorporated collective owners to lease out only part of the land, with committees of management organising the farming of the rest by tribespeople. The law allowed for tribal involvement, and chiefs were often represented on the management committees.

Moreover, from 1911 Ngati Porou had expanded its productivity plans, with provisions in the 1909 Native Land Act to be used for trail-blazing work on the consolidating of individualised shares. Painstaking work had begun on amalgamating the separate interests that any one person, family or related group owned in various fragmented blocks after Native Land Court rulings. Land to the appropriate value was to be consolidated as a single economic unit, allowing agricultural development to occur more easily.

Along with (an interrelated) tribal resurgence, this pioneering land-tenure reorganisation had helped revive the Maori economy on the East Coast. Ngati Porou was generally seen as the most successful farming tribe, and downstream factors such as renewal of pride in iwi membership and a healthy population increase were noted. The tribal leaders' objective had always been socio-tribal: hapu and whanau reconstruction, iwi strength, removal of justification for pakeha acquisition of 'idle Maori land', and (in the words of a later official report) 'full production for the benefit of the race' as well as of 'the Dominion in general'. By the post-war period, even the most pro-western of the Young Maori Party core members were reconsidering their previous enthusiasm for in-depth assimilation to European ways. Te Rangihiroa, having advocated individualisation of farming in a 1906 report, was by this time engaged in an intellectual journey that would end in vigorous opposition to it.

For him and others, the much-vaunted success of incorporation and consolidation on the East Coast constituted a significant factor along the way. It showed that in 'modernisation' the law could be used to preserve many of the traditional customs and lifestyle of Maori. Acutely aware of Crown as well as Maori perceptions, Ngata had known that in state eyes the problem with his tenurial and managerial reforms was that they *did* potentially foster communalism. He had thus proceeded cautiously, so much so that he hoped ultimately to get substantial state assistance. While stressing the downstream benefits for tribes from consolidation, for example, he also argued that it was the best solution to politico-bureaucratic worries over Maori land productivity.

The Crown had other reasons, too, for seeing 'public' advantages in consolidation. The process could make it easier, for example, once the Crown had purchased a 'strategic' mass of shares in a given area, to acquire usable blocks for on-sale to pakeha farmers. However, it came to see the force in Ngata's argument that Maori could often usefully farm on post-consolidation blocks, too. So long as the Maori-farmed consolidated units were not so communalised as to pose a conceptual threat to a Europeanised way of life, their productivity could contribute to the national economy – or, at the very least, subsistence farming could help keep people from the need to access state welfare coffers. It was the Ngati Porou experiment, in fact, which had helped embolden the Crown to sponsor large-scale model consolidation measures in the Urewera – the region still seen to need 'taming' despite the continued whittling away of its supposed autonomy. Imposing pakehaised 'order and regularity' on the Urewera could be achieved partly through the better economic base (for both Maori and pakeha) that would result from tenure restructuring.

The results of such consolidation experiments in the Urewera were so positive that the Crown was willing to sponsor similar exercises elsewhere. Gordon Coates, Native Minister from March 1921, was especially enthusiastic. The path was smoothed by the general acceptance by Native Land Court judges of Ngata's consolidation (and incorporation) guidelines in 1922. The Native Land Amendment and Native Land Claims Adjustment Act in the following year not only rationalised all legislation on land consolidation, but also authorised the minister (rather than the Governor-General) to approve projected schemes. In

1924 consolidation became firmly entrenched in government policy.

After their expansion from 1926, consolidation schemes would extend as far as Northland. Meanwhile, their validity was hotly contested among Maoridom. While some saw them as enabling rangatiratanga, others saw them as compromising or negating it. On the one hand, in the Urewera transactions, for example, the state's commissioners defined the consolidated form of the interests the Crown had purchased. Many non-sellers would be deprived of their ancestral connections with specific portions of land, which might include the best farming lands or areas of cultural and tribal significance to them. Whatever the overall benefits for Maori touted by the Young Maori Party, state-generated consolidation trampled on the rights of many Maori individuals and collectivities. On the other hand, compact, family-based farming units would benefit non-sellers through productivity gains. Less measurably, the fact that *some* tribespeople would remain on land within tribal boundaries/rohe meant a continuing base for socio-cultural pursuits.

Many Maori argued that rangatiratanga which resulted from Crown action was scarcely rangatiratanga at all. Moreover, it was noted that the state sponsored consolidation *only* where it assessed that it could promote what it defined as the interests of 'the country'. The consolidation schemes were established essentially to benefit the government and its settler constituency, not Maori – although Maori could gain from them, and many undoubtedly did. Primarily, consolidation made it easier for the state to carry out strategic purchasing of interests in desired areas. There were also spin-off effects, such as reducing the problem of rates left unpaid due to ownership fragmentation. The Crown became increasingly involved in consolidation, then, as the various benefits became clearer.

Consolidation also added to the gains from incorporation, which Maori leaders had seen as a good way of collectively organising productivity on land with fragmented title. A Carroll measure of 1903 had first focused on incorporation for farming purposes, and Maori had increasingly used it to improve their farming prospects and their collective aspirations, with Ngati Porou leading the way. 'By this device', wrote an historian looking back at its facilitation of Maori farming over several decades, 'the Maori tribal system could itself be used to put authority into the hands of some individual [or group able to farm the land efficiently] without infringing community rights'. Consolidation was another method, for some Maori collectivities, to own land legally in a 'traditional communal way', even though title had been divided into individual shares by the Native Land Court.

Dividends from incorporations' profits could be used for cultural purposes as well as to provide income. In fact, much original Maori support for the idea had been because the management committees would be hapu-based; many were indeed centred on tribal groupings of some nature, and some were dominated by chiefs. Once again, parliamentary mechanisms to alienate and decollectivise had been used by Maori to further their collective interests. As this contributed to national productivity and therefore to the 'public good', it was tolerated by the Crown.[75]

State-assisted land development

However much the consolidations might have benefited many, the schemes did not address the deep-rooted problem that the Native Land Court's succession procedures meant escalating title fragmentation among Maori landowners. Consolidation might be a solution to immediate problems relating to management, productivity and socio-political collective organisation, but ongoing fragmentation of title among inheritors of deceased estates was inevitable. The consolidation mechanism could not, moreover, address the major problem of lack of access by Maori to development capital. Lending institutions were generally resistant to Maori clientele at the best of times, and were particularly averse to providing loans to develop communally owned land, especially in a situation of actual or potential high ownership fragmentation. A landed resource that could provide a strong base to secure a stable socio-political future seemed as far away for many whose titles had been consolidated as it was for much of the rest of Maoridom.

Ngata and like-minded leaders, who believed that the key to Maori politico-cultural (as well as economic) advancement was development of the land, had put insistent pressure on the state to address the question of Maori access to development capital and expertise. Early in the century, the Crown had conceded in principle that it should assist Maori to develop farming operations, and this had been legislated for. Subsequently, little had happened, and Maori leaders had come to pin their hopes on an 'independent' source of development finance. The Public Trustee had for long been the sole legal owner of Maori reserves, administering them on behalf of their 'beneficial owners'. Normally, they had been leased out to pakeha farmers 'in the public good', in some cases in perpetuity. Many Maori viewed such trusteeship over their 'own' lands as antithetical to their rangatiratanga. In 1920 the Crown went some way towards acknowledging their concerns by conceding that managing assets held on behalf of Maori required a specialist Native Trustee. This office was set up in 1921 and, although attached to the Native Department, it operated autonomously. Its activities generated monies that could be invested for Maori purposes.

With the support of Ngata and Coates, the first Native Trustee (Judge W E Rawson) began to lend Maori Land Board funds vested in him to Maori owners or their lessees. These loans were pegged to land development and farming operations. By law no trustee could assume responsibility for the generalised good of an entire social sector, needing to be 'ever-mindful of the requirements of the trust deed' and the interests of its specified beneficiaries. The ability to take up generalised development, or to work on behalf of tribally based or wider groupings, was therefore restricted. But the Native Trustee's early assigning of mortgages and other devices to assist specific Maori co-operative endeavours, including some that were highly successful, contributed to Maori efforts to retain collective, resource-based control of their own destinies. From 1922, moreover, the Maori Land Boards themselves were allowed to provide mortgages to Maori or their lessees, and from 1926 they could (with ministerial permission) make loans for development.

Meanwhile, Ngata and others had been attempting to persuade the Crown of the need for state assistance for *large-scale* Maori land development. One of their trump cards, however, the success of pioneering experiments on the East Coast, was seen by many as suspect. The problem was that it aimed (in the words of a sympathetic pakeha observer) at 'reconciling Maori ideas of communal ownership with pakeha efficiency in working'. The Crown still preferred that most increase in production come from the sturdily individual pakeha or pakehaised farmer. But, as tribes outside the East Coast and Urewera began to take up consolidation and incorporation schemes, it increasingly appreciated that Maori-owned development might well be able to contribute to the 'national good'.[76]

In turn, Maori proponents of state-aided development, while seeking to underpin Maori identity through enhancing land-based rangatiratanga, increasingly directed their case to the Crown through the benefit to the economy as a whole for developing the land remaining to 'the race'. Additionally, they argued, the Dominion's treasury would benefit in other ways. Not only would Maori be better able to pay current and arrears rates, but also payments to the Crown outstanding because of low (or absent) yields from the land could now be made – for survey liens, for example.

Under great pressure from within both Maori (especially Ngataist) and pakeha (including local bodies affected by non-payment of rates) camps, the government made further moves towards greater state assistance to Maori development. In 1927 Ngata, already chair of the Native Affairs Committee of Parliament, was not only knighted but also appointed chairman of a Native Lands Consolidation Commission. This was charged with promoting to Maori and local bodies, especially those in Taitokerau and Waikato–King Country, the idea of state-led development in the context of consolidation. It would, among other things, mediate between Maori landowners and local bodies to procure rates compromises, preparing the way for extensive consolidation. At first, Maori in the target regions were often suspicious about accepting state-provided assistance, feeling that once the Crown had gained any leverage over their lands it would be exceedingly reluctant to concede unimpeded indigenous control, even after the completion of development. Ngata and his bureaucrats, however, provided assurances that state-imposed accountability would not be excessive, and significant numbers of communal landowners began to negotiate.

In December 1928 the government was defeated by Sir Joseph Ward's

United Party. Ngata then took on an even greater national leadership role with his appointment as Native Minister and a high Cabinet ranking. Although there was a template of success in cases where development finance had followed consolidation and incorporation, the lack of speed on Maori land development had been frustrating him. Endemic financing problems had been exacerbated by an uncertain economy. Ngata saw his mission as fast-tracking Maori land development by state aid on a *national* scale. He was to forge ahead despite the onset in 1929 of the Great Depression – and because of it, helped by pakeha fears that destitute Maori would become an enormous burden on the state.

The new minister shared the view of Maori generally that land development was a way of economically underpinning a communal mode of life based on tribal values and organisational principles. The Native Trustee's and other lending regimes had not encouraged such a perspective. Now, Ngata's 1929 Native Land Amendment and Native Land Claims Adjustment Act offered extensive state assistance for Maori farming development in a way that held potential for sustaining the nexus between the quest for rangatiratanga and the viability of retaining land. Indeed, to many people Crown-aided land development schemes seemed the best way to get some measure of land-based self-determination. The standard method was for a committee of management, representing the collective owners of a potentially developable block, to apply for assistance on their behalf. Advisory committees to the Crown could provide further tribal input. With prospects of both democratic self-management of the land, and the establishment of viable farming, many Maori who had originally been suspicious of Ngata's ideas were quickly won round and sought to participate.

The minister's guidance and control in the land development processes were ubiquitous. Once land had been gazetted for a scheme, for example, it could not be leased or sold without Ngata's permission. Further extension of his powers came in 1930 and 1931. One key aspect of ministerial intervention was to encourage Maori tribal leaders to offer themselves for positions in the schemes, such as foremen and (increasingly) supervisors. The Maori land development schemes soon came to be viewed in sections of Maoridom as 'the modern replacement of the authority and management of the chief in ancient Maori society', a 'stroke of genius', a way of preserving a communal ethos during a period of general state hostility. While the Crown saw state-assisted development as aiding a productivity-based public good, the process itself reflected collective identity and decision making.[77]

Politics of land

The first of the land development schemes showed that the United government's aim of incorporating Maori into the *economic* mainstream was not necessarily incompatible with the very communalism that the Native Land Court had been set up to erode. The state, pursuing its own agenda, was not deterred by widespread Maori celebration at the possibility of achieving their economic recovery by means which had a collective resonance. Ngata was invited to stay on as Native Minister in George Forbes' conservative ministry in 1930, and in the Depression-induced Forbes–Coates coalition government that followed it from September 1931. By then 41 schemes were operating, and policy relating to them remained unaffected by political change and national economic woes.

This was largely because, although the schemes had a collective orientation, they were very much the creatures of state direction. Ngata had preferred development to follow consolidation, but this had proved too slow. Massive state managerial control, albeit intended as temporary, was the price of a speedier approach. Land destined for development would be placed with the Native Department and associated specialist bureaucracies, the owners temporarily surrendering proprietary rights. The Native Department acted as both mortgagee and trustee, the 'mother and father' of the land and its owners, in the words of one bureaucrat. State control was pervasive. Scheme supervisors, for example, had to deal direct with the Native Minister even on detailed matters. He appointed the members of advisory committees, and in any case their consent was not necessary before a development proceeded. While the collective owners could nominate the 'occupiers' of sections, the final selection of 'competent' Maori to farm the developing lands was done by the state in order to protect its loan investment.

As the schemes proceeded, moreover, the occupiers gained a degree of protected legal status, so strengthening individualisation inside the Maori economy at the expense of the present and future rights of collective owners. This was contrary to initial Crown assurances that, once debts were repaid, land and stock would revert fully to the owners' collective control. Yet ultimate retention of full control over their own lands had been, a senior official later acknowledged, 'the most important part of the contract' for Maori owners.

The ramifications of state direction became increasingly clear, dismaying the many who had felt that state-assisted development would significantly promote land-based rangatiratanga. A foretaste of things to come occurred on the very first scheme under the 1929 legislation, at Horohoro, when the foreman treated the local hapu as 'strangers on the block' and ignored their views. Maori noted the preponderance of pakeha in key positions, and increasing bureaucratic intervention.

The Treasury, in particular, tried to ensure managerial regimes to its own liking, such as those with pakeha supervisors. In an effort to placate iwi that had suffered raupatu by restoring some kind of land base, moreover, resettlement to developing lands outside their rohe was sought, to the chagrin of the 'host' tribes. From 1933, for example, some Waikato were placed (along with Ngati Porou people with farm development expertise) on lands in Te Arawa territory. Separation of the great majority of owners from decision making or tilling contact with ancestral land in the development schemes frustrated many who wanted to use them to foster communal and cultural activity within Maoridom.

Other forces were also detrimental to the Maori search for Crown recognition of rangatiratanga. By 1932 the Native Trustee had lent beyond what was deemed prudent, and so his office was merged with that of the permanent head of the Native Department. The trusteeship was now virtually just another part of the state's Maori bureaucracy and was often used to provide an independent source of funding for the department, a situation which continued for half a century. At best the trustee's office had acted as a guardian, even a developer, of those Maori assets placed with it. Maori had generally seen it, however, as an inefficient user and distributor of their assets, even though it had enabled some land-based (or other) sustainability schemes to flourish. Many now noted an increasing caution and paternalism among the trustee bureaucrats in matters such as asset distribution, which added to the frustrations of the Maori quest for autonomy.

Conversely, initial pakeha suspicions of the schemes were placated by increasing state intervention in Maori affairs, as well as by success stories. The latter even helped to promote the idea that some tribally based collectivism might not necessarily equate with a 'degenerate race' practising 'communistic customs'. However much it was pitched for pakeha consumption, Ngata's vision remained inspired by a belief in the virtues of a rural and communal way of life that perpetuated Maori customs. While he envisaged Maori increasingly participating in the pakeha economy as individuals, they would retain their tribal ties and loyalties in their social lives. The development schemes would create a critical economic mass within a rohe, and thereby underpin a reflourishing of tribal institutions.

'Total assimilationists' had therefore been quick to counterattack. In response, from 1931 the Crown grew increasingly defensive. One official policy thrust, for example, stressed that an incorporation was, and should only be, a *temporary* expedient to enable the Crown to negotiate with a single body in a given area. New legislation, moreover, attempted to insulate issues of productivity for the 'national good' from those of tribal culture. Maori farming was to be mainstreamed as far as possible. Full assimilation was reaffirmed as ultimate state policy. And all the while the gap widened between socio-tribal control of the land in the schemes and the power of the bureaucrats (and some of their 'occupiers'). Maori hopes that the schemes' structures might prefigure a new kind of collectivist adaptation to modernity looked increasingly forlorn, dashed by the sizeable difference between promise and reality in operational control. Significant working community or tribal autonomy had seemed within reach, but once again this had proved to be a chimera.[78]

All the same, although Ngata was increasingly careful in his public statements, many pakeha were uneasy about the ultimate outcomes of the land schemes so long as he remained in charge of them. He was seen as a 'cuckoo in the state's nest'. The very success of some of the projects

(76 had been inaugurated by 1934) escalated such fears, even inside officialdom, where obstructions and moves to curb his power were under way. Some detractors took an opposite stance, deeming the schemes a failure for having proved inadequate to counteract the effects of the Depression on Maoridom. With three-quarters of adult Maori males unemployed, tangata whenua were regarded as a serious potential burden on the state.

Any criticism of land development that assumed it had been intended as a quick-fix panacea for the Maori economic plight was, of course, unfair. But the argument did reflect deep-rooted fears among pakeha. These were exacerbated by the Maori demographic recovery. This had first impinged significantly on pakeha consciousness when the 1921 census revealed that the total tribal population had increased to some 57,000, but many observers had still considered this a temporary phenomenon. A decade later, such a view was untenable. With land development unable to prevent such an increasing population from 'burdening the state', the amounts spent on it, and the policy itself, came under increasing scrutiny. Native Minister Ngata, the symbol as well as the controller of the schemes, came increasingly under fire.

Unfortunately for him, operation of the schemes had given his enemies ammunition. Unwilling to have his work impeded by red tape and minimal staff, Ngata had pressed ahead relentlessly. For him and many tribes, land development was far too important for their people to be held up by accounting and other niceties. The financial control departments of state began to be critical at an early stage, the more so as depression worsened. They and others focused on the very factors which had helped induce Maoridom to back Ngata's schemes: the speed of their implementation and the significance of input by tribal leadership and structures. In 1932, the National Expenditure Commission, established to reduce official spending, declared that Ngata's schemes had used excessive government funds.

In essence, while the various attacks personalised the issues to Ngata, they were directed at the *system* itself. Faults were contextualised as part of an alleged grave error in giving *any* minister (especially a Maori one) extensive powers to promote Maori interests. The fact that there was an element of 'tikanga Maori' in the implementation of the schemes merely gave further ammunition to those who objected to 'separatist policies' *per se*. Appointing people with mana and cultural competence, rather than necessarily with administrative skills, meant that official accounting and other bureaucratic requirements had often been neglected. A process of scrutinising and reducing Ngata's spending and decision-making powers began. The Native Land Settlement Board was established in 1932 to take hands-on control of the schemes. In 1933 the Controller and Auditor-General refused to approve the previous year's land development accounts, and apparent irregularities in field and district office accounts came under examination.

The Labour political opposition attacked Ngata vigorously, and Parliament's Public Accounts Select Committee launched an investigation. It felt that 'a lot of unnecessary fuss had been made', and the Auditor-General did not consider a public inquiry was necessary. However, the committee was under such political and media pressure that, in order 'to allay all suspicion and misunderstanding', it recommended that a commission of inquiry be appointed 'in the public interest'. In February 1934 the government, under similar pressure, established the Royal Commission of Inquiry into Native Affairs.

Many Maori feared the worst, and with good reason. The commission had no Maori representation, and comprised individuals known to be unsympathetic to continuance of a Maori way of life. It was headed by Judge David Smith, who was known to favour the emergence of individualised Maori farming and, concomitantly, to oppose the Ngataist stress on as much communal involvement in ownership and control of land as possible. Meanwhile, official New Zealand had been moving against Ngata. That same month he was forced, in line with a National Expenditure Commission recommendation, to relinquish oversight of both development policy and operations to the Native Land Settlement Board. In this way a direct and symbiotic relationship between minister and Maori 'was transformed into a bureaucratically driven process intended to generate a "national good".'

In such an atmosphere the commission of inquiry began its hearings in April 1934. The answer to its ostensible major question, whether

Ngata (and those close to him) had taken shortcuts in the administration of the land development schemes, was a foregone conclusion. It was far from secret that infractions in public service regulations had been required to counter bureaucratic inefficiency and resistance to the schemes. But the three-month investigation ranged far wider. Its broad agenda amounted to the exemplary disciplining of Ngata for his advocacy of a development path which accommodated tribal organisation and leadership, and ultimately for his 'break with assimilationism' which underpinned this. Both the schemes and the 'Maoritanga' he was conceptualising were seen as an impediment to full assimilation, and ultimately as a danger to the unitary state at both tribal and central or proto-nationalist level. Under hostile questioning, Ngata faltered. In any case, his attempts to balance his desire to preserve and promote key aspects of the Maori way of life with his duties as one of the highest members of the government were probably doomed in advance.

As a minister, he was forced into defending the state on its own terms. Development schemes, he proclaimed, were essentially to promote individualism among Maori, and relatedly for the good of the 'general public'. Certainly, he agreed, occupiers had to operate in the context of tribal leadership and the protocols of the whanau and hapu – but this needed to be within the competitive arena that had replaced the anachronistic 'communism' of the 'old world of Maoridom'. The commissioners were (rightly) unconvinced that Ngata's 'reconversion' to an individualistic agenda was genuine or fundamental. They noted with disapproval his clear attempts to promote Maori culture under the umbrella of the development schemes: the restoration of communal buildings as a focus for rebuilding Maori pride, to take one instance.

The commissioners noted that attempts to encourage, or even preserve, aspects of iwi or hapu self-determination pointed to the minister's agenda being collectivist rather than individualist. They expressed open disapproval of ministerial interventions in the schemes, both authorised and unauthorised, of Ngata being too much 'in a hurry', of his disregard of accountability mechanisms, of the 'wastefulness' of intertribal hui. Such matters were adduced as evidence to support the commission's aims, which amounted to an assault on rangatiratanga and an endorsement of full assimilation. The commissioners believed, as Smith said, that 'it is necessary to see that the whole system [of land development] is not given a communal bias . . . these schemes should not be used to give the Maori a basis of communal bias which would detract from the work of individual farmers'. They would not even endorse, Ngata noted, the concept of the 'nominated occupier' of land. The mere fact of multiple ownership by members of whanau and hapu was seen not just as economically unviable, but also as profoundly uncivilised and diverting Maori from a fully assimilationist future.

Experience of political power from the inside had shown Ngata that his former belief in Maori holding their own in a largely assimilationist polity was unrealistic. He was now urging that his people take greater proactive measures to control their own futures, using what was left of the land base to underpin such developments. In the view of the commission and its co-thinkers, bringing down the national figurehead for Maori aspirations would constitute a powerful actual and symbolic strike against the indigenous communal ethos. Although Ngata was absolved of personal corruption or wrong-doing, the commissioners sought out, and found, some 'minor graft', dubious ethical behaviour (such as 'favouritism' towards specific tribal groupings) and 'careless accounting' in the operation of the schemes. On this basis, in effect they declared that Maori socio-political objectives were ultimately incompatible with the designs of the state, which had allegedly tried to accommodate Maoridom and been rewarded by muddle, chaos and peculation.[79]

Some of Ngata's pakeha colleagues appreciated the difficulties he had faced in the past (such as inadequate back-up from the Native Department) and the commission's biases (its lack of contextualisation, for example, including any appreciation of the schemes' successes). But, because such importance had been attached to bringing him down by those operating the hegemonist agenda, those colleagues withdrew their public support. When the commission's report was tabled in the House, therefore, Ngata had little political support and resigned as Native Minister from 1 November 1934. He figured that this would be sufficient victory for the assimilationists, enabling the land development system to continue 'in the national interest'. While obviously the schemes would be under much greater state control, his resignation announcement urged his people not to falter in their goals.

In characterising the commission as a 'prosecution' from its very beginning, rather than an independent inquiry, Ngata did, however, emphasise the magnitude of the struggle. He knew that the whole affair had hindered Maori chances of pursuing autonomy through government bureaucracy. More broadly, it had reinforced stereotypes which would make it harder for Maori to continue their struggle by extra-official means. Even a sympathetic chronicler claimed that the results of the Ngata inquiry indicated that 'the ethics of accountability had no place in tribal morals and habits'. General public suspicion of state assistance of *any* type to Maori, and of Maori politicians achieving high office, was heightened. Almost four decades would pass before a Maori again assumed the ministerial portfolio for Maori issues.

Ngata continued informally to guide and inspire land development after his ousting. Not only did he believe deeply in the schemes, he felt that their ongoing success would help Maori 'prove' their capacity to assist the 'public good' while forwarding their own interests. He persuaded Forbes himself to take on the Native Affairs portfolio as a way of protecting the project, and in fact its scope soon expanded. But the rectification of inefficiencies highlighted by the commission, and widespread post-commission trumpeting of the ideological dangers of collectivism, meant that communalist elements in the system were increasingly sidelined. The Native Department took ever-greater control over the land incorporations, for example, and a Board of Native Affairs, established in April 1935, would supervise the whole land development process with the Crown's aims firmly in mind.

While the new board was given both sweeping powers and considerable finances to improve Maori land, sections of the legislation under which it operated disempowered Maori. In particular, the repeal of the local advisory committees, which Ngata had often used to ascertain the wishes of the Maori whose interests were involved, symbolised the direction of government policy. Three-person district committees, each including a Native Land Court judge, were established to replace them.

The emphasis was increasingly on coercing Maori to develop their land. The Board of Native Affairs had 'the power to do almost anything to bring Maori land under development'. If owners resisted the Crown's wishes, their views could be overridden. By the time the government was defeated at the polls in 1935, some Maori no longer saw the development schemes as a means of expressing even limited rangatiratanga. Some, indeed, saw state-led land development as trampling on it, or as the Crown having appropriated yet another Maori initiative.

Maori groupings did, however, fight back in a number of ways, including trying to use land development to rejuvenate collective endeavour. Some continued, for example, to convene the advisory committees unofficially. Others organised spontaneously to oppose (in a judge's words) 'any conception which inherently contains the possibility of dispossession' of their land. A Native Affairs officer noted of Far North Maori that there was 'a very strong suspicion that any scheme brought forward and sponsored by the Government has something behind it to their detriment'. Such feelings were widespread and continued well into the future, with stories circulating, for example, of officials violating undertakings to return developed blocks to the people. More immediately, volunteering land for development diminished, despite ongoing Crown proselytising. Many noted that government propaganda appealed to self and national rather than tribal or collective interests. After the official denigration of Ngata, and by extension of all Maori, many turned back to the counsel of those who had continued to operate within their traditional structures.

The development programmes had been envisioned by Ngataism as contributing to a revival and reorganisation of Maori life, helping to meld the 'best elements' of the cultures, mores and rhythms of life and work of both ethnicities. In a relatively short time, both friends and foes of the schemes had noted, the collective organisational component of the amalgam had been elevated by even the most pro-government of Maori leaders. Under Ngata's stewardship, they were no longer defensive about preserving 'the best in their ancestral past' as an integral part of a major 'reassertion of Maori *mana*'. The movement was not 'retrogressive in being retrospective', for it saw that developing the land along western farming lines was the final chance of securing at least some land base upon which to generate cultural and political revival. What it did insist on, however, was the right to conduct a way of life that took into account collectivist principles. It was this, antithetical to rapid and full assimilation in the rural areas as it was, which had caused the Crown to crack down on manifestations of assertive, land-based rangatiratanga within its purview.

The Maori resurgence continued regardless, based partly on the momentum gained from the development schemes and spurred on by Ngata's increasingly powerful commitment to rangatiratanga – the result of ministerial experiences that had led him to appreciate the full magnitude of the obstacles to modifying the official policy of assimilation. In 1935 the first Labour government was elected, and many Maori hoped that land development could be reclaimed for rangatiratanga. At first, such a prospect seemed viable. After Ngata persuaded the new Prime Minister to enhance the mana of the Native Affairs portfolio by taking it on himself, the theoretical parameters of the development projects were reviewed. This resulted in greater Maori input. Native Department officers, for example, were instructed to take into account the views of any informal 'committees fully representative of the local inhabitants'.

Despite such short-term developments, however, there was no political will to reverse the Crown's fundamental negativity towards the embodiment of meaningful communal, tribal or sub-tribal decision making in the schemes. On land-based matters, decisions were instead increasingly imposed from the politico-bureaucratic centre. When the Native Department declared that the voluntary committees would be used to 'communicate its intentions and views' to Maori, rather than the other way round, it was reflecting this ethos. Such a development was not, however, a fatal blow to the quest for rangatiratanga. For land-based development could only assist in *underpinning* the struggle for autonomy, particularly in communities which continued to hold suitable land. Rangatiratanga was in essence a political matter and needed to be primarily addressed as such.[80]

CHAPTER FIVE

TRIBAL AND PAN-TRIBAL RANGATIRATANGA

Crown negotiations with tribes

Maori efforts to regain land-based collective rangatiratanga had not proceeded far by the later 1930s, but there had been gains in other ways. The state was involved in some of these. A strengthening commitment to Maori physical well-being, an obvious prerequisite for resurgence, had been manifested in several ways: the establishment of nursing services targeted at Maori from 1911, the reconfiguring of the Maori Councils into health-oriented bodies in 1919–20, and the creation of the Maori Hygiene Division among them.

The latter two developments amounted to much more than a response to the huge Maori death toll in the great influenza pandemic of late 1918, which is the usual sole explanation for them. Government-sponsored Maori health initiatives indicated an increasing official recognition of the emerging demographic reality that Maori were far from a dying race. A more systematised approach to Maoridom and its problems was required. This was partly because such problems could be a drain on state coffers, but also because a 'strong native race' was regarded as useful for a range of reasons, including the performance of seasonal rural labour tasks.

However, government-initiated measures by the 1920s had little Maori involvement in decision making and were generally short of resources. Thus, the Crown's cross-tribal measures could not even partially compensate for the inability of pan-tribal organisation to achieve rangatiratanga. Many tribal groupings had therefore reverted to vocally reasserting their rights and aspirations *as tribes*. Their point of reference was essentially the Treaty of Waitangi and its promise of Crown acknowledgement of rangatiratanga. In 1922 Ngata noted that the Treaty was 'widely discussed on all maraes' in the country: 'It is on the lips of the humble and the great, of the ignorant and of the thoughtful.' Inadvertently reflecting a reversionary trend towards tribalist means, he labelled as 'wishful thinking' efforts to get 'Absolute Maori Authorities' through pan-tribal methods. Hui after hui around the country resonated with tribally based aspirations and organisation, seeking redress for the worst of the Crown's violations of rangatiratanga and support for its re-establishment. This was particularly the case among iwi and hapu which had suffered the most dramatically or materially: those which had seen their lands conquered and confiscated, for example, or Ngai Tahu, which had been deprived of most of the reserves promised in return for relinquishing much of the South Island.

In the period after Maori were deemed to be satisfactorily pacified, from the mid-1880s, European scholars had been propagating the notion that tangata whenua constituted a 'superior native race' of 'Aryan' origin. The colonial incursion could thus be seen as like a 'family reunion'. This set the scene, when Maori did not physically disappear, for an intended final episode in the process of 'civilising the natives' – cultural extinction, a prelude to full assimilation. This would come about partly through intermarriage with pakeha, legitimated by the 'European' origins of Maori. But one consequence of the 'Aryan Maori' and other such theses was that, if Maori were 'superior natives', the need for *full and final* assimilation would be less pressing. In such circumstances, one might expect considerable toleration for Maori cultural difference and organisational practices, and some in the Young Maori Party and other Maori milieus 'assisted' in propagating the thesis for this reason.

However, the Crown's general preference remained to deal with Maori as *individuals*. In its rejection of communalism, this was the most assimilationist of paradigms. Quite apart from the function and results of the Native Land Court, many measures reflected the individualist ethos. The South Island Landless Natives Act, for example, epitomised a perception of Maori as would-be assimilatees to an ethic of individualism (or, at most, western-style nuclear families), rather than as members of tribal, sub-tribal or other collectivities. Maori determination to retain collective social organisational ideals, and tribally based aspirations, frustrated and puzzled officers of state in particular and pakeha in general. Two 'liberal' pakeha historians writing in the 1930s reflected such perplexity in stating that 'sections of the Maoris still consider that they have grievances, and take curious steps to have them righted'. One Solicitor-General was not alone in depicting tribally based claims as 'absurd'.[81]

By the time of the First World War, some tribes had chosen to use the legal system in fighting for their cause. This could have ramifications for tribal dynamics, particularly as a result of 'modernising' and increasing the normal levels of interaction with the state in order to gain maximum leverage. From 1907, for example, the struggle for mana over the Rotorua lakes 'contributed to the institutionalisation of Te Arawa as a corporate group'. Other groupings, especially those at hapu or whanau level, had continued traditional, locally based protest methods. In the wake of the Maori war effort, the Crown could not entirely ignore collectivities engaged in such processes. In what would be a familiar pattern for decades, the government tended to respond to significant pressure by establishing 'independent' inquiries into the claims, expecting that these would both satisfy Maori that their concerns were being attended to and minimise Crown liability. In 1919 the Native Land Court's Chief Judge, Robert Jones, headed the first post-war inquiry, the Native Land Claims Commission. The Jones Commission told Parliament in 1920 that the Crown should have treated Ngai Tahu in a 'more liberal spirit' over the major South Island purchase, and that it now needed to offer redress.

The clear thrust of the evidence, such as it was, had put into perspective the state's belief that the 'landless natives' legislation had settled the South Island grievances. Jones' predecessor in the Native Land Court had recommended monetary reparation. The commission followed this up by declaring that the sizeable lump sum of £354,000 would be suitable compensation for Ngai Tahu. The government did not appreciate this recommendation, but neither was the tribe happy, wanting (in particular) return of land. Its fall-back position was cash payments in perpetuity, which would, among other things, be an ongoing reminder to the Crown of its past behaviour. The recommendation, however, gave Ngai Tahu a bargaining platform, although the government 'did not hasten' on the matter and the negotiations would take almost a quarter of a century to conclude.

Meanwhile, other tribes achieved success on specific issues. These reflected not only tribal pressure, but also the powerful political influence that Ngata could marshal, even from the back benches. This in turn both reflected and contributed to a gradual alteration of attitudes towards Maori. In the political field such changes were personified in Gordon Coates. The first pakeha politician to become a leader on Maori issues, he had devolved many of his duties to Ngata; the Liberal back-bencher was widely seen as the 'unofficial Native Minister'. When Coates became Prime Minister (as well as Native Minister) in 1925, Ngata penetrated the world of parliamentary committeedom even further, becoming chair of the Select Committee on Native Affairs in 1926. By this time, he had achieved several results which were to provide a precedent for Maori aspirations. He was instrumental, for example, in ending the legal struggles of two tribal confederations with regard to ownership and control of lakes, achieving compensation for the Crown's assumption of ownership of the lake beds and use of the waters. Such reparatory settlements bolstered the chances of tribes like Ngai Tahu attaining at least similar methods of compensation.[82]

Such compensation regimes fell far short of meaningful rangatiratanga, with its implication of ownership, or at least unfettered management, of key resources. But the first to sign, Te Arawa, had seen little other choice, given sustained Crown opposition to their claims of full ownership of the Rotorua lakes. Officials and politicians did fear defeat on the issue in the courts, but a judicial victory for Te Arawa could be negated by legislation: the iwi knew that in the end a political settlement was required. On the Crown's side, a negotiated political settlement was preferable to both legislative action or any settlement that was a response to a judicial decision. For one thing, the judiciary tended to be less frugal than the government when ordering or recommending transfers of 'public good' resources. Far more important, legislative overturning of a judgment would have put the spotlight on myths about the role of courts in a capitalist democracy.

In 1920, therefore, the Crown suggested an out-of-court, cash-based settlement, and on Ngata's advice Te Arawa decided to negotiate. After protracted negotiations, it agreed to relinquish claims to ownership of the Rotorua lakes. In return, from 1922 it would receive a perpetual annual payment of £6000, together with other concessions such as ownership of islands, management relationships and the right to catch indigenous fish. The income was not insignificant, and held out prospects of considerable future benefit for the tribal confederation. Indeed, many pakeha were surprised at its 'generosity'. It was perhaps relevant that Arawa, as Ngata noted, had been 'friendly' in the nineteenth century. But the state did not have a good track record in rewarding 'loyalty', as indicated by its rejection of Maori Parliament submissions or its treatment of Maori returned servicemen. Clearly, it saw advantages for the 'public good' in the deal; in particular, removal (or alleviation) of discontent among the iwi of the most strategically important tourist region of the Dominion.

Whatever the Crown's motivations, the 'Arawa Lakes' settlement embodied important precedents. First, the tribes viewed the payments as more than an annual reckoning for the Crown's past violations of the Treaty, seeing them as, in fact, a statement about their ongoing mana over the lakes. While the Crown took ownership, it was acknowledging a special tribally based nexus with the lakes and their associated resources. The deal thus gave multi-faceted benefits to the iwi. It provided a monetary resource base, it acknowledged some tribal involvement in control of waters and foreshores, and its conceptualisation of the lakes embodied Te Arawa's kaitiakitanga/guardianship. The tribes saw the settlement, then, as an assertion of rangatiratanga – not an ideal one, but an assertion nevertheless.

Second, the principle underlying the settlement was an important breakthrough in Crown concessions. The iwi *as a collectivity* was to be resourced, rather than the Native Trustee (for use on behalf of individuals) or Maori individuals. The tribal federation would be enfranchised to set up its own trust board. It was no accident that Treasury officials had opposed this model. Ostensibly, they claimed that the Native Trustee was quite capable of representing Maori interests, but their real reason was ideological: the state should relate to Maori as individuals rather than as people aggregated into a tribal or other collective grouping. The trust board solution was not acceptable to all Maori involved, with some seeing a state-imposed recognition of collectivism as a negation of autonomist aspirations. Since hapu remained 'the powerhouse of Maori society', some leaders sought hapu-level or other sub-tribal settlements. But the majority of Arawa decision makers accepted that, at least at the time, the iwi base was the only viable option. Because the proposal embodied the communal principle, its value as a precedent was enormous.

Third, the *type* of collective organisation created a precedent that would survive for the rest of the century. The state had sought a method whereby the iwi could receive and spend public monies in an accountable fashion. A trusteeship model which provided appropriate guarantees was selected. However, against the wishes of many assimilation-oriented pakeha involved in the negotiations, a *tribal* trust board comprising Maori representatives from the dominant descent groups was finally agreed on after hard bargaining.[83]

With the creation of the Arawa District Trust Board (later Te Arawa Maori Trust Board), other tribes now had a precedent for a state-sanctioned means of receiving compensation payments. The trust board model suited the Crown, for it legally constrained methods and outcomes for distributing compensation. Moreover, the state saw the Arawa precedent as providing for welfare resourcing which it would have needed to outlay in any case – on health, housing and the like. Ngata, in defending the annual payments against political opposition, declared that they were to be applied for education, health, farming and other public purposes. Although the board concept was not tied to managing welfare and similar issues, the Crown was reasonably confident that a significant portion of its monies would go towards social services, precisely because a need to do so existed. More broadly, officials and politicians believed that, at the very least, any state-accountable mobilisation of tribal energies would promote social and economic development, which would be good for the country in general as well as for iwi. In the event, the Arawa board did encourage farming and other enterprises, and took up housing, health, educational and other matters normally the province of the state.

In view of such developments, it was soon being argued that tribal authority was not being recognised in its own right through the new system. People began to emphasise that the trust board, far from being an organ of self-determination, had no more status in law than any corporate charitable trust, and that it was often, in its disbursement activities, acting in effect as a Crown agency. Yet Arawa confederation groupings, while aware of the limitations, sought to maximise their collective position through the board. In essence, they reappropriated what was a government appropriation of tribal organisational energies. At its initial meeting, the board appointed sub-committees, headed by 'ministers', to cover the portfolios of 'Marae and Pensions', land, education and special projects. The board 'saw itself as the parliament and government of Te Arawa' and 'fixed Te Arawa as the primary political unit of the inland Bay of Plenty and Maketu'. The various descent-group configurations saw the board, operating at a federal tribal level, as 'an alternative or accretion to their existing institutional resources'.

Despite the Crown's ultimate motives, through the board concept it had, in fact, acknowledged collective tribally based control of, and responsibility for, compensation monies and management functions. The board model was therefore seen by some tribes as a significant step towards state recognition and facilitation of tribal autonomy. There was great interest, for example, when the Arawa board decided, after discussions with Ngata, to establish a school of Maori arts and crafts in Rotorua. Under the trust board model, official recognition, in a *legal sense*, amounted in the eyes of some to a meaningful measure of self-determination. Not only was acknowledgement of the justice of compensation a breakthrough, but its administration system could, it was envisaged, be used to spearhead greater rangatiratanga. There was pressure on the Crown from within Maoridom to treat the Arawa case as a precedent.

The problem here was that the Crown, too, could see the autonomist potential. This cut across its desire to use the trust board concept to mobilise tribes for its own goals, rather than to empower them to effect theirs. From the beginning, in fact, the pioneering trust board was set up by the government in such a way that the state retained the upper hand – in details of administration and expenditure as well as in the broader sense of treating the board as a virtual agency of government. The Native Minister presided over the first board meeting so that its members could better grasp what would fall within their jurisdiction. Ngata warned that the board, while encouraging farming and similar activities among its people, should not engage in business activities for entrepreneurial profit. Such restrictions were intended partly to minimise the chances of inefficiency or peculation, since this was a radical experiment that would be closely scrutinised by hostile observers. The Crown also feared that an independent economic base might enable a trust board to gain leverage against it.

In 1926 the powerful Tuwharetoa tribe settled its grievances over the Crown's alienation of Lake Taupo in a similar way to the Arawa Lakes. The government had controlled the negotiations firmly, initially insisting, for example, on dealing only with paramount chief Hoani Te Heuheu Tukiao and his nominees. But there had been some tribal resistance, and hapu-based protest led to a widening of the Maori representation. After negotiation, too, the resources potentially available for tribal use were enhanced. Not only was a grant made to establish a trust board, but also income could increase in the future. The guaranteed annual payment was only half that of Arawa's, but Tuwharetoa's trust board would also receive, once a £3000 threshold had been reached, half of all annual licence fees for fishing Taupo and its surrounding waters. Such sums were not insignificant at the time.

Two years later, the trust board concept was extended to Ngai Tahu. The purpose of this board was not to receive monies, but to enable the tribe to facilitate negotiations with the Crown over the Jones Commission's recommendations, preparatory to compensation. As with the previous boards, the Crown had such great influence that its founding members were people the Crown could 'trust'. But already the existing boards were resisting Crown control. The government had been rebuffed in attempts to intervene in internal Tuwharetoa matters, such as the distribution of funding to marae. The Ngai Tahu trust board relationship with the Crown took on a similar trajectory.[84]

The trust board structure, along with the broad thrust of the settlements with historically 'friendly' or 'neutral' tribes, was eventually to become the key precedent for other tribes. Those which had fought against the Crown, and had nurtured land-based grievances as a result of their punishment for doing so, sought to boost their case for reparations by pointing to these tribal settlements and ways of administering them. Their prospects improved after a new development. Following pressure over land-centred grievances, especially from the tribes whose land had been confiscated, the Coates ministry (prompted by Ngata and others) in 1926 appointed a Royal Commission of Inquiry headed by Sir William Sim. Its terms of reference were narrow: in particular, it was to examine whether the confiscations were *excessive* (rather than wrong), although it was to gently subvert this brief in the light of damaging evidence against the Crown.

As with the Jones and later commissions, the government intended that the claims would not be substantially upheld. When the Sim Commission reported on 26 June 1927, however, the report's ramifications were so great that it was suppressed from the public. After pressure for its release, it was published in 1928, to considerable impact. A commentator sympathetic to Maori causes recalled, a quarter of a century later, that the 'Maoris were vindicated and the last black cloud removed from their sky. Sixty years' brooding and introspection must leave their marks, but for the new generation the road to economic and social equality with the Pakeha was open.'

The commission found that the Crown had been remiss with the major raupatu tribes, and recommended reparations which followed the 'lakes precedent' of cash in perpetuity. It recommended redress of £5000 a year to Taranaki for 'land unjustly confiscated' and £3000 a year to Tainui for 'excessive' confiscation. In response, during negotiations with the Crown in the late 1920s and 1930s, the tribes sought retrieval of a land base on which they could rebuild rangatiratanga. The Crown was not inclined to sponsor any resurgence in tribal life in this way. Indeed, under Treasury influence, it was even resiling from payment-in-perpetuity settlements, being more interested in discussing lump sums.

This concerned iwi, for whom land or annual payments embodied, respectively, a fundamental or continual acknowledgement of past wrong. Ngataists who remained influential in state circles advised that the aggrieved tribes would not make 'progress' until the 'mote in their eyes' was removed. The admission of wrong implicit in compensation, particularly in land or ongoing remuneration, was a prerequisite for this. The Crown was prepared, in name of a 'public good' emanating from the removal of deeply felt socio-racial grievances, to remain in discussions. But the possibilities it kept suggesting were rejected as inadequate in both kind and amount. Ngai Tahu, for example, was offered various lump sums (including one as low as £50,000), all of them falling far short of the Jones recommendation. However, the fact that royal commission recommendations for compensation had been made, and followed up, was seen by many tribes as a breakthrough in the long campaign for reassertion of rangatiratanga. Whatever the Crown resistance to the Jones and Sim findings and recommendations, then, these proved to be a significant weapon through the years.

The raupatu tribes, in fact, had been given sufficient ammunition by the commissioners' historical findings (crude as they appear, in retrospect) to argue that monetary settlements unjustly avoided the most pressing of their tribal aspirations, a return of at least some of the 'stolen' land. Non-raupatu tribes also took heart that independent inquiries had vindicated at least some Maori claims. Moreover, raupatu tribes which had not been treated sympathetically by the Sim Commission had begun to exert such pressure that their cause was taken up by the Maori MPs. Claimant tribes saw possibilities in Ngata's elevation to ministerial rank in a minority government that provided some potential influence for Labour.

By the beginning of the Second World War, the Crown's considerations of claims involved many tribes that lay outside the South Island and raupatu purview of most of the commissions' findings. In many eyes, the fact that the Crown now realised that tribally based claims could not be wished away constituted a considerable stride towards rangatiratanga. The state's willingness to negotiate owed much more to its desire to remove a Maori roadblock en route to 'national progress' than (as it would claim with Tainui) to 'enthron[e] justice above might'. But its perception of a significant roadblock reflected an intensifying of the Maori struggle in the period following the establishment of commissions and trust boards. Moreover, while the preferred destination of the 'Dominion journey' included an assimilated indigenous population, the fact remained that, meanwhile, tribes were the entities the state had to negotiate with. For many Maori, such a holding operation gave hope for an ultimate change in government strategy.

Moreover, increasing legal recognition was being given to tribal governance systems. The 1928 Native Land Amendment and Native Land Claims Adjustment Act established machinery to tackle the claims considered by the Jones and Sim Commissions, and Ngai Tahu's trust board (established in 1929) pioneered procedures for that model. Other parliamentary recognition of Maori followed. The 1931 Native Purposes Act, for example, explicitly authorised the government to settle the raupatu grievances. In the event, negotiations were intermittent and prolonged, partly because an economic depression was hardly a propitious time. But that same year the Taranaki federation of iwi, considered the most 'recalcitrant' in their pursuit of compensation for raupatu, accepted an interim settlement based on an annuity to be administered by a Taranaki Maori Trust Boad. By the time the Depression-era government went out of office in 1935, the Tainui federation, too, had accepted in principle an interim settlement offer which would have led to its own board and suspended its wish for return of land.

The trust boards, for all their inherent and operational problems, were seen as a compromise that both sets of signatories to the Treaty, Crown and Maori, could live with. They made life easier for the state by establishing legal entities to which it could hand settlement monies in an accountable way, and with which it could deal. There were less tangible benefits too. During the Second World War, for example, Ngata noted that official recognition of, and payments to, the Taranaki and lakes tribes had created a spirit that added value to their contribution to the war effort. It seems that, in general, Maori leaders regarded the trust board concept as a meaningful, if inadequate, step towards Crown recognition of rangatiratanga.

While the existence of a funded board was seen as assisting the pursuit of tribal self-determination, which was increasingly important even to Ngataism from the later 1920s, the fact remained that the boards existed because they served to contain tribal ambitions within state-imposed parameters. In the broader picture government policy remained unchanged: although tribal lifestyles and world-views could be tolerated temporarily in the interests of 'the nation', they should be kept firmly in check. Tribalism was destined ultimately to disappear, and its interim containment should preferably assist the Crown in its various aims.

This happened with some of the short- to medium-term goals, such as relieving the state of some of what would later be called its 'Article Three' Treaty obligations, those involving equality of various types for Maori. Given that the trust boards' very existence encouraged tribal autonomist ambitions, however, the state began to feel that it had been somewhat out-manoeuvred by Maori (even though this form of settlement had been a fall-back position for the tribes). But there seemed to be no better alternative, and the Crown's long-term strategy remained intact: removing the collectivity-based roadblock to assimilationist 'peace and good order'. The trust board system survived because, at the very least, it was not incompatible with eventual progress towards assimilation.[85]

The rise of Ratanaism

Some developments in defining and developing a Maori sphere of polity after the First World War were only partly based on tribal groupings. Others were not at all. These generally fell into one of two categories, intertribal (as with Kingitanga) or supra-tribal. The most powerful of the various pan-tribal movements was Ratanaism, which was not just stridently non-tribal, but anti-tribal. It began as a new strand of Christianity, another in a long line of Maori adjustment and protest movements based on religio-spiritual teaching. Maori churches splitting, or emerging separately, from mainstream Christianity often reflected recognition that traditional indigenous world-views were, by themselves, inadequate defence against socio-political and other types of marginalisation. Given the importance of spiritual practice in the traditional canon – the dominance of concepts such as mana, tapu/sacredness and mauri/life force – the emergence of syncretic religious movements melding the religion of the pakeha with that of indigenous theology and practice was logical.

Emergent doctrines were often contextualised within a search for new politico-cultural guidelines for everyday values and behaviour, and these frequently ignored or challenged some Crown 'requirements' or pakeha norms of behaviour while accepting others. In the nineteenth century, the politico-religious Pai Marire/'Hauhau' movement had sought, sometimes bloodily, to promote unity of action against Crown and settler encroachment. Resistance prophet Te Kooti's Ringatu Church had remained a focus of opposition to Crown intentions for the Urewera and neighbouring tribes. Kingite resistance to assimilation had been strengthened by its Tariao faith.

Most politico-religious movements, despite the frequency of unity-inspired aims and methods, had not been able to garner more than, at most, a handful of tribal bases. After the First World War, Tahupotiki Wiremu Ratana founded a religious movement that appealed not to trans-tribal federationism, but to the building of what was envisaged to be a non-tribal movement. This development reflected a growing feeling that traditional socio-organisational structures, and their unity movements, had failed to protect Maoridom from settler and Crown subsumption, and so something more than a mere overhaul of them was needed.

The way of the future was seen to lie in *superseding* the tribes. Ngataism had originated from a similar perception, but remained largely an elitist, top-down movement whose impact on Maori social life was largely indirect. And despite its supra-tribal beginnings, it had increasingly embraced tribally based solutions to the problems of Maoridom. 'Ordinary' Maori who were disillusioned with daily existence under its uneasy mix of capitalism and tribalism found in Ratanaism a leadership that was in touch with the reality of their everyday lives.

When Ratana took up what he believed to be God's command in 1918 to '[u]nite the Maori people', then, this was not to be brought about by the old method of federating tribes in a form of united front for specific or general purposes. Rather, unity of the 'Maori race' would come about through adherence to Ratanaism of masses of *individual* Maori – those who had renounced tribalism and opted for guidance by a movement that would eventually call itself 'The Union of the Maori

Race'. The popularity of its religious teaching was to have profound implications for both Maoridom and the Crown, especially when its leaders developed more overtly the political dimension that was implicit from the beginning.

For T W Ratana did more than reflect an alternative, holistic religious world-view in his preaching; he also addressed the socio-economic plight of the great majority of Maori, and seemed to understand their immediate wants and needs. In particular, he quickly came to voice the concerns of the poorest and most dispossessed within Maoridom, particularly the many subsistence farmers and contract labourers and their families. Expected by the Crown to assimilate, these sectors of Maoridom had gained very few of the material benefits of 'western civilisation'. Ratana gave them hope in his ringing endorsement of King Tawhiao's sentiments: 'Ko oku hoa, ko te humeka, te parakimete, te watimeta, nga kamura, nga pani, nga pouwaru . . . /My friends are the shoemaker, the blacksmith, the watchmaker, carpenters, orphans and widows . . .'[86]

Government concern at Ratanaism as a political movement increasingly overshadowed initial worry about its spiritual doctrines. Ratana argued that cutting tribal ties, followed by a recollectivised unity of purpose and approach, would create sufficient pressure on the Crown to force it to fulfil its obligations under the Treaty of Waitangi. In short, Ratanaist interpretation of rangatiratanga, and therefore of the state's obligations to Maori, was different from that of tribally based leaders, including those who continued to advocate unity in the sense of trans-tribal aggregation or activity for specific or general purposes. For Ratanaism, new politico-spiritual leaders would increasingly emerge from the tribal ashes. Insofar as there was collective organisation within the new politico-religious movement, it was the whanau grouping which was important.

Tolerating tribalism as a temporary necessity that, at best, it might be able to use in the meantime, the Crown had developed various mechanisms for coping with tribal pressure. On the surface, it might have been expected to welcome Ratana's anti-tribal teachings. Yet his movement was seen as a serious new potential mode of subversion. Its wish to unite all Maori, especially those who had suffered most from colonisation, on a policy platform that gave them politico-cultural as well as economically redistributive hope for the future was a greater threat to the body politic than the relatively quiescent Kingitanga and Kotahitanga. It also presented the possibility of an alliance with pakeha social-democratic and other organised labour movements. At a time of hysteria over bolshevism, these were considered sufficient threat to the political economy to be under close scrutiny by the intelligence agencies of state. The Ratana movement's desire to unite the poorest Maori was seen as threatening enough, let alone its potential as a new component in a broad left-wing front. It is scarcely surprising, therefore, that Ratanaism was viewed with great suspicion by conservative governments.

Some aspects of the Ratana movement suited the Crown, however. Members agreed to abandon elements of their tribal past that were seen by the state and Ratana leaders alike as anachronistic. This boded well for the assimilation agenda, and the government gave a good reception to the concept of Maori renouncing their tribal affiliations. Ratanaism, moreover, shared the antipathy towards tohungaism found in both Young Maori Party and state circles. Although Ratana's fame spread through his faith-healing message and successes, these were seen by his followers as a sign of his divine authority rather than adherence to traditional psycho-medical preachings and practices. The Crown, in particular, welcomed this. While Ngataism focused on the charlatanism which it perceived to have subverted tohungaism in the wake of colonisation, the state was in general accord with Ratanaism that all tohunga embodied outmoded tribally based mores and teachings. There was cautious official acceptance, then, of the Ratana movement's rejection of tohungaism and 'super-stitions' (despite the new prophecies and esoteric rituals that replaced them).

But official New Zealand (and Ngataism) remained exceedingly nervous of Ratanaism. Its concerns were several, in addition to anxiety about obvious resonances with the pakeha labour movement. Politicians and officials saw Ratana as a potential Te Whiti, whose attempt to create a mass passive-resistance movement across tribes had been viewed as subversive. Mere Rikiriki, who had raised Ratana, was a prominent supporter of Te Whiti and Ratanaism would adopt some of the policies of the Taranaki pacifist movement. Moreover, for state and mainstream religious authorities, Ratana's teachings and policies were eclectic, puzzling and seemingly contradictory; such people were apprehensive, even fearful, of the unknown. At first the prophet and his followers tried to operate through existing churches, but Ratana's belief that Maori were a 'chosen people', and his assumption of the title of Mangai/God's Mouthpiece, created enormous tension. Eventually, the movement came to stand alone.

Ratana's brand of faith healing reflected a popular international trend from the late nineteenth century, which had often come to the attention of the secular and religious authorities. Spiritual healing-based sects often propagated ideas deemed to subvert the authority of the state and its desired mores. Fraudsters heading or operating within them had frequently been exposed. In New Zealand, unease spread with Ratana's rapidly increasing popularity. Before long Ratana Pa, near Wanganui, had become *the* centre for faith healing in the country. The prophet's prioritisation of the needs of his own people applied even to his healing prowess, adding to church and state fears of Ratanaist 'race-separatism'. The movement would 'notify our Pakeha friends' in newspaper advertisements that 'you are absolutely barred from approaching our Brother, T.W. Ratana, at present until the Maoris have been treated'.[87]

The Crown was also concerned that Ratanaism was, at least passively and despite its intolerance of tohunga, resistant to many of the health-based reforms that were central to Ngataism. It opposed, for example, Te Rangihiroa's work as Director of Maori Hygiene. This was partly because Ratanaist spiritual practices were based on faith healing, but there were more profound reasons. In particular, the state-favoured Young Maori Party strand of Maoridom stood increasingly for tribal preservation as well as a 'beneficial' pakehaising of Maori. In contrast, Ratanaism campaigned overtly against iwi- or hapu-based lifestyles and in favour of a national, self-determinationist identity for a 'very Maori' Maoridom. Officials and politicians, of course, sought an assimilationist path that, while tolerating tribalism for the moment, attempted to do so in an appropriable form – a considerably 'lesser evil' than a mass movement of detribalised Maori.

Not only did Ratanaism increasingly become explicitly left-wing, but its quest for a transformed Maori future based on the actions and wishes of the morehu, the dispossessed and common people of Maoridom, took place within a firm Treaty of Waitangi framework. 'In one of my hands is the Bible; in the other is the Treaty of Waitangi.' The Treaty, signed with chiefs on behalf of their tribal groupings, was therefore to be used as the symbol for resolving all Maori grievances at a national, non-tribal level. This was a remarkable example of the selective adaptation of an iconic document for means (and ends) that might themselves be seen as subverting the Treaty's original embodiment of *tribal* rangatiratanga. The movement ignored or opposed any matters which might divert it from a national, supra-tribal Maori struggle for rights and the attainment of a new-style Maoridom.

Traditional tribal leaders resisted such a Treaty discourse, but so did the Crown, which – however much it endorsed the detribalisation message – preferred that the Treaty remain *sotto voce*. Notwithstanding this, Ratanaism attracted great publicity and continued to situate its various activities under the umbrella of its own interpretation of the Treaty. While making many demands on the state for redress of grievances, at its outset Ratanaism was careful to resist any sign of collaboration with the Crown on not just health but other issues too. It even declined to engage in any activity that might potentially be appropriated for state purposes.

All this created difficulties not only for the Crown, but for other Maori groupings. Ratana rejected, for example, Maori participation in the Ngataist consolidation and development schemes. In opposing the tribally based rangatiratanga on which most Maori leaders of the century had built their bases and their hopes, Ratana was from the beginning as implicitly political and challenging inside the Maori as the pakeha world. For this reason, for a time radical Kingite forces led by Taingakawa attempted to forge an alliance. By emphasising mass pressure as the main weapon to bear on the Crown, the Ratana movement offered a new means of deliverance from subordination, a rekindling of hope for recovery of what had been lost – or what, for at least some morehu, they had never had. As early as 1922, Ratana was well on the way to full appreciation that forcing the Crown to provide a better deal for the

Maori masses required supplementing spiritual with temporal actions. This meant modifying his initial policy of total non-engagement with the Crown. The movement petitioned the Crown and demanded that the Treaty be incorporated into statute, and Ratana leaders attempted to meet the King in England in 1924.

As politicisation progressed, the demands of the Mangai and his followers became increasingly radical. There was a bid, for example, to persuade the Crown to authorise the establishment of a unified Maori self-government regime. The movement quickly became the largest and most unified political movement among tangata whenua, reportedly touching every Maori community. In 1927 the Mangai estimated (and Ngata agreed) that Ratana membership was 21,500, or a third of all Maori. With many Ratanaists retaining tribal links despite the movement's teachings, its following is hard to calculate, but even official figures placed the percentage of adherence among Maoridom at around a fifth. Whatever the actual membership figures, it is clear that Ratanaism's flax-roots strength was enormous. That year William Baucke noted its intentions: 'The Ratana Movement has come to stay until the white man redeems his trust.'[88]

In the quest for such redemption, in 1928 the Mangai formally subsumed his spiritual mission beneath his temporal one. This decision included seeking engagement with the Crown at a parliamentary level. Many people, Maori and pakeha, had come to view the four Maori seats in the New Zealand House of Representatives as dominated by a complacent Maori elite. T W Ratana, in particular, had made very clear his opinion that the Maori MPs had, in recent times, been neglecting the interests of Maori, especially the morehu. At least three of the incumbent Maori MPs were felt to need replacing, so that the power the special seats were believed to have once had could be revived. Champions of indigenous rights could thereby 'find a place in the system of government and policy making which could help satisfy Maori needs and expectations'. Ratana's engagement in such debates had brought him round to the view that his extra-parliamentary movement might be able to concentrate its mass power through control of the Maori MPs in the 'pakeha parliament'.

While not rejecting the thrust of his founding methodology, then, the prophet added a new dimension: an attempt, on Ratanaism's own terms, at an accommodation with the pakeha political system. The movement would continue to concentrate on building its popular base but aim to use it as a lever into the pakeha political world. Ratana vowed to secure the Maori parliamentary seats for four chosen followers. The aim of this Four Koata/Quarters policy was integration of 'both grass roots representation and elite nationalism into a new form of group politics'. From 1928, then, Ratanaism came to refocus some of its energies on making its people-backed power more effective by gaining a voice in Parliament. At that year's election Ratana announced the fundamental policies of his parliamentary candidates: first, honouring the Treaty, and 'Secondly the Maori Self Government'.

The strategy was to work at first within the state system of indivisible sovereignty, and then ultimately to move outside it, in a way and to an extent not yet fully conceptualised. Along the route to power, the leadership realised, modifications would be needed. One came quickly, with Ratana and his advisers appreciating that, whatever the truth or otherwise of the Maori MPs once having wielded great influence, a minority voice in Parliament could do little on its own. The movement began, therefore, to explore the implicit linkages that its concerns for the poor gave it with the predominantly pakeha Labour Party. Increasingly, as a result, it would work towards a coalition with the party of the pakeha morehu.[89]

Ngataism

Meanwhile, until Labour could gain office, Ngataism rather than Ratanaism prevailed as the voice of Maori in high councils of state. Long after its institutional demise, the Young Maori Party had continued in the form of the Ngataist movement. However amorphous this was, it did focus intensely, as Ngata later put it, on 'the one goal, the conscious adjustment of Maori society in all its elements to the changed conditions and standards of life'. But it also increasingly emphasised the preservation of 'suitable' aspects of Maori culture. The initial downgrading of tribalism in Ngataist circles gradually gave way to an emphasis on marshalling discrete tribal entities for both general and specific purposes. This amounted to reconfirmation of the kotahitanga method, albeit in a less overtly political and structured way. A kind of pan-tribal 'collaboration' would complement tribal life, helping it adjust to the realities of a capitalist political economy and its hegemonic mores while at the same time promoting certain cultural forms. Even the most accommodationist parts of Maoridom, then, were increasingly declaring that complete assimilation was neither desirable nor irresistible. Progress would come from a 'judicious' selection and combination of 'elements of Western and Maori culture'.

Carroll had urged: 'Hold fast to your Maoritanga'. The tribally based approach of 'informal pan-tribal co-operation' generally came to be characterised by this rubric. Some Maori later saw all types of pan-tribalism as Crown-inspired replacements for failed 'divide and rule' policies. '[I]f you cannot divide and rule, then for tribal people all you can do is to bring them together and rule . . . because then they lose everything by losing their own tribal identity and histories and traditions.' Others have viewed Maoritanga's stress on Maori culture as a state-encouraged seeking of a 'safe' alternative to a politically organised or threatening Maori population. But in the 1920s and 1930s the Ngataist leadership portrayed an informally organised Maoritanga as a way of retaining all manner of tribally based forms and practices that were deemed worthy of preservation. These would constitute a foundation not for the disappearance of organised Maoridom, but for a modern Maori reconstruction, and aspects of this were not fully to the Crown's liking.

Several informal, tribally based unifying mechanisms were developing after the First World War, assisted by improvements in transport and communications. These moves towards co-operative advancement of tangata whenua interests were so pronounced that it is possible to talk of a significant 'renaissance' among Maori in the 1920s. Maori who had served overseas and acquired a fresh outlook during the war were particularly active in revival movements which stressed working together on as broad a basis as a tribal foundation would allow. Activities included intertribal hui to work out joint agreements on consolidation schemes, increasing contact between tribes at sports gatherings, cultural exchanges in various locations, arts and craft revivals. In 1928, for example, the Prince of Wales Rugby Cup competition was established within Maoridom. A series of intertribal hui culminated in a grand celebration of Maori arts on Waitangi Day in 1934 that aimed to strengthen links between Maori communities.[90]

In some of the developments of the 1920s, European ways were melded with tribal and pan-tribal approaches. A Maori leader commented that the 'spirit of the new movement is intensely Maori, even though externally it is adopting a *pakeha* guise and outlook'. This aided state tolerance of, and even assistance for, some developments. The Crown's aversion to formal political unity of the tribes could be accommodated by the looseness of the unifying mechanisms, despite some continuing unease that such arrangements could encourage the indigenous search for empowerment. Indeed, the state saw positive virtue in some loose, pan-tribal developments. In the 1920s it began to endorse and enhance their culture-based initiatives in an attempt to channel Maori energies in a 'safe' direction, away from political radicalism – especially Ratanaism.

Endorsement and assistance were not without difficulties for the Crown. Its establishment (following an approach by the Maori MPs to Coates) of the Maori Secondary Schools Aid Fund in 1922, of the Board of Maori Ethnological Research in 1923, and of the Maori Purposes Fund (to finance educational, community and cultural activities, such as building meeting houses) in 1924, all exemplified this. While these measures utilised unclaimed monies in the hands of the Maori Land Boards, and therefore cost the Crown little, they were nevertheless an implicit acknowledgement that rapid movement towards assimilation remained far away. In fact, state excursions into funding Maori cultural, educational and social activities, encouraged by Ngataism, helped foster a sense of separate identity for Maori – or Maoritanga. All the same, this was seen in state circles as preferable to other possibilities, especially Ratanaist ones.

In Coates' ministry, Ngataist influence increased enormously and, with it, state assistance for manifestations of Maoritanga. After much pressure, including Maori representations channelled through the

Ethnological Research institution, and considerable Crown consultation with Maori bodies, a 1926 Act established a board to encourage Maori arts and craft. The School of Maori Arts and Crafts at Rotorua followed in 1927, in conjunction with Te Arawa's trust board, and became heavily involved in adapting Maori cultural practices to hegemonic social conditions as a precondition for their strong survival.

To ensure that the Crown's perspective remained to the forefront of such developments, Coates charged the Native Department with social and cultural functions. The Ngataist approach, with modernisation proceeding hand in hand with preservation of the best of iwi- and hapu-based customs and the tribes coming together informally to pursue this, was seen by most pro-Maori pakeha observers as the way forward for Maori renaissance. They were soon waxing optimistic about 'hope of reconstruction' for Maoridom. One academic felt that both state and Maori were ensuring that 'aims' were 'clearly visioned' and 'problems' being 'courageously attacked'. He applauded the Young Maori Party-style leadership for resisting 'the superimposition of a highly-organised culture from above' on their people. Instead they were, at least for the moment, seeking to 'lay a basis for life's structure upon Maori *mana*' and doing so with the help of the Crown – which in turn could guide Maori energies towards appropriate modes of 'progress'. When Ngata, Pomare and Te Rangihiroa launched an offensive against Ratanaism in Wanganui in 1927, it was part of a bid to co-ordinate all 'progressive' forces in Maoridom.

That support for 'Maori progressiveness' within pakehadom came from the Prime Minister down, however, had aroused the suspicions of even Maori outside the Ratana fold. Some of them, in due course, changed their minds when they saw what could be achieved by working with 'the system'. By 1928 Ngata was able to argue that 'some of our aims and ideals' were being fulfilled. When he was installed in the ministerial seat that year, it was not just land development which benefited. For the first time a senior Maori politician within the western system who was *fully* committed to Maoridom was able to bring sizeable Crown resources to bear on many aspects of the lives of his people. These had a generally positive impact on tribal life, right down to the local level. Ngata argued tirelessly with MPs and bureaucrats for the principle that Maori, through their leaders, should have greater control of their own funds, lands and lives. His powers to deploy state resources among the tribes were strengthened when that part of the civil service that reported to him became, in 1930, indisputably 'the ultimate corporate entity for regulating and controlling Maori affairs'. This situation provided invaluable support for Ngata's 'brilliant strategy of subversive co-operation'.[91]

Maori Health Councils

The 1930 development also, however, helped the bureaucracy establish an even tighter control over Maoridom. Bureaucratic controls had remained tight for even the supposedly semi-autonomous Maori Councils/Maori Health Councils. In 1920, full administrative control of these passed from the Native Department to Te Rangihiroa's division of the health system. The Council apparatus had by this time become mostly absorbed within the government bureaucracy, a logical conclusion to its origins and evolution. The Maori Health Councils were to advise the District Health Officers and their superiors, and assist them with sanitary policies and operations. Te Rangihiroa reorganised many of the Maori Councils still in existence, and by April 1921 had established 20 Maori Health Council districts in the North Island. In 1922 the Health Department was assigned responsibility for appointments to the Councils, the Native Department having wished to divest itself of remaining responsibility for organisations which had only marginal relevance to its work.

Te Rangihiroa and his staff worked on new model bylaws, and supervised revival and reorganisation of the new-look Councils and their village committees. There was appreciation that community-based health workers and local Maori leadership support could play a significant role in achieving health goals, but the structure remained centralised. This was in line with a number of precedents: the Health Department's 1911 establishment of a tightly controlled Native Health Nursing Service, for example, rather than giving more resources to the combination of inspectors and volunteers within the Maori Councils (although the department was content to allow the voluntary Plunket Society to handle pakeha infant welfare).

Despite disincentives for local initiative, by 1923 all of the North Island Maori Health Councils were reportedly in good working order. Their brief included cultural and anthropological matters, with Maori health being interpreted on one level as 'working for the proper understanding and betterment' of the race. Shortages of funds, however, were chronic, especially when the Councils lost the power to collect dog-registration taxes and fines. There were also allegations that the bureaucrats had not ensured proper tribal coverage in appointments. But the system was deemed by the Health Department to be valuable enough to retain, and Maori continued working with and for it. Indeed, the Maori Health Councils were selected by Ratanaism as a site of contest, and state officials attempted to counter the movement's influence on them. In 1926, for example, the year before he left the department, Te Rangihiroa arranged with Native Health Inspector Takiwairoa Hooper for the revived, but Ratanaist, Kurahaupo Council to be supplanted by one comprising state nominees.

While the increasing officialisation of the Maori Councils/Maori Health Councils did not bode well for the Maori quest for recognition of rangatiratanga, Te Rangihiroa did provide inspiring leadership that promised concrete benefits for Maori. But the problems which had underlain the lacklustre performance of the Councils, even within their own spheres of reference, remained: constraints on initiative, and lack of government resources (including for training professional nurses). In 1927 a disillusioned Te Rangihiroa left the division he had created, but his work continued. By 1929, when the four South Island and Chathams Maori Health Councils were finally gazetted, virtually a national network existed, with only Waikato Maori holding out against jurisdiction by a Maori Health Council.

When Te Rangihiroa's successor resigned in 1930 the Maori Hygiene Division was abolished. The work of the Maori Health Councils was less appreciated after this action, forming as it did part of a restructuring intended to take an integrated national approach to health issues. When the division closed, it is said, '[w]ith it went the likelihood of a Maori health workforce closely linked to Maori communities, skilled in Maori approaches to health, and able to offer effective Maori leadership'. But the Maori Health Council institution was still assessed to be worth continuing, partly because of its flax-roots strength. In 1931, 260 village committees were operating under the Councils. The Director of Maori Hygiene, Dr Edward Pohau Ellison, described the network as comprising over 1400 'Maoris ever ready to assist in any emergency or cause the department may think necessary'. With some of the Maori Health Councils and their offshoots operating effectively well into the 1930s, it is too harsh a judgment to join most commentators in declaring the system a failure. In the later 1930s, indeed, the government considered reviving the Council movement, which it would scarcely have bothered to do had the existing system not had a viable base.

Caution won out, however, partly because of flax-roots robustness. Maori Health Councils that were flourishing often ignored their official limits and pursued their own independent agendas. Ngati Raukawa still operated its system of local governance in conjunction with the Councils, for example, and had even contemplated establishing a tohunga clinic – such was the resilience of tribal ways in the face of Crown wishes. In view of this as well as other factors, the state concluded that it should not revive the system – and meanwhile, had not made any sizeable investment in it. And so, except in the self-determinationist pockets, the original Maori Council cycle was repeated with the superimposed Maori Health Councils: decreasing numbers of Maori worked within the system and the Crown regarded it even more as of residual importance, starving it further of authority and resources.

New developments filled in some of the gaps which, as a consequence, opened up. Maori Women's Institutes had been established from 1929 in rural areas, for example, and from the early 1930s local health committees were formed in the Rotorua area, working closely with the local marae and hapu. In 1937 these formed the basis for the Maori Women's Health League/Te Ropu o te Ora, which had a higher professional nursing input than the Maori Health Councils. It soon spread into other rohe. Branches set up under its auspices tended to take over the functions of residual Councils, making the latter that much more marginal. Moreover, in another recurring pattern, these branches would themselves foster Maori cultural and other developments over many decades.

For Maori, the Maori Health Council system had played a not insignificant part in health, sanitation and other welcome reforms. Various tribes and regions had also used it to forward their aspirations for control over their own lives. The mere existence of the original Councils and their health-oriented equivalents, however truncated their powers, provided some hope that greater autonomous powers might be attainable even within an assimilationist paradigm. Moreover, despite their regional base and their supersession of Kotahitanga, the co-operation between and within councils may have assisted in forging the 'sort of proto-national culture' and intertribal cooperation among Maoridom that was to be highly significant in the future. During the Second World War the remnants of the Council system formed part of Maoridom's, as well as the Crown's, strategic adaptation to the dramatic circumstances of another international conflict. This was to be the final work undertaken within the Council system, and it was not insignificant.[92]

Tribalism

The Council system was, of course, just one example of Maori engagement with Maori issues under Crown auspices. Maori who had chosen to work within and through the state system did gradually get results – economic, health, social and cultural. Many others continued to consider gradualist engagement with pakeha politics and lifestyle to be compromised or ineffective. In addition to Ratanaism, alternative paths were explored, one of which was intra-tribal rebuilding. Such an endeavour could fit in with the Ngataist agenda by boosting the bases for pan-tribal and intertribal developments.

The work of Princess Te Puea in both rebuilding and uniting the Tainui tribes, in particular, was coming to national attention in the late 1920s. From 1927, her position in Kingitanga was consolidated against Tupu Taingakawa's camp. She also promoted her own initiatives for intertribal co-operation. She appreciated that, with the Crown willing to discuss compensation with raupatu tribes, the results could be enhanced by tribal co-operation. As with the Ngataists, accusations of 'selling out' were levelled against Te Puea, her colleagues and others seeking a reconciliatory way forward – on however principled a basis. She was called 'Mrs Kawanatanga', but pressed on regardless. The opening of the Tainui federation's Mahinarangi meeting house at Ngaruawahia in 1929 provided the occasion for the first national hui to be held in the Waikato. Goals for Maoridom and methods of attaining them were much discussed among its 6000 attendees.

While Kingitanga's Tainui focus was often seen in state and pakeha circles as relentless pursuit of tribally based rangatiratanga, and Te Puea's encouragement of intertribal contact and co-operation as containing unificatory dangers, the Crown preferred such developments to the political radicalism of Ratana. It believed that the 'steady and purposive re-organisation and co-ordination' sought by many tribally based Maori could be made to work towards the 'national good'. While it would of necessity encompass some self-determinationist aspirations, these were assessed to fall far short of the considerable degree of autonomy implied by Ratanaism. The state needed to attend to tribal and intertribal wishes more assiduously, in fact, to ensure that such energies were channelled in officially desired directions.

In 1928 Coates had left a memorandum for the incoming Ward government that the quicker settlements were reached with Maori over historical grievances, the sooner that 'feeling of silent resentment and passive resistance to progressive movements' which prevailed among 'backward' tribes would dissipate. The state, viewing trust boards as the best (though not perfect) 'compromise' between tribal control and accountability to the Crown, was not averse to establishing more and providing them with reparations-based or other resources. The problem for the Crown was to work out both the amount of resources that should be conceded to tribes deemed eligible, and how to ensure safeguards for its own interests.

The most unjustly treated tribal grouping of all, the Sim Commission had declared, was the Taranaki iwi. It was Native Minister Ngata, using a threat of resignation in the context of the 1930 Western Maori by-election (following Pomare's death), who got negotiations with the Taranaki federation moving. 'Native matters should not take a back seat all the time', he asserted. On the one hand, politicians and bureaucrats (especially Treasury officials) had been comfortable with neither the concept of an annuity nor the annual sum recommended by Sim. On the other hand, the tribes had sought return of confiscated land, or at the very least an interim settlement of £10,000 a year. It was a Ngataist compromise which emerged as the interim solution, in the face of the Treasury's preference for a lump sum: the annual sum to be administered by the trust board was that recommended by the Sim Commission, £5000.

Even if the state saw annual payments as compensation, tribes and Ngataists viewed them as ongoing acknowledgement of past wrongs to their rangatiratanga – in addition to, or perhaps until, restoration of a satisfactory economic base. As the tribes expected, while annuities did strengthen their revival efforts, these were insufficient to provide a platform for strong resurgence of tribal politico-economic power. The Taranaki groupings used their state-funded office to continue to press for a final settlement that could provide a base strong enough to enable significant tribal rebuilding. The board sought a payment of £10,000 in perpetuity in recognition of 'the sin' of raupatu, the return of land as partial recompense for the raupatu and re-establishment of its relationship with the Crown under the Treaty of Waitangi.

Immersed in economic depression, the Crown did not even fully pay what it owed the Taranaki board in the first year of the settlement. But at least an interim settlement of a raupatu grievance had been achieved, and this gave other tribes some hope of negotiating a deal that would involve resources and some control over them. The other major raupatu tribal federation, Tainui, sought parity with any final Taranaki settlement as a bottom line, despite the Sim Commission's recommendation that it should receive a lesser annual amount. In progress of sorts, departments of state increasingly accepted that Tainui might be eligible for something similar to the interim Taranaki solution. Just before the government left office, the iwi accepted an offer along these lines. All raupatu tribes, however, continued to seek land as part or all of their final settlements.[93]

Labourism and Ratanaism

The Labour Party, the major party of the pakeha working class, displayed
sympathy with the struggles of all marginalised people, Maori included.
MP Peter Fraser had called in 1923 for the 'spirit' as well as the 'letter' of
the Treaty of Waitangi to be 'carried out'. Maori were by then organising
within the Labour Party, but it was logical that the mass Ratana and
labour movements should move closer together. In 1924 the 'first official
gathering' between Maori and Labour Party representatives took place
at Parewanui Pa, near Bulls. Pakeha participants showed themselves to
be familiar with Maori customs, and expressed solidarity with tribal
grievances against the Crown. Party leader Harry Holland promised,
using the language of the Treaty of Waitangi, to restore lands that had
been unjustly taken.

Remedies, however, were to be on the condition that compensation
did not create injustices to New Zealanders as a whole. This was a matter
of interpretation, and some Maori noted that Labour's 'national good'
concerns remained principally with the European morehu. Holland did,
however, make some specific promises that gave hope to Maoridom.
When Labour gained office, for example, it would appoint a commission
to investigate 'native lands' and other matters. A dialogue between Labour
and Maori leaders ensued and a Maori Advisory Committee of the party,
headed by key Ratana follower Rangi Mawhete, was established. In
1925, with Ratana's support, Mawhete stood for Labour in the general
election.

While there was some Maori lobbying for Labour to endorse a separate
Maori parliament, this was too far from the party's platform of 'equality'
for it to contemplate. At the 1925 Labour Party conference the Maori
Advisory Committee made two submissions. The first reflected the long-
held view that Maori be enabled to run their own affairs. The second
built on Holland's pledge of a commission, advocating a high-level body
to settle Maori land problems within the Treaty relationship. A joint
committee of Maori and pakeha delegates reported favourably on the
proposals and they were adopted by the whole conference. The party's
policy statement for the general election of that year took the resolutions

into some account. It included not only provision for a Treaty-based royal commission into land claims, but also the 'revolutionary concept' of a Maori organisation to advise a Labour government on administrative, socio-economic and legislative matters.

The idea of such an organisation went some way towards acknowledging the advisory committee's concerns to procure Maori control, at national level, over issues relevant to Maori once office had been achieved. The importance of centralised Maori input into the political executive was stressed, partly because the regional institutions set up in 1900 had lacked national influence. Through a channelled role in advising on policy and its implementation, Maori would contribute to and eventually gain a share in political decision making. Labour's package of Maori proposals, although less radical than some of the ideas discussed at Parewanui and elsewhere, reflected both the pressure of Ratanaism and the propensities of a party of 'the underdog'. There had already been a drift into Labour of Ratana adherents who saw the similarities between the two movements. The party believed it had gone a long way towards meeting Maori desires, and its campaigners visited many Maori areas during the run-up to the election.

Labour's proposals were branded 'wild promises' by one of the most assimilationist of the former Young Maori Party leaders, Maui Pomare. Under competition for his seat from Mawhete, he counterattacked vigorously. In so doing he inadvertently acknowledged that Labour had been prepared to accommodate a number of Maori aspirations, particularly through his condemnation of 'one of [its] political catch-cries', the right to 'Mana Maori motuhake'. For him this was not just impractical, but also undesirable. He caricatured it as 'entirely separate Government for the Maoris [on] every matter affecting the native race'. But Labour's willingness to meet Maori aspirations lacked practical definition of ways to give effect to rangatiratanga. Pomare was therefore nearer the mark when he said on the hustings that the party's ideas did not amount to a 'clear cut policy'. In fact, some of its pakeha-oriented proposals seemed to cut across Maori interests. Some tangata whenua feared, for example, that its platform of 'land usehold' might prove to be another mode of confiscating Maori land. Pomare's retention of his seat may have reflected such concerns, as well as the fact that Ratanaism had yet to become a fully politicised movement. It was certainly far from ready to throw in its lot with an essentially pakeha party.

The Labour Party's Executive Council continued informally to reconfirm its 1925 'native policy', and did so formally in 1928, 1931 and 1934. While generally assimilationist in orientation, the party could see that neither rapid nor full assimilation was acceptable to Maori – that only a handful of Maori had taken advantage of the legislation enabling them to be legally designated European was just one of many indications. While it started out with such general appreciations, election results and other indicators helped it come to more specific conclusions. In particular, it realised that its Maori support might remain minimal unless it secured the formal backing of the Ratanaist mass movement, for which there seemed good grounds for optimism. Ratanaism's call for the removal of the constraints of tribalism, and its achievement (as a leading Labourite put it) of having 'broken down the strong barriers of Tohungaism', fitted well with Labour's emphasis on casting aside socially constructed bonds and rules which inhibited attainment of 'equality for all', or at least of 'equality of opportunity'. At the 1928 election, in fact, the thrust of Labour's Maori policies was not dissimilar to the positions of the four 'independent' candidates put up by Ratana: ratification of the Treaty, settlement of grievances and attainment of mana Maori motuhake. While the four were defeated, they did poll substantially. The Labour Party became even more interested in accommodation.[94]

By 1931, Maori members of both movements were increasingly co-operating at flax-roots level. The foundation for an alliance was already in place with a network of local Labour–Ratana committees, often headed by community leaders. Ratanaism reassessed its stand-alone politics, taking into account Labour's expanding strength, the synergies between their respective policies and the wishes of its members. That year the two organisations endorsed in principle Ratana involvement in the Labour movement, an 'informal alliance' based on Labour's support for the Treaty of Waitangi and its ramifications. During the 1931 general election campaign the Labour Party refrained from endorsing any candidates for the Maori seats, leaving the field clear for the Ratana candidates. In turn, these nominally independent candidates pledged to vote with Labour if they were elected.

The Labour–Ratana pact failed to persuade the Maori voters, perhaps partly (as Ngata believed) because of the early popularity of his government's land development schemes, and partly because the future of the combination seemed problematic. But in August 1932 Ratanaism entered the parliamentary scene when T W Ratana's principal disciple and organiser, Eruera Tirikatene, gained the Southern Maori seat in a by-election. He had done so with Labour support, after the party's intended candidate was deemed ineligible. When he was sworn in as an MP, the Labour whips acted as his sponsors. The new MP declared that he would work for the rights of all Maoridom, and he quickly began attending Labour caucus meetings and generally voted with Labour. Both inside and outside the House, Tirikatene tirelessly highlighted the significance of the Treaty and its promises to Maori. He demanded that it be incorporated into legislation, and a Ratana-organised petition to this effect gained over 30,000 signatures.

T W Ratana attended a 'Maori Labour Conference' in September 1932, along with party leaders, and assured it of his movement's continuing co-operation in ousting the government. The conference suggested establishing a nationwide organisation of Maori Labour branches but further consideration was postponed, partly because of rural Maori hostility to the party's anti-Ngata stance. A committee of Labourites continued the campaign, however, and informally co-operated with Ratana networks. Interest in the Treaty was growing in the Dominion at this time. Among other things, the 'Treaty House' at Waitangi was donated 'to the nation' by the Governor-General, who noted the Maori quest for 'justice, equality and peace'. The first official commemorative gathering in its grounds occurred in 1934, where the 1835 'Declaration of Independence' flag of the 'United Tribes of New Zealand', the symbol for Maori of unrelinquished or unrequited sovereignty, flew.

Despite such national interest, Labour, essentially a pakeha party, did not want to damage its election prospects by too close a Maori identification, especially following the fall of Ngata which it had helped engineer. It did not stress Maori matters while electioneering in October and November 1935, and they were not covered in its manifesto. But the fact remained that for over a decade Labour had been pledged to address Maori grievances, and this was now to be achieved in overall co-operation with Ratanaism. During the general election campaign, moreover, Labour leader Michael Joseph Savage promised equal treatment for Maori and pakeha, especially in policies to promote equality of economic opportunity. In effect a pledge to honour the Treaty's Article Three commitments, this was welcomed by many Maori, although some noted a certain resiling from the aspirations for autonomy that Maori sought under Article Two and for which Ratanaism overtly campaigned. At the election a second Maori seat fell to the Ratanaist movement when Tokouru Ratana took Western Maori. Labour gained office for the first time, and its leaders talked of their Maori 'partners'.[95]

CHAPTER SIX

RANGATIRATANGA AND SOCIAL DEMOCRACY

Labour into office

Naturally, Maori expected significant gains from Labour's accession to office. Their anticipation intensified with Prime Minister Savage's allocation to himself of the Native Affairs portfolio. After the Mangai visited him, the Ratana MPs were invited to attend the government's parliamentary caucus, which they then formally joined. The Labour–Ratana alliance, perhaps bringing nearly half of Maoridom (there were said to be up to 40,000 Ratana adherents at the time) under the purview of the party, was formally cemented on 24 April 1936. There was understanding among Maori that results would not be instant: the regime needed time to ponder how to put flesh on the skeletal statements it had issued over the years, culminating in a recent affirmation of 'equality with individuality'. But early on some tangata whenua noticed ominous signs.

The interim settlement that the previous government had offered to the Waikato–Tainui tribal federation, for example, came off the immediate agenda and was not replaced. This was said to be following officials' advice that Taranaki's settlement had been dubious from a legal perspective and that Tainui's was likely to be even more so. Such reasoning astounded those who knew that the Taranaki agreement was a political settlement negotiated without prejudice to either side (albeit fraught with misunderstandings), that the Crown had not raised this with Tainui before and that for a decade Labour had supposedly been working out mechanisms for resolving historical grievances and might therefore have been expected to know what to do on achieving office. Those who were alarmed included Ratanaists. While it eschewed tribalism, the movement strongly

161

advocated resolving tribally based historical claims as a prerequisite for the aggrieved parties moving on to constructive engagement with the modern world. Indeed, resolution of such grievances was one of the stated reasons for Ratana's agreement to work with Labour.

The new government, however, wanted to avoid putting its main Maori policy energies into tribally based segments of Maoridom. Instead, it was searching for a panacea for settling the problems faced by all Maori. It tended to prioritise trans-iwi activity, making the unificatory conceptual base of Ratanaism all the more attractive. The resultant reluctance to pursue further tribally based trust board settlements was encouraged by key officials it had inherited. Some were advising that, notwithstanding commission of inquiry findings, tribal claims had no moral, let alone legal, basis. Others were questioning the wisdom of further agreements based on annual payments.

The Labour government's initial intention (notwithstanding its attacks on Ngata's land development schemes) was 'getting the Natives settled on their lands'. This would be, then, a different approach from that of Ratanaism, despite the latter's non-tribal attributes. The people-centred rangatiratanga which dominated Ratanaism (although it too, of course, had land aspects) was seen as important but not sufficient. Labour also had a different approach from that of tribally based Ngataism. While expanding the land development schemes – regarded as the key to demarginalising Maori – involved an element of collectivity, this was seen as appropriately located at the most localised of levels. The schemes were therefore to be detribalised as far as possible (although few believed that collectivism could be entirely removed from the rural Maori agenda).

The decision to focus on land development might have had an element of administrative convenience about it, including dovetailing with Native Department officials' advice on the appropriate way to tackle Maori issues. But it also reflected Labour's quest for 'equality of opportunity' for all citizens. The government would 'as far as possible [do] anything' to make the individual Maori 'a settler', a reflection of assimilationist policies that 'assisted the whole nation'. Tangata whenua were allocated the role of contributing to the national economy through Europeanised farming techniques. Whatever their remaining connections with marae and tribe, they were supposed to opt for 'new ways' which stressed the ethos of individual expertise and effort. Such an approach would benefit Maori (as well as 'all New Zealanders') while not frightening a pakeha constituency which knew little of the Maori world, 'locked away' in its rural isolation.

Many Maori accepted the trade-offs involved in Labour's land development thrust, stressing its relative continuity with the Ngataist regime. The new government continued to appreciate the significance of turangawaewae, for example, however much it needed to be adapted for capitalist farming. From Ratanaist and other perspectives, however, the land focus contained retrograde elements. This was partly because it remained posited on sub-tribal groupings, and partly because the state's actions were ultimately for the 'public' rather than the 'Maori good'. The latter would be at best a subset of the former: the interests of a national pakeha collectivity overwhelmed those of the ethnic collectivity it had displaced. Even during Ngata's oversight of the schemes, and more so after it, Maori input into land development trended away from, rather than towards, significant participation. In any case, only a certain proportion of Maori could be assisted by land development. Most important of all from a Maori perspective, the emphasis on settling some people on the land, rather than attending to the needs and aspirations of all Maoridom, was at best only a single step towards autonomy. In fact, some who regarded the search for people-based autonomy as the only viable route for Maoridom saw the policy as backward-looking.

The Ratana movement perceived its presence within Labour to be primarily that of a watchdog on behalf of all Maoridom. Not only its mass base gave it kudos and strength, so too did the fact that for the first time a significant Maori movement had sought to persuade its people to vote for *policies* rather than to register adherence to candidates along traditional tribal lines. Even if Ratana had not been inclined to ally with it, the new government would not have been able to ignore his movement. The fact that Maori formed a disproportionate section of the poor, whom Labour's socio-economic policies aimed primarily to assist, meant that its organisation was a positive advantage to Labour. The medium-term prognosis for Ratanaist policies seemed favourable, then, whatever the Savage government's falterings at the beginning. Hope was raised, in fact, as early as January 1936, with a prime ministerial address at Orakei which pledged to uphold the letter and spirit of the Treaty. Government implementation of 'equality of status' between (and accordingly, equal treatment for) Maori and pakeha was stressed.[96]

Tensions and problems

A Maori Organising Committee, with Paraire Paikea as its secretary, finally emerged from the suggestions made at the Labour Party's 1932 conference. It presented its first report to the 1936 conference, and eventually became the party's high-powered Maori Advisory Council. Moreover, many new Maori branches of the Labour Party were formed after the Labour–Ratana alliance was formalised, helping inject Ratanaist vigilance and energy. But such matters constituted developments within the party rather than the government. As many rank and file activists have found over the years, a government's policies do not necessarily reflect the beliefs and wishes of its party's membership and followers. Before long, many Maori were pondering on the ramifications of Savage's commitment to 'equality of status' for Maori. Some began to wonder, despite the government's endorsement of the Treaty, if it meant the loss of the special relationship that Maori considered they had forged with the Crown in 1840.

Such ponderings were fuelled by policy drift. For at first there was little proactive making or implementation of policy on indigenous issues, except over land development. The Prime Minister's promise of a conference of Maori representatives to discuss policies and directions was not fulfilled. Before long Savage, burdened with the heavy responsibilities of office in a reforming government, began leaving Maori policy direction largely in the hands of the Minister of Lands, Frank Langstone. This reflected the Crown's renewed emphasis on land settlement policy.

Langstone pushed issues that were not directly relevant to his portfolio largely into the hands of Native Department personnel, where they tended to languish. The Ratana–Labour caucus (the two Ratana members of the House of Representatives had been joined by Rangi Mawhete on his appointment to the Legislative Council in 1936) could do little to counteract the conservatism of the bureaucracy. By the end of the first year of the Labour government, many Maori were revisiting their hopes of full implementation of more than a decade of promises. There *had* been problems of 'talking past each other', with Maori reading more into Labour's various statements than the party leadership had intended. It now seemed, however, as though even a minimal implementation of self-determinationist promises had been removed from the political agenda.

Not only were aspirations for even a small measure of autonomy put on the back burner, but there were other difficulties in the relationship with a Labourite Crown. Maori were frequently, for example, excluded by the politicians or bureaucrats from consultation over policies relevant to them, perhaps partly because Ngata's downfall had influenced pakeha perceptions of Maori capacity to contribute to matters of state. They were not invited in September 1936 to a key conference of departmental representatives and 'experts' in health, education and economics. The Maori reaction was anger. As a result, the Maori Organising Committee convened a three-day conference of Maori Labour supporters the following month.

The gathering was Ratanaist in orientation, and in preparing his keynote address Savage realised that mere reiteration of his government's focus on land development would be inadequate. Instead, he emphasised a developing theme within the government, one which both included farming development and drew on the rhetoric of equality: Labour would concentrate on implementing Article Three of the Treaty, incorporating this in its plans to establish the world's first fully fledged 'welfare state'. By ensuring that the welfare of *all* citizens would be looked after 'from the cradle to the grave' in health, housing, pensions, education and so forth, the government would, by definition, benefit all Maori. 'National good' arguments were being refined specifically to accommodate Maoridom.

For Labour, then, the fundamental problems facing Maori were caused

by poor living standards and, underpinning these, the economic base of
the country. The government regarded Maori as 'the rural equivalent of
the same groups that they were trying to provide an adequate standard of
living for in the towns'. The Crown's Treaty obligations, whatever words
the Labour leadership may have used in the past, were now oriented to
solving the socio-economic problems of 'the native race'. The government
was implicitly stressing that under Article One it was firmly in charge of
interpreting how it would 'honour' the Treaty. Although Ratanaist and
many other Labour supporters had been relying on the government to
implement, in some way or other, Article Two, this would clearly be
subsumed by Articles One and Three.

Article Three's focus on 'equality' was to be interpreted as 'equality
of status' for all *individuals*. As foreshadowed at Orakei earlier in the year,
the Savage government had added to its guiding socio-economic principle
of 'equality of opportunity' (particularly, for Maori, by developing their
remaining land) that of 'equality of treatment' for all individuals, Maori
and pakeha. While its vision was of a state-led, welfarist government
reflecting a collectivist ideology, this stance now referred to a form of
collectivism which did not fit well with the indigenous communalism
underlying Article Two.

A growing disquiet over such issues pervaded the October 1936
conference. While much of this was manifested in complaints about lack
of consultation over incipient policy direction, delegates also made it
clear that discussion with Maori would reveal that their people wanted
impending social security and other advances to be on Maori terms and
within a Maori context – which was not apparent in what was known
about the planned programmes. There was much appreciation that
Labour's principles derived from a social-democratic philosophical base
that was more inclined to be pro-Maori than were mainstream pakeha
political philosophies. But there were also firm statements that Maori
members of the party would not cease to prioritise their own Treaty-
derived principles, and that these centred on the collective-autonomist
approach of Article Two at least as much as on Article Three's implications
for 'equality' for individuals. Maori delegates expressed lack of confidence
in the system that now included 'their own' movement by calling for a

higher parliament to be formed – one that had representatives from both Maori and pakeha.

Pending this (or in lieu of it), they recommended other measures: the Labour membership's long-standing calls for a body to scrutinise Treaty-related matters should be implemented forthwith; all prospective legislation should be examined through a Treaty-based lens; and, to remove the bureaucratic impediments to their cause, the existing state bodies dealing with Maori should be replaced with 'virtually a separate Maori administrative wing of Government'. This new 'Native Administration Department' would have planning, strategic and co-ordinating functions throughout the public service, as well as providing operational and judicial services.

While the delegates' suggestions for senior Maori personnel in the new body seem modest – at least one Maori in a top position and Maori associates for senior European members – they were adamant about the need for in-depth Maori input into decision making. The new administration would, for example, consult with a network of Maori committees that would be established to provide a conduit for the views of 'ordinary people'. The delegates' concerns complemented those being expressed in other quarters of Maoridom. Around this time, for example, an Arawa-assembled meeting at Ohinemutu began planning for a 'Dominion Federation of Maori Organisations' to take pan-tribal perspectives to the government.

The conference recommendations reflected long-standing Ratana policies, which Savage and his key allies 'probably only dimly comprehended'. From this time the Ratana movement developed policies for a virtually separate Maori wing of government, to be administered by a board with sizeable Maori representation. But, while Labour was prepared to encompass a degree of 'special treatment' for Maori on the road to securing equality, it rejected the conference resolutions and their later manifestations. In doing so, it also ignored some non-radical ways of improving its relationships with Maori, such as better inter-departmental co-operation on Maori issues.[97]

Partly because of the welfare and 'equality' dimensions to Labour's policies, however, the new regime continued to be supported by

Maoridom in general. 'Maori Labour party committees came into being at almost every pa in New Zealand', with one candidate having 64 of them working on his behalf in the 1938 general election. To keep up Maori interest, party and government concessions were made. State thinking on the reparations issue, for example, was advanced together with the land development policies. A sector of the Crown, including even Langstone, was willing to consider handing back land to assist in settling tribal grievances, with groups receiving the land to be assisted to develop it.

Maori responses to this idea, which some had long been advocating, were enthusiastic. There were, however, some disturbing aspects to such thinking within the Crown. A senior official, for example, promoted the idea that the government could acquire blocks for use in reparations from tribes which had 'more land than is reasonably necessary'. Such misreading of the concept of turangawaewae was not untypical, and indicates why Maori felt frustrated at the government's propensity to listen to 'experts' who seemed to know little about their actual and hoped-for way of life. In the event, land-based reparations were again discarded as a solution, partly because of difficulties of land availability and rohe contestation.

Increasingly, Maori had little choice but to see the main benefit from the Labour government as being its commitment to formal equality for Maori and pakeha in the emergent welfare state. In line with Savage's Orakei speech, for example, from 1 June 1936 tangata whenua were placed on the same unemployment relief work rates as pakeha. Yet there were many indications that it would not be easy for Maori to attain the 'equality' promised in Article Three. While the Orakei announcement symbolised the political executive's intent, it was to be marred in its execution. Developing Maori land was designated as relief work for the unemployed, for example, and so brought in very little income. In some instances, the continuance of inequality was even more endemic and blatant.

Under social security legislation, for example, pensions for Maori remained smaller than for Europeans. This policy reflected pakeha perceptions – and to some extent the realities – of *difference*. It aimed to take into account continuance of collective-based Maori lifestyles in rural areas, which involved sharing resources, and support from whanau, hapu, marae committee or other groupings when their members got into difficulties. But the argument was explicated in public good terms. As Maori were not yet fully assimilated and contributing maximally to the economy, they should not reap the full fruits of the pakeha-based welfare state. In fact, to do so while receiving tribal support would, it was argued, privilege them over pakeha beneficiaries. The implication seemed to be that full 'equality' was a long-term goal whose achievement depended on full assimilation. This was contrary to the stated viewpoints of most Maori leaders, including many who sought both some autonomist separation *and* equality and even those who urged that the struggle for rangatiratanga should be downplayed until the 'full equality' of Article Three was achieved.

The number of competing and overlapping views within Maoridom about the current and future situations was increasing. Despite both government shortfalls in delivery and conceptual problems, many Maori – a meeting at Waitara in 1936 was typical – enthusiastically endorsed Labour's 'ultimate objective' of equality of treatment. Others interpreted differences in treatment between 'the races' as a back-handed recognition of rangatiratanga, given the assumptions that underlay, say, the differing rates in social security payments.

Whatever their strategies and tactics, however, most Maori groupings believed that the tasks before them were so great that state assistance would be needed to achieve their goals. This was a theme of a series of intertribal hui in the late 1930s. There was some official response to such Maori pressure, often couched in terms of problems over how any such help might be managed effectively. It was in this context that ministers and officials, for example, discussed a nationwide revival of the Maori Councils, some of which were still 'partially functioning' on the coat-tails of Maori Health Councils. While the motivation for such suggestions was largely to improve Maori health, talk of reviving the Councils held out hope of greater Maori participation in affairs of state. That was one of the reasons why nothing came of the idea: to formalise Maori input through organisations under the umbrella of the state could be seen to threaten the assimilationist 'equality of treatment' approach.

The trend was towards decreasing any 'separatist' aspects of government activity. The continued downgrading of Maori involvement in running the land development schemes was a case in point. Native Department officials, for example, gained greater day-to-day control from the 1936 Native Land Amendment Act. The Board of Native Affairs would use its power to declare any Maori land subject to state development, and 'advisors' would be appointed by the Crown in areas where advice from Maori quarters was deemed to be 'unworkable'. By such means the government was gradually de-emphasising the remaining legal and bureaucratic mechanisms by which Maori groupings might gain a more effective presence in a pakehaised New Zealand. The party that had its roots in collective organisation by the pakeha working class, then, was engaged in policies which, at the very least, did not encourage Maori collective endeavour within the political economy. Tribal structures, which had formed the basis of many of Ngata's original plans, such as 'supervision' of the schemes by local chiefs and other leaders, became increasingly irrelevant to breaking in Maori land.

These and politico-bureaucratic equivalents had not been accidental developments. A pre-Labour government draft of what became the 1936 Act had placed some emphasis on the welfare of Maori landowners collectively, but the final version's thrust was on development in the interests of 'national good' productivity. Langstone noted that the Board of Native Affairs would 'want to see that the most capable men are settled on the land' – regardless of the wishes of the owners, or whether those deemed 'the most capable' were from the local tribe or were even Maori at all, or whether the owners even knew that their land was being brought under the Act. It is well recorded that pakeha supervisors, reporting to and taking orders from Native Department officials, routinely ignored local indigenous wishes. Efficiency, as interpreted by the state, was accorded a greater priority than the wishes of the Maori owners and their communities. Ngata had initiated the land development schemes as 'part of a broader scheme for a cultural revival for Maori communities, a strengthening of Maori leadership and decision-making'. He became more and more vocal on these issues. By 1939 he was complaining of both the 'suppression' of Maori leadership involvement in the schemes, and the rise in importance of pakeha supervisors, shepherds, inspectors and the like. Many such personnel were, he believed, seeking opportunities for advancing their own careers rather than assisting Maori development.

The government did formally adhere to a policy on land development that incorporated cultural and ethnic revival and a degree of self-determination. Improving the yield from the soil would give Maori (in the words of the government's second-in-command, Peter Fraser) the 'chance to work out their own salvation' in multi-faceted ways. But it is clear that, increasingly, ministers felt that conceding any significant degree of autonomy would clash with the government's overriding commitment to 'equality' and assimilation. One commentator has detected a political shift under Labour from development of the Maori people to development of the land in the 'national good'. This is probably exaggerated, partly because state regard for Maori collectivity had never been high in the first place, but Maori political and socio-economic aspirations certainly took second place to policies of 'economic equality' for *all* individuals.

The emphasis on individual welfare helped the government see that developing the land might not be, after all, the panacea for reviving Maori fortunes. Ngataist wisdom on the matter was questioned in Maori circles as well. One reason was the differences over the best route to rangatiratanga. Another was that numbers of Maori (and pakeha) were gradually realising what became clear in retrospect: that a central focus on land development at this time was seriously flawed if the economic well-being of all Maoridom was the goal. So few Maori-held lands were left that, whatever the amount of state resources going into their development, only a minority of the people could be engaged in the process or benefit from its outcomes.

This problem was compounded by other factors. A sizeable number of Maori-owned properties comprised land that was at best only marginally developable. Moreover, those actually farming them did not necessarily support community life or endeavours. Many Maori could benefit only in the broadest sense of having a connection with communities where such land developments were occurring; many others, not at all. Even those involved in the schemes often found little advantage in them. Loan repayment requirements were often onerous, and the amount of training inadequate. In fact, in many places farming on the development schemes provided little better than a subsistence living. By the Second World War, farming supported directly (and often poorly) only a fifth of Maoridom, and rural Maori unemployment was, in the words of a contemporary observer, 'becoming acute'. Emerging demographic indications were that working the land was not a viable option for sustaining Maoridom.

While these problems were gradually being realised, not least by Labour politicians, no major economic alternatives for Maori emerged. In the absence of firm political direction to the contrary, the state departments continued the schemes with little regard to their various flaws. Most people, in fact, Maori included, continued to assume that the socio-economic future for Maori would remain farm-based. Some, however, both Maori and pakeha, began to draw the Crown's attention to problems in such assumptions. This was often in tandem with ongoing pressure for people-based rangatiratanga. These intertwined subjects began to be aired in public, including at a pan-Maori forum, the Young Maori Leaders Conference convened in 1939. The delegates heard, for example, Professor H Belshaw forecast widespread Maori migration to the urban areas. Internal migration had in fact already begun, and the conference discussed ways of better meeting Maori needs in Auckland – such as building on the experience of Wellington's Ngati Poneke Young Maori Club, whose establishment in 1937 reflected increasing numbers of Maori public servants.

Meanwhile, Maori leaders addressing the two key aspects of their people's aspirations, politico-cultural and socio-economic, remained torn by Labour's policies and practices, given that they involved the second subsuming the first. On the one hand, most agreed that Labour's welfarist and development policies, and its penchant for planning and centralising control of the economy, were helping some or all of their own people. Though so-called 'universal' assistance was less for Maori than for pakeha, for example, Maori started from a lower base and so made significant gains, especially from some targeted measures. On the other hand,

Labour's policies and practices not only downplayed rangatiratanga but seemed to some Maori leaders to cut across it. Even those inclined to praise the impact of social-democratic legislation on Maori living standards were often concerned lest welfarism, and other interventionist attempts to reduce class and status divisions, helped undermine Maori society. They saw in such developments the potential for weakening tribal leadership, collective responsibility and kinship ties, and subverting Maori cultural discourse. In short, they feared that, under Labour, Maori identity would be increasingly lost rather than, as they had hoped, endorsed and enhanced.

By the time war broke out in 1939, increasing numbers of Maori had joined Ngata and other leaders in criticising the seemingly constant encroachment of the state on Maori life and institutions. It is likely that, but for the war, the government would have come to see the need to address such concerns. At the very least, it would no doubt have registered the danger of having large numbers of Maori leave the land. If they could not find work elsewhere, they might become – especially those who had left their rohe – expensive dependants of the state. Possibly, then, increasing Maori pressure would soon have forced it to acknowledge that a focus on land development was not the only answer to meeting the economic aspirations of Maoridom – or even that welfare statism, however welcome for Maori marginalised by settler capitalism, was not a substitute for rangatiratanga.[98]

If new policies might have emerged as a result of the increasingly obvious inadequacies and inabilities of the old, signs of this, however, were few by late decade – especially of policies that acknowledged rangatiratanga in any fundamental way. In 1938, for the first time, a special Maori affairs section was included in Labour's election manifesto. This reaffirmed the commitment to raising Maori living standards, and in a general sense to recognising Maori as a not insignificant component of New Zealand society. But this was destined to be a minority role, and 'public good' matters were to take precedence over Maori aspirations. This was symbolised in the government's attitude towards the tribal complex at Orakei, where Savage had provided inspiration for Maori not long before. Now, so determined was the government to displace

Ngati Whatua from their ancestral land in favour of a state housing scheme that it established a tame commission of inquiry to give it the required 'independent' result.

Even welfarism was not doing as much for Maori, at the end of the decade, as might have been expected. The focus on land settlement had seemingly diverted the state from including tangata whenua in other state-planned and -assisted innovations. With no national plan for housing Maori, for example, many whanau continued to live in sub-standard conditions. Even the permanent head of the Native Department acknowledged that half of Maoridom was inadequately housed. The problem, moreover, had the potential to escalate as a result of demographic trends. In the decade to 1936, for example, the Maori population had increased by nearly three times the pakeha rate, despite high early mortality figures.

Langstone had taken over so much responsibility from Savage that he was eventually formally designated Acting Native Minister in addition to his major Lands portfolio. Maori noted that, in effect, he subordinated Maori policy to the quest for farming productivity and other matters prioritised by the 'national good' rationale. This did not occur without resistance, and pressure for a separate 'native administration' or polity remained. Labour's Maori organisation continued to base its activities on the platform of the initial Labour–Ratana alliance, even if it were honoured mostly in the breach. Such campaigns were paralleled in non-Labour settings. Even Ngata became an increasingly fierce proponent of an independently organised Maoridom within a bicultural country, a logical destination for the intellectual direction he had been taking since the late 1920s. In a sense he had led the camp which feared that Labour's emphasis on 'equality' would promote full assimilation.

But most Maori voices continued to support Labour's social-democratic ethos. Among the different strands and groupings which continued to advocate various platforms inside the Labour Party, Ratanaism remained the most notable. Pressure from the movement persuaded Labour to institute secret ballots for the Maori seats, to counter inbuilt advantages for chiefs and other tribal power figures in the previous system of transparent vote casting. This was introduced at the 1938 general election, in which Paraire Paikea's winning of Northern Maori and Ngata's near-ousting from Eastern Maori heightened the Ratana profile within the party. Three of the Four Quarters were in place, and the parliamentary strategy would be completed in 1943, when Ngata was finally defeated.

By 1938, however, much of the old Ratana influence, whatever the self-determinationism it formally retained, had been subsumed beneath the requirements of the powerful government machine. At the general election, for the first time the Ratana candidates stood as Labour Party members. In essence Ratanaism had seen that it could not get far in the political system as a separate body, even if it came to hold the four Labour seats. It had therefore coalesced with Labour, a logical development since this reinforced Labour's propensity to focus on socio-economic progress, across-the-board welfarism and de-emphasising tribalism. But, in becoming part of a larger, pakeha-dominated party, it had compromised on certain of its goals, only to see, in turn, many of those compromise pledges themselves unfulfilled. Through incorporation of one political movement into another, the government had partially appropriated the considerable energies of a mass movement that had once been set up to pose fundamental challenges to the state. Ratanaism's absorption into Labour became even greater when the movement's founder died in 1939, his personal vision now somewhat dissipated within the 'broad church' of the Labour movement.

Yet both Ratana and general Maori efforts within Labour had by no means been wasted. Through them tangata whenua had demonstrated the capacity to be a significant force in the Dominion's affairs. They had shown, moreover, that one way of doing so was to adapt Maori customary methods to the western organisational paradigm. The Labour conference heard in 1937, for example, that during the previous year Maori had formed over 160 komiti within the party. It was at this point that the Maori Organising Committee became the Maori Advisory Council, a change intended to prefigure greater consultation by the ruling party and its officials with Maoridom, and greater Maori influence within the party. The new body built on the flax-roots strength of the many party committees and developed the policies of its predecessor organisation.

The government was a different matter, but the party's advisory body was willing to flex its muscles, criticising – for example – the Crown's non-implementation of the 1936 special conference's recommendations. It openly deplored Langstone's dismissal of Maori aspirations to control their own lives, although giving him the dubious face-saving device of concluding that he had been 'wrongly advised by the Department'. However uphill the struggle, by 1939 Maori rangatiratanga aspirations were widely known and discussed within state and ruling party circles, and that in itself was a not inconsiderable achievement by Maoridom.[99]

Tribal pressure

Maori outside the party condemned Langstone even more strongly than those within. His focus on 'national good' land development, for example, revived fears dating back to original Labour policies that further raupatu, via land nationalisation, was on the government agenda. Petroleum legislation in 1938 added to their concerns. In the view of several leaders (including Ngata), this amounted to confiscation of natural resources from Maori. Thus, before most 'old grievances' had been attended to, new ones were being created in the 'public good'.

Waikato–Tainui's settlement, negotiated in the dying days of the Forbes–Coates administration, was to be one of parity with the Taranaki settlement, £5000 a year. It was the fact that a Kingmaker-led faction had opposed a monetary settlement in favour of land-based reparation that had given officials ammunition to 'take the initiative' in persuading the new Labour administration to withdraw from the arrangement. The iwi was possibly about to insist on a land transfer component, they argued – all the more reason why grievances should be conceded only if found to be legally sound. Ministers were not, in the event, prepared to go that far, recognising that the issue was in Maori eyes one of moral justice – and so needed to be met with political expediency rather than viewed legalistically. Savage would specifically reassure Waikato–Tainui leaders, in both 1936 and 1937, that postponement of their claim did not mean that the Crown was reneging on its promises, and that the settlement proposals of the previous government constituted his bottom line. But the officials' initiative meant that damage to Crown–tribal relations had occurred.

In the government's reaffirmation that it intended settling claims centred on historical grievances, regardless of whether or not it was legally obliged to, it accepted that settlements would be tribally based. This was neither an endorsement of the virtues of a collective lifestyle, nor the reflection of a desire to give iwi or sub-iwi groupings an economic base. Rather, it related to more practical concerns. In particular, settlements would, it hoped, repair the damage to the whole body politic caused by the existence of tribal grievances, which were regularly recited on marae and pervaded communal oral history. It was assessed that socio-racial (and therefore national) 'progress' would be impeded until they were resolved.

Another (if lesser) motivation was relieving the state of an actual and potential welfare burden. It was generally believed in official (and wider) circles that 'Maoris spend money like water'. This had been factored into decisions to pay benefits in lesser amounts for Maori. If tribes were given adequate resources, some felt, Maori could reprogramme their spending habits and even aspire to reach socio-economic parity with pakeha in a decade or two. Whatever the case, if reparations to tribal organisations could also help contain the total amount of welfare expenditure, two purposes could be served by one mechanism.

Such considerations dominated the bureaucrats' contributions to a 1937 government round-table conference to consider indigenous claims. As with similar affairs convened by earlier governments, the Maori delegates tended to be those the Crown felt comfortable with. To considerable protest, moreover, they were deemed by the organisers to represent specified groupings of tribes. Given their lack of meaningful mandate, there could be no tangible result. The Crown therefore considered taking a more conciliatory approach. In February 1938 it convened in Wellington a series of conferences with tribal representatives to secure agreement for 'final' settlements. Langstone reiterated the major government reason for seeking settlement. Following reparations, the customary 'meetings in Pas and talk of illustrious ancestors' would no longer need to dwell on the past actions of the Crown. 'Good Maoris' could stop 'looking backward' and instead, buoyed by state funding, progress towards modernity.

On this broad issue, Ratanaists and Ngataists were in accord with the government, feeling that, through compensation, Maori would stop brooding on the past and be able to participate in the opportunities presented by a country of 'equality'. Expression of such perspectives among generally pro-government Maori inspired Treasury and allied officials, since they were denied the option of refusing to settle, to present a new initiative: considering all claims at the same time, and fitting them into a totalised compensation sum. Reparations packages would be available to tribes only as lump sums – the preferred state option in its original offer to Waikato–Tainui. The reason was stated to be because annual sums would allegedly perpetuate negative memories and therefore 'backwardness', although financial factors were also involved. A 'discount for bulk' arrangement would save the state money in the long run, and a capital sum could be invested by its recipients to create a resource base. However attractive on the surface, the officials' initiative created new tensions in the Crown–Maori relationship. The suggestion not only introduced prospects of further delay, but incorporated an alarming argument: because of the establishment of the welfare state, any reparations needed to be only *minimal*.

It was clear that the actual grievances signified as little for the politicians who allowed officials to test out their new negotiating stances as for the Crown advisers themselves. Historical claims resolution was seen principally in terms of doing the minimum necessary to remove an impediment to achieving a society based on 'peace and good order'. This would lead to a country comprised of relatively socio-economically satisfied and hegemonised individuals whose aggregated happiness would lead to a 'normalised' daily existence in which profits could be pursued to maximal effect. At a Maori Labour conference in June 1938, Savage indicated acceptance of officials' advice that money alone would be offered as compensation, and stated that the government needed to work out how much could, in total, be afforded. Once this had been done, lump-sum claims would be compared, negotiated and settled. There was no longer to be even any *discussion* of return of land in compensation.

Quite apart from this, the unilateral settling of the parameters of negotiation, and Maori anger that the total amount of available compensation was to be assessed entirely in terms of what could allegedly be 'afforded' rather than what represented 'justice', yet another development was ominous from the perspective of rangatiratanga. When Koroki had become Maori King in 1933, he had authorised Tumate Mahuta to head the negotiations with the Crown. The Waikato–Tainui leadership had naturally continued to assume that it would select whomever it wished to represent it before the Crown. But the state's experience with tribally mandated representatives had not gone smoothly, and the tribes were now expected to agree that the Crown would decide on their representatives. The tension that ensued was exacerbated when Kingitanga reiterated its long-standing settlement guidelines: 'as land was taken so it shall be returned'. The relationship worsened further when it became clear that Labour's pledge to Tainui, that it would receive no less than the previous government's offer, was being interpreted in state circles as a promise to match the capitalised form of the previous regime's offer.

Aside from the issue of 'good faith' in negotiations, any formula to capitalise what would have been an in-perpetuity payment to a tribal confederation was more likely than ever to be exceedingly conservative in the context of a totalised compensation sum for all tribes. Indeed, by 1939 the Treasury was suggesting a total reparations payout of only £250,000. An intensified struggle with claimant tribes was clearly in the offing. If they were to accept the government's policy of lump-sum payments, Tainui and Ngai Tahu stated, they would require around £350,000–375,000 apiece. That Maori attitudes were hardening was reflected in the Labour Party itself, with growing disillusionment in a parliamentary leadership which – not very long before – had seemed to offer hope of positive action on behalf of, and in conjunction with, Maoridom. Only half of the Maori Labour committees were paying their affiliation fees, and a planned conference of Maori supporters had to be cancelled through lack of support.

Not only had the tribal rangatiratanga of the major raupatu confederations in particular been bruised, so too had the loyalty of the Maori party members been severely tested on this and other issues by the government. But they did retain some hopes, fed by new ideas such as Mawhete's suggestion that a commission of judges be appointed to examine compensation for breaches of the Treaty. With the advent of the Second World War, however, internal party criticism of the leadership became subdued and negotiations with iwi were postponed by mutual consent until the 'national emergency' was over.

All the while, the three tribal groupings which had signed deals with the Crown continued to receive annual payments that were used for tribal purposes. Although the sums seem small from a later perspective, at the time they were seen as useful. And, more important, the precedent they represented continued to provide hope for other parts of Maoridom. Moreover, such precedents might be improved on, especially given the interim nature of the Taranaki's arrangement. Tribal trust boards, based on regular income (however minimal and circumscribed), were regarded as possible harbingers of a degree of state-sanctioned autonomy.[100]

Contexts

There was an international as well as a national context to such hopes. Although the British Empire was at its territorial peak at this time and New Zealand remained a socio-economic and hegemonised colony of the 'Mother Country', in some quarters the old ties to empire were increasingly under scrutiny. While a postmodern identification of 1931 as the end of the period when the 'Empire was clearly the dominant state of mind' is premature, its selection reflects the entry of proto-nationalism into public discourse and a tentative and empathetic pakeha discovery of 'Maoriland' – the New Zealand 'Other'. Such perspectives, although unwittingly replete with the imperialist implications of what much later became known as 'orientalism', did move outside assimilationist assumptions about the future of Maoridom. While still operating within the hegemonic parameters of 'settler New Zealand', the Labour government notwithstanding, belief systems were gradually changing.[101]

This partly reflected the fact that Maori were painstakingly re-establishing a demographic, political and collective base from which to pressure the Crown to concede the rangatiratanga promised in the Treaty. Alongside and inside the pakeha world, and influencing its ideological direction, they were undoubtedly, if very gradually, becoming more empowered. But increasing numbers saw an implicit tension between social democracy's 'egalitarian' intentions and Maori aspirations to confirm and strengthen the cultural *differences* between their world and that of the pakeha. In retrospect, the two perspectives are not necessarily incompatible. Most Maori, for example, aspired to rather than rejected the material culture of mainstream New Zealand, and so aspirations for political or other autonomy did not necessarily mean rejection of Labour's welfare state. But, at the time, the relationship between Maori rangatiratanga and pakeha social democracy appeared to many from both cultures to be, at the very least, inherently troubled.

The Labour government did retain Maori support, however much that was tempered by dashed expectations. For it continued generally to work towards placing Maori on equal footing with pakeha and raising living conditions for both. That this should be done ideally without differential treatment between them lay deep in the roots of Labour ideology. Prominent Labour politician H G R Mason, who would later take charge of Maori Affairs, remained till the end of his life hostile in principle to any race-based proactivity by the state. Yet raising the living conditions of the poor required, by definition, disproportionate attention to Maori. And therefore, whatever the personal feelings of politicians, the state did attempt to address the marginalisation which colonisation had produced. Many Maori interpreted these as steps, however inadvertent on the Crown's part, towards state recognition of rangatiratanga and mana.

Such steps included, as well as rural land development, spectacular health improvements and developing educational policies. Under the guidance of the Senior Inspector of Native Schools (D G Ball) and of educationalist Dr C E Beeby (who became, in 1940, Director of Education), for example, the Education Department gradually moved its Native Schools policy away from the previous fully assimilationist approach. The strategy of producing replicated Britons having clearly failed, the schools were now increasingly covering subjects relevant to

Maori life and culture, including indigenous 'history' – albeit filtered through western notions such as racial hierarchy. The new approach, to be sure, focused on the *practical* relevance of a Maori workforce within a pakeha-dominated economy and culture, assuming, as with Labour's focus on the land, that Maori would continue to be rural dwellers. As the Director of Education had put it in 1931, the state aimed to produce for Maori 'a type of education that will lead the lad to be a good farmer and the girl to be a good farmer's wife'. When Native District High Schools were established from 1941, they concentrated on 'useful' agricultural and technical subjects for the boys and homemaking to prepare girls for servicing the desired social unit, the nuclear family of the pakeha social order.

While agricultural skills and other subjects were geared to perpetuating 'the race' at the bottom tiers of the political economy, the new emphases did recognise Maori as a distinct people rather than classifying them as aspirant brown-skinned whites, particularly when the Native Schools syllabus was broadened not only to include traditional Maori arts, crafts and culture but to involve the whole Maori community. Such developments did not happen in a vacuum. Some assumptions of the 'civilising mission', for example, had been challenged under the impact of Ngataist cultural resurgence. The state had now, therefore, to accommodate, and if necessary contain, the latter. This would give it time to work out subtler, longer-term strategies for assimilation.

These were ultimately conditioned by demographic and other developments within Maoridom. Complementing the official land-based prognosis for Maori, the indigenously oriented aspects of the syllabus in Native Schools reflected a tribally based 'differentness' that would soon become anachronistic for many Maori – and which would in time be modified. Factors such as the rapid rise in the indigenous population, Maoridom's small land base and deficiencies in the development schemes were resulting in not only a decreasing proportion of Maori working the land but also a migratory drift towards the towns and cities. It was noted at the 1939 Young Maori Leaders Conference that this trend was already being reflected in greater rates of offending and imprisonment. It was to increase considerably during and after the Second World War. The Crown was, however, slow to develop its new strategies. Even after the war, Education Department reports continued to opine that land was of the most 'vital importance' for the Maori future, and departmental assumptions generally ignored the wartime exacerbation of the 'urban drift'.[102]

That the state's education sector, and others equally important, was out of touch with significant aspects of the Maori experience did not bode well for Crown–Maori relations. Eventually, when officials and politicians realised that a land-based orientation for Maori policy was increasingly out of kilter with both the opportunities available in the countryside and the migration demographic, the resultant reorientation was not generally conducted through consultation with Maori. Unilateral measures included Crown encouragement of relocation to urban areas, where cheap Maori labour was needed for urban-based manufacturing expansion. Most fundamental, officialdom came to regard internal migration by Maori as a chance, at long last, for them to assimilate to a degree they had resisted when they had stayed largely in rural areas. In particular, it was seen that on the urban streets they would be far from the purview of tribal authorities and customs, and so collective bonds among large sectors of tribal membership would be loosened.

Urbanisation did, in the event, lead to a weakening of tribally based rangatiratanga. Maoridom, along with official New Zealand (albeit belatedly), had to adjust to the realities of population growth and socio-economic demands and opportunities. Its leaders increasingly realised that, however much their culture and aspirations were wedded to turangawaewae, the fact that the location, employment and lifestyles of many of their people were beginning to change fundamentally meant that the quest for autonomy needed restrategising. Wartime events had postponed full discussion of the ramifications of rural demographic overload and urban migration. But they were also to contribute significantly to shaping Maori politico-cultural adaptation to post-war industrialising New Zealand.

CHAPTER SEVEN

RANGATIRATANGA AND WORLD WAR TWO

The early Maori war effort

When war broke out in 1939, not just negotiations with tribes over historical grievances were placed on hold 'in the national interest'. So too were other developments in Crown–Maori relations. But the Crown had learnt some lessons from its First World War experiences. To maximise the Maori contribution to 'the emergency', it needed to make significant concessions to Maori aspirations for greater participation in public affairs.

As war was looming, Maori leaders had asked that approval be given for a Maori fighting unit, which they believed would provide an important contribution to the allied war effort. After the declaration of war, the Crown quickly conceded that Maori could indeed participate in the hostilities 'as a race'. In October 1939 it announced that a Maori infantry battalion would be raised. Those Maori who had already joined the army could remain in their existing units, but recruits would be sought for enlistment in the 28th (Maori) Battalion.

Pro-Crown tribes, eager to prove their loyalty and improve their image in a still largely pakeha New Zealand, had been at the forefront of the initial approaches to government. But others were also interested in having their young men serve. Some tribes argued that, whatever the recent frustrations, overall progress on Crown–Maori relations – such as the tribal trust board precedent – had been made since the First World War; their contribution would both reflect and enhance that. Recruiting was the responsibility of the wartime Maori Parliamentary Committee, comprising the four Maori MPs and Legislative Councillor Mawhete. It was headed by Paikea, Ratana's former private secretary, whose experience included building up the network of Labour Party Maori branches after the alliance was forged. There was no difficulty in getting sufficient volunteers for the all-Maori (except for pakeha in higher ranks) battalion to be formed.

After Ngataist pressure, the four field companies of the 28th Battalion were allowed to be organised along broadly tribal lines, despite problems caused by this issue during the First World War. The decision reflected, among other things, official recognition that tribal energies could be a valuable resource for the state. The battalion was to prove this in battle, gaining New Zealand and international fame. The Crown regarded it with increasing respect, dropping its insistence on pakeha in leadership positions, for example. While the initial recruiting drive was successful, ministers and their officials had longer-term concerns. One was that the more ambivalent tribes (especially those in the raupatu areas) and purist Ratanaists might resist if the need for military conscription arose. This would have the capacity to damage the war effort, as in the previous conflict. Soon after becoming Prime Minister on 1 April 1940, Peter Fraser turned his mind to the issue. After consulting with the Maori MPs, he affirmed that the Maori Battalion would continue to be entirely voluntarist. When military conscription was introduced in June 1940, Maori were exempted. There were also proactive measures designed to keep Maori enthusiastic about service to the state. From time to time, for example, the government reiterated that it did intend eventually to settle the historical claims of the tribes, and Fraser personally expressed particular interest in the raupatu issue. For these and other reasons, the prospect of tribe-based mass disobedience to the state was minimised.

Maori leaders were aware that their wartime co-operation, and the agreed hiatus in Crown–Maori negotiations, did pose a danger that tangata whenua concerns would largely disappear from the state's gaze. This was foreshadowed early on. 'The wartime emergency' muted the official celebrations planned for the 100th anniversary of the founding of the settler nation, but still provided the government with a chance to proclaim its 'public values'. As the planning and events unfolded, it became clear that little attention was being paid to Maori, except for exotic touches to distinguish New Zealand from elsewhere in the British Commonwealth. Coverage of Maori issues focused on touristic vignettes of pre-1840 life and crafts, with post-Treaty 'history' stressing progress from stone-age culture towards the ideal of assimilation to the ways of western civilisation. The official focus was firmly on 'a hundred years of progress' for white settlement. The Dominion was depicted as a sheltered, beautiful and quiet society, far from the evils of the old but possessing all of its (white) civic virtues. It was the best of all societies, a 'Better Britain' par excellence, in which Maori were fortunate to be able to share and to have the chance to become 'Britons'.[103]

The paucity of things Maori in Centennial Exhibition displays and official performances, functions and publications, except as decorative marginalia, was a fitting commentary on 100 years of post-annexation relations between Crown and Maori. During this time, the Treaty (if noticed at all) had been elevated in official and (to a degree) popular ideology to the status of the most enlightened 'founding document' in the world. Its Article Two ramifications, even under their most anodyne interpretation and despite ongoing Maori reminders, had been largely forgotten. Although the commemoration marked a greater appreciation of the Maori role in society than had the nation's half-century celebrations, which depicted the Treaty as a reflection of 'humanitarian' Colonial Office attitudes that had ceased to be relevant, it did not signify substantial progress towards autonomous control of the Maori destiny over the preceding 50 years. The official celebrations, therefore, reflected reality. But their 'disappearing' of Maori, even at a time of pro-war rhetoric and assistance from within Maoridom, did not seem to indicate any serious future efforts by the Crown to achieve a significant relationship with its indigenous people.

The celebrations drew some protest, both pakeha and Maori. At the Akaroa event, Ngai Tahu's paramount chief stressed the importance of its tribal claim, to Fraser's obvious discomfort. The raupatu tribes boycotted the North Island celebrations. Even Ngata's general praise of New Zealand race relations was qualified. Maori, he said, could scarcely be expected to be interested in celebrating the loss of most of their lands. He joined Paikea in suggesting that, although negotiations were voluntarily suspended, it would be appropriate in the centennial year to settle Maori grievances in principle. As an opposition MP, he went even further, opposing welfarist lumping of all New Zealanders together. This, he stated, implied anti-tribalism, whereas Maori cultural renewal, while reflecting a general unity of purpose, was based on a tribal vigour that augured well for the Maori contribution to New Zealand life. Ngata noted the paucity of Maori attendance at the celebrations, implicitly inviting the government to draw inferences. Other Maori spokespeople also embarrassed the Crown by querying the myths of assimilative harmony and stressing the need for a Maori-based future for their people.

In this 'Pacific haven' of 'peace and tranquillity', however, Maori objections to assimilationism and their reassertion of tribal energy were generally either resented or (more commonly) ignored. It was the 'intrepid' and 'dauntless' settlers who should be, and were being, celebrated – not their Maori foes (or allies). It was the pakeha 'pioneering spirit' that needed to be reforged for the nation's contribution to the international struggle against fascism. A supposed 'Maori warrior spirit' was seen as an interesting exotic touch, but not central to the war effort.

Overlying the patriotic fervour of the centennial events, which were tightly controlled by the state, was a celebration of beneficence: of 'British' governance in general, and of the Labour government and its policies in particular. Combining proto-nationalistic pride over socio-economic progress with the colonial and imperial mindset, Labour guaranteed both social security and 'preservation of freedom'. In Treaty terms, it promoted Article Three's emphasis on 'equality' over Article Two's respect for Maori differentness. In a national hegemony produced out of 100 years of privileged membership of empire, there was little role for indigenous self-determination. In the words of one cabinet minister at the 1940 celebrations, the government wanted, not tribalism, but 'Maori and pakeha to live side by side as brothers'.

The general Maori desire to assist, and to be seen to be assisting, the war effort was not, however, geared to winning a place in a homogeneously 'British' New Zealand. Rather, it was, as reflected in the title of Ngata's 1943 pamphlet 'The Price of Citizenship', a repeat of the Ngataist rationale for joining the previous international war effort. Proving that Maori were willing to assist the Dominion and 'the civilised world' in their darkest hours, even by the shedding of blood, would aid the tangata whenua struggle. This was a quest not just for the various manifestations of 'equality', such as socio-economic progress, but also for the autonomous control over their lives that had been implicit (and arguably, in Article Two, explicit) in 1840 when they signed up to British subjecthood. The Maori MPs, particularly, were conscious of the need for Maori to 'prove themselves' to be loyal subjects of the Crown as a prerequisite for pakeha public support for concessions from the state. In the absence of such backing, nothing much would happen in terms of Crown recognition of rangatiratanga.

The Maori Parliamentary Committee put great effort into stressing, particularly to the tribes with the major grievances, the potential political spin-off from enthusiastic and ongoing co-operation with the Crown. In turn it elicited grateful government responses to the many wartime initiatives from within Maoridom, and reported these back. Some concessions came early on. It was the Committee's insistence that the need to 'foster tribal unity' in the war effort could best be done in 'the traditional way' which had led to the government's acceptance of giving 'recognition to the principle of tribal leadership (consistent with military efficiency)' in the 28th Battalion. The Maori MPs worked hard to encourage voluntary enlistment and, when this flagged, set up an intensified recruitment campaign.

Even the leaders of the tribes which had resisted full collaboration during the First World War were now, their eyes strategically focused on post-war gains, careful not to be seen to be discouraging members from joining the military effort, although there was a relatively weak response to volunteering in raupatu regions. Maori became popular with pakeha as a result of publicity for the 28th Battalion. One observer later reminisced about the unusual experience of approval for her people during 'the Pakeha war': 'Maoris seemed to be heroes instead of "black niggers" . . . I will never forget the sight of the Maori Battalion as they marched through Wellington with all the other soldiers. The applause they received from the people was thunderous. You did not need an education to kill people. As long as you could pull a trigger you were fine.'

The Maori war effort was headed by the Maori MPs on the home as well as the fighting front. Here, too, there was strong Maori support for 'patriotic service'. Even Te Puea and the Waikato elders and people were enthusiastic in the production of food and materials for the war effort. The scale of the national challenge meant that, for the first time, 'Maori manpower' became an essential factor in the New Zealand 'national interest'. As a result of this, their military contribution and other home-front activities, Maori came to be seen by the state and pakeha as 'an asset' rather than a 'problem'.

At first, flax-roots contributions to both the home and fighting fronts were informally organised and loosely encouraged by the Maori politicians. These efforts were based on existing tribal structures, a traditional propensity to form komiti within these for specific purposes, and (to a lesser degree) what remained of the Maori Council system. After a year of disparate activities, the Maori MPs concluded that the tangata whenua effort needed to be more formally structured, and co-ordinated across all war-related activities. Their proposals gained widespread acceptance among Maoridom and, after considerable planning among the MPs and their networks, in May 1941 the government approved formalisation of the Maori contribution to the war. Military recruiting was to be its major focus. Paraire Paikea, pivotal to the Labour–Ratana alliance, had been appointed Member of the Executive Council Representing the Native Race on 21 January that year, in addition to chairing the wartime Maori Parliamentary Committee. He now became minister in charge of what was officially called the 'Maori War Effort'.[104]

The Maori War Effort Organisation established

Paikea and the other Maori MPs were well aware that the Native Department was generally regarded by their people as an oppressive agency of racial control. It could not therefore act as the central institution needed to co-ordinate and regulate the regional and local Maori war effort activities. They proposed, therefore, to create a structure that would be independent of the department and built on the existing, mostly informal, groupings. The latter generally approved the Maori Parliamentary Committee's propositions, whose autonomist slant reflected their own views and activities.

There were also some concrete reasons of state for a separate Maori body to run the war effort. One was a record-keeping problem: the Crown was unable to obtain accurate lists of Maori eligible for war service. It had not compiled Maori electoral rolls, and social security registrations covered only a quarter of the Maori workforce. Tribal knowledge was the best way of accessing such information. But tribal leaders were scarcely going to give this priority, or even assist at all, if departmental officers were presiding over the exercise.

It took a considerable time to establish the concept of the Maori War Effort Organisation. This reflected the difficulties of systematising so many disparate, far-flung and often relatively inchoate institutions. It was also hampered by hesitancy from bureaucrats about the possibility of Maori taking control of things Maori. From the state's point of view, caution was essential for a number of reasons. One was efficiency. Another was that the informal, quasi-formal and tribal Maori wartime organisations that had sprung up or taken on new forms or tasks had often refused to have anything at all to do with the Native Department. Their spontaneity and independence made them a potentially untameable, and therefore troubling, force. Most politicians and advisers, however, came to appreciate that establishing a centralised co-ordination mechanism, even if outside the conventional bureaucracy, might help bring the wartime komiti under some control. This would be a better option, on efficiency grounds, than an imposed bureaucracy that would engender little enthusiasm or co-operation. If it could also establish firm linkages with existing state machinery, that would be a bonus. The bureaucrats concerned with both containing and using Maori organisational energies focused many of their in-house discussions on ways of encouraging this.

In line with imperial norms, the New Zealand state had always been adept at appropriating indigenous movements that were too powerful to suppress or which might aid Crown goals. Native Minister John Ballance had typified this phenomenon when referring in 1885 to unofficial Maori komiti as the equivalents of local government. By officially franchising them as such, he had proposed, they might become useful instruments of state rather than problems for it. Since then there had been many actual or attempted appropriations, and such matters were now on the Crown agenda again.

Many Maori leaders, however, especially the MPs Paikea and Tirikatene, saw maximising the Maori contribution to the war as a means of pursuing rangatiratanga in a way that would assist both peoples of Aotearoa/New Zealand. They believed too that Crown acceptance of virtually autonomous Maori control of their war effort would help ameliorate long-standing suspicions of the state among Maoridom. This might herald a new chapter in Treaty relations and lead to an eventual working partnership. The Maori Parliamentary Committee went to work at once, setting up *ad hoc* centralising and controlling measures to provide thinking time for the best way to harness the methods, organisations and enthusiasms which had developed since the beginning of the war. Their efforts increased with the perceived threat of Japanese invasion after Pearl Harbor was bombed, and they were ready to submit a proposal for a fully fledged scheme by May 1942. The Maori War Effort Organisation (MWEO) was approved by the War Cabinet as a six-month experiment on 3 June 1942.

The Maori Parliamentary Committee, still chaired by Paikea during his time as Minister in Charge of the Maori War Effort in the War Administration of June–October 1942, was to superintend it. The general plan was to establish, in each electorate, Maori organisations representing the main iwi groupings. They would report to and interact with politicians and departments through liaison officers seconded from the army, a reflection that their main initial task was military recruiting. Tribal customs and configurations were taken into account in selecting committee areas and military recruiting zones. Selection of both the 21 zones and the recruiting officers often involved departing from military and administrative norms, adding to delays, but during the six-month experimental period the MWEO structure was fine-tuned. In the event, politicians and officials were satisfied with the level of efficiency which ensued, including in committee work other than recruiting, and the life of the organisation was extended.[105]

The Maori War Effort Organisation's operations

The informal komiti which had sprung up early in the war had generally been rooted in iwi, hapu, whanau and other tribally based collective groupings. The structure of the new organisation built on them. The network of official 'Tribal Committees' which emerged was testimony – especially in view of the pan-tribal Ratanaist background of the organisers – to the continuity of tribal power in Maoridom. A contemporary scholar assessed that the authorities had gone beyond merely tolerating Maori traditional organisation, and were actually 'encouraging Maori co-operation along the lines of the Maori people's own traditions'. The tribal committees were 'to function entirely under Maori control and according to Maori ideas'. Although this discounted the fact that these were official structures, it is clear that under the MWEO Maori had gained unprecedented responsibility in the administration of their own affairs. At the very least, the tribal committees embodied the ideas of the October 1936 Labour Maori Conference's call for a network of komiti at the interface between Maori and government. An executive layer above enabled them to have an influence beyond the merely local.

The MWEO rapidly made an undoubted contribution to the war effort, beginning with improving Maori enlistment rates. As time went on, Maori demonstrated that they could efficiently run the largest tangata whenua organisation ever to be established under Crown auspices. It was, Paikea proclaimed, a 'revolutionary experience' for his people. Even under considerable media and other scrutiny, it did much to dispel, at least in the short to medium term, pakeha concerns about the Maori capacity to organise efficiently. Bureaucrats would have preferred more rigid state control mechanisms, but failing this had sought the appointment of 'reliable' military personnel to work with the MWEO.

At the top level, an officer was attached to the Maori Parliamentary Committee to liaise with the recruiting networks. Completely independent from the military in his seconded position, Lieutenant-Colonel H C Hemphill reported direct to Paikea. He had been selected partly because of his capacity to understand the tribal resonance of the organisation, and he quickly perceived the advantages of virtually autonomous operation in the field. After consulting with Maori, more-over, he strongly advised the Crown that the principle of tribal organis-ation and leadership should be entrenched in all military services, including (as eventually happened) the Territorial Forces and the Home Guard.

By March 1943, the MWEO had enlisted 5178 men for overseas war service, 2088 for home-based military service and 10,229 for the Home Guard – making a total of 17,495 enlistments in the armed forces of New Zealand. This was seemingly done with good will between the Maori War Effort Organisation and officials, despite initial suspicions on both sides. When Hemphill stepped down in 1944 a northern kaumatua's farewell noted that Maori had seen him as their 'bulwark' in Wellington. The man put in place to help control Maori had been converted by his experiences to such an appreciation of Maori organisational capacity that he had been prepared to risk unpopularity with other Crown agencies.[106]

While the tribal committees had been founded mainly for military and related purposes, from the beginning 'general service' at home and abroad had been involved. It had always been clear, moreover, that both the basis of operations and the measures of success would reflect Maori values and goals. The network of tribal committees, therefore, almost seamlessly continued the 'home front' activities that their informal predecessors had engaged in, whatever the official requirements. This had been expected – and encouraged – by the Maori MPs. By March 1943, for example, the tribal committees had put thousands of extra acres of land into production. Accolades were many, and two 1944 assessments were typical: 'The story of the Maoris' total war effort . . . is one that it will be difficult to parallel anywhere in the world.' 'The Maori people are behind the country's war effort with a willingness and enthusiasm which in proportion to their numbers, would be hard to equal even by the pakeha.'

When the National Service Department began the task of national distribution of 'manpower', especially to 'essential industries', it received huge support from the tribal committees. It quickly set up Maori sections in its offices in centres of Maori population. The tribal committee and executive recommendations to officials embodied extensive knowledge and authority. These contributed to the National Service Department's considerable successes with Maori manpowering, such as the placing of 10,825 Maori in essential occupations within six months. As a result, the MWEO committees soon secured the task of formal registration of Maori for the national manpowering operation, and it became mandatory for departmental manpower officers to consult with them before issuing decisions relating to Maori personnel. The two divisions of state, National Service Department and MWEO, worked together to place large numbers of Maori in workplaces such as freezing works, sawmills and dairy factories, and in shearing gangs and on construction sites. Workplace direction and control were, in fact, to become the biggest responsibility for the MWEO committee network. On 1 April 1945 some 15,000 Maori were working in essential industries.

By the end of the initial six-month MWEO experiment, a total of 315 tribal committees had been formed, each with a maximum of two representatives on one of the 41 district 'Tribal Executive Committees' which co-ordinated the tribal committee efforts. Maori leaders had never considered that the MWEO would be a short-term affair. Its successes had given them ammunition for extending the organisation's life beyond the experimental period. The Maori MPs had led the campaign, arguing that the MWEO's franchise should not only be renewed but broadened. The government, appreciating that its own interests as well as those of Maori were being advanced by the organisation, endorsed Paikea's formal approach for an extension.[107]

In view of the Crown's past actions, many Maori (including some of the informal war effort collectives) had at first been cautious about participating in a formally franchised war effort organisation. But when it emerged that the MWEO would be Maori-dominated and operated in Maori ways, with minimal pakeha bureaucratic interference, the enthusiasm level rose remarkably. Tribal committees not only investigated and provided for the needs of essential industries, they liaised and negotiated with various government departments, intervened in employer–employee relations in situations where production was affected, sought ways of maximising land use, promoted education and vocational training among their people, assisted in rehabilitating returned Maori servicemen, raised relief monies, oversaw expanded food production and collected 'agar seaweed – the new Government industry which has been organised to supply the British Empire with this valuable medicinal and purifying commodity'. Before long, moreover, many of the committees were taking on the functions of local bodies, assuming powers previously exercised by the Maori Councils/Maori Health Councils and their village committees (a few of which continued a separate existence outside the MWEO, though in relation to it). They did so 'with considerable success' – not only from their own perspective but also, at times, from that of the state.

The tribal executive committees played a more formal role. At first they focused on co-ordinating military recruiting, and later their energies were concentrated on directing and controlling labour. They presided over a huge mobilisation, and by March 1943 some 29,000 Maori (out of a total of 95,000) were in military services or appropriate industries. At a less formal level, and with or without official mandates, they steadily expanded their range of activities. In many instances, together with their tribal committees they were doing – unpaid – the work of the state. This was sometimes overt, as with their registration of all Maori of specified ages, with its obvious potential for pressured military service, or their tackling of such problems as absenteeism or changing jobs under false names. 'Cases of failure to comply with direction orders, absenteeism, etc., are dealt with by the tribal executive, which sits in conjunction with the Manpower authorities.'

Increasingly, moreover, the MWEO was being asked to intervene in the lives of Maori who were deemed to be behaving improperly in their private lives – those who had 'mis-spent' their family benefit allowances, for example – or to investigate 'cases where Maori beneficiaries . . . are capable of giving manual service'. As some Maori noted, this seemed proof that through the MWEO the Crown was in effect appropriating the flax-roots initiatives of Maori. With elements of the organisation being increasingly viewed as coercive agencies of the state, resistance from within Maori communities grew – especially towards the tribal executive committees, the main channel through which the Maori Parliamentary Committee and the central bureaucrats kept general control over the network.

But Maori mostly kept faith with 'their' organisation. The fact that the MWEO's committees received no state payments or subsidies might be seen as yet another example of Crown parsimony. Yet there was no pressure for payment, a reflection of the main Maori motivation for the MWEO – the desire to control their own contribution to the war effort. In the aftermath of Ngata's fall from grace, officials, politicians and the media were more determined than ever that, where state monies were involved, Maori organisations needed strong state oversight and stewardship. As the wartime committee system's financing was based mostly on fund-raising activities alone, however, the tribal executive committees could exercise general authority over the Maori war effort with a minimum of direct intervention by the Crown. Under this general supervision, flax-roots tribal committees did practically whatever they felt they needed to do.

Carried along by abundant local energy, the tribal committees moved, almost inexorably, into community-based activities which bore little or no relationship to their formal tasks. Some began providing social welfare support for their people, for example, particularly on issues in which the Native Department showed little interest. MWEO bodies handled, for example, the 'plight of Maori girls' who had arrived in the larger centres of population by directing them into 'productive or essential employment', finding them accommodation and warning them of the 'moral danger' from 'predatory' soldiers and 'professional seducers'. Maori and pakeha scholars and observers alike, at the time and since, have depicted the MWEO as embodying 'authority of a form unprecedented for Maoris' in post-1840 New Zealand and as 'an unprecedented empowering of the Maori people to manage their own affairs'. Hemphill, typical of contemporary officials, noted to Paikea that 'never before has so much direct responsibility been given to the Maori people'.

Whatever the reservations about and resistance to the MWEO among some of the Maori leaders and people, it is difficult to overestimate its impact within Maoridom. Its extensive autonomy meant that even the tribes with the most vocal grievances against the Crown could take part enthusiastically. In the face of suspicions among intelligence officials, based mostly on memories of the First World War, Princess Te Puea herself headed the Waikato tribal executive committee, which eventually supervised the largest number of tribal committees in any of the MWEO regions.

While the state was always apprehensive about unauthorised ventures by its agencies, some of the 'extra' MWEO activities proved to be so useful that they were formalised. Following a conference on Maori welfare in 1943, for example, the organisation took on the role of advising Maori recipients on the best use of welfare benefits. While this might well be seen as (and in some instances certainly became) a coercive supervision, it was appreciated in a number of tribal milieus. The Crown increasingly appreciated such interventions, too, and would make auxiliary appointments to assist committee work. From early 1943, following MWEO recommendations to the National Service Department, 'lady welfare officers' were appointed in cities (and later in large towns) to complement efforts to ease the adjustment of recently arrived women. Other auxiliary appointments aimed to help hard-pressed urban Maori committees provide assistance to young male migrant workers 'cast adrift' in the cities. And all along, the committees worked alongside pakeha voluntary contributions to the war effort.

MWEO committees, pakeha committees and state institutions had in effect combined to turn local effort into a national mission. Accordingly, as the MWEO's work escalated 'a degree of acceptance of Maori values' grew among pakeha. This led, in turn, to increasing Maori confidence in operating collectively in a society dominated by other cultural and organisational modes – boosting that which had been inspired by the MWEO in the first place and, more broadly, by the emerging pre-war 'sense of Maori unity'. The results of the MWEO's work, then, enhanced the perceived benefits to both the country and Maoridom from the tangata whenua operating, in some contexts, 'as a race'. One observer referred to 'a unity unparalleled in the history of the tribes'. 'For the first time', an historian has noted, 'one organization had successfully co-ordinated Maori efforts and had brought within its ranks all the accepted Maori leaders. Maori were moving into participation in the mainstream of New Zealand life but on their own terms.'

Alongside increasingly favourable publicity depicting the MWEO's work as a nationwide Maori collective endeavour, calls for a structured revival of kotahitanga were increasing. A temporary Crown enfranchising of Maori self-organisation, to assist 'the nation' by placing spontaneous and informal effort under some formal control, had increased the potential for Maori unity of action and (possibly) organisation – all of which would most likely aid the quest for autonomy. Such autonomist implications were present at sub-national levels too. The degree of freedom for the tribal committees and their executives that was needed to ensure success had led, in a sense, to reappropriation by Maori at regional and especially local levels.

Pakeha officials, politicians and others who regarded any manifestation of Maori self-determination as inherently dangerous were alarmed at such propensities within the MWEO. The organisation was seen as particularly problematic *because* such a large proportion of Maoridom placed such significance on it. Paikea felt the 'Maori War Effort' to be so significant that, he told the Prime Minister, it was 'the greatest thing that has happened in the history of the Maori people, since the signing of the Treaty of Waitangi'! Whereas the military bureaucracy were not alone in feeling that the MWEO should be disbanded once it had performed its recruiting function, he and other Maori leaders were quickly arguing that it continue through to the end of the war. The extra tasks that they encouraged it to take on, in fact, increasingly included preparations for the peacetime relationships and organisation of Maori. Moreover, since the MWEO was a model that Maori greatly preferred to that of the Native Department, Paikea and others urged that the organisation itself be extended into peacetime.

This particularly alarmed the professional Native Department bureaucrats, upon whose activities the MWEO's work had quickly and inevitably encroached. In contrasting the two organisations, Maori people generally had their views confirmed about the paternalistic, controlling and Wellington-centred focus of the department. They had therefore increasingly bypassed the old bureaucracy, going straight to the MWEO committees for advice and to offer assistance. The provision of adequate housing was one area where the Native Department was seen as particularly deficient, and where the bottom-up concerns and activities of the MWEO were appreciated. The clear (though not universal, because of its location within the state) success and popularity of the MWEO, coupled with the increasing push to extend its energies into post-war reconstruction, implicitly threatened even the continued *existence* of the Native Department. A scholar opined that the 'fundamental problem of finding the right place for a fast-multiplying native people in the modern social and economic system' lay more with the Maori-initiated and -run MWEO than with the old-style bureaucrats. The organisation was being hailed for its potential to enable Maori to address issues of 'economic and cultural adjustment', and to give 'the Maori race as a whole both renewed confidence and an instrument of its own through which the people may by their own efforts go far toward solving the "Maori problem"'.[108]

Opposition and fightback

Langstone had been confirmed as Native Minister by Fraser, but relinquished the position in late 1942. The Minister of Justice and Attorney-General, H G R Mason, took over the responsibility from him and was formally confirmed in the portfolio on 7 July 1943. Mason had little knowledge of Maori and was even less disposed than Langstone to empathise with their aspirations. He relied a great deal on his departmental officials' advice. Even at this relatively early stage of the MWEO, their tack was generally to stress the danger that the indigenous war effort could lead Maori to affirm what one observer called 'a nationality of their own'.

Langstone, Mason and the Native Department all appreciated, however, that the MWEO was both too successful and too popular to be dismantled at once. While it should certainly be disbanded at the end of the war, its powers should meanwhile be curbed – although, in the interests of the national war effort, the community involvement which characterised it could not be seriously truncated. Senior officials, such as Mason's private secretary, Michael Rotohiko Jones, worked through several possibilities for 'taming' it.

One, advocated by influential figures such as Judge George Shepherd (who became, from February 1944, the Native Department's permanent head) was particularly favoured. Shepherd agreed that the Crown would probably have to meet a post-war demand for Maori community participation in affairs of state, but felt that this process could by-pass the MWEO. Indeed, it could begin at once, based on the pre-war plans to revive Maori Councils. When these became entrenched, the MWEO committees would merge with them. As the new bodies would be under the firm tutelage of the minister and his department, the MWEO's implicit challenge to the state's authority would be a thing of the past and a smooth transition to peacetime could occur.

When Paikea died on 6 April 1943, Fraser called him 'irreplaceable' in view of his pivotal role in mediating between Crown and Maori. Mason and his officials moved quickly to take advantage of the resulting hiatus at the top of the Maori War Effort Organisation. The aim was to seize control of the agenda for future Crown–Maori relations, and push through the Maori Councils model (or something like it) as a means of implementing this at flax-roots level. A month after Paikea's death, politicians and officials attended a 'summit meeting' to discuss Maori wartime organisation. M R Jones and the Native Department representatives presented a draft Bill to re-establish a Maori Council system and locate it firmly in the department. The MWEO officers present at the meeting had not been consulted beforehand and they and the Maori MPs vigorously opposed the proposal. Both groupings noted that the plan 'took away the autonomy they had secured in various aspects of Maori affairs' and heavily reinserted the state into Maori decision making.

Fraser could see the dangers in circumventing the representatives of organised Maoridom, especially during a national emergency, and agreed that Maori needed to be widely consulted before any actions were taken. He upset the Native Department 'old hands' by declaring that the MWEO mechanisms could be used as legitimate conduits for passing on Maori views about the future of organised Maoridom to the government. Tribal executive committee meetings were called to consider the Maori Councils proposal. When the consultation process was completed, the Crown was notified that there had been unanimous tribal opposition to it.

Whatever the departmental misgivings about possible 'stacking' of MWEO-convened meetings, there could be no doubt about the general feeling in Maoridom.

Tirikatene had in effect taken over control of the MWEO on Paikea's death, and soon succeeded him as Member of the Executive Council Representing the Native Race. Knowing full well what the outcome of the consultation on reviving Maori Councils would be, he had quickly convened an informal 'select committee' to produce or examine alternative proposals. This looked beyond the end of the war and envisaged a post-war Maori organisation that would retain the considerable autonomy already built up. The main proposal was for a 'Ministry of Maori Welfare' to preside over a continuation of the wartime network of tribal committees and executives. Given the delicate circumstances, this plan was a paler version of the 1936 proposals for a new ministry to be the liaison and co-ordination point for *all* Crown–Maori interaction. But it did reflect the innovations of the 1940s, which seemed far more promising than the idea of breathing new life into experiments from the beginning of the century which had not proved durable.

In face of the entrenched might of the MWEO and its political backers, based as this was on popular enthusiasm for the Maori war effort, Mason and the Native Department soon made a tactical withdrawal. A final decision on Maori Councils was postponed indefinitely. In the meantime, the MWEO continued to occupy the moral high ground in its support from the Maori people. Tirikatene, Mawhete and others sought new ways of using this to extract concrete concessions in relation to the Labour Party's long-standing formal commitment to mana Maori motuhake. They began working on details of their plan for a department of state to service and enhance networks of tribally based committees. One radical proposal helped emphasise the collective basis of decision making in Maoridom: the projected Ministry of Maori Welfare would report to the combined Maori MPs. Although the plans did not call for the scrapping of the Native Department, its very existence was more than ever under adversarial scrutiny within Maoridom.

Whereas the department's primary aim was to serve the interests of the Crown, Maori continued to see the MWEO, and by extension any successor to it, as essentially *their own* organisation. This is not to say that they did not cavil at its flaws – and indeed there were increasing numbers who disagreed, for example, with its intrusion into people's lives. But the problems could be addressed in a Maori way through use of customary methods such as hui. As Maori support for continuing the MWEO in some form increased, opposition within the state grew accordingly. While Mason's Maori Councils proposal had been put on hold 'for further consideration', so too had all other proposals. This gave ministers and officials time to develop grounds for querying the need for the MWEO to continue even to the end of the war. Reasons were eagerly seized on – that the army declared it had no further need for Maori recruiting efforts, for example. By the end of 1943, both Native Department officials and their minister had begun openly arguing for the almost immediate disbanding of the MWEO. Their campaign was strengthened by the support of, in particular, the Treasury, which saw grave dangers to the fabric of the state from the continuance of an organisation that was potentially difficult to control.

The fact remained, however, that the MWEO was continuing to deliver services required during the wartime emergency, at a time when the Native Department's concentration on matters such as land develop-ment schemes had made it increasingly more reluctant and inefficient in performing many of its other allocated tasks. Among the MWEO's vocal supporters, for example, were returned servicemen who had received more (and more willing) assistance from the tribal executive committees and their community-based committee networks than from the lumbering department. Sectors within the Crown appreciated the value of MWEO work which the department could not, or would not, undertake. They also saw that to dismantle the MWEO immediately would lead to an enormous Maori backlash. The MWEO continued on, protected in particular by the Prime Minister, who had been persuaded in February 1944 to become Minister in charge of the Maori War Effort.[109]

Fraser's motives in agreeing to the additional portfolio did not, however, add up to a message of unqualified support for the MWEO. He could not ignore much advice that there was a risk to the state that the organisation might attempt to establish and perpetuate itself as a 'a state within a state'. He could now keep a closer eye on the MWEO, begin to curb those of its powers which concerned him, and if necessary intervene quickly to contain the situation. As the result of an ongoing official review, from March 1944 the MWEO was progressively instructed to truncate aspects of its operations. Some of these directions merely reflected that many of its initial purposes had been fulfilled – in July, for example, its recruiting officers were reduced from 21 to 15. But others were, in effect, instructions to keep away from matters under Native Department jurisdiction – or even to give up certain activities, including certain welfare functions, altogether.

Despite such setbacks, the Maori War Effort Organisation continued to thrive. In September 1944, for example, 51 tribal executive committees and 398 tribal committees were operating, and the figures were to peak at 61 and 407 respectively. Based as it was on communal organisation, the MWEO had developed its own internal dynamic. Since this had positive implications for the 'national good', Fraser continued to extend its life, in an implicit bargain. The state wanted to continue to use such power and energy in the 'public interest', so long as it could be restricted to outcomes desired by the Crown; Maori wished to continue working through the MWEO for the national war effort as well as for their own reasons. However many restrictions the government attempted to impose, Maori maintained their feeling of empowerment within the MWEO. Tirikatene declared that continuing control by Maori of things Maori was 'the most vital matter being discussed both generally and politically on every Maori Marae in New Zealand at the present time'.

Preparations for peacetime

In many parts of New Zealand during 1944, the MWEO held meetings to promote further flax-roots action on Maori issues, with long-term improvement in Maori governance in mind. At four conferences hosted that year by the Maori MPs, support for continuance of the organisation after the war was overwhelming. Such enthusiasm was not confined to Maori or non-official channels. Rehabilitation authorities were among those anxious to continue using the services of the Maori committees.

At the Labour Party conference in 1944, delegates adopted post-war socio-economic reconstruction proposals which included a role for such an organisation. The remaining proponents of a Maori Councils-style replacement had once again to defer the matter – in the event, permanently.

That year Tirikatene chaired a working party centred on Maori MPs which further developed the proposal for a co-ordinating ministry to be in overall charge of Maori welfare, broadly defined. Paikea had argued, just before his death, that statutory embedding of a permanent MWEO-type structure would lead to enthusiastic Maori sharing of the burden of administering their own affairs. Although there was a danger of state appropriation of Maori energies, this would be counteracted by vigilance and flax-roots energy. In any case, a limited degree of government intervention would be offset by autonomist, and other, benefits to Maori. While such ideas influenced drafts of 'Maori Social and Economic Reconstruction' legislation being shepherded by Tirikatene through the working party, the members were conscious of the need to avoid giving too much ammunition to their powerful opponents in the political and bureaucratic establishment. They therefore proposed, for example, that while the MWEO-style committees would 'retain their degree of autonomy' under a new ministry's umbrella, they should be brought 'within public service requirements'. Blueprints for the ministry were cautious.

At a 'Maori summit conference' chaired by Labour Party President Jim Roberts at Wellington's Ngati Poneke Hall on 18–20 October 1944, it was clear that the Maori MPs' concessions were insufficient to deflect widespread opposition to the legislative proposals within state circles. Fear of officially franchised committees 'running rampant' or intruding on bureaucratic patches was openly voiced. Native Department officials, in particular, at a time when their inefficiencies in farming, housing and rehabilitation were being widely criticised, were worried about their future if any kind of new ministry was established alongside them. Other officials and political advisers, while not necessarily opposing a welfare ministry to complement (or even replace) the existing department, had joined in the opposition on various grounds (including ethnocentrism and racism), concerned to counter any Maori future that enhanced state recognition of rangatiratanga.

The Prime Minister's opening address to the summit conference attempted to reconcile the two broad strands of opinion, those for and against continuation of MWEO-style autonomy. But the sheer amount of distrust within the state and the party at the ability of Maori to control their own affairs had strengthened his initial caution about the *extent* of the powers that should be entrusted to Maori organisations. His thrust was, therefore, to contain rather than mandate rangatiratanga. The committees of the Maori collective wartime endeavour should certainly be extended into the peacetime world, he declared, but the Native Department was the only appropriate medium for regulating the ongoing relationship between state and Maori. Any committee system would have to operate under its auspices and in accordance with its rules.

In his support for continuance of MWEO-style committees, the most powerful man in New Zealand's political structure had once again revealed himself to be more in empathy with Maori aspirations than many of his colleagues. But now that he had taken heed of advice that a modified MWEO under a new co-ordinating ministry was 'far too radical' for peacetime normalcy, it was clear that the organisation's current embodiment of rangatiratanga, however limited, would not be contemplated once the wartime emergency was over – not even subsumed within a new Ministry of Maori Welfare/Administration. But the mood of the more than 400 Maori representatives at the summit was clear from the beginning: the principle for post-war indigenous reconstruction should be that Maori had control over Maori affairs.[110]

Thus the delegates responded vigorously to the Fraser 'compromise', knowing that a Native Department-controlled structure for the MWEO's successor committees would largely neutralise the collective power that Maori had been rebuilding under the umbrella of the state. While his proposal was, in their eyes, greatly preferable to the draft Maori Councils Bill which Mason was still promoting whenever he could, they still resoundingly rejected it. Not only that, they also rejected the compromises of the Maori MPs, demanding *more* power for the tribal and executive committees than they currently exercised. This would provide 'permanence and increased effectiveness to the Maori tribal and racial unity in the service of our race and of our country'.

In what was becoming a disparate debate, such stark differences between the delegates and those associated with government, Parliament and bureaucracy helped focus attention on fundamentals. On the one hand, Maori were attempting to transcend the paradigm of undivided sovereignty, and most felt that an enhanced MWEO system was a suitable starting-point for a collectivity-oriented future. Through the delegates, Maoridom was telling its MPs, and the government supported by most of its people, that anything less would be unacceptable. On the other hand, the politico-bureaucratic mainstream, while appreciating that Maori collectivism could not only not be ignored but might even be harnessed, wanted to claw back many of the powers Maori had gained during the wartime emergency. Insofar as Maori communal energies could be endorsed, they were to be placed and controlled firmly within the indivisible sovereignty that the government saw as being embedded in Article One of the Treaty of Waitangi. Whatever Article Two meant, it could not be interpreted as encompassing in the medium or long term even MWEO-style rangatiratanga.

Officials and politicians, buoyed by the Prime Minister's support for the Native Department to take over the tribal committee network, began to explore ways of taming Maoridom by this means. The exploration became intertwined with an incipient debate on 'urban drift'. There was an increasing feeling in some state circles that the wartime movement of young Maori to the urban centres might prove difficult to reverse. With Native Department officials continuing to view the future of Maoridom as suppliers of rural product and labour, this was perceived as problematic. Some advisers, however, began to believe that reversal of the urban migration might not be *desirable*. The fact that Maori were mingling with pakeha in large towns and cities, well away from their tribal support mechanisms, could have the result of weaning them from tribalism – a major step en route to the elusive goal of assimilation.

Few officials as yet advocated active encouragement of permanent urbanisation, but some believed that positive results might flow if the state took a hands-off approach. If younger Maori wanted to opt for the 'civilisation' and work prospects of the cities rather than the constraints of the marae, the political economy would be helped. Welfare payments for rural dwellers unable to make a living off the land would be avoided, internal migrants could contribute to an industrialising national workforce and the processes of hegemony would be enhanced. That permanent urbanisation would lead to detribalisation, and therefore assimilation, became an increasing theme in public and official discussion. Some of those advocating the benefits to the nation of such a development believed that continuance of strong MWEO-style institutions would hinder indigenous urbanisation, postpone the loosening of tribal bonds and impede the Crown's long 'civilising project'. While the assimilationist agenda could accommodate some 'interesting trappings' of 'native culture', the continuing existence of tribally based institutions with significant autonomy was not conducive to 'Maori progress'. If there *had* to be some form of official Maori committees, these should be confined to the rural areas where, as *tribal* committees, their negative impact on progress towards full assimilation might be minimised.

Such incipient rethinking took place amid longer-standing consider-ations. If collective tribal grievances could be ameliorated, for example, assimilation might speed up even in rural areas. In particular, the continuation of tribally based demands for Crown recompense for past injustices remained a major roadblock on the route to an assimilationist future. With the end of the war seemingly in sight, such demands should be addressed. Doing so might even be sufficient to subdue opposition to the Crown's hobbling of the MWEO and its successor organisation. Government representatives at the 1944 summit conference had therefore made some concessions on settling historical grievances, and these made a favourable impact on delegates.

But the fact remained that the overwhelming demand of the summit conference was for substantial Maori autonomy in the future, building on the semi-autonomy of the MWEO. Overarching this, but related to it, was the renewed feeling of the potential of power through 'close-knit unity' which had permeated much of Maoridom. The MWEO was clearly being increasingly seen as an emergent form of kotahitanga revival. The summit delegates' strong self-identification with such developing unity, however, served to heighten the government's alarm. Unity was desirable for certain state purposes, but only if it were containable; a kotahitanga that was an aggregation of more or less autonomous bodies, even if they were technically under state auspices, could 'get out of hand'. State decision makers were the more determined, then, that the wartime institutions, thrown up autonomously, appropriated by the state and then in some ways reappropriated by Maori, should be brought firmly under Crown control and partially disempowered.

The Native Department had continued assiduously to lay the groundwork for such developments. It had put much effort into working on ways of gradually taking back, or taking over, functions performed by the tribal executive committees and their community-based committees. In September 1944, for example, the department had begun to strike back against MWEO encroachment into the welfare area. While it had been prepared to devolve welfare activities to the proposed Maori Councils, now that these were highly unlikely to eventuate it had created the position of chief welfare officer. A veteran of the Maori Battalion, Major Te Rangiataahua Royal, was appointed to the position, and quickly began developing a structure by which the Native Department would handle all indigenous welfare functions. By 1945, the department's welfare work was already expanding greatly, its officers working closely with other Crown agencies interested in Maori welfare. Mason was soon ready to present the plans for a Native Department welfare branch whose operational purview looked very much like the welfare functions of the MWEO. In mid-year Tirikatene noted that the MWEO, bereft of the state-funded resources of the department, was steadily being squeezed out of social welfare.

The MWEO attempted to meet such challenges in various ways. Many of its members and supporters believed that, in view of the political leadership's clear intention to place their institutional network under the Native Department, it was time to fight with gloves off. They openly called for the old bureaucracy to be disbanded and replaced by a co-ordinating body that would be an umbrella for autonomous flax-roots organisations as well as a more efficient and empathetic all-purpose department of state for Maori affairs. This was a rearguard action with risks. When – as seemed the most likely scenario – the MWEO committees came under Native Department control, critics in them could scarcely expect sympathetic treatment from those they had adjudged to be wanting.

The best that the pro-autonomy forces could realistically hope for was to protect the concept of a communally based committee system and ensure that central bureaucratic control over it was of relatively moderate degree. With increasing numbers of Maori coming to realise this, and so becoming more conciliatory, the Maori MPs presented new proposals which embodied greater compromise than the blueprints presented to the summit conference. In doing so they hoped to gain (no doubt, grudging) acceptance from the anti-MWEO milieu within the party (whose rhetoric was generally that of the Labour imperative of 'equality') as well as from those fighting on for a significant degree of Maori popular control, despite the intensification of the struggle on these issues between Maori and Crown. In the event they satisfied few on either side, debate raged on, and the MPs continued to work on watering down their proposals in an effort to get official endorsement of at least some kind of flax-roots involvement in Maori affairs of state. When the war ended in August 1945, a decision on the long and hotly debated issue of the future of the Maori War Effort Organisation could be delayed no longer.[111]

CHAPTER EIGHT

LIMITING RANGATIRATANGA
AFTER WORLD WAR TWO

The Maori Social and Economic Advancement Act

By the end of the war, Tirikatene had consulted widely and persuaded many Maori that sacrifice was needed if the wartime gains were to be in any way preserved. He convened a Maori working group drawn from different parts of the country and, as a result, on 20 September 1945 sent the Prime Minister yet another compromise proposal. His new draft Maori Social and Economic Reconstruction Bill attempted to replicate the tribal committee and tribal executive system, but within a departmental structure very similar to the existing Native Department. This Department of Maori Administration would in effect be the old Native Department with new co-ordinating and other powers, but there would also be wide scope for flax-roots influence on decision making.

The proposed legislation was designed to meet both Labour's 'equality' imperatives, through focusing on promoting rapid socio-economic development, and Maori desires to run their own affairs. While Tirikatene and his fellow Maori MPs knew that it was unrealistic to expect the existing Native Department administrators to be discarded, they stressed that many needed to relearn their roles or take up new functions. In particular, the ethos of the new department would need to incorporate the 'self administration and discipline' which Maori had demonstrated in the war. Building on the successes of the MWEO, he emphasised to the Prime Minister, would mean that both Maori and the state benefited – and therefore the whole nation.

In particular, it was crucial that the reconstituted bureaucracy heed the views of Maori at community and marae level, via tribal committees. The draft legislation provided for each of these to select two delegates to a tribal executive, as with the MWEO. But the executive in turn would elect a delegate to one of four district councils. The latter were to be a senior-level mechanism for passing flax-roots views onto the country's decision makers, and so would also contain representatives from the bureaucracy and Parliament. Each district council would elect two of the members of a Board of Maori Social and Economic Reconstruction, which would also include officials and politicians.

At officials' level, the new structure would be given wider terms of reference than the Native Department. Key MWEO functions would be added, and enhanced by the appointment of officers assigned to liaise between department and people. Government insistence on full accountability to head office by the community-based parts of the department was met, but there was a *quid pro quo*: the Crown would amply resource the tribal committees and their superior bodies, in contrast to the wartime emergency committees, Maori Councils and other such bodies in the past. Government resourcing was seen by some as a risk to autonomy, but measures to prevent undue head office or political leverage by this route were planned.

It was a big compromise from a Maori perspective, for it in effect endorsed continuation of the Native Department bureaucracy under a new name and in a powerful position over the network of Maori committees. In the eyes of those in the political ascendancy, however, the draft Bill had not sufficiently departed from previous proposals which 'clearly placed the future authority in the hands of Maori controlled organisations'. Mason, in charge of planning Maori reconstruction, vetoed the Bill as a government measure. However, he and senior Native Department officials could see that continued Maori non-co-operation with the Maori Councils proposal had doomed that as a viable alternative. The draft Bill alone was on the drawing board, and time was tight.

After consulting with his inner circle, Mason announced that he and his staff would set about forging a state-acceptable compromise out of the Maori compromise. While they claimed to be working on modifying Tirikatene's proposed legislation, in fact they were fitting it and aspects of the MWEO organisation into the framework of their own Bill (although without consulting the MWEO or the Maori MPs). The redrawn Bill which emerged was therefore closer to the Maori Councils draft legislation than to that of the Tirikatene's working group. In essence, the minister was promoting a 'compromise', based on his own 1943 plans, to counteract a Maori 'compromise' that still embodied elements of the fundamental concept of the MWEO – community control of Maori affairs. The title of the new draft had replaced 'Reconstruction' with 'Advancement'. The latter looked towards a fully assimilationist future, in contrast to the former's implication of reconstituting elements of Maori socio-political organisation. The Native Department was to stay. While it was to be formally charged with co-operating with tribes, in essence it was to survive intact, with the 'old hands' firmly guiding Maori towards a non-Maori future. The Maori MPs' plans for regional and national representative bodies had been rejected, removing any high-level means of co-ordinating pressure on the government from official institutions with aspirations for rangatiratanga.

However, while the Mason draft removed Tirikatene's proposal for higher representation, its authors could not avoid retaining a network of tribal committees and a layer of what were now called 'tribal executives' above them. It differed from the working group's version of these, however. Survival of the old department had been inevitable in some form after the Prime Minister's statement at the 1944 conference, but Tirikatene and other Maori leaders had tried to preserve a significant degree of autonomy for the community-based and executive committees. This had largely disappeared in the new draft: all committees under the scheme were to be constituent parts of the Native Department rather than coming loosely under a departmental umbrella. The key people in the new committee structure were to be the department's district officers, who would be in hands-on charge of all activities and structures in their areas. The Mason draft, moreover, omitted any mention of the proposed new board, so the old, ethnocentric Board of Native Affairs retained ultimate bureaucratic control of the committee structure.

The Fraser government opted, unsurprisingly, for Mason's Bill. Most commentaries have depicted the resulting Maori Social and Economic Advancement Act of 1945 as a 'compromise' between Maori aspirations and departmental control. But it fitted that description only insofar as

Mason and his officials had been forced to retain some aspects of the MWEO system. The new structure, to be operative from 1 April 1946 (though some institutional transitioning began at once), was thus essentially a victory for the old bureaucracy. More broadly, it represented a triumph for the many in governing circles and pakeha society who opposed the prospect of the MWEO's evolution into a peacetime embodiment of rangatiratanga. The tribal committees that were to form part of the Native Department were not given the politically led task of exercising 'comprehensive economic and social power', as Maori had asked. Instead, they gained very limited powers, mostly in connection with 'Maori well-being and perpetuating Maori culture'. The tribal executives could promulgate by-laws on such matters as sanitation, health and housing, fishing grounds and water reticulation, but these powers were similar to those of the 1900 legislation.

Yet most analyses tend to see the Act as an 'enlightened' drawing upon of the MWEO experience, an attempt to 'recognise officially and standardise the procedure of [previous] unofficial councils of elders . . . in most Maori communities'. More critical accounts still tend to interpret it as a *genuine* compromise. Usually reflecting wishful thinking analysis, these are inclined to regret the government's 'mistake', through accident, compromise or loss of courage, in letting pass yet another opportunity to offer a real share in governance to Maori. A 'great policy initiative' ends up as 'ultimately sterile'.[112]

It is clear, however, that the politicians acted deliberately to curb the generally successful, and therefore 'dangerous', quest for autonomy that wartime conditions had fostered. The process of incorporating the MWEO into the state's machinery had disturbed a number of Maori, either because it intervened in their personal lives or was thought to intrude on tribal rangatiratanga. Yet this process had not been enough to defuse the inherent challenge to the indivisible and ultimately assimilationist state that Maori aspirations were seen to represent. The latter were so powerful that it would have been difficult to crush the communal energies unleashed within the wartime committees, and in any case, subdued and channelled use of such energies was beneficial for state purposes. A tighter form of appropriating Maori energies, which controlled them far more than the MWEO central mechanisms had been designed or able to, had therefore been put in place. It is possible, in fact, to conclude that, at a formal level, the 1945 legislation 'appeared to give fewer powers' to Maori than had the 1900 Maori Councils Act. What can definitely be concluded is that, in the context of its times, the new Act reduced the power Maori had recently attained in the political economy. Maori reappropriations of the Crown's early wartime appropriation had themselves been incorporated into the state under stricter conditions.

The new Act, however, did require the Native Department to broaden its activities in a way that took into account the organised expression of Maori flax-roots views. The new structure, then, had some potential for Maori as well as for the state. Although they cavilled against the legislation in private, the Maori MPs praised it in public: the new MWEO-influenced organisation could be used, even in its bastardised form, to pursue rangatiratanga. The Acting Prime Minister's announcement of the new structure to Maori attempted to ensure their participation by taking just such a perspective. He endorsed a Ngataist co-existence of cultures: 'It is not for you to be as we are, but for you to be as you could and would be, with all the advantages that the Pakeha may have had.' The Maori MPs urged Maori not only to continue to participate in official committees, but to ensure that their activities were as expansive as possible within the limits laid down. To complement this, Tirikatene in particular lobbied the Native Department to tolerate broad definitions for the committees' work.

Many Maori accepted their leadership's arguments that, taking a long-term perspective, the Act represented progress for rangatiratanga. For all its inherent problems for Maoridom, the Act forced the department into a peacetime co-operation with Maori 'that would have been unthinkable in the [pre-war] years'. As with the MWEO (although within stronger constraints) a subtle expansion of permitted committee activities would quickly begin after the new structure was formally set up. It was soon noted that, whatever the government's intentions for the committees, the legislation 'seems to have empowered them to take an interest in anything at all'. Glowing contemporary Labour Party claims for the legislation reflected a not inconsiderable participatory ethos. A 1946 election campaign pamphlet proclaimed that, with the Maori Social and Economic Advancement Act, Labour's 1925 promise of mana Maori motuhake had been fulfilled. Although this assessment was highly exaggerated, it could be so boldly stated partly because Maori *had* accepted that some Crown recognition of rangatiratanga, however reluctant, had survived the war.

To conclude that the transplanted MWEO structure had, under the new legislation, 'lost its overall acceptability to the Maori people' seems too drastic. However, although the Maori MPs and other leaders urged co-operation, an immediate reaction to the legislation among many Maori was to withdraw their services from the state. A number of the existing tribal committees and tribal executive committees went into recess, or even formally disbanded, rather than reorient or subdue their energies in conformity with the requirements of a Native Department-based regime. When the department's Maori Social and Economic Welfare Organisation (soon called the Maori Welfare Organisation, or often just the welfare organisation) formally replaced the Maori War Effort Organisation, then, the committee system it inherited was considerably less impressive than the network operating during the war.

The initial wartime quest for expressing rangatiratanga in a way that assisted both Maoridom and the nation in general had remained too autonomous for the authorities to contemplate as a long-term prospect, even after it had been brought under state auspices. Parliament had seen fit, therefore, to tame it as part of the post-war reconstruction. It remained to be seen how severe was the bite of the tamed beast, and how often and under what circumstances official New Zealand would let it bite.[113]

Wartime trust board settlements

The protracted negotiations resulting from the findings of the Jones and Sim Commissions had been terminated by mutual consent with the onset of the Second World War. But tribes and Maori MPs had continued to remind the Crown that this could be only a pause in the struggle for compensation. From time to time the government, despite the demur of

·some ministers and officials, publicly reaffirmed its intention to settle eventually. The case for reparations was strengthened by the Maori contribution to the war effort. But Maori knew from experience that it was not easy extracting compensation from the Crown. Ngata was blunt in reminding Mason that, while 'the British empire' was pleased enough to accept the aid of colonised indigenes, they were still awaiting 'justice' – even in New Zealand.

Justice included some form of self-determination. Ngata was just one of many Maori leaders who warned the Crown that its propensity to appropriate successful Maori endeavours would be, in the long run, self-defeating. Any Crown takeover of Maori organisational energies would lead not to abandonment of the quest for rangatiratanga, but to its taking different forms. He recalled that, at the local level, the development schemes had often fallen into the hands of pakeha management, leaving Maori with only seasonal and labouring work on and near their tribal homelands, or migration to the urban areas, as the means of survival. His 'high spirited people', he argued, were 'disappointed in their vision of enlarged opportunities' from their land bases. Despite all the gains of the land settlement schemes, Maori had not been able to establish a series of resource bases from which they could greatly enhance the chances of realising their politico-cultural aspirations. They would strategise accordingly.

At the national level, as one response to their people's enthusiastic support of the war effort, Maori leaders had argued for at least a degree of *actual* self-determination in the future – rather than versions that had been emasculated by the Crown. They urged that tribal reparations form part of this, with adequate resources (land or otherwise) and powers given to the tribes which had been the most violated by past Crown actions. By 1943 the major tribes involved in the 1930s negotiations, empowered by favourable reaction to the Maori contribution to the war, were discussing reparations in the context of post-war reconstruction and the reconstitution of tribal fortunes. Although the Crown had consistently refused to assess claims in Treaty of Waitangi terms, some Maori sought to peg issues of extent and kind of compensation specifically to Article Two's promise of rangatiratanga. While the government might continue to dismiss such arguments, it could not ignore an increasing demand that it address the historical grievances as part of its planning for the post-war world.

With a general election looming, in June 1943 Mason and Fraser held discussions with Tirikatene and Mawhete. As a result, Mason was asked to investigate how much the tribal claims might cost – the Crown assumed that compensation would be in money. He reported back his officials' calculations in August: a total of £81,550 immediately and £17,000 annually (partly in perpetuity and the rest for specified periods). There was a possibility that some 'surplus land claims' compensation would also be needed. In view of these relatively modest sums, in the 1943 general election Labour pledged an 'early and complete settlement' of Maori claims against the Crown. At the polls the last of the non-Ratana Maori seats fell to the Labour–Ratana alliance. That it was the ubiquitous, powerful and highly respected Ngata who was ejected from Parliament was a telling indication that the Maori people preferred Labour, whatever its faults, to the conservative alternative. This was no doubt due generally to the collectivist and welfarist philosophy which had enabled Ratanaism to forge an alliance with it, but also perhaps partly to Labour's sanctioning of the MWEO's activities.

There was a lesson for Labour, however, in the ousting of an MP of such great mana, after nearly four decades of service to his people: nothing should be taken for granted in Maoridom. Even Ngata's increasing propensity to make statements on the need for the state to recognise rangatiratanga had been insufficient to save him. The Maori vote was important to the governing party, and the 1943 culmination of the 'Four Quarters' strategy reinforced appreciation among Labour politicians and their advisers that Maori demands for recompense for the Crown's 'past sins' needed to be addressed. As soon as Tirikatene had entered Cabinet, he urged that it was time for a 'final settlement' of Maori historical grievances, beginning with the longest-running major claim, that of his own Ngai Tahu. He opened discussions with Mason at once, and he and his staff worked hard to persuade ministers and other officials of the need to settle, even if only out of expediency. In 1944 Mason reopened formal negotiations.

At that year's Maori summit conference the delegates endorsed the Maori MPs' demand for rapid action over historical claims. Proposals for doing so followed clear official signals that, in the Crown's view, the trust board system was the only viable way of controlling settlement resources. Delegates agreed that boards, if properly established, could be sufficient to provide 'an avenue for the self-expression of, and the assumption of responsibility by, the Maori Race'. It was this relative moderation, along with continuing publicity for the Maori contribution to the war effort, that helped persuade the government to respond favourably on the issue of settlements. Moreover, it was willing to settle even before the war ended, so long as difficulties over which collectivities it should deal with, and which leaders had the mandate to represent them, were resolved. In light of this, many kaumatua and rangatira felt it best to forge ahead, even if offers were small, in order to take advantage of what might be only a temporary government willingness to settle.

Others demurred. Many Maori still envisaged compensation as helping to re-establish a land-based rangatiratanga. Officials had consistently advised the government that there was insufficient available Crown land for a land component to be included in the compensation packages, an argument incorporated into Mason's costing exercise. Iwi spokespeople were angrily noting that the government was readily enough able to contemplate land for rehabilitation of (mostly) pakeha returned soldiers. Even Mason was embarrassed by such a blatant double standard. By now, however, the government had finally agreed on its intentions for reparations. It had abandoned as impractical any thought of a total settlement sum into which all claims would be fitted. It had opted for precedent: tribal trust board governance, the boards receiving annual money payments (or their capitalised equivalents).

While many Maori remained unhappy about both the control and financial aspects of such packages – especially those in raupatu tribes, whose fundamental demand remained the return of ancestral land – some noted that the situation could have been far worse. Fierce disputes within various institutions of state had centred on attempts to lower the sums previously discussed or proffered. The Treasury, for example, had argued that government social welfare policies were partial recompense for the

Crown's past inflictions on Maori, and so amounts previously on the table should be lowered. The ministers had rejected such advice in favour of more realistic appraisals of likely Maori reaction, and confirmed that they would be generally guided by the Sim and, to a lesser degree, Jones Commission recommendations.

In the negotiations with tribal leaders, however, the Crown reiterated its long-standing insistence that compensation monies were essentially to be used, as well as for administration, to pursue such matters as health, education, housing and welfare. Mason, indeed, put forward a paler version of the Treasury argument. A sizeable portion of compensation monies, he stated, needed to be used as a substitute for 'other Government expenditure, possibly from the Social Security Fund'. The Crown, then, to use later Treaty parlance, was attempting to offset compensation for violations of its Article Two/rangatiratanga obligations against its Article Three/equality responsibilities to Maori. Many tribal leaders were emphatic, however, that the boards should be able to do with reparation monies whatever their people wished, subject to democratic scrutiny by their constituents. They envisaged, for example, rebuilding marae complexes as foundations for politico-cultural revitalisation.

Bearing in mind the pre-war experience of long years of negotiation, some prominent Maori leaders argued that the Crown's conditions on use of monetary compensation should be accepted. Some restrictions were both inevitable and a small price to pay if they guaranteed settlement, and in any case draconian conditions could later be alleviated through discussion or negotiation. They stressed that, however welcome a land base would be, the tribal collectivities would survive without one – and be able to use some of the reparations income to restore turangawaewae. Some even declared that there could be gains for rangatiratanga in developing the government's proposals: if welfare resources were provided, control of their distribution could be seen as reflecting at least a degree of autonomous tribal power. The point was that tribally based organisations, even if established and run under the auspices of the state, would be firmly in charge of internal resource allocation. Those who advocated quick settlements, however inadequate these might be, turned out to constitute the great majority.

One potential impediment to the settlements reflected the level at which the Crown dealt with Maori. Some hapu and sub-hapu leaders believed that the government's willingness to negotiate only with broadly based tribal entities was a violation of indigenous rights, given that most Maori collective decisions were generally at hapu or whanau level. Iwi and tribal federation leaders, however, argued that, given the Crown's history of stalling on even broadly based settlements over a long period, chances of success lay only with the tribal-wide or federal arrangements currently on tentative offer. There were other arguments as well, quite apart from practical ones relating to timeframe and other difficulties if the Crown had to deal with the large numbers of hapu. In particular, it was noted that, given the size of past offers to iwi, any realistic sub-iwi agreements could scarcely provide meaningful resources to the communities involved. Such arguments generally prevailed among the people of the tribal groupings at the forefront of the claims, as they had with those involved in the 'lakes settlements' of the 1920s, so long as – within the realms of possibility – sub-iwi groupings gained representation on the trust boards.

The first major grouping to negotiate a settlement with the government in 1944 was the iwi confederation which had already obtained an interim settlement along the lines desired by the Crown. Representatives of the Taranaki tribes discussed a Crown offer to make permanent the temporary arrangement which reflected the Sim Commission's findings. They were fully aware that these findings were from time to time heavily contested within officialdom and by politicians, and that there was a danger of this occurring once again – especially if the wartime 'spirit of co-operation' dissipated. They therefore decided to abandon their quest for compensation in land, and accept the existing £5000 a year in settlement of their grievances. They saw the payment as an annual reminder to the Crown of 'the sin' of the land confiscations, a lesson whose repetition in perpetuity would help preclude any replay of the Crown's past adversarial actions. Even Ernest Corbett, for the conservative opposition, depicted the settlement as 'a permanent recognition of the wrong' done by the Crown.

The Taranaki Maori Claims Settlement Act of December 1944

depicted the settlement as 'final'. The payments were not enough to enable major rebuilding of tribal resource bases. But the main concern of iwi members was Crown endorsement of their mana, tribal dignity and rangatiratanga. They had assessed that perpetual payments and the state's implicit acknowledgement of its breaches of tribal rights embodied these. The Crown's guilt over past wrong-doing was symbolically reinforced by an additional payment of £300 for the destruction that had resulted from the sacking of Parihaka in 1881. Tribal leaders noted that, although limitations on ways of spending the annuities remained in place, as a result of discussions considerable flexibility was possible. Mason stated when the Act was being passed that the monies could be distributed 'as visioned' by the Taranaki tribes.

Ngai Tahu had pioneered the new round of settlement talks, but its negotiations had proved problematic because of the size of the Jones Commission's lump-sum recommendation. Treasury and other officials argued that, in view (among other things) of the constrained wartime financial situation, any possible total sum for Ngai Tahu could be nowhere near the £354,000 recommended by Jones. The last figure offered had been £100,000 in 1935. As the Taranaki negotiations progressed, a relativity argument entered.

Ngai Tahu's tribulations were viewed as being of lesser magnitude than Taranaki's, since it had not experienced armed invasion, death and post-conquest confiscation at the hands of the coercive forces of the Crown. A lump sum had seemed to some iwi leaders to be an attractive proposition in principle, as it would provide development capital. However, to secure a settlement approaching Jones Commission magnitude, Tirikatene and the other tribal leaders had indicated that they were prepared to accept payment over time. The Crown accepted in principle, preferring a cut-off date to perpetual payments – so long as officials' calculations ensured that the total figure represented lesser compensation than that given Taranaki. A compromise sum of £300,000, to be paid out over 30 years, was agreed upon, pending later confirmation by the tribal communities. This was legislated into effect on the same day as the Taranaki settlement, and the Native Trustee held the monies pending creation of a reconstituted Ngai Tahu Maori Trust Board in

1946. The board's powers reflected the outcome of more negotiations, including acquiring and managing land for the benefit of its members and expenditure on projects to enhance tribal or community life.

Later, Taranaki and Ngai Tahu argued that their settlements were, in view of the magnitude of the Crown's acts and omissions, greatly inadequate – and the Crown eventually agreed. But by 1944 they had fought for a long time and the outcome of the wartime negotiations seemed the best they could get in the foreseeable future. They were certainly much better than some powerful elements within the state wanted. Ex-minister Langstone grumbled, in the context of the Ngaitahu Claim Settlement Act, that many Maori grievances were imaginary: New Zealand was 'the only country that understands how to treat its Native people'. And, in terms of the values of the times, the monies could be quite significant for the tribes and their people.

Moreover, the settlements embodied the Crown's acknowledgement that a *tribal collective* was more than just the remnant of an historical entity affected by the violations of the past. It was also the institution with which the Crown needed to develop a relationship in the future. Trust boards were recognised by law as bodies corporate representing sizeable descent-based populations. For this reason, among others, Maori saw the arrangements as Crown recognition of tribal rangatiratanga. Most tribespeople accepted (or at least did not oppose) the settlements. Makere Love, Tirikatene's private secretary, said in 1946 of the Ngai Tahu arrangement that 'no Maori land claim settlement has been so thoroughly well discussed' by its potential beneficiaries – although acceptance was no doubt influenced by the lack of an alternative offer on the negotiating table.[114]

Post-war tribal settlements

Kingitanga tribes had held out from settling with the Crown by the end of the war. As with other raupatu tribes, they had always wanted recompense based on the return of seized land. It had only been in the face of firm government rejection of land reparations that they had previously been prepared to discuss monetary compensation. Given the

Crown's wartime willingness to find farmland to settle returned servicemen, the tribal leaders had again stressed their strong preferences for compensation in land. This stymied any possibility of agreement on reparations during the course of the war. Disquiet among such an important tribal grouping was regarded as a serious impediment to post-war reconstructive progress. After the war Fraser had appointed M R Jones to be Maori Liaison Officer. He was to concentrate on overseeing implementation of the Maori Social and Economic Advancement Act, but was also named as the chief official for negotiating tribal compensation.

Despite its ability to procure lands for other purposes, the government remained adamant that money alone would be offered in settlement of grievances. This would avoid both a precedent for future settlements and demands for reopening the existing 'final' settlements. Some of the most traditional elements within Kingitanga, encouraged by the generally favourable race relations climate in wartime, argued for holding out indefinitely for Crown recognition of a version of rangatiratanga centred on return of raupatu land – and also for statutory recognition of their king as a leader of international status. Jones and his staff, however, assiduously canvassed tribal leaders with the message that land and independence were not on the agenda.

The Sim Commission's recommendation that Waikato receive a smaller annual compensation than Taranaki had been overturned long ago. If it *had* to give up its claims for land reparations, however, Kingitanga hoped to negotiate a better deal than Taranaki's. The government stressed that the sum of £5000 a year in perpetuity was the maximum possible, in view of the settlements already reached, but offered extra payments as arrears to cover the decade since parity with Taranaki had been conceded. The proposals were put to a huge hui at Turangawaewae marae at Easter 1946 by both the tribal leadership and a government team comprising Fraser, Mason and Tirikatene. Some quarters voiced opposition to such a settlement, including Ngati Maniapoto and Ngati Haua representatives; others who agreed to accept the proffered settlement pledged to continue the fight for return of confiscated land still in Crown hands. But the great majority supported what was seen as the best possible deal for the times, and the Tainui tribes generally saw the resulting Waikato–

Maniapoto Maori Claims Settlement Act as a Crown endorsement of rangatiratanga.

At the beginning of this new settlement era in the 1940s, in fact, there was great optimism among, and even some concrete gains for, the recipient iwi. Indeed, it has been said that the 'quality of life' in the Waikato 'markedly' improved as a result of the settlement. Moreover, insofar as the trust boards embodied state recognition of collective tribal control, they constituted contested territory on which rangatiratanga could be advanced (or set back) during engagement with the Crown. Tainui's board, for example, established itself at Turangawaewae House in Ngaruawahia, which had been opened as Kingite headquarters in 1919. It operated alongside and in conjunction with other Kingitanga governing institutions such as Te Kauhanganui, Te Kaumarua (kaumatua advisers to the King) and the Runanganui (council of delegates from marae committees). All were involved in Tainui's socio-political revival.[115]

From 1946, when Labour gained increased Maori votes, other outstanding claims were investigated. Further settlements were negotiated, including with Whakatohea, a tribe which had not emerged as well from the Sim Commission as others. It settled over what had been deemed to be some 'excessive' confiscation, and thus created a new precedent for tribal compensation. The Crown assessed that its reparations should be low in relation to the other raupatu tribes, and so an annual payment would not have been meaningful. A one-off lump sum of £20,000 was negotiated instead, enough to give the new tribal trust board a capital base.

Treasury and other officials, and politicians, saw this as a positive development: the slate was wiped clean in a 'discount for bulk' deal, and ongoing relations with the iwi would not be complicated by an annual monetary reminder of past events. It was a precedent for 'smaller settlements' for tribes in the negotiating queue. Over time, these negotiations led to other lump-sum reparation payments. In 1949 it was agreed, for example, that £20,000 should go to the Wairoa Maori Trust Board in compensation for transactions over the Kauhouroa Block. In the following year compensation of £38,000 and £50,000 was negotiated with regard to the Patutahi and Aorangi Blocks.

Annuity and lump-sum reparations did not mean that tribes had abandoned their quest to expand turangawaewae, whether or not the Crown and Parliament billed settlements as 'full and final'. In 1949, for example, a significant claimant hui had reiterated that, ideally, land should be provided in compensation for past losses. But the government's only concession had been to allow trust boards to operate commercially with regard to land: if tribes wanted to rebuild land holdings, they could purchase on the open market when properties became available, even if these were Crown lands that had become surplus to state requirements. But such purchases were seldom within reach, even for iwi with settlement incomes.

Trust boards were charged with providing, from their settlement monies, a broad range of services for their people, including social and economic welfare, education and health. Although the tribes hoped to do all this and more, particularly financing politico-cultural revival, in the long run they were able to provide few social services except for some welfare and educational assistance to individuals. The realities of the situation meant, for example, that Tainui's board could not begin to develop a commercial focus until the 1970s, and this was made possible only by negotiating capitalisation of 20 years' worth of the annual grant. But, in general, the results of renegotiations were of little import. When inflation made the various trust board incomes of little value, the state conceded no more than small annuity rises and the perpetualising of Ngai Tahu's payments.

Compensation payments, then, provided the trust boards with little more than basic monies to run tribal affairs and enhance their politico-cultural dimension as best they could, and beyond that to provide assistance to needy or deserving tribal members. As officially sanctioned institutions, under trustee law and various legislative provisons the boards had obligations as well as powers, and these added to their difficulties. In 1955, moreover, the trust board system was consolidated and further regulated by the Maori Trust Boards Act. Despite Crown control over their activities, however, the boards continued to be seen by many Maori as representing a significant degree of official recognition of tribally based collective autonomy.

Conversely, the government had hoped that settling with the tribes which had the largest and most persistent grievances would be sufficient to remove some major remaining blockages to assimilating Maori into the dominant culture and the capitalist economy; concomitantly, they would be assisted to move gradually towards socio-economic parity with pakeha within the welfare state. Maoridom welcomed efforts to close the disparities in living standards between the two peoples. But it reiterated that it wanted more than this, including both freeing up the trust boards and Crown recognition of mechanisms of autonomy for those many tribes which lacked boards.

The Maori summit conference of 1944 had requested investigation of all remaining grievances as part of redefining the place of Maori in post-war society. Official representatives had been obliged to take note, leading to a greater impetus for various tribes to press their claims. The government finally met such pressure by establishing what had been discussed for a long time: a general commission into grievances that were not already settled or on the negotiating table. But this would focus on the 'surplus lands' issue, involving those lands which had been deemed not to have been validly purchased from Maori before annexation, but the ownership of which had been assumed by the state rather than being passed back to the original Maori owners. Many other claims had been deemed to be insignificant or 'frivolous' by officials, and the government had generally accepted their advice. When the commission was announced on 5 October 1946, therefore, it had limited terms of reference. This was greeted with anger by Maori, and the Crown was forced to announce that other claims with *prima facie* substance would not be overlooked. In 1947 it specifically added some new claims to the work of the 'Surplus Lands Commission'.

Many grievances, however, continued to remain outside the state's interest. And, in the event, the commission's findings and subsequent Crown actions were far from satisfying for the various claimant groups. The commissioners had 'followed a well established pattern of not using historians to thoroughly investigate the circumstances surrounding the early purchases', and they recommended low levels of compensation. The small tribal reparation payments which resulted from negotiations reflected the continued lack of Crown knowledge of and empathy with tribal grievances. This did not augur well for an ideal relationship between kawanatanga and rangatiratanga. But it needs to be balanced by the fact that some tribes considered that they had made significant gains in reclaiming a degree of autonomy before and during the period of post-war reconstruction. While some hopes had been dashed, others had been partly fulfilled, and this had fortified many Maori in their 'struggle without end': 'ka whawhai tonu matou'.[116]

Post-war social policy

As the end of the war had approached, the government turned its attention to socio-economic revival. Elements within the state were increasingly realising that this was not unproblematic in terms of indigenous policy. Over a decade, the number of Maori living in urban areas had doubled. It had been generally expected that most Maori who went to the cities and big towns for wartime purposes, or overseas with the military, would return to their tribal homeland areas. But the land-based Maori development schemes were insufficient to sustain the rising Maori population which had stayed in rural areas, let alone provide an economic base for a mass return of urban dwellers and former soldiers. The cities, moreover, required cheap labour for a country gearing itself for greater economic diversity, and their social life attracted people whose horizons had been extended by wartime travel. Thus, both 'push' and 'pull' factors meant that movement back to the tribal rohe was considerably less than anticipated.

Maori leaders, uneasy about the implications for tribal cohesion and progress if large numbers of their young people were to stay permanently in the urban areas, were not alone in their worries. Some state authorities had begun welcoming the trend to urban relocation as leading towards assimilation, but many others were concerned about the possible destabilising consequences of *rapid* change. A senior magistrate in Auckland in 1945 was just one of the commentators concerned about a 'serious Maori problem' in the biggest urban area. There had been, it was believed, too swift a transition from rural to urban, creating a problem that was likely to be more than ephemeral. While the government continued largely to see Maori as a rural people, the demographic trend towards urbanisation, and its consequent problems, led sections within the state increasingly to promote social and economic development for Maori people *wherever* they were. It was felt that state links with tribal headquarters should be, if anything, reducing in favour of diversified interaction with Maori.

This trend in official thinking was a logical outcome, in any case, of the government's 'equality'-based policies. Reducing socio-economic disparities would improve the lot of Maori as individuals. There would be benefits for their existing institutions along the way, but this was not the Crown's major intention or priority. A smooth arrangement of socio-economic life in New Zealand, the modern effecting of the 'order and regularity' that had been the state's overriding imperative ever since 1840, could be best achieved in Maori policy by building on the founding principles of the Labour Party. Devolving a degree of self-determination to tribal groupings was not integral to this, although expedience decreed it was necessary in some circumstances and to some degree. The thrust of the Crown's intention towards Maori was in the opposite direction: the pace of assimilation was to be quickened.

At the 1946 Labour Party Conference, Fraser reinforced this general assimilationist strategy by reiterating that 'full equality' was the hallmark of the party's Maori policy. The ramifications were considerable, quite apart from the overt issue of the potential negative impact on tribal rangatiratanga. Implementing 'equality', for example, could manifest itself in assimilationist ways that had no place for positive discrimination policies aimed at removing systemic inequalities. When the National Employment Service was established in 1946, there was neither differentiation between Maori and non-Maori nor even Native Department involvement. The decision makers had wanted a close interrelationship between the methods and the goal of full employment for all citizens. But some Maori noted that the tangata whenua's initial disadvantage could well be perpetuated by a system which did not pay special attention to their needs and circumstances.

Debates on full assimilation and its connection with urbanisation had been mostly speculative and tentative through to the immediate post-war years. While waiting for political and demographic trends to firm up, many of the Maori affairs policy makers seemingly continued to operate on the premise (or the hope) that 'urban drift' would prove to be a temporary phenomenon, and that the department's focus should therefore remain firmly on rural Maori. As the end of the wartime emergency approached, they (along with some leading tribally based Maori, including Ngata) made plans to concentrate their energies more intensely than ever on land development. Responding to the fears of social dislocation caused by urbanisation, some even began to work on 'back to the land' incentives.

As it turned out, the main disagreement with a land thrust for 'Maori policy' came from the National Employment Service itself, a department little influenced by official sub-cultural supposition and wishful thinking from the past. Its officials argued that a serious lack of employment for Maori in rural areas was imminent, and that the state should therefore take positive action to help actually or potentially affected individuals to adjust to the realities of post-war New Zealand. Among other things, new educational and vocational opportunities, and initiatives geared to other than the requirements of farm development and labouring, needed developing. At the end of 1947, an interdepartmental education and employment committee was established to explore possible solutions. In the event, policy developments which emphasised the individuals constituting Maoridom, rather than Maori grouped as rural collectivities, proved to be of greater overall economic benefit to tangata whenua than the relatively static policies of the 'old Native hands'.

Yet the Native Department, whatever its predictive and policy faults, had continued to understand that tribally based rangatiratanga did remain significant in Maoridom. The government knew, too, that the relatively unified Maori contribution within the wartime national consensus had been posited on the old tribal structures. Although the official emphasis was now increasingly on equality for all citizens, and some state sectors saw that changing Maori demographics required rethinking policies, ministers were reminded of the ongoing significance to Maori of their tribal links by Maori affairs policies and structures. Post-war reconstruction policy needed to involve continuing use of tribal energies, as well as non-tribal policy developments. The tribal committees and tribal executives to be established under the Maori Social and Economic Advancement Act, however far short they fell from what was desired by Maori, would be important for both Crown and tribes.

Fraser declared that the Act's structures were to be 'as self-controlling and autonomous as possible'. The caveat 'as possible' was scarcely noticed at the time or by later commentators, but it was of considerable significance when placed alongside other qualifying remarks. In particular, the welfare organisation needed to be 'always stipulating for efficiency', a criterion envisaged in terms of 'equality', 'national good' and (ultimately) assimilation. There were people, both Maori and pakeha, who had been arguing that that there was no inherent incompatibility between rangatiratanga (or Maori 'race consciousness') and the 'progressive' politics of the labour movement, but their voices tended to be increasingly drowned out.

The state's weightier involvement in the Maori Welfare Organisation than in its wartime predecessor reflected an ongoing assessment that too permissive a regime for the committees could lead to indigenous developments that were hard to control. Fundamentally, such a fear had underpinned rejection of the original proposals for building on the MWEO structure. Official endorsing of a Maori committee network did acknowledge that the powerhouses of Maori decision making were collective and tribal in orientation. But, given that the welfare organisation's locally based and executive committees would both be securely incorporated into Native Department structures and their activities monitored and controlled by departmental officers, the tribes, sub-tribes and marae organisations were denied ultimate control of decision making.

Despite the missing dimension of rangatiratanga, for Maori there was no viable political alternative to the ruling party, and they were well aware that they had made considerable socio-economic gains under it. Few demurred when the 1946 Labour Party election pamphlet 'The Maori Way of Life' lauded Maori progress under social democracy. At a formal level, moreover, there was still talk of some form of self-determination. That year the party even pledged that its policies would fulfil 'the self government of the Maori'. Tangata whenua flocked to vote Labour in the knowledge that, however far practice fell short of rhetoric, the party continued to offer much more than the National Party opposition. Because of the government's Maori policies, in fact, danger of a pakeha backlash was in the air.

With the parties split 38–38 in the general constituencies following the 1946 election, the four Ratana–Labour Maori MPs were depicted in the media and by National as holding the balance of power, Labour retaining office via a 'Maori mandate'. This was not strictly correct, as Labour held the four most marginal seats and all were in the general constituencies. But the perception was that Maori were propping up the government and extracting a price for their political support. Because this was politically damaging for Labour, in turn it became problematic for tangata whenua aspirations, with the government under increasing pressure to distance itself from any 'pandering' to Maori 'political blackmail'.[117]

The Maori Welfare Organisation

The machinery that had been established by the Native Department to rival MWEO welfare activities had become the base for departmental 'social and economic advancement' operations under the 1945 Act. M R Jones, overseer of the Act, had been instrumental in the efforts to revive the Maori Councils rather than build on the relative spontaneity of the MWEO. He had then become a powerful player in superimposing a Maori Councils ethos upon Tirikatene's draft legislation. The establishment period for the new structure did not augur well for the future of even a 'second best' rangatiratanga. Implementation of the legislation was slow and lacklustre. Keynote positions in the new organisation were given to career public servants, rather than (as many had hoped) to individuals who had helped ensure the wartime success of the MWEO.

A Maori scholar summed up the implementation of the Maori Social and Economic Advancement Act: the 'heat and spirit of the Maori War

Effort Organisation was discarded in favour of the orthodoxy of the Native Department'. The situation was worsened by a lack of resources for 'Maori Welfare'. The Minister of Finance, Walter Nash, was mindful of the need for reconstructive austerity, and his philosophical opposition to differential treatment between 'races' reinforced the scarcity of government funds available to set up and run the system. Even within the limits of Labour's truncated version of meeting Maori aspirations, the government's performance was widely criticised by tangata whenua.

Such criticism increased after the opposition's 'Maori mandate' campaign led the government to place the welfare organisation on an even tighter rein than it might otherwise have been. After the 1946 general election, with Mason's performance on Maori issues under scrutiny, pressure came from senior departmental officers for the Prime Minister to take over the Native Affairs portfolio. This was partly to ensure that the Maori MPs did not take control of the portfolio through their nominee, Tirikatene. This would have boosted the collective profile of 'the Maori Caucus' and encouraged the official committees to try to claw back some of the relative autonomy of operation that they had exercised through the MWEO. The officials' suggestion of Fraser's overlordship of Maori policy and operations, then, was intended to reduce the potential influence of rangatiratanga.

There would also be an upside for Maori. Prime ministerial mana would shelter the portfolio from public attack, and Fraser was generally considered to be empathetic with Maori wishes. In view of the mana involved, there was popular as well as official Maori support for the Prime Minister to take on the task. Jones expressed the views of many in feeling that Fraser 'governed with his heart rather than his head' on Maori issues. While some disagreed, he clearly did have a degree of empathy with Maori aims (especially socio-economic 'uplift'); and he had not been fully satisfied with Mason's handling of the welfare organis-ation. He agreed to take up the portfolio and, unlike Savage, did not delegate responsibility for Crown–Maori relations to a minister with less interest. On balance, Maori believed, they had gained from the situation.

Fraser relied heavily for welfare organisation policy advice on Jones, who, though closely involved in Langstone's and Mason's policies, had also moved in Ngataist circles. As a result, the person steering the welfare organisation was becoming influenced by Ngata's and others' increasing belief that (inevitable) assimilationist tendencies needed strong counter-balancing by rangatiratanga. It was on Jones' advice that Fraser agreed to take on the new ministerial responsibility. He worked at once with the new minister to push through semantic changes symbolic of Crown recognition of the mana of Maoritanga. Replacing the 'Native Minister' in December 1946, Fraser became 'Minister of Maori Affairs'. From January 1947 his department became the Department of Maori Affairs. The word 'native', in fact, was to be removed from official discourse as having demeaning implications. In the following year Fraser, in the face of (pakeha) bureaucratic opposition, appointed Tipi Ropiha to the position of under-secretary of the department, the first Maori to head a department of state.

While such developments indicated a degree of state accommodation of Maori aspirations, however, the 'Maori bureaucracy' was generally able to operate much as before. The welfare organisation represented an addition of functions to the department, rather than a change in institutional culture. The incorporation of some MWEO attributes and personnel into the department was actively resented in some of its corridors, especially at head office in Wellington. While some efforts were made to thwart the organisational transfer of Maori wartime energies to peacetime reconstruction, however, in most departmental quarters the initial fears of 'excessive' flax-roots influence were quickly allayed when the small amount of rangatiratanga involved was revealed.

The ethos of the department remained, then, firmly assimilationist rather than autonomist, with professional bureaucrats in control of the welfare organisation activities. In turn, as the department noted in 1949, the welfare organisation 'gives general direction to [all of] the activities' of the Maori Social and Economic Advancement Act. Its three dozen paid welfare officers were the key individuals within the 22 zones established under the legislation. The chief welfare officer, Royal, had been assigned to assist Jones in establishing the welfare organisation and setting its operating parameters. In 1946 he became, in the terms of the Act, Controller of Maori Welfare.

Royal's style was very much that of the military from which he had emerged, in contrast to the participatory methods of the MWEO. He had publicly doubted the viability of parts of the 1945 Act which depended on MWEO-style organisation, particularly those concepts of community empowerment which had, in theory, survived the transition to the welfare organisation. As the key implementer of the Act alongside Jones, he was instrumental in stamping the departmental brand on the new regional and local structures. Furthermore, through careful selection of the welfare organisation's permanent staff he created a section of the department in his own image. The list of welfare officials reportedly 'read like a who's who of the [Maori] battalion', people used to giving or receiving orders. While they were attached to tribal executives, they were clearly defined as Native/Maori Affairs officers. Indeed, they were 'not responsible in any formal sense' to tribal or sub-tribal groupings.

Since their task was, however, to promote 'race uplift', at least some (military background or not) saw themselves as responsible to 'the people' (usually through their relationship with tribal committees) as well as to the controller. This did not accord with departmental wishes, and some of them quickly ran into difficulties. Their first point of tension was generally with the departmental officials in charge of the seven districts into which the country was divided, through which all communication between the field and head office had to pass.

The department emphasised decision making by officialdom, rather than government participation in, response to or tolerance of flax-roots policy formation. With the welfare organisation's committee network placed so firmly within the department, even the small number of autonomist-leaning 'compromises' inherent in the Act were rapidly being compromised. There was, however, a group of ministers who, for various reasons, wanted the organisation to involve the Maori communities in meaningful ways – at the very least by listening to their concerns and ideas and investigating them. For some, this was a matter of expedience. Fraser himself had several motivations, including appreciation of the wartime effectiveness of the MWEO committees as social control agencies. On taking up the Maori affairs portfolio, he declared that the department had been too negative towards consultation with, or even popular participation by, Maori. By the department drawing the line in the wrong place, where it did not fully reflect the intentions of the legislators, efficiency had suffered.

Affinity with subjugated people may have influenced Fraser's assessment of departmental performance; he had reportedly 'never forgotten the experience of the crofters' being dispossessed in his native Scotland. In early 1947, dismayed at the domination of the welfare organisation by the department which he found on taking up the portfolio the previous December, he ordered compliance with the tribally based participatory ethos that had supposedly underpinned the formal structures and functions of the Maori Social and Economic Advancement Act. In short, Maori communities were to be involved in its implementation without delay. Welfare officers in the Department of Maori Affairs were to be akin to the recruiting and liaison officers of the MWEO system, the crucial link between government and people, not superior officials supervising subordinates. They were to implement a genuine two-way flow of information and advice rather than act as nothing more than departmental control agents.[118]

That the 'Maori Social and Economic Welfare Organisation must not be looked upon as merely another branch of the Maori Department' was scarcely a message welcomed in mainstream officialdom. But it gave heart to committee members – and to those welfare officers who were not content to be mere implementers of state-imposed ways of doing things in Maori communities. Yet all still had to operate under an Act that considerably constrained marae or tribally based initiative. The administrative districts followed Maori Land Court boundaries, which were often contentious within Maoridom. The world of the district officers and that of officials in the bureaucratic layer beneath was essentially a pakeha one. The Maori presence operated mostly at the voluntarist level of the tribal committees and the tribal executives.

With the latter, however, there were some problems from a rangatiratanga perspective. Although the tribal executives comprised two representatives from each committee, for example, the boundaries of the areas they oversaw did not necessarily reflect what were, in iwi and hapu eyes, appropriate groupings. Even some tribal executive members argued that the only authentic representative voices in the entire welfare organisation network were those of the marae-based tribal committees. Furthermore, as well as flaws in tribal executive boundaries and mandating, the absence of the high-level representational machinery (district councils, and roles for Maori MPs) that had been envisaged in Tirikatene's Bill impeded further development within the welfare organisation of the wartime kotahitanga which had flourished within the MWEO.

The Prime Minister would frequently state that the organisation's committees were to be as 'independent', 'self reliant' and 'autonomous as possible'. But the fact remained that the only part of the hierarchy with a relatively uncontested claim properly to represent sections of the Maori people, the voluntarist tribal committees, comprised the lowest level of a bureaucratic hierarchy run firmly from Wellington. Whatever Fraser said or believed, the tribal committees and tribal executives were integral parts of the Maori Affairs hierarchy, and its paid officials chose to highlight the caveats he attached to his words about the supposed autonomy of committees – that they were to be independent 'to a very large extent' and only to be as separate 'as possible' from the professional bureaucracy.

And so 'instructions' to the various sections of the welfare organisation went out frequently from the Maori Affairs head office, via its district officers, often after little or no consultation with the flax-roots. Before long the welfare officers were being (in the words of the historians of Maori Affairs) 'treated as the pack horses for other divisions of the Department', rather than – as they had expected to do – mediating between community initiatives and head office and government responses. The equine analogy derived from Fraser, who in 1948 instructed that the department discontinue treating its welfare officers as 'pack-horses' for carrying all manner of Maori Affairs requirements into the community. The minister would, from time to time, lament that departmental attitudes tended to 'nullify the purpose of the legislation'. As late as September 1949, not long before the general election that ousted Labour, he was warning that it was important that the welfare organisation should not be absorbed by the department. But, as an embattled Prime Minister at a time when Labour was losing political ground to both right and left, he had little time or energy to intervene, beyond occasional guideline pronouncements.

In any case, Fraser's public attitude was somewhat disingenuous. While it does seem that he was genuinely frustrated that the welfare organisation constituted little more than 'merely another branch' of the department, this amounted to being hoist with his own petard. It was his own government's choice to support departmentally inspired legislation, rather than opt for the 'compromise' produced by the Maori MPs and their supporters. Moreover, he had been at the political head of the process which gave the existing bureaucracy the opportunity to reshape the former MWEO system into an approximation of its own image. This had not been an accidental development. The fact was that the Prime Minister's idea of the appropriate role for Maori in relation to the state fell far short of the rangatiratanga sought by most tangata whenua, including his own Maori MPs.

Yet from the government's point of view, departmental control of the subordinate levels of the welfare organisation came to pose problems. In particular, Fraser and some ministers came to regret the opportunities for paid officials to be highly interventionist and prescriptive. One consequence was that the processes established by and under the Maori Social and Economic Advancement Act did not prove an effective way for the political executive to hear the views of the flax-roots. Some politicians and officials, at least, realised that it was important for the politico-bureaucratic centre to know what Maori in the communities were thinking, if only to anticipate future difficulties. Other appreciated that Maori should handle their own affairs, albeit 'with assistance from government officials to back them up when required'. The Education Department's Superintendent of Child Welfare had noted during the war years that 'the Maoris themselves must be given a large share in the responsibility of providing for the betterment of families'. The system did not encourage this. And the lack of higher representative bodies in the welfare organisation meant that Maori views were usually interpreted to central government, if at all, through briefings by departmental officers. Many of these had preconceived institutional and cultural perspectives, or career imperatives, which precluded them from being able or willing to pass on critical or autonomist views from within Maoridom.[119]

Politics, autonomy and welfare

While Fraser's stated wishes for a degree of self-determination for Maori were thwarted by the legislation and its implementation, his Maori caucus continued to work assiduously for rangatiratanga. With the wartime emergency over, Ratanaism might have been expected to revert to non-tribal operation. Its formal and centralised institutions (Te Komiti Kura for education, Te Komiti a Iwi/The People's Committee, and Te Komiti Marae for local organisation) were already constituted on that basis. However, the movement appreciated that the vigour needed to get things done lay at the local level – which often meant, in reality, a strong tribally based infusion. The self-supporting and autonomous Ratanaist committees at community level resembled those which had underpinned the MWEO (and now, to some extent, the welfare organisation), with their strong tribal resonance. There was often co-operation and overlap between Ratana and official committees. More broadly, the Maori Social and Economic Advancement Act had taken, via the Maori MPs' wordings at drafting stage, some of its operating principles from practices on Ratana marae, helping lock the movement's political leadership into its structures and processes.

Ratanaism's flax-roots activities formed a non-official mass base for the movement's centralised attempts to strategise and co-ordinate action on issues pertaining to 'Maori progress'. The Ratana–Labour caucus in Parliament continued to push for a special Maori co-ordinating department of state, to focus now on *fully* exploring all possibilities in implementing the 1945 legislation. It would report to Tirikatene, who, however marginalised he might be in governing circles, had retained his membership of the Executive Council and the designation 'Minister Representing the Maori Race'. The Ratana–Labour MPs continued to stress to their own government that Maori harboured 'antagonistic feelings' towards a Department of Maori Affairs whose institutional culture was antithetical to community autonomy. In the absence of any official body with an overarching role to co-ordinate all Maori issues, moreover, the welfare organisation, or at least the ideals that supposedly characterised it, would remain sidelined. In short, the MPs reflected a general Maori perspective that the new organisation could never flourish inside a mainstream department that remained, however broad its welfarist scope, committed to the land-oriented and controlling gaze of pre-war officialdom. Tirikatene was blunt: 'the Maori world is moving away from the Department as quickly as it is possible for them, the Maori people, to do so'.

The Maori MPs took their case to Labour's parliamentary caucus in May 1947. At this time the Ratana movement was re-examining its compact with Labour after experiencing well over a decade of its governance. Reflecting this, its MPs questioned the Fraser ministry's commitment to what, in the final analysis, Maori sought. In doing so they went considerably beyond their usual attack on the implementation of the Maori Social and Economic Advancement Act. At the macro-policy level, they noted that, whatever Labour had claimed at the elections, its Maori policy had been characterised by an 'equality' that homogenised and pakehaised rather than by the politics of self-determination. The members of the Maori caucus reminded their pakeha colleagues that, if they were pushed too far, they could turn the mythical 'Maori mandate' into a reality and bring down the government. They asked the assembled pakeha Labour MPs: 'have you enquired as to whether you are giving the Maori crumbs from the Pakeha's table, when the Maori is asking for nothing from your table, but is yearning to get his feet under his own table for a change?' The party caucus, worried at the ramifications of such disaffection, endorsed the concerns of its Maori members.[120]

The government was also, however, mindful of potential pakeha backlash. Ministers knew, too, that Maoridom would not welcome its political representatives toppling a government that, at the very least, provided more crumbs from the pakeha's table than promised to be the case with the conservative opposition. Fraser exhibited some flexibility, but essentially called the Maori MPs' bluff. His immediately proffered concessions were not great: boosting Tirikatene's role and status, for example, or placing Maori representatives (Tirikatene and fellow MP Tiaki Omana) on the Board of Maori Affairs for the first time. As a measure of the significance or otherwise of these moves, it is sufficient to note that the latter did not prevent the board from continuing to operate mostly as a rubber stamp for departmental policy. Yet Cabinet had been shaken by the strong Ratanaist stand, and a series of small but ongoing concessions eventuated. The Prime Minister himself, for example, encouraged the easing of urban adjustment problems by supporting the idea of community centres to help retain Maori cultural identity in cities, and preparations began in 1948 for one in Auckland's Freemans Bay.

While the Maori caucus had no real choice but to stay with Labour, it continued to put up a sustained fight on behalf of its people. The MP for Western Maori, Matiu Ratana, would sometimes defy the party whip to symbolise the frustration of the Maori politicians. Outside Parliament, the party's Maori Organiser (and Secretary of the Maori Advisory Council), Oriwa Haddon, resigned from Labour and helped form an independent Maori party on a self-determination platform. This and other such efforts, however, were abortive. Most Maori members and supporters of Labour decided to stay on in the party and retain at least some capacity to influence government policy. Drip-fed concessions had made the Maori caucus, in particular, more determined to get greater gains. But it had to put on hold its 'prime objective', placing Maori matters in Maori hands, co-ordinated by a Maori minister presiding over a more amenable bureaucracy.

Fraser worked hard to persuade Maori to give priority to Labour's plans for a more equal society. In particular, he sought to enlist the welfare organisation's assistance in procuring a Maori focus on socio-economic 'uplift', thus marginalising its pursuit of politico-cultural matters that were unique to Maoridom. He urged that the 'Tribal Committees, the Tribal Executives and the Welfare Officers must think out proposals and plans for the advancement of the Maori people in all directions'. Once the committee system had assisted the state in its general goal of raising the living standards of all disadvantaged New Zealanders, he implied, *then* Maori institutions might be able to evolve towards certain types of self-management. This did not involve rethinking of the long-term Crown project of full assimilation. Rather, it implied a state view that further developments in the exercise of rangatiratanga were premature, and that when they did occur they would have to be in sanitised form. In any case, it was believed, even mild forms of autonomy would not ultimately endure in the face of socio-economic and hegemonic forces.

Such issues were involved in the Prime Minister's early announcement that there was a *quid pro quo* for that degree of Crown support of Maoridom which existed. In its ongoing endeavours, the welfare organisation – and by extension future approved Maori institutions – must not become a drain on the state. The Maori Welfare Organisation should be to 'a very large extent independent and self reliant' in its resourcing. Not only would this assure the Crown that it would not have to bear an undue welfare burden, but also Maori would see the organisation as their 'own' institution and, therefore, the state's assistance to it would not be 'wasted'. This was conceptually difficult territory, given the assimilationist agenda. So Fraser did not couch his formulations of possible future autonomist developments in terms of tribal identity and resourcing. Instead, there was a clear implication of the temporary nature of the existing tribally based institutions; and a future was posed in which Maori might gain local government powers by dint of their tendency to live in proximity to each other, in whatever circumstances that might involve.

The welfare organisation, then, could evolve into or give way to an institution which Maori 'could control locally' rather than tribally – 'a form of local expression, direction and control'. Indeed, he opined, the committee system could, 'up to a point', lead to 'a measure of local government in matters affecting the living conditions, housing, health and the general welfare of the Maori people'. Even if the state's willingness to foster such a possibility was believed, the question was whether it was a sufficient goal, in terms of indigenous aspirations for self-determination, to encourage enough Maori to work within the welfare organisation to make state support worthwhile.

The beginnings had not been auspicious. Given its superseding of the MWEO, at first mostly members of iwi with a history of strong loyalty to the Crown had considered coming under the scheme, and only a minority of those (such as Ngati Porou) had opted in quickly. When Fraser assumed ministerial control he instructed his bureaucrats to proselytise among iwi and hapu likely to be persuadable. The Ratana–Labour MPs and other Maori leaders complemented these efforts: a second-best route towards recognition of rangatiratanga it might be, but it was the only one the Crown would travel. Moreover, a committee system flourishing under the Maori Social and Economic Advancement Act could bring considerable influence to bear on the Department of Maori Affairs from within the public sector. And there could be concrete benefits from gaining easier access to various policy and operations divisions of the bureaucracy. After the initial hiatus, membership of the welfare organisation rapidly increased.

Some of the communities which opted in felt that while opportunities for autonomous development through the organisation would be slight, they would sign up to pursue lesser advantages; others believed that doing so might be a way of preserving some of the collective gains they had made during the war. But some were determined to use the welfare organisation's institutions to move towards re-establishment and state recognition of rangatiratanga, emphasising the need to take advantage of all opportunities presented by the system. Tribal executives could purchase land, for example, and so those able to raise funds could work towards recreating tribal resource bases.

Whatever the motives and conceptual and other difficulties, early results in some of the regions that opted in surprised many people, Maori and pakeha. These sometimes reflected the fact that tribal committees, especially those MWEO committees which had seamlessly transferred to the new system, quickly became adept at undertaking a range of activities not envisaged by the Act. It was soon being noted, in fact, that if they were determined enough they could gain a local mandate that was, in a later assessment, 'as wide as they chose to make it'. And where state resources could be procured, it was noted, communities would often thrive: 'social security offices observed healthy children' in areas which had made the committee system work for them. At community level, committee membership often reflected the pre-existing authority of traditional leaders, their work enhanced by access to state personnel and resources. The thriving of some of the pioneering welfare organisation's institutions indicated to initially cautious tribal leaders that the new system, whatever its shortcomings, could be used to pursue welfarist and other policies of benefit to the people.

Successful functioning of tribal executives and tribal committees often coincided with efforts to pursue traditional tribally based rangatiratanga agendas. Whatever the Crown's ultimate intentions, in fact, the new structures were quickly able to produce considerable gains for autonomist causes as well as for 'approved' work. Some rural marae were able to revive their politico-cultural identity on the basis of official help, through the committees, for extending and improving management and productivity of local farming. Such autonomist developments did not concern the authorities too much, because of the 'public good' aspect that was involved. Pakeha had long been vocal about 'idle' Maori-owned land, a campaign renewed in the context of post-war resource scarcity. Independently, pressure for better land use was mounted from within Maoridom after 1947, when an official survey revealed that the area of land farmed by Maori remained small.

Pakeha elements in the welfare organisation structure worked alongside Maori on the land issue. They sought systemised ways of ensuring Maori use of lands that had been 'locked up' through such problems as multiple and absentee ownership and the fact that so much Maori-owned land was farmed by pakeha who were often only loosely controlled by the land management regimes (many of which were deemed to be far from efficient). They shared the widespread assumption that people farming their own land would have greater production incentive. This belief meshed well with the importance to tangata whenua of turangawaewae, although Maoridom's preferred methods of ownership and farming differed from those of the pakeha farming lobby. All considered that urgent action was needed to improve farming productivity by extending it to land that was currently being under-utilised or 'wasted'. In 1949 the Crown, and Maori working within the welfare organisation structure, finalised plans for using the system to expand farming by Maori. Rural Maori leaders looked forward to reaping political and cultural as well as economic benefits for tribal collectivities.

Because of the various perceived benefits from official assistance, tribal opting in to the welfare organisation's committee structure escalated remarkably. In terms of declared boundaries, by 31 March 1948 over 85 per cent of the Maori population had come formally under its coverage. A year later, the welfare organisation comprised 381 tribal committees and 63 tribal executives. By this time the leaders of Waikato–Tainui, the last tribal area to hold out, were continuing reconciliation with the state after settlement of their historical claims. At mid-century, all areas of the country had been officially gazetted under the 1945 Act. While this formal coverage of all Maoridom by the new institutions did not reflect universally whole-hearted support, or even support at all in some areas, it represented a general Maori take-up, without illusions, of the best that the Crown had on offer at that time.

Committees able to get state funding for specific, approved projects in fields such as welfare and farming could provide considerable help to their people. But there were many problems, partly because access to official resources required processes that were often long, complex and time-consuming. Frequently, in the event, they had to find funding and personnel from within their own communities, and so the amount, extent and value of their activities reflected the availability of time, expertise and fund-raising capacity. Securing basic funding and time was not necessarily a great problem at flax-roots committee level, but getting sufficient resources to make a difference in people's lives was a different matter. Access to appropriate expertise could be difficult where traditional leadership had reasserted itself in the face of an educated 'new rangatira' stratum which had previously been gaining ground (as a result of such factors as the secret ballot and wartime experience). The work of tribal executives particularly suffered from resourcing constraints, and as a consequence some became dominated by paid officials – especially the welfare officers.

The tribal executives could in theory meet together at district level but there were no means or encouragement to do so. In the absence of vigorous representation and adequate funding for tribal executives, and of any higher representational institutions, the welfare officers (whose official tasks included advising, helping and steering the committees) were the major intermediaries between the communities and the Wellington-based decision makers. Although this was not necessarily of their making, for they were obliged to take instructions from the controller at Maori Affairs head office, the flow was often in one direction – downwards. Such a high professional bureaucratic profile in the welfare organisation's committee system might have been seen by some communities as a relatively small price to pay if the system had achieved fundamental socio-economic progress. Certainly, successes continued to be reported beyond the first flush of enthusiasm among those iwi which had opted in early on. But, although all state departments were supposed to have a Maori component in their activities and goals, the welfare officers found it difficult to get a number of them to co-operate. This was not helped by a continued lack of will at Maori Affairs to divert itself from its core business to give any great priority to the work of the welfare organisation.

Although the marae-based committees, in particular, could operate successfully in some areas and endeavours, the 1945 Act and its institutions had not, by mid-century, achieved *dramatic* or across-the-board changes in Maoridom. So pronounced was this that Ngata could declare the Act to be a 'botch' from the perspective of seriously forwarding Maori aims – even those of attaining socio-economic improvement, let alone rangatiratanga. The fundamental problem was that, in essence, the welfare organisation existed to do the Crown's bidding, rather than to find out what Maori wanted and how to implement this in conjunctiom with them. The state's definition of goals and methods that were good for Maori differed, according to the statements of many Maori leaders, from that of the Maori people. Through the welfare organisation, then, the Crown worked to bring Maori into line with what was perceived to be best for them. Ropiha inadvertently acknowledged this in 1949 when assessing that, after a great deal of official guidance, the tribal committees were 'settling down to a better appreciation of their functions'.

The 1950 annual Department of Maori Affairs report talked of the goal of its welfare organisation as achieving tangible, state-desired objectives. When it had succeeded in this, it could then move on to more 'abstract' matters. Such talk had given hope to some welfare organisation participants that real self-government, even some form of self-determination, might be in the Crown's mind. But statements about future goals reflected other Crown agendas, such as appropriate, assimilatory education of Maori children. The overarching policies of the welfare organisation, reflecting the lines of official control, continued to be dictated from the pakeha-dominated centre. Despite some relatively minor devolution to tribal and sub-tribal level, they lay generally within the assimilationist paradigm. In the struggle between the representatives of two 'diametrically opposed philosophical bases', it was the Crown that remained in control.[121]

CHAPTER NINE

RANGATIRATANGA INITIATIVES AND CROWN CONTAINMENT TOWARDS MID-CENTURY

Assimilation and rangatiratanga

From the late 1930s, the indigenous population of New Zealand began to increase very rapidly, largely because of 'a sharp decrease in Maori mortality'. The trend reflected a number of the developments discussed in this book, culminating in the Labour government's aims to include Maori in all the benefits of the welfare state. Assimilationist policies not only gelled with these Labour aspirations to raise the living standards of all disadvantaged New Zealanders, but also appeared to an increasing number of policy makers to suit the post-war indigenous situation particularly well and should therefore be accelerated. Not only were growing numbers of Maori physically separating themselves from their homelands, but other trends were relevant too – such as aspects of the ongoing reorganisation of farming of Maori-owned lands. Those which fitted official ideology were encouraged by the state, sometimes in turn feeding into the accelerated assimilation thesis. With regard to those Maori staying in the tribal regions, for example, the Department of Maori Affairs noted in 1949 that population concentration through consolidation was 'being widely promoted' because it 'had the advantage of being the most comprehensive method of approximating the goal of individual, or at least compact family titles'. This would bring Maori closer to the European model of land ownership and lifestyle modes.

In view of the multi-faceted strengthening of assimilationist pressures, Maori leaders and others promoting rangatiratanga had, at times, to adopt temporary fall-back positions as the major focus of their effort – such as saving selected aspects of Maori culture from obliteration. But they never ceased to stress that their grand goal remained Maori self-determination. Thus Tirikatene, in his capacity as the highest official representative of his people, had cause to remind the Prime Minister that 'the fusion of the Maori people into the community of New Zealand as an integral part of it does not mean that the movement is to turn the Maori into a pakeha'.

For the state, in contrast, assimilation not only remained the ultimate item on the strategic agenda for Maori, but it also now seemed more achievable. An increasing number of bureaucrats and politicians believed that demographic, urbanising, farming and other trends within Maoridom held out hope that tangible progress could be made on this elusive goal. The Maori Welfare Organisation, a temporary measure in any case, might be able to assist assimilatory progress through its assigned work on socio-economic levelling and equalising.

Conversely, one question being asked in many Maori circles in the later 1940s was how far the welfare organisation could be used to *resist* assimilationist imperatives and pressures – or, better still, to *assist* autono-mist impulses and strategies. Even if it might be an exaggeration to assess that the new committees were, from a Maori point of view, 'only a shell of the effective organisations' of the MWEO, the task faced by those attempting to harness them to the cause of rangatiratanga was huge.

Self-determinationists often did not think the effort worthwhile. In some quarters, for example, Maori leaders or rank and file continued to work through organisations which had been operating in wartime, officially or unofficially, and which remained in place informally. In some places these constituted effective rivals to welfare organisation committees, while in others they complemented them – or filled a space where official committees had not gone (sometimes because the unofficial institutions were there first). Because of the stigma within Maoridom that resulted from getting too close to the government, some of the welfare organisation committees resisted direction from head office, risking loss of access to resourcing.

Some of the fiercely independent branches of the Maori Women's Health League also functioned as local expressions of rangatiratanga, however limited their formal aims might be. Yet such was the level of post-war Maori suspicion of a government which had dashed so many of their hopes that, because league groups needed to have some dealings with the authorities and because Maori Affairs tried to woo them, they too were sometimes viewed as creatures of 'pakeha Wellington'. All the same, they formed one section of a remarkable new development, the beginnings of a pan-tribal movement among Maori women.

Given that the tribal committees were mostly male-dominated, Maori women often tended to group together to focus on things of most interest to their own lives – issues such as family, health and housing. They were particularly inclined to organise as a result of their 'liberating' experiences during the war, when – especially when the men were away – they were often crucial for the success of the MWEO. In some areas Maori komiti wahine/women's committees had been created to assist the official war effort, and some of them continued on after the war.

Royal and other officials came to see the usefulness of women's groupings able to assist the tribal committees in 'aspects of welfare which are the prerogative of women', and encouraged existing ones to flourish and new ones to form. Maori Affairs and government alike, however, noted that such groups had thriven despite being outside the tribal executive and tribal committee structures – and perhaps sometimes because of it. The results were so positive that from 1949 the welfare officers were formally charged with assisting activist Maori women to establish a network of women's welfare committees.

The committees' main role was officially stated as bringing 'professional guidance' to Maori women in both home and marae settings. Royal had intended that they would eventually merge with the Maori Women's Health League, but the latter was cautious, fearing that this would add to perceptions that its autonomy was under threat. Moreover, the Crown's assimilationist agenda continued to worry some of the league branches: while they wished to acquire western expertise, they also aimed to incorporate tikanga Maori. Conversely, elements in the department feared that any such merger would lead to domination by the branches.

Despite their increasing official links, the women's welfare committees were often able, in effect, to operate autonomously. They could concentrate on their own agendas rather than on those of the Crown's agents to a degree that the more entrenched and elected official tribal committee members could not. They were assisted in this capacity by the broad-ranging nature of their 'welfare' brief, which allowed them to work under the auspices of the 1945 Act without too much tension, and which fostered a sense of nationwide unity – their goals were uncontestable. A feeling soon grew, in fact, that the committees would be more effective if they acquired a united voice. Some began to talk of a national body that could become a powerful tool for distilling the experiences of its flax-root members and creating policies and platforms that could influence the government's words and deeds.

Some officials and politicians could see that such a body could also be a useful conduit for information flow, upwards and downwards, so long as there were some minimal safeguards. A national Maori women's organisation was seen as highly unlikely to challenge the indivisible authority of the state, a general reflection of the prevailing mores about the place of women in society, although there were others factors too. Several leading members of the welfare committee movement, for example, were educated, urban-based and interested in the practical realities of the migration experience. Their perspectives were far different from those of the traditionalist men who dominated many of the tribal committees and tribal executives, and the state could see their significance for assisting in the social adjustment to city life.

While the united voice of the women's welfare committees might sometimes put uncomfortable pressure on the government, then, it could also assist official aims of various types, including assimilationist ones. The league dropped out of preparatory discussions in reaction to the high profile of Maori Affairs in the developments, but welfare officers continued to encourage the women's committees to consider forming a nationwide organisation with a central secretariat. Over time, informal discussions led to official consultation, and a draft constitution was developed and then adopted at a conference in Rotorua in 1950. Female welfare officers, in particular, put a great deal of energy into taking this initiative further, helping establish district councils on a regional basis preparatory to setting up a national body.

By March 1951 there were 160 welfare committees, with 14 district councils co-ordinating their activities, and membership was around 2500. That September a general conference of the welfare committees was held in Wellington, with delegates from what had now grown to 187 branches which reported to district organisations, and 27 independent 'isolated branches'. There had been a last effort to persuade the Maori Women's Health League to attend, but it remained sceptical that it could retain its decentralised structure and independence in the face of Maori Affairs' overview. A draft constitution was presented and endorsed, and the Maori Women's Welfare League, a powerful force for rangatiratanga, was founded.

Inside the Maori Welfare Organisation, rangatiratanga had made considerably lesser progress. In 1946 a book of instruction for American soldiers about New Zealand was republished. It pointed out that Maori communal endeavours and organisations 'live on persistently, to the puzzlement of Europeans, who are unaccustomed to seeing their scale of values cheerfully ignored'. The activities of some committees fitted this syndrome. While used to resistance to assimilation, the government would sometimes intervene when such tribal committees began to utilise the welfare organisation system to promote their own, autonomist perspectives – those trying, in effect, to reappropriate that which the Crown had bequeathed them from 'their' wartime organisation. Denial of any support was one method, and while some independently inclined committees did thrive despite this and other forms of state remonstrance, others 'found themselves floundering'.[122]

Maori wardens

Some committees which asserted independence were tolerated because they provided the government with services it needed. These included the valuable (and cheap) provision of adjunct services for enforcement of 'order and regularity' in Maori localities and districts. As well as the Maori Council policing system, other Maori coercive forces had operated in the twentieth century, some of them endorsed by the state. Ratanaism's early development had itself been nourished with the help of its own policemen, or katipa, once headed by an Irish 'Chief of Police'. This was one of many similar efforts by Maori groups to exercise control over activities of importance to them. These generally assisted, albeit indirectly, Crown as well as Maori authority. To help it face the challenges of the Second World War period, the government had acquiesced in many informal social control mechanisms at village or marae level – as indeed it had often done before. With the war nearing an end, many Maori leaders wanted the right to continue such activies in peacetime. The government appreciated that Maori self-policing could assist to maintain order during the reconstruction period and beyond.

In supporting the inclusion of coercive apparatus and authority in drafts of the Maori Social and Economic Advancement Act, the government was aware that, in a legal sense, it was going beyond the powers given to the MWEO, and that this might be a fraught and ambiguous exercise. But the legislation sought to regularise and exercise control over current self-policing arrangements, placing tight formal limits on tribal coercive capacity. The jurisdiction of the 'Maori police', and of those they reported to in the welfare organisation system, was constrained. To emphasise this, although they were referred to bluntly within the department as a 'police force', the personnel involved were to be given the euphemistic title of 'Maori Wardens' (a term used in a Rotorua experiment, implemented in 1937, with which Te Arawa's trust board was associated). While wardens were to be nominated and superintended by tribal executives and work with the tribal committees, they were to be appointed by the minister (with advice from the officials) and he would be in overall control of their activities. Whatever the formal hands-off position of the state once wardens were appointed, it was always implicit, in their terms of reference, that they were to pay attention to the control and enforcement priorities of the Crown.

Just as various Maori movements had retained or developed their own order institutions and functions for their own purposes, however, many welfare organisation committees intended to – and in the event frequently did – use the position of warden to pursue community aims. This was generally tolerable for the state, because in their primary enforcement orientation the committees' views tended to coincide with those of the Crown. Both regarded liquor control, in particular, as a priority, regarding the amount of Maori consumption as detrimental to both the national good and Maori communities. The problem was exacerbated in Crown eyes by Maori moving to live in close proximity with pakeha in the towns and cities – race relations, work productivity and 'public order' were all considered to be under strain. Elders and other Maori leaders were just as concerned; they had seen, for example, that new drinking habits acquired by some who had gone away during the war added to domestic and community problems after their return home. By mutual consent, therefore, from the beginning it was intended that a central focus for the wardens would be regulating alcohol consumption.

The idea of wardens, in fact, was generally received more enthusiastically in Maori communities than within the state. Some elements of the state system opposed it from the beginning, on philosophical grounds related to 'societal equality'; others had second thoughts after the 1945 legislation was passed. The New Zealand Police, who had vetting functions for the 'Maori police', had previously indicated concerns over the spread of 'unprofessional' policing by blocking any expansion of the Rotorua experiment. Since well before the end of the previous century, Maori had essentially been policed, at least on an official level, by pakeha constables, and the final remnants of the part-time 'Native Constable' position within the force were dispensed with in 1945.

Police wariness at reintroducing 'Maori policing Maori' was widely shared among officials on a number of grounds. Among them was a feeling, that Maori police would, for tribal reasons, be loath to enforce certain laws against members of their own community – laws which, for example, negated customary fishing or birding practices. Anecdotal examples of such reluctance by Maori constables in the past were often cited. In effect, Maori police were considered unreliable when rangatiratanga came into conflict with the law. As a result, the welfare organisation's policing regime stalled at its very outset: when the Maori authorities put forward nominations for wardens' positions, confirmation of appointment was deferred.

But pressure was applied by other state elements as well as the tribal authorities, especially in the context of post-war review and reform of the liquor legislation. Eventually, waverers were persuaded by the argument that, with appointments to be 'probationary', the experiment could easily be abandoned if it proved unsatisfactory. The first nominations were formally approved in 1949, and the complement of wardens numbered well over 100 before the year was out. Their services came quickly to be appreciated by Crown and Maori authorities alike, and their numbers soon rose considerably. Their operating principle has been described as 'aroha ki te tangata' (love for the people): wardens' services were unpaid and, given the paucity of resources of the welfare organisation, they were seldom reimbursed for even out-of-pocket expenses. The motivations of the individuals who took on the task were generally similar to those of the leaders of the Maori search for indigenous control of indigenous matters. They were described by a Maori parliamentarian as people with 'a social conscience [making] a positive contribution to the life of the people', and most Maori seemingly viewed them that way. They represented one model of how an institution could operate in a way that satisfied many requirements of both rangatiratanga and the state.

The liquor question

Wardens became particularly important in tackling difficulties arising out of Maori migration to towns and cities in the quarter-century after the war, especially after this gained huge magnitude from about 1950. Maori leaders were as worried as the state and 'public opinion' (if not more so) by 'anti-social' behaviour by their people in population centres. Far from their traditional socio-tribal support structures, many (especially young) Maori used heavy alcohol consumption as a coping mechanism, which often led to problems with 'the law'. Migrated Maori who rose to provide leadership of their people in the new environment, often in conjunction with city-based welfare officers as well as with leaders 'back home', began to use the Maori warden system to complement their informal efforts to 'recreate community' in the urban areas and, increasingly, their building of welfare organisation institutions there.

But there were endemic problems. The major role for policing in

New Zealand was designed to be preventive, based on a highly visible or accessible patrol-based presence. Policing personnel were distinguished from other citizens in that they possessed at all times and in all circumstances a legally sanctioned power to coerce. The informal, collective social control structures of the villages often minimised any necessity for wardens to employ force. But their intervention in disorderly urban incidents was more likely to be overtly coercive, creating tension. Over and above this, there was some resentment among Maori at what was seen as 'double-policing' of their people.

More broadly, an institutional focus on regulating *Maori* alcohol consumption had been foreshadowed as a conceptual problem at planning stage. There was a general wartime and post-war mood, among 'progressive' thinkers of both major ethnicities, to eradicate all 'race discrimination'. As the war had progressed, there was increasing demand for legal 'equality' in liquor consumption to be enshrined in legislation, and this campaign escalated at the beginning of post-war reconstruction. Many rank and file Maori supported it, their views spearheaded by returned servicemen whose eyes had recently been opened to new possibilities of social and lifestyle equality. Urban migrants, too, had experienced a 'colour bar' as a result of gaining a more visible profile in what had been largely white towns and cities. Many Maori and pakeha believed that legal discrimination in something as important to New Zealand popular culture as drinking helped to legitimise racist behaviour.

Some Maori, moreover, saw equal access to and control of liquor, freed of special stigma for tangata whenua, as an achievable next step in the struggle to gain recognition of mana from the Crown – and therefore a further base from which to continue the struggle for rangatiratanga. An MWEO-organised conference in Rotorua in 1945 had noted that discriminatory liquor legislation applied exclusively to Maori (not even to other indigenous people who had migrated to New Zealand). The delegates declared that, given the equality of sacrifice in the war effort, removal of discrimination was more necessary than ever for restoring the 'mana of the race'.

In some rural areas especially, however, such a move was regarded by tribal leaders as potentially impeding the quest for rangatiratanga. To them, the struggle for self-determination had been weakened by excessive use of alcohol among their people, who needed 'protection' against its scourge. Kingite leaders such as Koroki (who took a huge delegation to Parliament on the issue) and Te Puea held such views, as did the King Country's tribal executive, the East Coast prohibitionist movement and groups elsewhere in the country. Some leaders, then, had sought retention or strengthening of discriminatory practices as one way of warding off modernising influences that disturbed the tenor of tribal life.

Such a strategy not only tended to discount or ignore some pertinent cultural and migratory factors, but could lead to complications. The right to 'otherness' that Maori leaders were claiming could, for example, gain some strange bedfellows when it included discriminatory liquor regulation – including ethnocentric pakeha conservatives (and even white racists). A witness at the 1946 Royal Commission on Licensing answered his own question as to whether Maori should be 'treated differently to the Pakeha in [alcohol] matters': they should be, he argued, because 'the Maori is different. The Maori has no history, traditions, or ingrained customs, or generally accepted rules of conduct, regarding many commonplaces of European ways of life and habits'.

In short, there were two broad methods of approaching rangatiratanga in relation to the liquor question: in favour of or opposing discrimination in law and policing. In the event, it was almost inevitable that legal 'equalising' should win out in the immediate post-war climate of 'equality'. The Labour Party's philosophical roots emphasised all citizens being of equal status: 'the Maori' was (in Walter Nash's words) 'good enough, strong enough, and able enough to stand on his own feet, and he will not reach the heights we would like to see him reach' through continuing to inhabit a 'protected' position. Increasing numbers of pakeha, in fact, had been coming to the same conclusion. A policeman summed up such perspectives by arguing before the royal commission that 'Maoris should be treated the same as any other citizens' and that anything else was both 'a slur on the Maori at this stage of his history' and a bar to assisting Maori to 'stand on his own feet'.

The commissioners agreed, and after much debate the government too decided in favour of equalisation. Even the long-established prohibition in the King Country would soon disappear, following the commission's recommendation to make the area subject to the same rules as the rest of the country: a regional referendum failed to get the required 60 per cent vote for continuing the no-licence regime. Whatever its origin and evolution, the 'sacred pact' between the Crown and tribal leaders, who had equated it with 'our mana and our rangatiratanga', was overturned.

But the main result of the commission was the 1948 Liquor Licensing Act. Under it, Maori consumers of alcohol were put on an equal legal footing with their pakeha counterparts. Maori women were now allowed to drink in public bars, Maori men were entitled to equal access to liquor away from licensed premises, and several other racially based discriminations regarding consumption were repealed. But the interventionary power of the wardens in effect continued a separate surveillance and enforcement regime for Maori, given that they were especially charged with controlling alcohol intake and suppressing liquor-related disorder. Wardens could, for example, order Maori to leave licensed premises or prevent publicans serving liquor to them. From time to time they received extra powers from the government to pursue its desired goals on such issues. In 1951, for instance, wardens gained greater control over drinking on marae, particularly during hui, a development welcomed by some in rangatiratanga terms and opposed by others promoting the same cause in different ways.

The main liquor-related order problem, however, was increasingly seen to be in the towns and cities. Here it took time for warden policing to make an impact. Meanwhile, greater Maori visibility in urban areas had not only reminded pakeha that full assimilation had not arrived, but led many to depict Maori 'differentness' in derogatory terms – especially because of alcohol-related disorder. It was widely believed that Maori both drank excessively and 'could not hold their liquor' and so special coercive attention was required beyond that of the warden system. In the event, a 'progressive' reaction against such ethnocentric perspectives meant that demands for much greater Crown controls on Maori than on pakeha were not fulfilled. But, along the way, various Maori requests to operate their own control measures independently of the state were also rejected. Deployment of wardens, then, remained as close as Maori leaders and communities were to get in terms of special, officially sanctioned regulatory powers over their own people.[123]

Labour and rangatiratanga

All of these debates had occurred in the context of both major political parties, Labour and the conservative National, stressing full assimilation as the ultimate goal, though the former wanted to remove 'negative' discrimination while the latter was prepared to continue it if necessary. In the run-up to the 1949 general election, as expected, Labour sought the Maori vote on the basis of its record on the search for (assimilationist) 'equality': tangata whenua had benefited from the party's implementation of 'social and economic uplift' through housing, education, social security and other policies. This campaign summed up the thrust of the government's policies, even though it had been forced to accommodate aspects of self-determination for the foreseeable future. Its social-democratic base had continued to lead it to the fundamental conclusion that the problems facing Maori would ideally be dealt with by equality before the law, and especially by raising the living conditions of all citizens in need – to do which special interventionary attention would be needed in the meantime.

Labour's identification with Ratanaism had not modified this strategy very much, for that movement's emphasis on the Treaty was tempered by both its formal rejection of tribalism and its determination to provide the morehu with satisfactory living conditions. Although Labour had paid some attention to Maori as a socio-political grouping, it continued to see them essentially as collective beneficiaries of 'general progress' (strengthened in this by the popularisation of the Ngataist concept of 'Maoritanga') and, even more so, as individuals who tended to be disadvantaged and were therefore particularly eligible for welfare assistance that allowed them 'to stand on [their] own feet'.

Insofar as Labour leaders had been prepared to go some way towards meeting non-Ratanaist aspirations to rangatiratanga, especially with the

MWEO and the welfare organisation, it was a cautious and constrained engagement. Fully aware of the propensity of tribally based movements to seek out as much independence from the Crown as possible, the government needed to place them under greater or lesser control. But as mid-century approached, the Labour Party leaders had strongly reasserted their central equalising message, which they felt to be even more relevant in view of the 'urban drift' among Maori. The tangata whenua would benefit best from non-ethnic social and economic 'levelling-up', from removing negatively discriminatory legislation, and ultimately from full assimilation to the ways and mores of the dominant culture.

The government, then, had reasserted the assimilationist policy that the Crown had never essentially departed from since the 1840s, despite the hopes and efforts of Maori (and the wishful thinking of many a modern historian). This analysis makes no judgment on the beliefs, efforts and motivations of politicians and officials (and members of the pakeha public) who pursued and supported an assimilationist agenda at this time – nor on those Maori who co-operated with the Crown's endeavours. Assimilation was in the New Zealand hegemony generally believed to be a correct and (in an international context) enlightened policy, rectifying the problems of poverty and disadvantage among Maori.

In the first half of the century, developments in such matters as health, housing and social security had undoubtedly led to considerable improvement in the Maori way of life, forming the base for the 'massive population explosion' of the second half. With the help of Ratanaism, the Labour regime had accelerated progress towards, even if falling far short of, various manifestations of 'equality' and 'levelling upwards'. But its policies and practices were situated in 'western' paradigms of progress to which a hegemonic, monocultural 'civilisation' was central. In terms of ultimate outcomes, this vision was incompatible with that of rangatiratanga. But Labour policies *had* been prepared to take into short- and medium-term account Maori collectivist striving for politico-cultural distinctiveness. From 13 December 1949 a new government held office, representing a party which considered even temporary accommodations with rangatiratanga to be of dubious merit.[124]

New developments at mid-century

After the war the indigenous population was well on its way to tripling since its late-nineteenth-century nadir, and it would be recorded in 1951 as 115,676 (out of a total population of 1,938,032). By then, increases in and transfers of the Maori population were adding to the enormous strains on tribal organisation that had followed colonisation. In 1936, 83 per cent of Maori lived in rural communities, and at the time of the population adjustments at the end of the war this proportion was calculated to be still at a relatively high three-quarters. But the wartime 'urban drift' continued during peacetime, and after 1950 it became a deluge; from around 1960 Maori 'became a predominantly urban people', involving a change in lifestyle of 'staggering' proportions.

As urban migration had gathered momentum, tribal leaders had increasingly seen that it would be a struggle to retain strong traditional structures. Some felt that the survival of Maoritanga itself was already under threat. Not only had sizeable numbers of their people left for the large towns and cities, but also these had few tribally based (or indeed Maori-based) support mechanisms in their day-to-day lives. Displaced individuals and families mostly had to interact with, and often came largely to conform to, cultural norms that were largely alien to their rural and tribal upbringing. One later observer believed that 'the abrupt resumption' of close interracial contact from the 1940s, heralding a 'post-withdrawal stage', led to 'a more traumatic, conflictful, and anxiety producing adjustment process than in situations where the contact had been gradual and continuous over a long period of time'.[125]

Although it was slow to appreciate the nature of the problems that resulted from urbanisation, the state would increasingly come to encourage internal migration; among other things, this would be taken as an opportunity to return accelerated assimilation to its strategic agenda as a seemingly achievable item. In such circumstances, Maori Affairs did little to encourage robust development of the tribal executive and committee system, except in law enforcement. Maori leaders, however, were increasingly appreciating that the welfare organisation apparatus could be useful for general collectivist as well as tribal collectivist purposes.

Although the official committees were originally rurally and tribally oriented, moreover, a number of Maori leaders, including some marae-based rangatira, saw that expanding the committee system onto urban streets might be useful for such matters as promoting race relations (or at least stopping their deterioration), assisting 'at danger' youth and creating a Maori collectivist ethos beyond the home marae or tribal headquarters.

In mid-century discussions it was already appreciated that setting up committees under the welfare organisation in the cities could be achieved only (except for urban tribes, or in towns or city suburbs with large concentrations of people from a particular tribe, usually based nearby) by pan-tribal or, more usually, decidedly non-tribal committees. The latter naturally gelled with the Ratanaist strand that had been so influential for some two decades. The beginning of urbanisation among Maori, therefore, added a complication to hopes of using the 1945 system as a beach-head for tribally based autonomy. From a tribal autonomist perspective, urban-based committees could be at best only a holding measure, helping Maoritanga survive, if not flourish, in a harsh new environment. The tribal focus would have to be kept up through informal social contact, tribal communication with dispersed members and 'visits home' for occasions such as weddings, holidays, whare runanga/meeting house openings and tangi/funerals. Incipient urbanisation, then, added yet another challenge for the many tribal leaders determined to further the autonomist agenda through welfare organisation committees.

But the most fundamental challenge remained that of the official policy of assimilation. While Fraser's 1949 report as Minister of Maori Affairs stated that his goal was 'an independent, self-reliant and satisfied Maori race working side by side with the Pakeha', in that year's general election campaign Labour had offered the same 'equality'-based policies as in the past. In the grand scheme of things, even the welfare organisation constituted only a minor policy and operational thrust. But this essentially assimilationist platform did not go far enough for the increasing numbers of Europeans who found the *rhetoric* of Maori self-determination, and even the sight of Maori socio-economic 'uplift' (which *was* significant in the period 1938–49), to be alarming. During the election campaign, the opposition made great gains by emphasising its continuing allegation that the government was being held to ransom by the 'Maori mandate'. This may have been one reason why sufficient pakeha switched their votes to the National Party at the polls to bring Labour down.

When Sidney Holland's National ministry took office, Maori were understandably dismayed. His party had highlighted during the campaign that it was offering less to Maori than had Labour. This was across the board: an attack on both 'welfarist' state interventionism and – especially given its even greater stress than Labour on rapid assimilation – the quest for Crown recognition of rangatiratanga. Moreover, New Zealand now had a ruling party in which Maori were not represented at parliamentary level, for the first time since the provincial period in the third quarter of the nineteenth century. With no Maori in the political executive, a six-decade political tradition ended and, in addition, the office of Member of the Executive Council Representing the Maori Race was abolished. While the principal activities of the Department of Maori Affairs continued to be overseen by the Board of Maori Affairs, this no longer contained a Maori MP.

The reasons for such developments are complex and varied. A racial backlash against the increasingly visible Maori presence in urban areas may have played its part. Race relations could be deemed to be 'the best in the world' when most pakeha knew Maori only at a distance, but when Maori moved into their neighbourhoods and brought unfamiliar ways of behaviour with them the relationship could well degenerate. Whatever the reasons, there was an increasingly ethnocentric mood in pakeha New Zealand, and the policies of the incoming government reflected this trend. One of its ministers had said, when National opposed removing liquor discrimination, that Maori 'are Natives to me, and I will call them what I like': they should be treated 'like children'.

Similar comments were increasingly being made in public in a number of quarters, sometimes using language reminiscent of the previous century. At the same time, post-war assisted immigration from Europe, especially from Britain, aimed to increase the population on the basis of white 'kith and kin' who would fit in with the dominant culture of the nation. This clearly did not bode well for Maori aspirations for recognition of and respect for rangatiratanga. While it is true that Labour had 'no long term commitment to empowering the Maori people', National was decidedly *against* such empowerment. If anything, it stood for disempowering Maori.

Faced with Maori agency, however, members of the new cabinet proved to be pragmatic. A few ministers reflected a feeling in some National Party circles, for example, that, although one era of Maori development was finishing, another was beginning – and they were not too concerned that the participants continued to identify as Maori. One reason for this was that an emergent new Maori leadership was able to work within the pakeha as well as the indigenous world. It was assumed, in any case, that in the longer term the process of absorbing Maoridom would be facilitated by increasing numbers of such Maori 'modernisers'.

In a broader sense, however, it might be said that time was on the side of Maori in fulfilling at least some of their aspirations for self-determination. The half-century from the 1890s to the 1940s had been characterised in Maoridom by enormous social, economic, demographic, cultural and political developments. Despite the beginnings of 'urban drift' towards its end, since the 1920s much had happened to affirm the vibrancy and adaptability of the Maori people, their organisational modes and their culture. At mid-century, many marae-centred communities were thriving and others were being reconstructed. The pace of tribal and cultural reconstruction had been assisted by socio-economic gains under Labour, which had done 'more for the material well-being of the Maori people than any other Government or Party'. That this had occurred without Labour 'really understanding Maori culture' indicates that, intentionally or otherwise, significant autonomist advances were quite possible under governments which had a poor appreciation of Maori perspectives. Governments would do whatever matters of state required. If political pressure, or national economic production, required measures that would also assist Maori fortunes or aspirations, the need to intervene would qualify – for as long as was expedient – hegemonic, pakeha-oriented ideology and strategy.

Expedience proved to be as much a characteristic of National as of Labour, whatever its rhetoric and formal policies. The new government, for example, continued inherited agricultural and pastoral developments which promised benefits for Maori that were also in the 'public good'. The situation was not entirely clearcut, and some National suggestions for such reform clearly violated rangatiratanga. The Labour MPs fought attempts, for example, to facilitate compulsory rationalisation of land ownership for, in Tirikatene's words, that 'hits right into the heart and soul of Maori mental sentiment and Mana i.e. the alienation of his lands without his consent . . . It is not the value of the land that counts but the principle'. But the Crown was, after the 1949 general election, prepared to continue working through the Maori Welfare Organisation and other Maori institutions when it believed that the benefits to Maori would further its own aims and objectives. The struggle for rangatiratanga would keep operating within as well as outside and against the state.

One issue faced by the Crown which would ultimately assist Maori in their pursuit of rangatiratanga was New Zealand's role in the international community. Again, while Labour and National ideologies clashed, both had to face certain global realities. While 'empire' had reached its greatest-ever geographical spread in the 1930s, the subsequent war had been a catalyst for the beginning of global decolonisation. The New Zealand Labour Party had taken a relatively 'progressive' stance on such issues, and its record on the international decolonisation movement had been followed within Maoridom. From the 1950s, whatever National's formal foreign policy, the world experience of 'national liberation' struggles would be increasingly closely monitored by New Zealand. That Maori leaders were attuned to these issues did not go unnoticed in state circles, although the ramifications for New Zealand would take decades to work through – and in the eyes of many remained unresolved by the end of the century.

Such debates and developments were already present in incipient form in mid-century New Zealand. Repatternings of Maori leadership to meet post-war challenges and changes were being observed in the 1940s. Some of the new generation of Maori leaders that was emerging had qualifications and approaches which reflected urbanisation, higher across-the-board educational standards (resulting from the reforms of the 1930s), the increase in quality of life among Maori set in train by Labour's equalising policies, and the opportunity for leadership thrown up by the experiences (and deaths) of wartime. Post-war leaders, who were not necessarily of traditional rangatira stock, assisted with, and were sometimes at the forefront of, the operation of the 1945 legislation – either on behalf of the Crown, especially at head office in Wellington, or out in the field on behalf of their tribes.

Those in the Labour camp, in particular, focused on achieving full equality in society for Maori, while at the same time seeking to promote those aspects of Maoridom which had survived assimilationist colonisation and were deemed worthy of preservation, revival or adaptation. In this sense, they had taken on board the ideas of the mainstream Young Maori Party milieu, which had long been developing a vision of two peoples in one nation. Ngata had insisted in 1929, for example, that Maori demanded to remain ethno-culturally distinct, and that aspects of traditional culture which should be retained (including the language) needed proactive protection.

Wherever and however the post-war Maori leaders operated, however assimilated they appeared to be (or not), most reflected the general desire of their people to retain their 'differentness', and seek Crown respect for rangatiratanga, at the same time as participating increasingly in mainstream New Zealand. They were, then, heirs to a long effort to come to terms with the state and its political economy while at the same time attempting to rebuild organised Maoridom. The Crown was fully aware that the 'Maori problem' had not gone away.[126]

CONCLUSION

This book has stressed the resilience and adaptiveness, in the face of great odds, of Maori political and cultural forms and aspirations. It has focused on the enduring Maori quest for Crown recognition of rangatiratanga, and the Crown's responses to this. Ever since 1840, whenever Maori demands for autonomy were asserted with any strong organisational backing, the colonial and post-colonial state sought to defuse or deflect them. Frequently it did so by incorporating organisational and ideological aspects of such movements into its own structures and apparatus – from officialised runanga, komiti and other Maori institutions in the nineteenth century through to the Maori War Effort Organisation and its successor towards the middle of the twentieth.

Crown acceptances or incorporations of degrees of tribally based organisational and cultural revival and development represented strategies and tactics in pursuit of its hegemonic goals. In turn, Maori used the state's offerings and institutions to promote their own autonomist aims and aspirations. The first half of the twentieth century witnessed an endemic clash of cultures and misapprehensions between disparate world-views in New Zealand – as had occurred before 1900 and would continue after 1950. But the leadership of the two major peoples knew in general what each other wanted, and strategised to maximise their own position in such knowledge. These manoeuvrings involved accommodations and compromises as well as confrontations.

In their complicity with the colonising gaze, generations of 'traditional' historians missed the fundamental point that the state possessed overwhelming power and would always use this to pursue its own agenda; and that its goals had little connection with issues of indigenous justice

CONCLUSION267

or rights – unless policies which appeared to be empathctic to these
happened to suit it at the time. Nationalist historians and many later
revisionists, among them members of the 'wishful thinking/lost
opportunity' school, have also failed to address adequately the relationship
between the state and indigeneity. It is timely to appreciate that the
colony of New Zealand was, whatever its particularities, an integral part
of a global imperialism that possessed great expertise in modes of socio-
racial control and assimilation; that the Dominion of New Zealand applied
the same general assimilationist policies from its establishment in 1907;
and that the application of hegemonic policies not only continued but
intensified after New Zealand became constitutionally independent from
Britain four decades later.

Historical revisionism has correctly overturned a previous tendency
to highlight and laud the Crown and its personnel and actions, but in
rescuing 'the people' from obscurity it has tended to overlook or deny
the essentially coercive and hegemonic might of the state. By channelling
itself into inward-looking race (and gender, and a few class) studies, much
revisionist work, insofar as it relates to the state, has had a tendency to
throw out the scholarly baby with the decidedly dirty bathwater. The
consequent scholarly loss has included any great capacity to perceive the
fundamental nature of, and interrelatedness between, resistance and that
which was resisted. The task of revising revisionism must, therefore,
emphasise the continuingly powerful role of the state and its unswerving
determination – whatever the temporary concessions along the way – to
pursue its hegemonic agenda.

Scholarly neglect of the coercive power of the state and the interests
it primarily represents, and of its hegemonic aims and strategies, has often
manifested itself in a lack of understanding of the sheer pervasiveness and
intensity of the Crown's assimilationist mission – which prevailed until
the last quarter of the twentieth century, and perhaps beyond. A modern
historiography that at least implicitly rehabilitates Maori resistance to
acculturation and subsumption, but makes only uneasy murmurs about
assimilation, actually underplays the enormous determination of that
resistance in the face of overwhelming odds. Conversely, such work
underestimates the subtleties and efficiencies of the state's strategies and

tactics of control. It thus conspires, albeit inadvertently, in the official view that the Crown is a body that is not intentionally antithetical to rangatiratanga. While the state is seen to get almost *everything* wrong (whether by accident or inefficiency) in a series of missed opportunities for 'partnership' with the tangata whenua, it is believed to have been at least potentially full of good intentions towards Maori and their aspirations.

In actuality the state, in its various manifestations, has been highly instrumental in imposing and implementing strategic and tactical policies to effect its own definition of the 'national good'. As has been stressed, from the beginning the Crown's key Maori policy – resonant with an attitude shared by most pakeha – was that tangata whenua should assimilate fully to 'superior' European mores, beliefs and ways of doing things. Whatever the retrospective longing of many a scholar, while indigenous customs and institutions were often tolerated or incorporated from 1840, this was seen as a temporary expedient until Maori had been Europeanised. This latter process entailed subjecting Maori fully to the will of the Crown: removing practices deemed to be 'repugnant to morality', stripping the tangata of most of the whenua, coercing and socialising Maori into appropriate ways of thinking, seeing and doing. While such policies and actions were continually adapted to changing circumstances, they essentially continued to the end of the nineteenth and throughout the first half of the twentieth centuries, and beyond.

But even the Maori milieu deemed to be the most accommodationist of all, that of the Young Maori Party/Ngataism, believed that Maoridom should preserve appropriate elements of its own culture and institutions at the same time as taking up the many desirable ideas, technologies and lifestyles of the pakeha. Far from being fully assimilationist, then, the Young Maori Party programme of mutual self-respect between the 'two races' of Aotearoa/New Zealand included preservation and enhancement of key aspects of Maori ways and culture. There should be, in Ngata's words, 'an experiment in cultural adaptation' that melded the best elements of both cultures and polities and included some concrete form of rangatiratanga that the state could recognise and work with and alongside. Other Maori movements in the first half of the twentieth century attempted to progress autonomy in many, varied and often more forthright ways.

Great hope was raised with the Labour–Ratana alliance and Labour's accession to office in 1935. Maori leaders and institutions became quickly aware, however, that their campaign for autonomy needed to take into account that, at that time, the ideological configuration of the dominant culture's political leadership had changed. The triumph of social democracy meant that notions of socio-economic levelling upwards, or at least of reducing the glaring disparities between groups and classes in society, were in the ascendancy. These coalesced neatly with the material and social aspirations of Maori, both of 'ordinary people' wishing for a better life and of leaders who emphasised Ngataist, tribalist or Ratana policies, but official concentration on such labourist aspirations did not allow much room for enhanced recognition of rangatiratanga.

Maori autonomy seemed closer when, during the Second World War, a state effort was made to harness the energies of 'the race'. Maori people and their leaders gained greater Crown-endorsed power than ever before in the history of the nation. But hopes that the wartime gains made for rangatiratanga would be extended substantively into peacetime were dashed. The post-war welfare organisation did provide some capacity for Maori empowerment, but its flax-roots committee system was tolerated only because something like it was regarded by politicians and bureaucrats as temporarily unavoidable.

Moreover, it was established in such a way as to have the potential to divert Maori energies away from 'undesirable' socio-political pursuits and towards safer activities – preferably those that would advance state policies. These would, in turn, lead Maori towards an assimilationist future, one in which the welfare organisation and all its parts would become redundant, along with tribal collectivism and even Maoritanga itself. In the post-war period, as previously, Maori resisted such an agenda, and that resistance included the familiar pattern of using tools provided or endorsed by the state – the welfare organisation itself, for example, or the women's welfare committees.

Whenever Maori progressed towards powerful autonomist forms that the Crown would not easily be able to counteract, then, the state would seek to appropriate their energies to further its own goals; and, in turn, the continuing Maori search for Crown recognition of rangatiratanga would include efforts to reappropriate the appropriated modes of organisation. By 1950, however, despite the gains of the war years, Maori collectivist institutions, vibrant and adaptive as many of them were, remained embattled within the wider polity of New Zealand and at a grave disadvantage in relation to the strength of the state. The general subsuming of Maori matters reflected many socio-economic, cultural, demographic and political factors, including loss of land and an intense Crown desire for the disappearance of all things indigenous (except perhaps for some 'cultural' and tourist-oriented marginalia).

Yet despite the state's ultimate aim for Maori, and whatever Labour's reliance on equality policies and National's extreme aversion to 'separatism', politicians and officials could see that collectivism remained the key organisational mode (however altered by colonial and other experiences) of the tangata whenua and the foundation of their aspirations. Certainly, both Maoridom as a whole and its various organisational expressions could not be wished away. The 'Maori race' had not faded or disappeared, as expected; the 'Race That Would Not Die' was still there, insistently and interactively so, constantly engaging with new socio-political and cultural developments and adapting its organisational forms to suit the times.

In 1950 the path that the quest for meaningful exercise of rangatiratanga would take was unclear. Ngata died in the middle of that year, while Labour and its Maori allies were still adjusting to being in the political opposition; Ratana had died long before, and Te Puea would die two years later. While Ngataism, Kingitanga and Ratanaism continued strongly, some of the ways and teachings of their former leaders were seen to be no longer appropriate. Their successors, along with many other Maori leaders and rank and file, sought to develop new ways of expressing rangatiratanga in the greatly altered circumstances of a post-war New Zealand in which Maori were rapidly urbanising.

Internal migration to the urban areas gave official New Zealand new cause to believe that the aspiration for rangatiratanga could finally be assimilated out of existence. Decision makers had long been searching for signs that this terminal process was about to begin. Officials had seized on such sentiments as Te Puea saying to her followers: 'Our relationship between the Maori and the Pakeha is such that we are basically one people.' But, as so often, this was a 'talking past' situation, and the Kingitanga leader's comments needed contextualising by her follow-up statement: 'In the future, remember, we are to walk side by side with our Pakeha friends.' What was sought was far from assimilation, but rather separate ethno-cultural identities and polities interacting and co-operating with each other – in general terms, 'two peoples in one nation' based on (using later terminology) an exemplary 'bicultural partnership' between rangatiratanga and the Crown.[127]

Whatever the specific types of autonomy desired by the various Maori movements, however, these seemed particularly far away at mid-century. Even 'equality' had not yet arrived. To take one example, it was not accidental that almost all police were pakeha. Maori were not considered to have a responsible enough 'temperament' to do such an important job. The state believed (in the words of a senior sergeant in 1950) that the 'average European would strongly resent being corrected or repri-manded by a Maori'. One thing that all involved in the interface between the two peoples of Aotearoa/New Zealand could agree on was that the way ahead in 'race' and Crown–Maori relations would be far from unproblematic and untroubled. This was no small matter in what was officially and popularly considered to be one of the most tranquil societies in the world – perhaps *the* most peaceful of all.

Yet, although the two major peoples of New Zealand often 'talked past each other' over the next half-century, dialogue did continue and results of sorts did occur. Organisational developments tended to conform to the long-established pattern: significant exercise of Maori agency would be followed by Crown appropriation, and this in turn would be succeeded by Maori attempts to reappropriate the appropriation. All the while, despite the discrepancy between the enormous coercive and hegemonic power of the state and the relative lack of resources of Maori organisations, discussions, debate and sometimes consultation or negotiations occurred. Such engagement continued through a period of increasing, urban-based intermarriage, and gathered momentum during the 'Maori Renaissance' of the 1970s and 1980s, when pakeha and governments had scant choice but to listen more closely to the raised voices of Maoridom and respond in various ways to its autonomist strategies and the tactics it was developing to pursue them.

What they were hearing was, in essence, what Maori had been saying throughout the first half of the twentieth century – indeed, since the beginning of colonisation. In turn, the Crown, at least until the 1970s– 80s, and in some interpretations also thereafter, sought what it had always aimed for: a society of fully assimilated Maori (and other non-pakeha ethnicities). While the two visions might be ultimately incompatible, the search continued for a *modus vivendi* – in the Crown's eyes a temporary one, but in Maoridom's eyes a lasting one which would entrench state recognition of rangatiratanga. Interactions between Crown (and more broadly, pakeha) and Maori remained, accordingly, highly complex.

The state continued to attempt to defuse or deflect autonomism, often using methods which engaged with and incorporated the organisational and other manifestations of rangatiratanga. Despite both this and urbanisation, Maoridom continued to focus on achieving autonomy, often borrowing from pakeha modes, concepts and structures along the way, and sometimes working to 'take back' (or at least make use of) Maori-based institutions which had been officialised. Despite its strength, and favourable demographic and other factors, the Crown was unable to effect its grand strategy of fully incorporating and then superseding rangatiratanga.[128]

All through the period under review – and well into the future – Maori collective organisation, in its myriad of tribal, pan-tribal, sub-tribal and non-tribal expressions, adapted and flourished in the face of great odds, and Maori culture survived, adjusted and revived as demographic recovery proceeded. Maoridom had not, as the Crown wished, withered away, however bleak its future had seemed as the twentieth century approached. Despite urban migration and state containment, it remained vibrant in 1950, and the Crown, whatever its assimilationist vision, had no choice but to continue to engage with Maoridom's aspiration for full exercise of rangatiratanga. The struggle had no end in sight for either of the signatory parties to the Treaty of Waitangi.

BIBLIOGRAPHY OF CITED SOURCES

A Maori View of the 'Hunn Report', Christchurch, 1961.

'A Native Prince', *Mana*, June–July 1999.

'Aid to Maoris', *New Zealand Herald*, 21 June 1944.

Adams, Peter, *Fatal Necessity: British Intervention in New Zealand 1830–1847*, Auckland, 1977.

Akenson, Donald Harman, 'No Petty People: Pakeha History and the Historiography of the Irish Diaspora', in Fraser, Lyndon (ed), *A Distant Shore: Irish Migration and New Zealand Settlement*, Dunedin, 2000.

Anderson, David M and Killingray, David (eds), *Policing the Empire: Government, Authority and Control, 1839–1940*, Manchester, 1991.

Andrews, C Lesley, 'Aspects of Development, 1870–1890', in Kawharu, I Hugh (ed), *Conflict and Compromise: Essays on the Maori Since Colonisation*, Wellington, 1975.

Appendices to the Journals of the House of Representatives (AJHR).

Armstrong, David, 'Land for Landless Natives', Waitangi Tribunal Document Wai 27, M16.

Armstrong, David and Stirling, Bruce, 'A Summary History of the Wellington Tenths: 1839–88', Wellington, 1992.

Attwood, Bain and Magowan, Fiona (eds), *Telling Stories: Indigenous History and Memory in Australia and New Zealand*, Wellington, 2001.

Ausubel, David P, 'The Maori: A Study in Resistive Acculturation', in Webb, Stephen D and Collette, John (eds), *New Zealand Society: Contemporary Perspectives*, Sydney, 1973.

———, *Maori Youth: A Psychoethnological Study of Cultural Deprivation*, New York, 1961.

Awatere, Donna, *Maori Sovereignty*, Auckland, 1984.

Baker, J V T, *The New Zealand People at War: War Economy*, Wellington, 1965.

Baker, Paul, *King and Country Call: New Zealanders, Conscription and the Great War*, Auckland, 1988.

Ball, D G, 'Maori Education', in Sutherland, I L G (ed), *The Maori People Today: A General Survey*, Wellington, 1940.

Ballara, Angela, *Iwi: The Dynamics of Maori Tribal Organisation from c.1769 to c.1945*, Wellington, 1998.

———, 'Ratana, Haami Tokouru', in *Dictionary of New Zealand Biography*, vol 4, Wellington/Auckland, 1998.

———, 'Ratana, Tahupotiki Wiremu', in *Dictionary of New Zealand Biography*, vol 3, Wellington/Auckland, 1996.

Barrington, J M and Beaglehole, T H, *Maori Schools in a Changing Society: An Historical Review*, Wellington, 1974.

Bassett, Heather, Steel, Rachel and Williams, David, *The Maori Land Legislation Manual*, vol 2, Wellington, 1994.

Bassett, Michael, *Coates of Kaipara*, Auckland, 1995.

Bassett, Michael and King, Michael, *Tomorrow Comes the Song: A Life of Peter Fraser*, Auckland, 2000.

Beaglehole, Ernest and Pearl, *Some Modern Maoris*, Wellington, 1946.

Belgrave, Michael, 'Something Borrowed, Something New: History and the Waitangi Tribunal', in Dalley, Bronwyn and Phillips, Jock (eds), *Going Public: The Changing Face of New Zealand History*, Auckland, 2001.

Belich, James, 'Colonization and History in New Zealand', in Winks, Robin W (ed), *The Oxford History of the British Empire: Volume V: Historiography*, Oxford, 1999.

——, *'I Shall Not Die': Titokowaru's War, New Zealand 1868–1869*, Wellington, 1989.

——, *Making Peoples: A History of the New Zealanders from Polynesian Settlement to the End of the Nineteenth Century*, Auckland, 1996.

——, 'Myth, Race and Identity in New Zealand', *New Zealand Journal of History*, 31(1), April 1997.

——, *The New Zealand Wars and the Victorian Interpretation of Racial Conflict*, Auckland, 1986.

——, *Paradise Reforged: A History of the New Zealanders from the 1880s to the Year 2000*, Auckland, 2001.

Bennion, Tom, 'The Maori Land Court and Maori Land Boards 1909–1952', Waitangi Tribunal Rangahaua Whanui Series Working Paper, Wellington, 1997.

Biggs, Bruce, 'Humpty Dumpty and the Treaty of Waitangi', in Kawharu, I Hugh (ed), *Waitangi: Maori and Pakeha Perspectives of the Treaty of Waitangi*, Auckland, 1989.

Binney, Judith, 'Encounters Across Time: The Makings of an Unanticipated Trilogy', in Attwood, Bain and Magowan, Fiona (eds), *Telling Stories: Indigenous History and Memory in Australia and New Zealand*, Wellington, 2001.

——, 'Te Mana Tuatoru: The Rohe Potae of Tuhoe', *New Zealand Journal of History*, 31(1), April 1997.

——, 'The Maori and the Signing of the Treaty of Waitangi', in Green, David (ed), *Towards 1990: Seven Leading Historians Examine Significant Aspects of New Zealand History*, Wellington, 1989.

——, 'Maori Oral Narratives, Pakeha Written Texts: Two Forms of Telling History', *New Zealand Journal of History*, 21(1), April 1987.

——, *Redemption Songs: A Life of Te Kooti Arikirangi Te Turuki*, Auckland, 1995.

—— (ed), *The Shaping of History: Essays from the New Zealand Journal of History*, Wellington, 2001.

Binney, Judith, Chaplin, Gillian and Wallace, Craig, *Mihaia: The Prophet Rua Kenana and His Community at Maungapohatu*, Wellington, 1979.

Blythe, Martin, *Naming the Other: Images of the Maori in New Zealand Film and Television*, Metuchen, 1994.

Boast, Richard, 'Lawyers, Historians, Ethics and the Judicial Process', *Victoria University of Wellington Law Review*, (28)1, March 1998.

———, 'Maori Land and the Treaty of Waitangi', in Boast, Richard, Erueti, Andrew, McPhail, Doug and Smith, Norman, *Maori Land Law*, Wellington, 1999.

———, 'The Mohaka–Waikare Confiscation Consolidated Report: Vol 1: The Mohaka–Waikare Confiscation and Its Aftermath', a report for the Waitangi Tribunal, Wellington, 1995.

Boast, Richard, Erueti, Andrew, McPhail, Doug and Smith, Norman, *Maori Land Law*, Wellington, 1999.

Bollinger, Conrad, *Grog's Own Country: The Story of Liquor Licensing in New Zealand*, Wellington, 1959 (1967 ed).

Boenisch-Brednich, Brigitte and Hill, Richard S, 'Biculturalism in New Zealand/Aotearoa', in Csukas, Gyorgyi, Kiss, Reka, Kristof, Ildiko, Nagy, Ilona and Szarvas, Zsuzsa (eds), *Times, Places, Passages: Ethnological Approaches in the New Millennium*, Budapest, 2004.

Brookfield, F M, *Waitangi & Indigenous Rights: Revolution, Law and Legitimation*, Auckland, 1999.

Brooking, Tom, '"Busting up" the Greatest Estate of All: Liberal Maori Land Policy, 1891–1911', *New Zealand Journal of History*, 26(1), April 1992.

———, *Lands for the People? The Highland Clearances and the Colonisation of New Zealand: A Biography of John McKenzie*, Dunedin, 1996.

———, 'Review', *People's History*, March 2000.

Brown, Bruce, *The Rise of New Zealand Labour*, Wellington, 1962.

Bryder, Linda, *A Voice for Mothers: The Plunket Society and Infant Welfare 1907–2000*, Auckland, 2003.

Burdon, R M, *The New Dominion: A Social and Political History of New Zealand 1918–1939*, Wellington, 1965.

Butterworth, G V, 'Aotearoa 1769–1988: Towards a Tribal Perspective: Report for Department of Maori Affairs', Wellington, 1988.

———, 'Apirana Ngata: The Politics of Adaptation', typescript, nd.

———, 'The Health of the Body, the Health of the Land: A Comparative Study of the Political Objectives and Careers of Wiremu Ratana and the Ratana Movement, and Sir Apirana Ngata', a report for the Crown Forestry Rental Trust, Wellington, 2000.

———, 'The Politics of Adaptation: The Career of Sir Apirana Ngata 1874–1928', MA thesis, Victoria University of Wellington, 1968.

———, 'A Rural Maori Renaissance? Maori Society and Politics 1920 to 1951', *Journal of the Polynesian Society*, 81(2), June 1972.

———, *Sir Apirana Ngata*, Wellington, 1968.

———, 'Trustee Law and the Trust Deed: Their Implications for Governance', unpublished manuscript, Wellington, 1998.

Butterworth, G V and S M, *The Maori Trustee*, Wellington, 1991.

Butterworth, G V and Young, H R, *Maori Affairs/Nga Take Maori*, Wellington, 1990.

Byrnes, Giselle, *The Waitangi Tribunal and New Zealand History*, Melbourne, 2004.

Campbell, S K L, 'Land Alienation, Consolidation and Development in the Urewera 1912-1950', a report for the Crown Forestry Rental Trust, Wellington, 1997 (Waitangi Tribunal Document Wai 36, A9).

————, 'National Overview on Land Consolidation Schemes 1909–1931', a report for the Crown Forestry Rental Trust, Wellington, 1998.

Clark, Margaret (ed), *Peter Fraser: Master Politician*, Palmerston North, 1998.

Cody, Joseph F, *Man of Two Worlds: Sir Maui Pomare*, Wellington, 1953.

Collins, Heeni, 'Nga Tangaroa Awarua', *National Oral History Association of Aotearoa New Zealand Journal*, 1999.

Committee of the Maori Members of Parliament, 'A Description Concerning the Maori Contingent of Aotearoa and Te Waipounamu Who Took Part in the Great War', in Pugsley, Christopher, *Te Hokowhitu a Tu: The Maori Pioneer Battalion in the First World War*, Auckland, 1995.

Condliffe, John B and Airey, Willis T G, *Short History of New Zealand*, Auckland, 1938 (rev ed).

Condliffe, John B, *Te Rangi Hiroa: The Life of Sir Peter Buck*, Christchurch, 1971.

Consedine, Robert and Consedine, Joanna, *Healing our History: The Challenge of the Treaty of Waitangi*, Auckland, 2001

Cox, Lindsay, *Kotahitanga: The Search for Maori Political Unity*, Auckland, 1993.

Crawford, John (ed), *Kia Kaha: New Zealand in the Second World War*, Melbourne, 2000 (2002 ed).

Curnow, Jenifer, Hopa, Ngapare and McRae, Jane (eds), *Rere Atu, Taku Manu! Discovering History, Language and Politics in the Maori-language Newspapers*, Auckland, 2002.

Dalley, Bronwyn, *Family Matters: Child Welfare in Twentieth-Century New Zealand*, Auckland, 1998.

Dalley, Bronwyn, and Labrum, Bronwyn (eds), *Fragments: New Zealand Social and Cultural History*, Auckland, 2000.

Dalley, Bronwyn, and Phillips, Jock (eds), *Going Public: The Changing Face of New Zealand History*, Auckland, 2001.

Dawson, Richard, *The Treaty of Waitangi and the Control of Language*, Wellington, 2001.

Department of Maori Affairs, *The Maori Today*, Wellington, 1949.

Department of Maori Affairs Report for Year Ended 31 March 1950, *AJHR*, 1950, G9.

The Dictionary of New Zealand Biography, *Te Kingitanga: The People of the Maori King Movement*, Auckland/Wellington, 1996.

The Dictionary of New Zealand Biography, vol 1, 1769–1869, Wellington, 1990.

The Dictionary of New Zealand Biography, vol 2, 1870–1900, Wellington, 1993.

The Dictionary of New Zealand Biography, vol 3, 1901–1920, Auckland/Wellington, 1996.

The Dictionary of New Zealand Biography, vol 4, 1921–1940, Auckland/Wellington, 1998.

Doig, Suzanne, 'The Battle for the Whanganui River 1840–1998', *History Now*, 4(2), October 1998.

Dow, Derek A, *Maori Health and Government Policy 1840–1940*, Wellington, 1999.

Dunstall, Graeme, *A Policeman's Paradise? Policing a Stable Society 1918–1945*, Palmerston North, 1999.

————, 'The Social Pattern', in Oliver, W H and Williams, B S (eds), *The Oxford History of New Zealand*, Wellington, 1981.

Durie, E T J, 'Custom Law', unpublished paper, [Wellington], 1994.

————, 'Ethics and Values', in *Indigenous Peoples and the Law*, 1999, http://www.kennett.co.nz/law/indigenous/1999/39.html.

————,'Maori Autonomy: Preventing Power Games', *Stimulus*, May 1998.

————,'The Treaty in Maori History', in Renwick, W L (ed), *Sovereignty and Indigenous Rights: the Treaty of Waitangi in International Contexts*, Wellington, 1991.

Durie, Mason, *Te Mana, Te Kawanatanga: The Politics of Maori Self-Determination*, Auckland, 1998.

————, *Whaiora: Maori Health Development*, Melbourne, 1994 (2nd ed, 1998).

Edwards, Mihi, *Mihipeka: Early Years*, Auckland, 1990.

Else, Anne (ed), *Women Together: A History of Women's Organisations in New Zealand: Nga Ropu Wahine o te Motu*, Wellington, 1993.

Elsmore, Bronwyn, *Mana from Heaven: A Century of Maori Prophets in New Zealand*, Tauranga, 1989.

Evison, Harry C, *The Long Dispute: Maori Land Rights and European Colonisation in Southern New Zealand*, Christchurch, 1997.

Fairburn, Miles, *The Ideal Society and Its Enemies*, Auckland, 1989.

Fanon, Frantz, *The Wretched of the Earth*, New York, 1963.

Farland, Bruce, *Coates' Tale: War Hero, Politician, Statesman, Joseph Gordon Coates, Prime Minister of New Zealand, 1925–1928*, Wellington, 1995.

Fleras, Augie, 'A Descriptive Analysis of Maori Wardens in the Historical and Contemporary Context of New Zealand Society', PhD thesis, Victoria University of Wellington, 1980.

————, *From Village Runanga to the New Zealand Maori Wardens' Association: A Historical Development of Maori Wardens*, Wellington, 1980.

————, 'Maori Wardens and the Control of Liquor Among the Maori of New Zealand', *Journal of the Polynesian Society*, (90)4, December 1981.

Frame, Alex, *Salmond: Southern Jurist*, Wellington, 1995.

Fraser, Lyndon (ed), *A Distant Shore: Irish Migration and New Zealand Settlement*, Dunedin, 2000.

Freire, Paulo, *Pedagogy of the Oppressed*, 1970 (New York ed, 1988).

Gardiner, Wira, *Te Mura o te Ahi: The Story of the Maori Battalion*, Auckland, 1992.

Gilling, Bryan D, 'Engine of Destruction? An Introduction to the History of the Maori Land Court', *Victoria University of Wellington Law Review*, 24(2), July 1994.

————, *Government Valuers*, Wellington, 1996.

————, '"The Mana of Their Own Land": Rangatiratanga and the Maori Land Council Regime, 1900–1905', draft paper, Treaty of Waitangi Research Unit, 2004.

Gilling, Bryan D, and O'Malley, Vincent, *The Treaty of Waitangi in New Zealand History*, Wellington, 2000.

Gilling, Tui, 'Rangatiratanga and the Crown in the Twentieth Century: Case Study Three', draft paper, Treaty of Waitangi Research Unit, 2003.

Gould, Ashley, 'Maori and the First World War', in McGibbon, Ian (ed), *The Oxford Companion to New Zealand Military History*, Auckland, 2000.

————, 'Maori Land Development 1929–1954: An Introductory Overview with Representative Case Studies', a report for the Crown Forestry Rental Trust, Wellington, 1996.

Grace, Patricia, Ramsden, Irihapeti and Dennis, Jonathan (eds), *The Silent Migration: Ngati Poneke Young Maori Club 1937–1948*, Wellington, 2001.

Greenland, Hauraki, 'Ethnicity as Ideology: The Critique of Pakeha Society', in Spoonley, P, Macpherson, C, Pearson, D and Sedgwick, C (eds), *Tauiwi: Racism and Ethnicity in New Zealand*, Palmerston North, 1984.

Gump, James O, 'A Spirit of Resistance: Sioux, Xhosa, and Maori Responses to Western Dominance, 1840–1920', *Pacific Historical Review*, February 1997.

Gustafson, Barry, *From the Cradle to the Grave: A Biography of Michael Joseph Savage*, Auckland, 1986.

Hamer, David, *The New Zealand Liberals*, Auckland, 1988.

Harris, Aroha, 'Maori Land Title Improvement Since 1945: Communal Ownership and Economic Use', *New Zealand Journal of History*, 31(1), 1997.

Harrison, Noel, *Graham Latimer: A Biography*, Wellington, 2002.

Head, Lyndsay, 'The Pursuit of Modernity in Maori Society: The Conceptual Bases of Citizenship in the Early Colonial Period', in Sharp, Andrew and McHugh, Paul (eds), *Histories, Power and Loss: Uses of the Past – A New Zealand Commentary*, Wellington, 2001.

Heelas, Paul, Lash, Scott and Morris, Paul (eds), *Detraditionalization: Critical Reflections on Authority and Identity*, Oxford, 1996.

Henderson, J McLeod, *Ratana: The Man, the Church, the Political Movement*, Wellington, 1972 (2nd ed).

Hill, Richard S, *Anti-Treatyism and Anti-Scholarship: An Analysis of Anti-Treatyist Writings*, Wellington, 2002.

———, 'Autonomy and Authority: Rangatiratanga and the Crown in Twentieth Century New Zealand: An Overview', Wellington, 2000.

———, *The Colonial Frontier Tamed: New Zealand Policing in Transition, 1867–1886*, Wellington, 1989.

———, *Enthroning 'Justice Above Might'? The Sim Commission, Tainui and the Crown*, Wellington, 1989.

———, 'The Future of Rangatiratanga', *Future Times*, 8, 2003 (fuller version at: http://www.futurestrust.org.nz/e-FutureTimes/e-FTVol8.html#anchorhill).

———, *Introducing Policing into the Rangatiratanga Discourse: An Historical Overview of the Role of Maori Police Personnel*, Wellington, 2003.

———, *The Iron Hand in the Velvet Glove: The Modernisation of Policing in New Zealand, 1886–1917*, Palmerston North, 1995.

———, 'The Policing of Colonial New Zealand', in Anderson, David M and Killingray David (eds), *Policing the Empire: Government, Authority and Control, 1839–1940*, Manchester, 1991.

———, *Policing the Colonial Frontier: The Theory and Practice of Coercive Social and Racial Control in New Zealand, 1767–1867*, Wellington, 1986 (two-book set).

———, *Settlements of Major Maori Claims in the 1940s: A Preliminary Historical Investigation*, Wellington, 1989.

———, *The Treaty of Waitangi Today*, Wellington, 2000.

———, 'Worthington, Arthur Bently', in *Dictionary of New Zealand Biography*, vol 2, Wellington, 1993.

Hill, Richard S and O'Malley, Vincent, *The Maori Quest for Rangatiratanga/Authority, 1840–1920*, Wellington, 2000

Hippolite, Joy, 'Rangahaua Whanui District 11C: Wairoa', a report for the Waitangi Tribunal, Wellington, 1996.

Hogan, Helen M, *Hikurangi ki Homburg: Henare Kohere and Terei Ngaitai with the Maori Coronation Contingent 1902*, Christchurch, 1997.

Hohepa, P W, *A Maori Community in Northland*, Wellington, 1964 (1970 ed).

Holt, James, 'Compulsory Arbitration in New Zealand, 1894–1916', in Binney, Judith (ed), *The Shaping of History: Essays from the New Zealand Journal of History*, Wellington, 2001.

Hunn, J K, *Report on Department of Maori Affairs: with Statistical Supplement*, Wellington, 1961.

Hutt, Marten, *Te Iwi Maori me te Inu Waipiro: He Tuhituhinga Hitori/Maori and Alcohol: A History*, Wellington, 1999.

Hutton, John, 'Archival Material Relating to the Maori Land Boards 1900–1952', a report for the Crown Forestry Rental Trust, Wellington, 1996.

———, 'The Operation of the Waikato–Maniapoto District Maori Land Board', in Loveridge, Donald M (ed), 'Twentieth Century Maori Land Administration Research Programme', a report for the Crown Forestry Rental Trust, Wellington, 1996 (rev ed 1998).

———, '"A Ready and Quick Method": The Alienation of Maori Land by Sales to the Crown and Private Individuals, 1905–30', in Loveridge, Donald M (ed), 'Twentieth Century Maori Land Administration Research Programme', a report for the Crown Forestry Rental Trust, Wellington, 1996 (rev ed 1998).

Johnston, R J (ed), *Urbanisation in New Zealand: Geographical Essays*, Wellington, 1973.

Jones, Pei Te Hurinui, 'Maori Kings', in Schwimmer, Erik (ed), *The Maori People in the Nineteen-Sixties*, Auckland, 1968.

Jones, Reimana R, 'Jones, Michael Rotohiko', in *Dictionary of New Zealand Biography*, vol 4, Auckland/Wellington, 1998.

Kaa, Wiremu and Te Ohorere (eds), *Apirana Turupu Ngata*, Wellington, 1996.

Kaati, John Reihana, *Rohe Potae and Wahanui Paramount Chief*, Te Kuiti, nd.

Kawharu, I Hugh, *Maori Land Tenure: Studies of a Changing Institution*, Oxford, 1977.

——— (ed), *Conflict and Compromise: Essays on the Maori Since Colonisation*, Wellington, 1975.

——— (ed), *Waitangi: Maori and Pakeha Perspectives of the Treaty of Waitangi*, Auckland, 1989.

Keenan, Danny, 'Bound to the Land: Maori Retention and Assertion of Land and Identity', in Pawson, Eric and Brooking, Tom (eds), *Environmental Histories of New Zealand*, Melbourne, 2002.

———, 'Ma Pango Ma Whero Ka Oti: Unities and Fragments in Maori History', in Dalley, Bronwyn and Labrum, Bronwyn (eds), *Fragments: New Zealand Social and Cultural History*, Auckland, 2000.

———, 'Predicting the Past: Some Directions in Recent Maori Historiography', *Te Pouhere Korero Journal*, March 1999.

Keesing, Felix M, *The Changing Maori*, New Plymouth, 1928.

Kernot, Bernard, 'Maori Buildings for the Centennial', paper presented to *Celebrating the 1940 Centennial* conference, Stout Research Centre for the Study of History, Society and Culture, Wellington, 1999.

———, *People of the Four Winds*, Wellington, 1972.

Kersey, Harry A Jr, *Indigenous Sovereignty in Two Cultures: Maori and American Indians Compared*, Wellington, 2000.

King, G S R, 'Assimilation or Separation? The Kotahitanga Parliament Movement 1891–94', in Reilly, Michael and Thomson, Jane (eds), *When the Waves Rolled in upon Us: Essays in Nineteenth-Century Maori History*, Dunedin, 1999.

King, Michael, 'Between Two Worlds', in Oliver, W H and Williams, B S (eds), *The Oxford History of New Zealand*, Wellington, 1981.

———, *Maori: A Photographic and Social History*, Auckland, 1983.

———, *Moriori: A People Rediscovered*, Auckland, 1989.

———, *Nga Iwi o te Motu: One Thousand Years of Maori History*, Auckland, 1997.

———, *The Penguin History of New Zealand*, Auckland, 2003.

———, *Te Puea: A Biography*, Auckland, 1977.

——— (ed), *Tihe Mauri Ora: Aspects of Maoritanga*, Auckland, 1978

———, *Koroki – My King*, [Ngaruawahia], 1999.

Labrum, Bronwyn, '"Bringing families up to scratch": The Distinctive Workings of Maori State Welfare, 1944–1970', *New Zealand Journal of History*, 36(1), October 2002.

Lange, Raeburn, *A Limited Measure of Local Self-Government: Maori Councils, 1900–1920*, Wellington, 2004.

———, *May the People Live: A History of Maori Health Development 1900–1920*, Auckland, 1999.

Love, R Ngatata, 'Policies of Frustration: The Growth of Maori Politics: The Ratana/Labour Era', PhD thesis, Victoria University of Wellington, 1977.

Loveridge, Donald M, 'Maori Land Councils and Maori Land Boards: A Historical Overview, 1900 to 1952', Waitangi Tribunal Rangahaua Whanui Series, Wellington, 1996.

Loveridge, Donald M (ed), 'Twentieth Century Maori Land Administration Research Programme', a report for the Crown Forestry Rental Trust, Wellington, 1996 (rev ed 1998).

McCan, David, *Whatiwhatihoe: The Waikato Raupatu Claim*, Wellington, 2001.

Maclean, F S, *Challenge for Health: A History of Public Health in New Zealand*, Wellington, 1964.

McClure, Margaret, *A Civilised Community: A History of Social Security in New Zealand, 1898–1998*, Auckland, 1998.

McGibbon, Ian (ed), *The Oxford Companion to New Zealand Military History*, Auckland, 2000.

McHugh, Paul, 'Constitutional Myths and the Treaty of Waitangi', *New Zealand Law Journal*, September 1991.

———, 'Law, History and the Treaty of Waitangi', *New Zealand Journal of History*, 31(1), April 1997.

———, *The Maori Magna Carta: New Zealand Law and the Treaty of Waitangi*, Auckland, 1991.

McRae, Jane, 'Participation: Native Committees (1883) and Papatupu Block Committees (1900) in Tai Tokerau', MA thesis, University of Auckland, 1981.

Mahuta, Robert, 'The Maori King Movement Today', in King, Michael (ed), *Tihe Mauri Ora: Aspects of Maoritanga*, Wellington, 1978.
———, 'Tainui, Kingitanga and Raupatu', in Wilson, Margaret A and Yeatman, Anna (eds), *Justice and Identity: Antipodean Practices*, Wellington, 1995.
Maori Councils Act 1900 (No 48).
Maori Land Settlement Act 1905 (No 44).
Maori Lands Administration Act 1900 (No 55).
Maori Social and Economic Advancement Act 1945 (No 43).
'Maori War Effort Unexcelled Anywhere: A Voluntary Organisation Achieves Grand Record', *Standard*, 28 September 1944.
'Maoris Farewell Liaison Officer', *Northern Advocate*, 18 July 1944.
Marr, Cathy, 'The Alienation of Maori Land in the Rohe Potae (Aotea Block), 1840–1920', a report for the Waitangi Tribunal, Wellington, 1996.
———, 'The Alienation of Maori Land in the Rohe Potae (Aotea Block), Part 2, 1900–1960', a report for the Waitangi Tribunal, Wellington, 1999.
———, 'Crown Policy Towards Major Crown/Iwi Claim Agreements of the 1940s and 1950s', a preliminary report for the Treaty of Waitangi Policy Unit, Wellington, 1990.
———, 'An Overview History of the Taranaki Confiscation Claim: From the Sim Commission to the Submission of Taranaki Claims to the Waitangi Tribunal', a report for the Waitangi Tribunal, Wellington, 1991.
Martin, John F and Taylor, Kerry (eds), *Culture and the Labour Movement: Essays in New Zealand Labour History*, Palmerston North, 1991.
Martin, R J, 'The Liberal Experiment', in Pocock, J G A (ed), *The Maori and New Zealand Politics*, Auckland, 1965.
Mead, Sidney Moko, *Landmarks, Bridges and Visions: Aspects of Maori Culture*, Wellington, 1997.
Meek, R L, *Maori Problems Today: A Short Survey*, Wellington, nd.
Melbourne, Hineani (ed), *Maori Sovereignty: The Maori Perspective*, Auckland, 1995.
Meredith, Paul, 'Hybridity in the Third Space: Rethinking Bi-cultural Politics in Aotearoa/New Zealand', *He Pukenga Korero*, 4(2), Ngahuru/Autumn 1999.
Metge, Joan, *The Maoris of New Zealand: Rautahi*, London, 1976 (rev ed).
———, *New Growth from Old: The Whanau in the Modern World*, Wellington, 1995.
———, *A New Maori Migration: Rural and Urban Relations in Northern New Zealand*, London, 1964.
Metge, Joan, and Kinloch, Patricia, *Talking Past Each Other: Problems of Cross-cultural Communication*, Wellington, 1978.
Middleton, Sue (ed), *Women and Education in Aotearoa*, Wellington, 1998.
Milne, Jonathan, 'War Inquiry into Ratana Members', *Sunday Star-Times*, 26 January 2003.
Morris, Paul, 'Community Beyond Tradition', in Heelas, Paul, Lash, Scott and Morris, Paul (eds), *Detraditionalization: Critical Reflections on Authority and Identity*, Oxford, 1996.
Mulgan, Richard, *Maori, Pakeha and Democracy*, Auckland, 1989.
Murray, Tom, Taylor, Kerry, Tepanaia, Joe and Rameka, Nora, 'Towards a History of

Maori and Trade Unions', in Martin, John F and Taylor, Kerry (eds), *Culture and the Labour Movement: Essays in New Zealand Labour History*, Palmerston North, 1991.

Native Department Report on the Working of the Native Land Courts, Native Land Boards, and Native Land Purchase Board for Year Ended 31 March 1920, *AJHR*, 1920, G9.

Native Land Act 1909 (No 15).

Native Land Amendment Act 1913 (No 58).

New Zealand Government, *The New Zealand Official Handbook 1892*, Wellington, 1892.

——, *The New Zealand Official Yearbook, 1951–52*, Wellington, 1952.

——, *Report of Royal Commission on the Courts*, Wellington, 1978.

Ngaitahu Claim Settlement Act 1944 (No 33).

Ngaitahu Trust Board Act 1946 (No 33).

Ngata, Apirana T, 'Maori Land Settlement', in Sutherland, I L G (ed), *The Maori People Today: A General Survey*, Wellington, 1940.

——, 'The Price of Citizenship', Wellington, 1943.

——, *Te Tiriti o Waitangi*, Hastings, 1922 (1950 ed, Christchurch).

O'Brien, Anne-Marie, 'Taihoa: The Stout–Ngata Native Land Commission, 1907–1909', in Reilly, Michael and Thomson, Jane (eds), *When the Waves Rolled in upon Us: Essays in Nineteenth-Century Maori History*, Dunedin, 1999.

O'Connor, P S, 'The Recruitment of Maori Soldiers, 1914–1918', *Political Science*, 19(2), 1967.

O'Malley, Vincent, *Agents of Autonomy: Maori Committees in the Nineteenth Century*, Wellington, 1997 (rev ed, 1998).

——, *Indigenous Land Rights in an International Context: A Survey of the Literature Relating to Australia, New Zealand and North America*, Wellington, 2000.

——, 'Progressive Paternalism: Maori and the First Labour Government', *Race Gender Class*, 14, 1992.

Office of Treaty Settlements, *Healing the Past, Building a Future: A Guide to Treaty of Waitangi Claims and Negotiations with the Crown*, Wellington, nd (2nd ed).

Oliver, W H, 'The Future Behind Us: The Waitangi Tribunal's Retrospective Utopia', in Sharp, Andrew and McHugh, Paul (eds), *Histories, Power and Loss: Uses of the Past – A New Zealand Commentary*, Wellington, 2001.

Oliver, W H and Williams, B S (eds), *The Oxford History of New Zealand*, Wellington, 1981.

Olssen, Erik, *The Red Feds*, Auckland, 1988.

Orange, Claudia J, 'An Exercise in Maori Autonomy: The Rise and Demise of the Maori War Effort Organisation', *New Zealand Journal of History*, 21(1), April 1987.

——, 'Fraser and the Maori', in Clark, Margaret (ed), *Peter Fraser: Master Politician*, Palmerston North, 1998.

——, 'A Kind of Equality: Labour and the Maori People, 1935–1949', MA thesis, University of Auckland, 1977.

——, 'Maori War Effort Organisation', in McGibbon, Ian C (ed), *The Oxford Companion to New Zealand Military History*, Wellington, 2000.

——, 'The Price of Citizenship? The Maori War Effort', in Crawford, John (ed), *Kia Kaha: New Zealand in the Second World War*, Melbourne, 2000 (2002 ed).

————, *The Treaty of Waitangi*, Wellington, 1987.

Orbell, Margaret (ed), *He Reta Ki Te Maunga: Letters to the Mountain*, Auckland, 2002.

Ormsby, M J, 'Maori Tikanga and Criminal Justice', a report for the Ministry of Justice, Wellington, nd.

Owen, Graham, 'Case Study 1: Tikitere Development Scheme', in Gould, Ashley, 'Maori Land Development 1929–1954: An Introductory Overview with Representative Case Studies', a report for the Crown Forestry Rental Trust, Wellington, 1996.

Parsonson, Ann, 'The Challenge to Maori Mana', in Rice, Geoffrey (ed), *The Oxford History of New Zealand*, Auckland, 1992 (2nd ed).

Pawson, Eric and Brooking, Tom (eds), *Environmental Histories of New Zealand*, Melbourne, 2002.

Pearson, David, 'Biculturalism and Multiculturalism in Comparative Perspective', in Spoonley, Paul, Pearson, David and Macpherson, Cluny (eds), *Nga Take: Ethnic Relations and Racism in Aotearoa/New Zealand*, Palmerston North, 1991.

————, *A Dream Deferred: The Origins of Ethnic Conflict in New Zealand*, Wellington, 1990.

————, *The Politics of Ethnicity in Settler Societies: States of Unease*, Basingstoke, 2001.

Pere, Rangimarie Rose, 'Te Wheke: Whaia te Maramatanga me te Aroha', in Middleton, Sue (ed), *Women and Education in Aotearoa*, Wellington, 1998.

Phillips, Jock, 'Reading the 1940 Centennial', paper presented to *Celebrating the 1940 Centennial* conference, Stout Research Centre for the Study of History, Society and Culture, Wellington, 1999.

Pocock, J G A (ed), *The Maori and New Zealand Politics*, Wellington, 1965.

Pool, Ian, *The Maori Population of New Zealand 1769–1971*, Auckland, 1977.

Poulsen, M F and Johnston, R J, 'Patterns of Maori Migration', in Johnston, R J (ed), *Urbanisation in New Zealand: Geographical Essays*, Wellington, 1973.

Pratt, John, *Punishment in a Perfect Society: The New Zealand Penal System 1840–1939*, Wellington, 1992.

Prichard, Ivor and Waetford, Hemi, *Report of the Committee of Inquiry into the Laws Affecting Maori Land and Powers of the Maori Land Court*, Wellington, 1965.

Pugsley, Christopher, *Te Hokowhitu a Tu: The Maori Pioneer Battalion in the First World War*, Auckland, 1995.

Raureti, Moana, 'The Origins of the Ratana Movement', in King, Michael (ed), *Tihe Mauri Ora: Aspects of Maoritanga*, Auckland, 1978.

Reilly, Michael and Thomson, Jane (eds), *When the Waves Rolled in upon Us: Essays in Nineteenth-Century Maori History*, Dunedin, 1999.

Renwick, W L (ed), *Sovereignty and Indigenous Rights: The Treaty of Waitangi in International Contexts*, Wellington, 1991.

Report of Royal Commission on 'Confiscated Native Lands and Other Grievances', *AJHR*, 1928, G7 [Sim Commission].

Report of Under-Secretary for Maori Affairs for Year Ended 31 March 1950, *AJHR*, 1950, G9.

Reports of the Commission on 'Native Lands and Native-Land Tenure', *AJHR*, 1907, G1–G1E and 1908, Gi–iii, and G1A–1T [Stout–Ngata Commission].

Rice, Geoffrey, *Black November: The 1918 Influenza Epidemic in New Zealand*, Wellington, 1988.

—— (ed), *The Oxford History of New Zealand*, Auckland, 1992 (2nd ed).

Riddell, Kate, '"Improving" the Maori: Counting the Ideology of Intermarriage', *New Zealand Journal of History*, 34(1), April 2000.

Rigby, Barry, 'Historians and Lawyers in the Public Arena', paper presented to New Zealand Historical Association Conference, Hamilton, 1999.

Ritchie, James E, *The Making of a Maori: A Case Study of a Changing Community*, Wellington, 1963.

Rogers, Anna and Simpson, Miria (eds), *Te Timatanga Tatau Tatau/Early Stories from Founding Members of the Maori Women's Welfare League as Told to Dame Mira Szaszy*, Wellington, 1993.

Roth, Bert, *Trade Unions in New Zealand Past and Present*, Wellington, 1973.

Round, David, *Truth or Treaty? Commonsense Questions about the Treaty of Waitangi*, Christchurch, 1998.

Royal, Te Ahukaramu Charles and Jamison, Tom, 'Royal, Te Rangiataahua Kiniwe', in *Dictionary of New Zealand Biography*, vol 4, Wellington/Auckland, 1998.

Said, Edward W, *Orientalism*, New York, 1978.

Scott, Dick, *Ask That Mountain: The Story of Parihaka*, Auckland, 1975.

Schwimmer, Erik (ed), *The Maori People in the Nineteen-Sixties: A Symposium*, Auckland, 1968.

Sharp, Andrew, *Justice and the Maori: The Philosophy and Practice of Maori Claims in New Zealand since the 1970s*, Auckland, 1997 (2nd ed).

Sharp, Andrew and McHugh, Paul (eds), *Histories, Power and Loss: Uses of the Past – A New Zealand Commentary*, Wellington, 2001.

Simon, Judith (ed), *Nga Kura Maori: The Native Schools System 1867–1969*, Auckland, 1998.

Simon, Judith and Smith, Linda Tuhiwai (eds), *A Civilising Mission? Perceptions and Representations of the Native Schools System*, Auckland, 2001.

Simpson, Tony, *Shame and Disgrace: A History of Lost Scandals in New Zealand*, Auckland, 1992.

Sinclair, Keith, *A Destiny Apart: New Zealand's Search for National Identity*, Wellington, 1986.

——, *A History of New Zealand*, Harmondsworth, 1959.

——, 'Why Are Race Relations in New Zealand Better Than in South Africa, South Australia, or South Dakota?', *New Zealand Journal of History*, 5(2), October 1971.

Sissons, Jeffrey, 'The Post-Assimilationist Thought of Sir Apirana Ngata: Towards a Genealogy of New Zealand Biculturalism', *New Zealand Journal of History*, 34(1), April 2000.

——, *Te Waimana/The Spring of Mana: Tuhoe History and the Colonial Encounter*, Dunedin, 1991.

Smith, Linda Tuhiwai, *Decolonizing Methodologies: Research and Indigenous Peoples*, Dunedin, 1999.

Sorrenson, M P K, 'How to Civilize Savages: Some "Answers" from Nineteenth-Century New Zealand', *New Zealand Journal of History*, 9(2), October 1975.

————, 'The Purchase of Maori Lands, 1865–1892', MA thesis, University of Auckland, 1955.

————, 'Towards a Radical Reinterpretation of New Zealand History: The Role of the Waitangi Tribunal', in Kawharu, I Hugh (ed), *Waitangi: Maori and Pakeha Perspectives of the Treaty of Waitangi*, Auckland, 1989.

———— (ed), *Na To Hoa Aroha: From Your Dear Friend. The Correspondence between Sir Apirana Ngata and Sir Peter Buck 1925–50*, 3 vols, Auckland, 1986–88.

Soutar, Monty, 'Maori War Effort Overseas in the Second World War', in McGibbon, Ian C (ed), *The Oxford Companion to New Zealand Military History*, Wellington, 2000.

Spiller, Peter, Finn, Jeremy and Boast, Richard, *A New Zealand Legal History*, Wellington, 1995.

Spoonley, P, Macpherson, C, Pearson, D and Sedgwick, C (eds), *Tauiwi: Racism and Ethnicity in New Zealand*, Palmerston North, 1984.

Spoonley, Paul, Pearson, David, and Macpherson, Cluny (eds), *Nga Take: Ethnic Relations and Racism in Aotearoa/New Zealand*, Palmerston North, 1991.

Stokes, Evelyn, Milroy, J Wharehuia and Melbourne, Hirini, *Te Urewera: Nga Iwi te Whenua te Ngahere: People, Land and Forests of Te Urewera*, Hamilton, 1986.

Sutherland, I L G (ed), *The Maori People Today: A General Survey*, Wellington, 1940.

Taranaki Maori Claims Settlement Act 1944 (No 32).

Taylor, Nancy M, *The New Zealand People at War: The Home Front*, Wellington, 1986.

Te Awekotuku, Ngahuia, 'Conclusion', in Spoonley, P, Macpherson, C, Pearson, D and Sedgwick, C (eds), *Tauiwi: Racism and Ethnicity in New Zealand*, Palmerston North, 1984.

Te Puni Kokiri, *Discussion Paper on the Review of the Maori Community Development Act 1962*, Wellington, 1998.

Thomson, Jane, 'The Rehabilitation of Servicemen of World War II in New Zealand 1940 to 1954', PhD thesis, Victoria University of Wellington, 1983.

Tirikatene, E, 'Maori Purposes Bill', memo of 30 November 1945, AAMK 869, 692e, Archives New Zealand, Wellington.

Turbott, H B, 'Health and Social Welfare', in Sutherland, I L G (ed), *The Maori People Today: A General Survey*, Wellington, 1940.

Veracini, Lorenzo, *Negotiating a Bicultural Past: An Historiographical 'Revolution' in 1980s Aotearoa/New Zealand*, Wellington, 2001.

————, 'Negotiating Indigenous Resistance in the South Pacific: Australia, Aotearoa/New Zealand and Kanaky-New Caledonia, Three Cases in Historical Redescription', PhD dissertation, Brisbane, 2001.

Waikato–Maniapoto Maori Claims Settlement Act 1946 (No 19).

Waitangi Tribunal, *Ngai Tahu Report 1991*, 3 vols, Wellington, 1991.

————, *Raupatu Document Bank*, vol 137, Wellington, nd.

————, *The Taranaki Report: Kaupapa Tuatahi*, Wellington, 1996.

Walker, Ranginui J, *He Tipua: The Life and Times of Sir Apirana Ngata*, Auckland, 2001.

————, *Ka Whawhai Tonu Matou: Struggle Without End*, Auckland, 1990.

————, 'Maori People Since 1950', in Rice, Geoffrey W (ed), *The Oxford History of New Zealand*, Auckland, 1992 (2nd ed).

————, 'The Politics of Voluntary Association: The Structure and Functioning of a Maori Welfare Committee in a City Suburb', in Kawharu, I Hugh (ed), *Conflict and Compromise: Essays on the Maori Since Colonisation*, Wellington, 1975.

Walsh, Pat (ed), *Trade Unions, Work and Society*, Palmerston North, 1994.

Ward, Alan, 'Carroll, James', in *Dictionary of New Zealand Biography*, vol 2, Auckland/Wellington, 1993.

————, 'Commentary: The Treaty and the Purchase of Maori Land', *New Zealand Journal of History*, 22(2), Oct 1988.

————, *National Overview: Waitangi Tribunal Rangahaua Whanui Series*, 3 vols, Wellington, 1997.

————, *A Show of Justice: Racial 'Amalgamation' in Nineteenth Century New Zealand*, Auckland, 1995 (rev ed).

————, *An Unsettled History: Treaty Claims in New Zealand Today*, Wellington, 1999.

Wards, Ian McL, *The Shadow of the Land: A Study of British Policy and Racial Conflict in New Zealand 1832–1852*, Wellington, 1968.

Waymouth, Lyn, 'The Bureaucratisation of Genealogy', *Ethnologies Comparées*, 6, Printemps 2003.

Weaver, John C, *The Great Land Rush and the Making of the Modern World, 1650–1900*, Montreal/Kingston, 2003.

Webb, Stephen D and Collette, John (eds), *New Zealand Society: Contemporary Perspectives*, Sydney, 1973.

Webster, Peter, *Rua and the Maori Millennium*, Wellington, 1979.

Webster, Steven, *Patrons of Maori Culture: Power, Theory and Ideology in the Maori Renaissance*, Dunedin, 1998.

Wharemaru, Heeni and Duffie, Mary Katharine, *Heeni: A Tainui Elder Remembers*, Auckland, 1997.

Willan, Rachael, 'Maori Land Sales, 1900–1930', in Loveridge, Donald M (ed), 'Twentieth Century Maori Land Administration Research Programme', a report for the Crown Forestry Rental Trust, Wellington, 1996 (rev ed 1998).

Williams, Charlotte, *The Too-Hard Basket: Maori and Criminal Justice Since 1980*, Wellington, 2001.

Williams, David V, *Te Kooti Tango Whenua: The Native Land Court 1864–1909*, Wellington, 1999.

Williams, John A, *Politics of the New Zealand Maori: Protest and Co-operation, 1891–1909*, Auckland, 1969.

Wilson, Margaret and Yeatman, Anna (eds), *Justice and Identity: Antipodean Practices*, Wellington, 1995.

Winks, Robin W (ed), *The Oxford History of the British Empire: Volume V: Historiography*, Oxford, 1999.

Wood, F L W, *This New Zealand*, Hamilton, 1946.

Yeatman, Anna, 'Justice and the Sovereign Self', in Wilson, Margaret and Yeatman, Anna (eds), *Justice and Identity: Antipodean Practices*, Wellington, 1995.

Young, David, *Woven by Water: Histories from the Whanganui River*, Wellington, 1998.

NOTES

1 Hill, Richard S, 'Autonomy and Authority: Rangatiratanga and the Crown in Twentieth Century New Zealand: An Overview', Wellington, 2000 (for a short summary see Hill, Richard S and O'Malley, Vincent, *The Maori Quest for Rangatiratanga/Authority, 1840–1920*, Wellington, 2000). The terms 'authority' and 'autonomy' have often been used conjointly in recent times to reflect Maori aspirations: eg, Sorrenson, M P K, 'Towards a Radical Reinterpretation of New Zealand History: The Role of the Waitangi Tribunal', in Kawharu, I Hugh (ed), *Waitangi: Maori and Pakeha Perspectives of the Treaty of Waitangi*, Auckland, 1989, p 159, refers to the chiefs in 1840 viewing the Treaty as 'a guarantee of their autonomy and authority'. My practice is to use 'autonomy' as an approximation of rangatiratanga and 'authority' as a shorthand for state authority and all it implies, including coercive and hegemonic functions.

2 Smith, Linda Tuhiwai, *Decolonizing Methodologies: Research and Indigenous Peoples*, Dunedin, 1999, p 1 (for 'privilege' quotes); Freire, Paulo, *Pedagogy of the Oppressed*, 1970 (New York, 1988), especially chs 1, 4; Fanon, Frantz, *The Wretched of the Earth*, New York, 1963; Sutherland, I L G (ed), *The Maori People Today: A General Survey*, Wellington, 1940, p 10 (for 'sad story' quote).

3 Akenson, Donald Harman, 'No Petty People: Pakeha History and the Historiography of the Irish Diaspora', in Fraser, Lyndon (ed), *A Distant Shore: Irish Migration and New Zealand Settlement*, Dunedin, 2000, pp 13–15 (includes 'bi-culturally' quote); Meredith, Paul, 'Hybridity in the Third Space: Rethinking Bi-Cultural Politics in Aotearoa/New Zealand', *He Pukenga Korero*, 4(2), 1999, pp 12–14 (for 'reconceptualisation' quotes); Simon, Judith (ed), *Nga Kura Maori: The Native Schools System 1867–1969*, Auckland, 1998, p 2.

4 The literature on resistance is vast. For a brief attempt at comparative resistance of relevance to New Zealand, see Gump, James O, 'A Spirit of Resistance: Sioux, Xhosa, and Maori Responses to Western Dominance, 1840–1920', *Pacific Historical Review*, Feb 1997. For other comparative work, see Kersey, Harry A Jr, *Indigenous Sovereignty in Two Cultures: Maori and American Indians Compared*, Wellington, 2000; Weaver, John C, *The Great Land Rush and the Making of the Modern World, 1650–1900*, Montreal/Kingston, 2003; and O'Malley, Vincent, *Indigenous Land Rights in an International Context: A Survey of the Literature Relating to Australia, New Zealand and North America*, Wellington, 2000. For Maori armed resistance and military response, see Belich, James, *The New Zealand Wars and the Victorian Interpretation of*

Racial Conflict, Auckland, 1986. For a perspective regarding ongoing resistance in New Zealand, and the Crown's coercion-based responses, see Hill, Richard S, *Policing the Colonial Frontier: The Theory and Practice of Coercive Social and Racial Control in New Zealand, 1767–1867*, Wellington, 1986 (two-book set); *The Colonial Frontier Tamed: New Zealand Policing in Transition, 1867–1886*, Wellington, 1989; and *The Iron Hand in the Velvet Glove: The Modernisation of Policing in New Zealand, 1886–1917*, Palmerston North, 1995. These books form the first three volumes in 'The History of Policing in New Zealand' series. For the fourth, see Dunstall, Graeme, *A Policeman's Paradise? Policing a Stable Society 1918–1945*, Palmerston North, 1999. See too Spoonley, P, Macpherson, C, Pearson, D and Sedgwick, C (eds), *Tauiwi: Racism and Ethnicity in New Zealand*, Palmerston North, 1984, pp 103–4.

5   The amount of literature on the Treaty of Waitangi is sizeable and ever expanding. For a starting point, see Orange, Claudia, *The Treaty of Waitangi*, Wellington, 1987; for a brief account, Gilling, Bryan and O'Malley, Vincent, *The Treaty of Waitangi in New Zealand History*, Wellington, 2000.

6   Ward, Alan, *An Unsettled History: Treaty Claims in New Zealand Today*, Wellington, 1999, p 1 and Parts I and II; see too Alan Ward's 1974 work *A Show of Justice: Racial 'Amalgamation' in Nineteenth Century New Zealand*, Auckland, 1995 (rev ed), and Durie, Mason, *Te Mana, Te Kawanatanga: The Politics of Maori Self-Determination*, Auckland, 1998. Several works since the 1960s have challenged the historiography of the past and led to a paradigm shift. See especially James Belich's works: *New Zealand Wars*; *'I Shall Not Die': Titokowaru's War New Zealand 1868–1869*, Wellington, 1989; *Making Peoples: A History of the New Zealanders from Polynesian Settlement to the End of the Nineteenth Century*, Auckland, 1996; and *Paradise Reforged: A History of the New Zealanders from the 1880s to the Year 2000*, Auckland, 2001 (whose themes inform significant aspects of this book). See also Parsonson, Ann, 'The Challenge to Maori Mana', in Rice, Geoffrey (ed), *The Oxford History of New Zealand*, Auckland, 1992 (2nd ed); Veracini, Lorenzo, *Negotiating a Bicultural Past: An Historiographical 'Revolution' in 1980s Aotearoa/New Zealand*, Wellington, 2001; and Ballara, Angela, *Iwi: The Dynamics of Maori Tribal Organisation from c.1769 to c.1945*, Wellington, 1998, p 336.

7   Ward, *Show of Justice*, is a ground-breaking work in its detailing, *inter alia*, of Maori agency and aspiration; for other aspects of this and the Crown reaction, see Hill, *Iron Hand*, Introduction and ch 1; O'Malley, Vincent, *Agents of Autonomy: Maori Committees in the Nineteenth Century*, Wellington, 1997 (rev ed, 1998); Belich, *New Zealand Wars*; McHugh, Paul, *The Maori Magna Carta: New Zealand Law and the Treaty of Waitangi*, Auckland, 1991, p 64; a number of reports within the Waitangi Tribunal/Treaty claims resolution processes stress such themes.

8   McHugh, *Magna Carta*, pp 46, 95; Metge, Joan, *New Growth from Old: The Whanau in the Modern World*, Wellington, 1995, pp 310–11; Dawson, Richard, *The Treaty of Waitangi and the Control of Language*, Wellington, 2001, p 59; Morris, Paul, 'Community Beyond Tradition', in Heelas, Paul, Lash, Scott and Morris, Paul (eds), *Detraditionalization: Critical Reflections on Authority and Identity*, Oxford, 1996, pp 238–46; Durie, E T J, 'The Treaty in Maori History', in Renwick, W L (ed),

Indigenous Rights, 1991; Andrews, C Lesley, 'Aspects of Development, 1870–1890', in Kawharu, I Hugh (ed), *Conflict and Compromise: Essays on the Maori Since Colonisation*, Wellington, 1975, p 93; Love, R Ngatata, 'Policies of Frustration: The Growth of Maori Politics: The Ratana/Labour Era', PhD thesis, Wellington, 1977, pp 8–9, 23, 26, 31; Sinclair, Keith, *A Destiny Apart: New Zealand's Search for National Identity*, Wellington, 1986, p 208; Yeatman, Anna, 'Justice and the Sovereign Self', in Wilson, Margaret and Yeatman, Anna (eds), *Justice and Identity: Antipodean Practices*, Wellington, 1995, p 209; Awatere, Donna, *Maori Sovereignty*, Auckland, 1984, pp 16, 20 (including 'no justice' quote); Armstrong, David, and Stirling, Bruce, 'A Summary History of the Wellington Tenths: 1839–88', Wellington, 1992; Rigby, Barry, 'Historians and Lawyers in the Public Arena', paper presented to the New Zealand Historical Association Conference, Hamilton, 1999, p 2; Biggs, Bruce, 'Humpty Dumpty and the Treaty of Waitangi', in Kawharu (ed), *Waitangi*, argues that the two Treaty versions are in effect different documents altogether.

9   Durie, in Renwick (ed), p 157 (for 'integrity' quote); Biggs; Belich, *New Zealand Wars*; Ward, Alan, 'Commentary: The Treaty and the Purchase of Maori Land', *New Zealand Journal of History* (*NZJH*), 22(2), Oct 1988, p 173 (for 'laws and processes' quote); Binney, Judith, 'The Maori and the Signing of the Treaty of Waitangi', in Green, David (ed), *Towards 1990: Seven Leading Historians Examine Significant Aspects of New Zealand History*, Wellington, 1989, esp p 29 (for 'mutual benefit' quote); Parsonson, in Rice (ed), p 197 (for 'loss of autonomy' quote).

10   Belich, *Making Peoples, passim* and p 306; Orange, *Treaty*; Walker, Ranginui, *Ka Whawhai Tonu Matou: Struggle Without End*, Auckland, 1990; Waitangi Tribunal, *The Taranaki Report: Kaupapa Tuatahi*, Wellington, 1996, p 6. Pockets of 'Maori autonomy' persisted for a long time, some of them having some means of coercion. Rua Kenana's establishment of a new Zion in the Urewera, and its bloody invasion and dismantling by the state in 1916, may be seen as the last manifestation of overt separationist autonomy and its crushing: see Binney, Judith, Chaplin, Gillian and Wallace, Craig, *Mihaia: The Prophet Rua Kenana and His Community at Maungapohatu*, Wellington, 1979; Hill, *Iron Hand*, pp 382–90; Webster, Peter, *Rua and the Maori Millennium*, Wellington, 1979.

11   It is instructive to compare the first edition of *The Oxford History of New Zealand*, Wellington, 1981, edited by W H Oliver and B S Williams, and the second, revised version, edited by Geoffrey Rice, Auckland, 1992; see especially Rice's preface to the second edition, p ix. (Refer also to Veracini, *Bicultural Past* and Smith; and to Sissons, Jeffrey, *Te Waimana/The Spring of Mana: Tuhoe History and the Colonial Encounter*, Dunedin, 1991, p 289 for the 'seeking to decolonise' quote.) I do not argue that modern historiography, including the various types of Treaty claims resolution reports, necessarily or always constitutes (or is intended to constitute) 'sound history'; on the contrary, I find much of it wanting in certain key aspects. There is the beginning of a debate on such issues. The Waitangi Tribunal, for example, has been seen as depicting a 'retrospective utopia' whereby settlement 'should and could have led to a regime characterised by partnership, power-sharing and economic well-being for Maori as well as for Pakeha', a 'counterfactual history' of 'policies and institutions' which were *not* put in place and of 'presentist' judging

of the Crown's past actions. This is seen as a political divergence from 'academic' ways of examining the past: Oliver, W H, 'The Future Behind Us: The Waitangi Tribunal's Retrospective Utopia', in Sharp, Andrew and McHugh, Paul (eds), *Histories, Power and Loss: Uses of the Past – A New Zealand Commentary*, Wellington, 2001. Prior discussions of relevance include Rigby's 'Historians and Lawyers' and R P Boast's 'Lawyers, Historians, Ethics and the Judicial Process', *Victoria University of Wellington Law Review*, (28)1, March 1998. This is not the forum to engage in debate about the quality and purpose of the Tribunal's reports, though it might be noted that since these reflect evidence from 'experts', including 'academics', if there is within them a shortfall in academic standards, this might partly reflect developments within 'the academy'. I should note that as this book was going to press, Giselle Byrnes' critique *The Waitangi Tribunal and New Zealand History*, Melbourne, 2004, was published. (See too endnote 16.)

12   Durie, 'Treaty in Maori History', p 160 (for 'dogged determination' quote); Durie made a number of such statements during the seminal years when he headed the Waitangi Tribunal, and autonomy is central to his privately circulated paper 'Custom Law' in January 1994, which he backgrounds in 'Ethics and Values', in *Indigenous Peoples and the Law*, 1999, http://www.kennett.co.nz/law/indigenous/1999/39.html; see too his 'Maori Autonomy: Preventing Power Games', *Stimulus*, May 1998. Orange, Claudia J, 'A Kind of Equality: Labour and the Maori People 1935–1949', MA thesis, Auckland, 1977, p 7 (for 'separatist trend' quote). For some initial guidance on state–indigenous relationships, see Winks, Robin W (ed), *The Oxford History of the British Empire: Volume V: Historiography*, Oxford, 1999. I use the term 'post-colonial' in this section in a technical sense to mean the period after New Zealand ceased formally to be a colony; this is quite different from its increasing (and very useful) application to the period following the time when the country remained informally tied to Britain – in other words, either from soon after the Second World War onwards, or (following James Belich's formulation, in his 1996/2001 general history of New Zealand, of 'recolonisation' from the 1880s to the 1970s) from the time Britain joined 'Europe'. And, of course, it is a separate usage from that employed in 'post-colonial discourse studies'.

13   That the state aim was assimilation is unmistakable; the 1844 Native Trust Ordinance, for example, stood for 'assimilating as speedily as possible the habits and ways of the Native to those of the European population', as noted in the Record of Documentation for Claim WAI 145, Waitangi Tribunal, document B4, p 27. Many scholars have been misled by Crown rhetoric, and by Crown actions that were designed only as temporary expedients. Refer to Part 1 of Hill, *Policing the Colonial Frontier*; Ward, *Show of Justice*, p viii; Sorrenson, M P K, 'The Purchase of Maori Lands, 1865–1892', MA thesis, University of Auckland, 1955, p 236; Ball, D G, 'Maori Education', in Sutherland (ed), p 276; Orange, 'Equality', p 7. It is instructive to trace Keith Sinclair's views through time: eg, compare *A History of New Zealand*, Harmondsworth, 1959, Part 1 (such as 'The Treaty of Waitangi was intended to lay a basis for a just society in which two races . . . could live together in amity', p 73; see too p 67 for 'noble beginning' quote), with 'Why Are Race Relations in New Zealand Better Than in South Africa, South Australia, or South Dakota?',

NZJH, 5(2), October 1971, and *Destiny Apart*, p 200 (which includes citation of 'experiment' quote from the *New Zealand Herald*, 1906). On the issue of alignment of humanitarianism with settler interests, see Sorrenson, M P K, 'How to Civilize Savages: Some "Answers" from Nineteenth-Century New Zealand', *NZJH*, 9(2), October 1975; Adams, Peter, *Fatal Necessity: British Intervention in New Zealand 1830–1847*, Auckland, 1977; and especially Ward, *Show of Justice* (including p viii for 'simply assumed' quote). For a pioneering account of the implicit and explicit use of coercion in annexation and colonisation of New Zealand, see Wards, Ian McL, *The Shadow of the Land: A Study of British Policy and Racial Conflict in New Zealand 1832–1852*, Wellington, 1968; and Hill, *Policing the Colonial Frontier*, ch 1.

14   Te Awekotuku, Ngahuia, 'Conclusion', in Spoonley *et al* (eds), *Tauiwi*, p 245 (for 'devaluation' quote); Mead, Sidney Moko, *Landmarks, Bridges and Visions: Aspects of Maori Culture*, Wellington, 1997, p 130 (for 'disease' quote). A less catastrophist view from that of those quoted can be taken, in the context of imperial practice: if Maori wanted a 'full engagement' with the benefits brought by the colonisers, as seems to have been the case, some form of assimilation might have been a preferable option to the segregated reserves of other settler colonies: Ward, *Show of Justice*, p viii.

15   King, Michael, 'Between Two Worlds', in Oliver and Williams (eds), p 280; Riddell, Kate, '"Improving" the Maori: Counting the Ideology of Intermarriage', *NZJH*, 34(1), April 2000, p 83; Turbott, H B, 'Health and Social Welfare', in Sutherland (ed), p 263 (for 'good Europeans' quote); Belich, James, 'Colonization and History in New Zealand', in Winks (ed), p 184, and *Paradise Reforged*, ch 6; Walker, Ranginui, *He Tipua: The Life and Times of Sir Apirana Ngata*, Auckland, 2001, p 289 (for 'beastly communism' quote); Pugsley, Christopher, *Te Hokowhitu a Tu: The Maori Pioneer Battalion in the First World War*, Auckland, 1995, p 29 (for 'dark races' quote).

16   Evison, Harry C, *The Long Dispute: Maori Land Rights and European Colonisation in Southern New Zealand*, Christchurch, 1997, p 338 (for 'Englishman' quotes). For major coverage of official runanga, see Ward, *Show of Justice*, ch 9; Pratt, John, *Punishment in a Perfect Society: The New Zealand Penal System 1840–1939*, Wellington, 1992, pp 46ff; and Hill, *Policing the Colonial Frontier*, ch 10. For war and sovereignty, see Belich, *New Zealand Wars*, ch 4 and *passim*, and Orange, *Treaty*, ch 8. My depiction of a 'school' of wishful thinking/lost opportunity scholars was outlined in 'Autonomy and Authority' in 2000, and is covered later in this book. Suffice it to say here, its focus is different from that of recent critiques which assert that the Waitangi Tribunal displays 'a historical mentality less concerned to recapture past reality than to embody present aspiration': Oliver, 'Future Behind Us', p 9. Rather than engaging with the Tribunal and its reports, it addresses the work of modern historians and suggests that many of them fall short of fully appreciating the essentially coercive and hegemonic nature of imperialism, colonisation and capitalism, and greatly underestimate the complexities of the state's social (including 'racial') control mechanisms. (See too endnote 11.)

17   Brooking, Tom, '"Busting up" the Greatest Estate of All; Liberal Maori Land Policy, 1891–1911', *NZJH*, 26(1), April 1992, p 97 (this essay is reprinted in Binney,

Judith (ed), *The Shaping of History: Essays from the New Zealand Journal of History*, Wellington, 2001, as '"Bursting up" the Greatest Estate of All'; references in the current work are to the *NZJH* article); Oliver, 'Future Behind Us'; McHugh, Paul, 'Law, History and the Treaty of Waitangi', *NZJH*, 31(1), 1997, pp 45, 54–5, and 'Constitutional Myths and the Treaty of Waitangi', *New Zealand Law Journal*, September 1991; Ward, *Unsettled*, p 159; King, G S R, 'Assimilation or Separation? The Kotahitanga Parliament Movement 1891–94', in Reilly, Michael and Thomson, Jane (eds), *When the Waves Rolled in upon Us: Essays in Nineteenth-Century Maori History*, Dunedin, 1999, pp 163–4 (for 'chiefs' quote). (A milder version of 'lost opportunity' is to view the Crown's policies as ever wavering between pressure from settlers and its trusteeship duties towards Maori, and this can be seen in a number of reports in the Treaty settlement processes.)

18 Ball, p 276 (for 'native policy' quote); Mulgan, Richard, *Maori, Pakeha and Democracy*, Auckland, 1989, p 23 (for 'many degrees' quote); Orange, *Treaty*; Curnow, Jenifer, Hopa, Ngapare and McRae, Jane (eds), *Rere Atu, Taku Manu! Discovering History, Language and Politics in the Maori-language Newspapers*, Auckland, 2002; Orbell, Margaret (ed), *He Reta ki te Maunga: Letters to the Mountain*, Auckland, 2002.

19 This is not, of course, to argue that the Crown's unwillingness to give Maori a meaningful share in government should not be charted. For an example of such works, see Orange's account in a key twentieth-century period in 'Equality', *passim* and pp 220–2 (eg, 'Reluctance to allow Maoris a real share in Government is a consistent theme of New Zealand history'), and O'Malley's *Agents*.

20 Smith, pp 2–4 (including 'spaces' quotes). For the 'struggle without end' from a Maori scholar's perspective, see Walker, *Ka Whawhai*. See too Hill, 'Autonomy and Authority', ch 7. Note that decontextualised history sometimes reflects the beliefs of those who, under what they perceive as postmodernist scholarship, resile from the scholarly norm of perceiving patterns in things.

21 For the question of ethnocentrism, see Keenan, Danny, 'Predicting the Past: Some Directions in Recent Maori Historiography', *Te Pouhere Korero Journal*, March 1999, p 26; Melbourne, Hineani (ed), *Maori Sovereignty: The Maori Perspective*, Auckland, 1995, p 32 (for 'sovereignty' quotes); for a full working through of the 'revolutionary' interpretation, see Brookfield, F M, *Waitangi & Indigenous Rights: Revolution, Law and Legitimation*, Auckland, 1999.

22 Hogan, Helen M, *Hikurangi ki Homburg: Henare Kohere and Terei Ngaitai with the Maori Coronation Contingent 1902*, Christchurch, 1997, p 114 (for 'English flag' quote); Ausubel, David P, 'The Maori: A Study in Resistive Acculturation', in Webb, Stephen D and Collette, John (eds), *New Zealand Society: Contemporary Perspectives*, Sydney, 1973, p 100 (for 'reservation-like' quote); Belich, *Making Peoples*, p 270 (for 'impact of Europe' quote); Pearson, David, 'Biculturalism and Multiculturalism in Comparative Perspective', in Spoonley, Paul, Pearson, David and Macpherson, Cluny (eds), *Nga Take: Ethnic Relations and Racism in Aotearoa/New Zealand*, Palmerston North, 1991, p 205; Keenan, 'Predicting the Past', p 29 (for 'independence of identity' quote); O'Malley, *Agents*; Ballara, *Iwi*.

23 Head, Lyndsay, 'The Pursuit of Modernity in Maori Society: The Conceptual Bases of Citizenship in the Early Colonial Period', in Sharp and McHugh (eds),

p 97. (Head believes that making autonomy the 'organising principle' of race relations in the early years of the colony has led to much ignoring or demonising of Maori who were neutral towards or assisted the state; the treatment of the word in this book does not do this); Ward, *Show of Justice*, p ix (for 'understood' quote); O'Malley, *Agents*; Durie, 'Ethics and Values'; Ballara, *Iwi* (includes 'political unit' quote, p 19); Sharp, Andrew, *Justice and the Maori: The Philosophy and Practice of Maori Claims in New Zealand since the 1970s*, Auckland, 1997 (2nd ed).

24   Meredith; Collins, Heeni, 'Nga Tangaroa Awarua', *National Oral History Association of Aotearoa New Zealand Journal*, 1999; Ballara, *Iwi*, pp 19, 282; see Office of Treaty Settlements, *Healing the Past, Building a Future: A Guide to Treaty of Waitangi Claims and Negotiations with the Crown*, Wellington, 2nd ed, nd, p 44, for the 'large natural groups' concept; for discussion of 'indigenous history telling', see, eg, Binney, Judith, 'Encounters Across Time: The Makings of an Unanticipated Trilogy', and other contributions to Attwood, Bain and Magowan, Fiona (eds), *Telling Stories: Indigenous History and Memory in Australia and New Zealand*, Wellington, 2001.

25   Boenisch-Brednich, Brigitte and Hill, Richard S, 'Biculturalism in New Zealand/ Aotearoa', in Csukas, Gyorgyi, Kiss, Reka, Kristof, Ildiko, Nagy, Ilona and Szarvas, Zsuzsa (eds), *Times, Places, Passages: Ethnological Approaches in the New Millennium*, Budapest, 2004; Hill, Richard S, *The Treaty of Waitangi Today*, Wellington, 2000; Hill, Richard S, 'The Future of Rangatiratanga', *Future Times*, 8, 2003 (see http:/ /www.futurestrust.org.nz/e-FutureTimes/e-FTVol8.html#anchorhill for a fuller version); Binney, Judith, 'Maori Oral Narratives, Pakeha Written Texts: Two Forms of Telling History', *NZJH*, 21(1), April 1987, p 16.

26   For the above paragraphs refer particularly to O'Malley, *Agents*; see too Young, David, *Woven by Water: Histories from the Whanganui River*, Wellington, 1998, ch 6; Belich, *New Zealand Wars*; Ward, *Show of Justice*; Hill, *Policing the Colonial Frontier* and *Colonial Frontier Tamed*; Andrews; Gilling, Bryan, 'Engine of Destruction? An Introduction to the History of the Maori Land Court', *Victoria University of Wellington Law Review*, 24(2), July 1994; Love, p 35; Edwards, Mihi, *Mihipeka: Early Years*, Auckland, 1990, p 7.

27   King, Michael, *Te Puea: A Biography*, Auckland, 1977, pp 263–4; Marr, Cathy, 'The Alienation of Maori Land in the Rohe Potae (Aotea Block), Part 2, 1900– 1960', a report for the Waitangi Tribunal, Wellington, 1999, *passim* and ch 1.

28   King, *Te Puea*, pp 29, 67; Doig, Suzanne, 'The Battle for the Whanganui River 1840–1998', *History Now*, 4(2), October 1998; Belich, *New Zealand Wars* and *I Shall Not Die*; Hill, *Frontier Tamed* and *Iron Hand*; Love, pp 99, 102; McRae, Jane, 'Participation: Native Committees (1883) and Papatupu Block Committees (1900) in Tai Tokerau', MA thesis, University of Auckland, 1981, pp 33–4 (for Maori MPs' statement); Williams, John A, *Politics of the New Zealand Maori: Protest and Co-operation, 1891–1909*, Auckland, 1969, chs 3–4 (includes 'rights' quote, p 43); Jones, Pei Te Hurinui, 'Maori Kings', in Schwimmer, Erik (ed), *The Maori People in the Nineteen-Sixties: A Symposium*, Auckland, 1968, pp 137ff (includes 'called a king' quote, pp 138–9); personal communication from Tamihana Te Winitana.

29   Belich, James, 'Myth, Race and Identity in New Zealand', *NZJH*, 31(1), April 1997, p 16; Cox, Lindsay, *Kotahitanga: The Search for Maori Political Unity*, Auckland,

1993; McRae, pp 31–2; Walker, *Ka Whawhai*, pp 165–6; Parsonson, p 197; Cox, p 67; Kernot, B, *People of the Four Winds*, Wellington, 1972, p 64 (for 'four winds' concept); O'Malley, p 213 (for 'murmuring' quote); Orange, *Treaty*, pp 217, 224–5; personal communication from Tamihana Te Winitana. For a summary of the argument that by the mid-1880s both pakeha and Maori were deemed by the state to be generally 'tranquil' and orderly, see Hill, *Colonial Frontier Tamed*, pp x–xiii, and for an influential and relevant interpretation of pakeha society in the nineteenth century, see Fairburn, Miles, *The Ideal Society and Its Enemies*, Auckland, 1989.

30 Belich, *Paradise Reforged*; Ward, *Show of Justice*, p 303; Williams, David V, *Te Kooti Tango Whenua: The Native Land Court 1864–1909*, Wellington, 1999, p 7; Marr, 'Rohe Potae, Part 2', p 5; Report of the Commission on 'Native Lands and Native-Land Tenure', *AJHR*, 1907, G1C, esp p 5; Orange, *Treaty*, pp 7–8; New Zealand Government, *Report of Royal Commission on the Courts*, Wellington, 1978, p 2 (for 'English derived law' quote).

31 Sinclair, *Destiny Apart*, p 204 (for 'one people' quote); New Zealand Government, *The New Zealand Official Handbook 1892*, Wellington, 1892, p 275; Greenland, Hauraki, 'Ethnicity as Ideology: The Critique of Pakeha Society', in Spoonley *et al* (eds), *Tauiwi*, pp 96–7; Cox.

32 Cox, pp 67–8; Walker, *Ka Whawhai*, pp 165ff; Else, Anne (ed), *Women Together: A History of Women's Organisations in New Zealand: Nga Ropu Wahine o te Motu*, Wellington, 1993, pp 4–5; O'Malley, *Agents*, p 212; McRae, pp 31–2; Orange, *Treaty*, pp 217, 222–5; Parsonson, p 197 (for 'parallel institutions' quote); Butterworth, G V and Young, H R, *Maori Affairs/Nga Take Maori*, Wellington, 1990, p 57. The 'good Native policy' statement by a Bay of Islands MP is cited in: Hutton, John, '"A Ready and Quick Method": The Alienation of Maori Land by Sales to the Crown and Private Individuals, 1905–30', in Loveridge, Donald M (ed), 'Twentieth Century Maori Land Administration Research Programme', a report for the Crown Forestry Rental Trust, Wellington, 1996 (rev ed, 1998), p 32.

33 Stokes, Evelyn, Milroy, J Wharehuia and Melbourne, Hirini, *Te Urewera: Nga Iwi Te Whenua Te Ngahere: People, Land and Forests of Te Urewera*, Hamilton, 1986, p xiv; Webster, p 125; Butterworth, G V, 'Aotearoa 1769–1988: Towards a Tribal Perspective: Report for Department of Maori Affairs', Wellington, 1988, ch 6, p 12; Ballara, *Iwi*, pp 300–1; Walker, *Ka Whawhai*, p 157; Binney, Judith, 'Te Mana Tuatoru: the Rohe Potae of Tuhoe', *NZJH*, 31(1), April 1997.

34 Pearson, David, *A Dream Deferred: The Origins of Ethnic Conflict in New Zealand*, Wellington, 1990, pp 219–20 and *passim* (and for an internationalised discussion see his *The Politics of Ethnicity in Settler Societies: States of Unease*, Basingstoke, 2001); Spiller, Peter, Finn, Jeremy and Boast, Richard, *A New Zealand Legal History*, Wellington, 1995, pp 155–6; Love, pp 103–4, 117, 121; Williams, *Politics*, pp 158–9; Hill, *Iron Hand*, p 246; O'Malley, *Agents*, pp 193ff; Orange, *Treaty*, p 55 (for Hobson quote).

35 Belich, *Paradise Reforged*, pp 200ff; Ballara, *Iwi*, p 332 (for 'Maori people' quote); Walker, *He Tipua*, p 107; Pocock, J G A, 'Introduction', in Pocock, J G A (ed), *The Maori and New Zealand Politics*, Wellington, 1965, p 5. For demographics, see

Pool, Ian, *The Maori Population of New Zealand 1769–1971*, Auckland, 1977; see too Butterworth, G V, 'The Health of the Body, the Health of the Land: A Comparative Study of the Political Objectives and Careers of Wiremu Ratana and the Ratana Movement, and Sir Apirana Ngata', a report for the Crown Forestry Rental Trust, Wellington, 2000, p 110 (this report should be consulted for material of relevance to several themes of this book).

36 Butterworth, G V, 'Apirana Ngata: The Politics of Adaptation', typescript, nd, *passim* and ch 2, p 9 for 'material welfare' quote (this work is a fuller and revised version of G V Butterworth's 'The Politics of Adaptation: The Political Career of Sir Apirana Ngata 1874–1928', MA thesis, Victoria University of Wellington, 1968, and is the version mostly used for this book; see also Butterworth, G V, *Sir Apirana Ngata*, Wellington, 1968); Walker, *He Tipua*, p 81 and *passim*; Kaa, Wiremu and Te Ohorere (eds), *Apirana Turupu Ngata*, Wellington, 1996, np (for the Ngata proverb; this standard translation was passed onto the present author by Taingunguru Walker); Sissons, Jeffrey, 'The Post-Assimilationist Thought of Sir Apirana Ngata: Towards a Genealogy of New Zealand Biculturalism', *NZJH*, 34(1), April 2000, pp 54ff.

37 Walker, *He Tipua*, p 176; Keesing, Felix M, *The Changing Maori*, New Plymouth, 1928, pp vii, 157, 166; Lange, Raeburn T, *May the People Live: A History of Maori Health Development 1900–1920*, Auckland, 1999, pp 77–8, 92, 95, 119–20; Orange, 'Equality', p 8; King, 'Between Two Worlds', pp 288–9; see Veracini, Lorenzo, 'Negotiating Indigenous Resistance in the South Pacific: Australia, Aotearoa/New Zealand and Kanaky-New Caledonia, Three Cases in Historical Redescription', PhD dissertation, Brisbane, 2001, for comparative discussion.

38 Butterworth, 'Apirana Ngata: Politics of Adaptation', ch 4, p 10 and ch 5, p 5; King, 'Between Two Worlds', p 289 (for 'no alternative' quote); Sutherland (ed), pp 37ff; Love, pp 53–4, 138 (for 'death trap' quote); Walker, *He Tipua*, pp 118; Butterworth, 'Health of the Body', pp 63, 115; Keesing, pp vii, 157, 165–8 (including 'accumulation', 'decadence' and 'race-pride' quotes); Butterworth, *Apirana Ngata* and thesis, pp 16ff; Condliffe, John B, *Te Rangi Hiroa: The Life of Sir Peter Buck*, Christchurch, 1971, pp 8, 105, 220 (for 'partnership' quote); Cody, Joseph F, *Man of Two Worlds: Sir Maui Pomare*, Wellington, 1953, pp 21, 37, 44 (includes 'wisdom' quote). For later developments of Young Maori Party views in detailed ways, see Sorrenson, M P K (ed), *Na To Hoa Aroha: From Your Dear Friend. The Correspondence between Sir Apirana Ngata and Sir Peter Buck 1925–50*, 3 vols, Auckland, 1986–8.

39 Butterworth, 'Apirana Ngata: Politics of Adaptation', ch 2, p 16 (for 'keep the peace' quote); Love, pp 114ff, 133; Walker, *He Tipua*, pp 86ff; for context, see Martin, R J, 'The Liberal Experiment', in Pocock (ed).

40 Williams, *Politics*, pp 107–8, 111–12, 123–4 (including 'detestation' quote); Walker, *He Tipua*, pp 83ff, 98; Butterworth, 'Apirana Ngata: Politics of Adaptation', ch 2, ch 5, p 11, ch 7, p 2; King, *Maori: A Photographic and Social History*, Auckland, 1983, p 162; Butterworth and Young, p 8; Cox, p 96; Walker, *Ka Whawhai*, p 175; Ormsby, M J, 'Maori Tikanga and Criminal Justice', a report for the Ministry of Justice, Wellington, nd, p 11.

41   Maori Councils Act 1900 (No 48); Else (ed), p 5; Butterworth, 'Apirana Ngata:
     Politics of Adaptation', ch 9, pp 28–9; Ormsby, p 12; Walker, *He Tipua,* ch 4;
     Fleras, Augie, *From Village Runanga to the New Zealand Maori Wardens' Association:
     A Historical Development of Maori Wardens,* Wellington, 1980, ch 2; Hill, Richard S,
     *Introducing Policing into the Rangatiratanga Discourse: An Historical Overview of the Role
     of Maori Police Personnel,* Wellington, 2003.
42   O'Malley, *Agents,* ch 10; Cox, p 96; Hill, *Iron Hand,* pp 129, 134–7; Love, pp 104,
     122, 129–31, 368; Lange, *May the People Live,* ch 7; Butterworth and Young, p 60;
     Walker, *He Tipua,* pp 91–2; Butterworth, 'Apirana Ngata: Politics of Adaptation',
     ch 6, p 11.
43   Walker, *He Tipua,* pp 93–4; Cody, pp 45, 70; Ward, *Show of Justice,* ch 9; Brooking,
     Tom, 'Review', in *People's History,* March 2000, p 5; Brooking, 'Busting', pp 92,
     97–8 (for 'lost an opportunity' quote); Pearson, *Dream;* Boast, Richard P, 'The
     Mohaka–Waikare Confiscation Consolidated Report: Vol 1: The Mohaka–Waikare
     Confiscation and Its Aftermath', a report for the Waitangi Tribunal, Wellington,
     1995, p 1398; Ward, Alan, 'Carroll, James', in *Dictionary of New Zealand Biography,*
     vol 2, Wellington, 1993, pp 78–81; Awatere, p 89 (for 'destiny' quote); Love,
     pp 54, 59 (for 'doomed' quote); re assimilation, see Williams, *Politics,* p 111; Belich,
     New Zealand Wars, esp p 302; King, Michael, *The Penguin History of New Zealand,*
     Auckland, 2003, p 468 (for 'best race relations' quote); Consedine, Robert and
     Consedine, Joanna, *Healing our History: The Challenge of the Treaty of Waitangi,*
     Auckland, 2001, p 101. For state and unions, see Hill, *Iron Hand,* pp 76–7; Holt,
     James, 'Compulsory Arbitration in New Zealand, 1894–1916', in Binney (ed);
     Walsh, Pat (ed), *Trade Unions, Work and Society,* Palmerston North, 1994; and Roth,
     Bert, *Trade Unions in New Zealand Past and Present,* Wellington, 1973.
44   Butterworth and Young, p 61; Walker, *He Tipua,* pp 96–9 and *Ka Whawhai,* p 175;
     Butterworth thesis, ch 3; Cox, p 96; Hill, *Iron Hand,* pp 127–8; King, 'Between
     Two Worlds', p 290; Cody, pp 57 (for 'every step' quote), 72; Dow, Derek A,
     Maori Health and Government Policy 1840–1940, Wellington, 1999, p 101; Williams,
     Politics, pp 114–15.
45   Walker, *He Tipua,* p 97; Cody, pp 37, 57, 72–3; Love, p 144; King, 'Between Two
     Worlds', p 289; Butterworth and Young, p 61; Condliffe, p 80 (for 'communism'
     quote); Lange, *May the People Live;* King, Michael, *Moriori: A People Rediscovered,*
     Auckland, 1989; Dow, pp 128–30; Durie, Mason, *Whaiora: Maori Health
     Development,* Melbourne, 1994 (2nd ed, 1998), pp 42–3; King, *Te Puea,* p 32.
46   Cody, p 71; Ballara, *Iwi,* p 312; Butterworth thesis, ch 2; Cox, pp 75, 96; Hill, *Iron
     Hand,* pp 247–8 (for 'suppress' and 'gaol' quotes); Sissons, *Te Waimana;* Walker, *He
     Tipua,* pp 95ff, 162–3 (for 'cultural adaptation' quote); Butterworth, 'Apirana Ngata:
     Politics of Adaptation', ch 6, pp 6, 9–12 and ch 9, p 4; Love, pp 104, 122; Lange,
     May the People Live, pp 204–5, 258; Hunn, J K, *Report on Department of Maori
     Affairs: with Statistical Supplement,* Wellington, 1961, p 84. As this book was going
     to press, the Treaty of Waitangi Research Unit published Raeburn Lange's *A Limited
     Measure of Local Self-Government: Maori Councils, 1900-1920,* Wellington, 2004,
     and this should be referred to for detailed information about the Maori Councils.
47   Keenan, Danny, 'Bound to the Land: Maori Retention and Assertion of Land and

Identity', in Pawson, Eric and Brooking, Tom (eds), *Environmental Histories of New Zealand*, Melbourne, 2002, p 250 (for 'paramount' quote); Walker, *Ka Whawhai, passim*; Love, pp 47, 150 (for 'problem' and 'cornerstone' quotes); Ward, *Unsettled* and *National Overview: Waitangi Tribunal Rangahaua Whanui Series*, 3 vols, Wellington, 1997; Kaati, John Reihana, *Rohe Potae and Wahanui Paramount Chief*, Te Kuiti, nd, p 58 (for 'People have come and gone . . .'); Melbourne (ed), pp 28–9 (includes 'disempowered' quote); Greenland, p 88 (for 'key symbol' quote); Kawharu, I Hugh, *Maori Land Tenure: Studies of a Changing Institution*, Oxford, 1977, pp 251, 274; King, 'Assimilation or Separation?', p 162 (includes 'chaos' quote); O'Brien, Anne-Marie, 'Taihoa: The Stout–Ngata Native Land Commission, 1907–1909', in Reilly and Thomson (eds), pp 178–9.

48 Loveridge, Donald M, 'Maori Land Councils and Maori Land Boards: A Historical Overview, 1900 to 1952', Waitangi Tribunal Rangahaua Whanui Series, Wellington, 1996, ch 1; Butterworth and Young, pp 52, 56–7; Walker, *He Tipua*, p 109; Brooking, 'Busting'; Hutton, 'Ready and Quick', p 16; O'Malley, *Agents*, pp 243–4; Cody, p 37 (for 'rehabilitation' and 'communistic' quotes); Hippolite, Joy, 'Rangahaua Whanui District 11C: Wairoa', a report for the Waitangi Tribunal, Wellington, 1996, p vii. For 'new' leaders, see Binney, Judith, *Redemption Songs: A Life of Te Kooti Arikirangi Te Turuki*, Auckland, 1995, and Walker, *He Tipua*.

49 Loveridge, 'Land Councils and Land Boards', pp 7–8, 12ff, 70, 153; Walker, *He Tipua*, pp 89, 122; Williams, *Politics*, p 108; Butterworth and Young, p 59.

50 Maori Lands Administration Act 1900 (No 55); Butterworth, 'Apirana Ngata: Politics of Adaptation', ch 5, p 16; Loveridge, 'Land Councils and Land Boards', pp 12ff; Brooking, Tom, *Lands for the People? The Highland Clearances and the Colonisation of New Zealand: A Biography of John McKenzie*, Dunedin, 1996, p 134; Walker, *Ka Whawhai*, p 90 (for 'small degree' quote).

51 Maori Lands Administration Act 1900 (No 55); Butterworth, *Sir Apirana Ngata*, p 30 (for 'retention' quote); Loveridge, 'Land Councils and Land Boards', ch 2; Butterworth and Young, p 59; Walker, *He Tipua*, p 90; Lange, *May the People Live*, ch 4; Willan, Rachael, 'Maori Land Sales, 1900–1930', in Loveridge (ed), 'Twentieth Century Programme', p 7; Butterworth, 'Apirana Ngata: Politics of Adaptation', ch 5, p 16; Ward, *Unsettled*, p 159.

52 Hutton, 'Ready and Quick', pp 8–12; McRae, pp 65ff (including '*mana*' quotes, pp 78–80); Marr, 'Rohe Potae, Part 2', pp 2–7, 15; Williams, *Politics*, pp 108–9 (for 'real autonomy' and 'legal control' quotes); Loveridge, 'Land Councils and Land Boards', pp vii, ch 2, 21–2, 29–30; Walker, *He Tipua*, p 90; Cox, p 96; Boast, 'Mohaka–Waikare', p 1400; Spiller *et al*, p 158 (for 'creative', 'alienation' and 'restrain' quotes); Ward, *Unsettled*, p 161 (for 'long way' quote); Maori Lands Administration Act 1900 (No 55); O'Malley, *Agents*, pp 244–5.

53 Loveridge, 'Land Councils and Land Boards', chs 2–4 (includes 'deprived' quote, p 36); Reports of the Commission on 'Native Lands and Native-Land Tenure', *AJHR*, 1907, G1–G1E and 1908, Gi–iii, and G1A–1T ['Stout–Ngata Commission'] (see G1C, p 6 for 'deprived' quote); Willan, p 7; O'Malley, *Agents*, pp 244–7; Williams, *Politics*, p 118; Marr, 'Rohe Potae, Part 2', pp 6–7; Marr, Cathy, 'The Alienation of Maori Land in the Rohe Potae (Aotea Block), 1840–1920', a report

for the Waitangi Tribunal, Wellington, 1996, p 147; McRae, pp 67, 78–9 (for
other Stout–Ngata Commission material), 94 (for 'reap the benefit' quotes) and
passim; Butterworth and Young, p 62; Gilling, Bryan D, '"The Mana of Their
Own Land": Rangatiratanga and the Maori Land Council Regime, 1900–1905',
draft paper, Treaty of Waitangi Research Unit, 2004.

54 Butterworth, 'Apirana Ngata: Politics of Adaptation', ch 6, pp 16ff; Loveridge,
'Land Councils and Land Boards', pp 153–4; McRae, pp 79, 93–4, 97; Hutton,
'Ready and Quick', pp 12–13; Marr, 'Rohe Potae, Part 2'; Butterworth and Young,
p 62; Boast, 'Mohaka–Waikare', pp 1398–9; Brooking, 'Busting'; Ward, *Unsettled*,
p 160; Gilling, 'Mana of Their Own Land'.

55 Ward, *Unsettled*, pp 155, 161; Butterworth, 'Apirana Ngata: Politics of Adaptation',
ch 6, p 18; Love, p 139 (for 'Maori ideal' quote); Loveridge, 'Land Councils and
Land Boards', pp 43–8, 70; Walker, *He Tipua*, pp 132–3; Gilling, 'Mana of Their
Own Land'; Hutton, 'Ready and Quick', p 17 (for 'idleness' quote); Spiller *et al*,
p 158; Boast, 'Mohaka–Waikare', p 1400 (for 'transforming' quote); 'A Native
Prince', *Mana*, June–July 1999, p 48 (for 'communism' quote).

56 Hutton, 'Ready and Quick', pp 12–13, 17; Gilling, Bryan D, *Government Valuers*,
Wellington, 1996, p 53; Boast, 'Mohaka–Waikare', pp 1400ff; 'A Native Prince',
Mana, June–July 1999; Love, p 139; Brooking, 'Busting'; Loveridge, 'Land Councils
and Land Boards', pp vii, 43–8, 62–3, 67; Butterworth and Young, p 63; Ward,
Unsettled, p 155; Walker, *He Tipua*, p 133; Maori Land Settlement Act 1905 (No
44); Walker, *He Tipua*, p 108; Williams, *Politics*, p 128.

57 Loveridge, 'Land Councils and Land Boards', pp 63–4; Boast, 'Mohaka–Waikare',
pp 1041–3; Hutton, 'Ready and Quick', pp 22–5; O'Malley, *Agents*, pp 245–6;
Hutton, John, 'Archival Material Relating to the Maori Land Boards 1900–1952',
a report for the Crown Forestry Rental Trust, Wellington, 1996, p 8; Hutton,
John, 'The Operation of the Waikato–Maniapoto District Maori Land Board', in
Loveridge (ed), 'Twentieth Century Programme', p 8; Marr, 'Rohe Potae, Part 2',
p 23; Gilling, *Valuers*, pp 53–4 (for 'laudable provision' quotes); Williams, *Politics*,
p 134.

58 Reports of the Commission on 'Native Lands and Native-Land Tenure', *AJHR*,
1907, G1–G1E and 1908, Gi–iii, and G1A–1T; Loveridge, 'Land Councils and
Land Boards', ch 6 (includes 'own land' quote, p 50) and pp 71–2; Butterworth
and Young, p 66; Walker, *He Tipua*, pp 131ff; O'Brien; Butterworth, 'Aotearoa',
ch 6, p 25 (for 'mediating' quote); Love, p 139 (for 'Maori ideal' quote); Hunn,
p 60 (for 'hierarchy of chiefs' quote).

59 Walker, *He Tipua*, pp 134ff; Loveridge, 'Land Councils and Land Boards', ch 6
and p 67; O'Malley, *Agents*, pp 244ff; Reports of the Commission on 'Native
Lands and Native-Land Tenure', *AJHR*, 1907, G1–G1E and 1908, Gi–iii, and
G1A–1T; King, 'Between Two Worlds', p 289 (for 'European interests' quote);
Butterworth, 'Aotearoa', ch 6, pp 25ff; Hutton, 'Ready and Quick', pp 27–8 (for
'mana' quote).

60 King, *Maori*, pp 159–60; Boast, 'Mohaka–Waikare', p 1404; Butterworth, 'Aotearoa',
ch 6, pp 21–2; Hutton, 'Ready and Quick', pp 26–30; Love, pp 137–9; O'Brien;
Marr, 'Rohe Potae, Part 2', pp 21–2, 24, 27; Waitangi Tribunal, *Ngai Tahu Report*

1991, 3 vols, Wellington, 1991, pp 993–9; Evison, p 389; Armstrong, David, 'Land for Landless Natives', Waitangi Tribunal Document WAI 27, M16, Wellington, nd, p 55 (for 'unsatisfactory resolution' quote); Williams, *Politics*, p 117.

61 For the whakatauki, see Williams, Charlotte, *The Too-Hard Basket: Maori and Criminal Justice Since 1980*, Wellington, 2001, p vi. Conflation of land and collective identity fuels 'anti-Treatyist' writers and publicists, who claim, for example, that it is 'impossible to see how . . . tribal self-management could outlast the sale of land': Round, David, *Truth or Treaty? Commonsense Questions about the Treaty of Waitangi*, Christchurch, 1998, p 101. For the anti-Treaty writers, see Hill, Richard S, *Anti-Treatyism and Anti-Scholarship: An Analysis of Anti-Treatyist Writings*, Wellington, 2002.

62 Campbell, S K L, 'Land Alienation, Consolidation and Development in the Urewera 1912-1950', a report for the Crown Forestry Rental Trust, Wellington, 1997 (Waitangi Tribunal Document Wai 36, A9), pp 8–9, 25 (for 'hindrance' quote), 62 (for 'tribal holdings' quote), 106 (for 'tribal administration' quote), 147; Spiller *et al*, p 156; Stokes *et al*, pp xiv (includes 'breach' quote), 55ff, 160 (for 'foreign territory' quote); Ward, *Unsettled*, p 157; Walker, *He Tipua*, pp 195–8; Ballara, *Iwi*, p 301; O'Malley, *Agents*, pp 236ff.

63 Campbell, 'Urewera', pp 20ff and *passim*; King, Michael, *Nga Iwi o te Motu: One Thousand Years of Maori History*, Auckland, 1997, pp 49–50 (for 'potentially' quote); O'Malley, *Agents*, ch 9; Stokes *et al*, pp 86, 95 (including 'Kick the Maoris out' quote).

64 Williams, *Politics*, pp 120–2, 140–3; Murray, Tom, Taylor, Kerry, Tepanaia, Joe and Rameka, Nora, 'Towards a History of Maori and Trade Unions', in Martin, John F and Taylor, Kerry (eds), *Culture and the Labour Movement: Essays in New Zealand Labour History*, Palmerston North, 1991, pp 55–6. For the background and significance of the 'great strike', see Olssen, Erik, *The Red Feds*, Auckland, 1988 and Hill, *Iron Hand*, chs 18, 20.

65 Scott, Dick, *Ask That Mountain: The Story of Parihaka*, Auckland, 1975; Hill, *Colonial Frontier Tamed*, pp 327–31; King, 'Between Two Worlds', p 288; Dictionary of New Zealand Biography (DNZB), *Te Kingitanga: The People of the Maori King Movement*, Wellington/Auckland, 1996, pp 92ff; Williams, *Politics*, pp 118–19, 137–9, 144; King, *Te Puea*, pp 67–8, 102–3; Orange, *Treaty*, p 227; Hill, Richard S, 'The Policing of Colonial New Zealand', in Anderson, David M and Killingray, David (eds), *Policing the Empire: Government, Authority and Control, 1839-1940*, Manchester, 1991, p 67 (for 'absorption' quote); Love, pp 104–5, 144–5; Gould, Ashley, 'Maori Land Development 1929–1954: An Introductory Overview with Representative Case Studies', a report for the Crown Forestry Rental Trust, Wellington, 1996, p 59 (for 'averse' quote); McCan, David, *Whatiwhatihoe: The Waikato Raupatu Claim*, Wellington, 2001, pp 173–4.

66 Belich, *Making Peoples*, pp 263–4; Hutt, Marten, *Te Iwi Maori me te Inu Waipiro: He Tuhituhinga Hitori/Maori and Alcohol: A History*, Wellington, 1999, pp 61, 67, 83–4 (p 67 includes 'the man' quote; for a slightly different version, see Walker, *He Tipua*, p 218); Marr, 'Alienation', chs 3–4 and 'Rohe Potae, Part 2'.

67 Loveridge, 'Land Councils and Land Boards', pp 69, 76–8; Butterworth, 'Aotearoa',

ch 6, pp 26ff; Walker, *He Tipua*, pp 149–50; Frame, Alex, *Salmond: Southern Jurist*, Wellington, 1995, pp 112–14; Boast, Richard, 'Maori Land and the Treaty of Waitangi', in Boast, Richard, Erueti, Andrew, McPhail, Doug and Smith, Norman, *Maori Land Law*, Wellington, 1999, esp pp 282ff; Native Land Act 1909 (No 15); Hutton, 'Ready and Quick', p 31 (for 'Native lands' quote).

68 Hamer, David, *The New Zealand Liberals*, Auckland, 1988, pp 306–7; Willan, p 12; Walker, *He Tipua*, p 137–8; Loveridge, 'Land Councils and Land Boards' (includes 'integrated system' quote, p vii); Butterworth, 'Aotearoa', ch 6, pp 27–8 (for 'safeguards' and 'significant recognition' quotes); Butterworth, 'Politics of Adaptation', ch 9, pp 10ff; Hutton, 'Ready and Quick', pp 5, 14, 16 (for 'due consideration' quote), 30–1, 41; Campbell, S K L, 'National Overview on Land Consolidation Schemes 1909–1931', a report for the Crown Forestry Rental Trust, Wellington, 1998, ch 3; Love, pp 54, 139 (for 'reversal' and 'trading' quotes); Marr, 'Rohe Potae, Part 2', pp 8–9; Butterworth and Young, pp 66–7 (includes 'legal recognition' quote).

69 Ward, *Unsettled*, pp 159, 169; Butterworth and Young, pp 66–7; Loveridge, 'Land Councils and Land Boards', pp 75, 84ff, 115, 118; Walker, *He Tipua*, pp 172, 184; Butterworth, 'Apirana Ngata: Politics of Adaptation', ch 10, pp 4, 23 and 'Aotearoa', ch 6, p 31 (for 'proprietorship' quote); Hutton, 'Waikato–Maniapoto', p 30 (for 'agent' quote); Bennion, Tom, 'The Maori Land Court and Maori Land Boards 1909–1952', Waitangi Tribunal Rangahaua Whanui Series Working Paper, Wellington, 1997, p 40 (for 'facilitators' quote); Hutton, 'Ready and Quick', p 44 (for 'juggernaut' quotes).

70 Loveridge, 'Land Councils and Land Boards', pp 108 (for 'marginally' quote), 126–7 (includes 'check', 'the Judge' and 'vestige' quotes), 132; Butterworth, 'Aotearoa', ch 6, pp 32–9; Walker, *He Tipua*, p 184; Butterworth and Young, pp 68–9; Willan, p 13; Hutton, 'Waikato–Maniapoto', pp 17, 23, 25, 30 and 'Ready and Quick', pp 18, 44, 46; Bennion; Campbell, 'National Overview', pp 55ff; Marr, 'Rohe Potae, Part 2', pp 9–13, 28–9; Native Land Amendment Act 1913 (No 58); Love, p 148 (for 'steeped' quote).

71 Gardiner, Wira, *Te Mura o Te Ahi: The Story of the Maori Battalion*, Auckland, 1992, pp 13–22; Else (ed), pp 5–6, 23–4; Walker, *He Tipua*, pp 186–7; Gould, Ashley, 'Maori and the First World War', in McGibbon, Ian (ed), *The Oxford Companion to New Zealand Military History*, Auckland, 2000; Butterworth, 'Aotearoa', ch 7, pp 43–4, 50; O'Connor, P S, 'The Recruitment of Maori Soldiers, 1914–1918', *Political Science*, 19(2), 1967; Committee of the Maori Members of Parliament, 'A Description Concerning the Maori Contingent of Aotearoa and Te Waipounamu Who Took Part in the Great War', in Pugsley, Christopher, *Te Hokowhitu a Tu: The Maori Pioneer Battalion in the First World War*, Auckland, 1995, ch 1 [English translation] and chs 2–3 (includes 'good enough' quote, p 35).

72 Gould, 'First World War'; Walker, *He Tipua*, p 188; Gardiner, pp 16–22; King, *Te Puea*, p 81; Butterworth, 'Apirana Ngata: Politics of Adaptation', ch 11, pp 5–7; Pugsley, pp 45ff.

73 King, *Te Puea*, pp 77, 84–7; Butterworth, 'Aotearoa', ch 7, p 48; Walker, *He Tipua*, p 189; DNZB, *Kingitanga*, esp pp 95, 105, 114, 120; Baker, Paul, *King*

and Country Call: New Zealanders, Conscription and the Great War, Auckland, 1988;
King, 'Between Two Worlds', pp 285, 288; Hill, Iron Hand, pp 382–90; Pugsley,
pp 66–81.

74 Loveridge, 'Land Councils and Land Boards', pp 130–1; O'Malley, Vincent,
'Progressive Paternalism: Maori and the First Labour Government', in Race Gender
Class, 14, 1992; Butterworth, 'Aotearoa', ch 7, p 55; Butterworth and Young,
p 72; Walker, He Tipua, p 190; Thomson, Jane, 'The Rehabilitation of Servicemen
of World War II in New Zealand 1940 to 1954', PhD thesis, Victoria University of
Wellington, 1983; Native Department Report on the Working of the Native Land
Courts, Native Land Boards, and Native Land Purchase Board for Year Ended
31 March 1920, AJHR, 1920, G9, pp 2–3 (for 'small area', 'suitable' and 'occupation'
quotes).

75 Hunn, p 46 (for 'allowed to remain' quote); Butterworth, 'Aotearoa', ch 6, pp 20–1,
ch 7, pp 59, 64; Walker, He Tipua, pp 112–13, 230; Harris, Aroha, 'Maori Land
Title Improvement since 1945', NZJH, 31(1), April 1997, pp 135–6 (includes 'full
production' quotes); Bassett, Michael, Coates of Kaipara, Auckland, 1995, p 75;
Butterworth, 'Apirana Ngata: Politics of Adaptation', ch 12, pp 18–19; Ward,
Unsettled, pp 150–2; Prichard, Ivor and Waetford, Hemi, Report of the Committee of
Inquiry into the Laws Affecting Maori Land and Powers of the Maori Land Court,
Wellington, 1965, p 119 (for 'fractions of ownership' and 'farming' quotes); Wood,
F L W, This New Zealand, Hamilton, 1946, p 173 (for 'authority' quote); Love,
p 60 (for 'traditional' quote).

76 Butterworth, G V and S M, The Maori Trustee, Wellington, 1991, p 57 and Appendix
1; Hunn, pp 50, 54; Campbell, 'Urewera', ch 2 and 'National Overview', ch 3;
Gould, 'Land Development', pp 14, 21, 34; Butterworth, G V, 'Trustee Law and
the Trust Deed: Their Implications for Governance', unpublished manuscript,
Wellington, 1998 (includes 'requirements' quote); Wood, p 172 (for 'reconciling'
quote); King, Maori, p 200; Loveridge, 'Land Councils and Land Boards',
pp 137–40; Department of Maori Affairs, The Maori Today, Wellington, 1949, p 8.

77 Butterworth and Young, pp 73–4; Butterworth and Butterworth, pp 57–8; Walker,
He Tipua, p 233; Gould, 'Land Development', pp 13, 23, 72–3, 83; King, Te Puea,
pp 149–50, 156; Butterworth, 'Apirana Ngata: Politics of Adaptation', ch 12; Ngata,
Apirana T, 'Maori Land Settlement', in Sutherland (ed), p 96; Butterworth,
'Aotearoa', ch 7, pp 65–6; A Maori View of the 'Hunn Report', Christchurch, 1961,
p 23 (for 'replacement' and 'genius' quotes).

78 Walker, He Tipua, pp 241, 253; Loveridge, 'Land Councils and Land Boards',
pp 141–2; Department of Maori Affairs, The Maori Today, p 8; Wood, p 174;
Durie, Te Mana, p 141; Campbell, 'Urewera', pp 117–18; Gould, 'Land Development', pp 7, 21, 23, 34, 37, 49, 52–3, 72–3, 83–4; Owen, Graham, 'Case Study 1:
Tikitere Development Scheme', in Gould, 'Land Development', pp 93ff; Orange,
'Equality', p 81 (for 'mother and father' quote); Butterworth and Butterworth, ch
2ff; McClure, p 26 (for 'communistic' quote).

79 Burdon, R M, The New Dominion: A Social and Political History of New Zealand
1918–1939, Wellington, 1965, p 283 (for 'fuss' and 'allay' quotes); Walker, He
Tipua, pp 274ff (pp 287–8 for 'hurry' and 'communal bias' quotes); Gould, 'Land

Development', p 84 (for 'important part' and 'transformed' quotes); Love, pp 156ff; Butterworth and Butterworth, p 58; King, 'Between Two Worlds', pp 286–7, Butterworth and Young, pp 77–8; Butterworth, 'Aotearoa', ch 7, p 67; Walker, King, *Te Puea*, p 156–8; Sissons, 'Post-Assimilationist Thought', pp 54ff.

80   Butterworth and Young, pp 78–9; Burdon, pp 283–4 (for 'ethics' quote); Walker, *He Tipua*, pp 299ff, 315; Gould, 'Land Development', pp 32, 35, 40, 43–6, 49 (for 'committees' and 'communicate' quotes), 51 (for 'suspicion' quote), 69 (for 'dispossession' quote), 84; Love, pp 158–60; King, 'Between Two Worlds', p 293; Orange, Claudia, 'Fraser and the Maori', in Clark, Margaret (ed), *Peter Fraser: Master Politician*, Palmerston North, 1998; Orange, 'Equality', pp 17–18, 70–1 (for 'power' quote), 74–5; Hohepa, P W, *A Maori Community in Northland*, Wellington, 1964 (1970 ed), p 51; Sissons, 'Post-Assimilationist Thought'; Keesing, p 169 (for 'mana' quotes); Simpson, Tony, *Shame and Disgrace: A History of Lost Scandals in New Zealand*, Auckland, 1992, ch 8.

81   This discussion owes much to James Belich, esp 'Myth, Race and Identity', pp 18ff, and *Paradise Reforged*, pp 206ff. See also Else (ed), p 7; King, *Te Puea*, pp 98–9; Ngata, Apirana, *Te Tiriti o Waitangi*, Hastings, 1922 (1950 ed, Christchurch), pp 2, 8 (for 1922 and 'wishful thinking' quotes); Orange, *Treaty*, p 229; Rice, Geoffrey, *Black November: The 1918 Influenza Epidemic in New Zealand*, Wellington, 1988, ch 6; Armstrong; Condliffe, John B and Airey, Willis T G, *Short History of New Zealand*, Auckland, 1938 (rev ed), p 138 (for 'curious steps' quote); Butterworth, 'Aotearoa', ch 6, p 39 (for 'absurd' quote).

82   Walker, *Ka Whawhai*, p 191; Ballara, *Iwi*, p 312 (for 'institutionalisation' quote); King, 'Between Two Worlds', p 281; Marr, Cathy, 'Crown Policy Towards Major Crown/Iwi Claim Agreements of the 1940s and 1950s', a preliminary report for the Treaty of Waitangi Policy Unit, Wellington, 1990, pp 8, 43; Butterworth and Young, p 71; Burdon, p 279 (for 'hasten' quote); Butterworth, 'Apirana Ngata: Politics of Adaptation', ch 12, p 1; Evison, p 344; Armstrong; Hill, Richard S, *Settlements of Major Maori Claims in the 1940s: A Preliminary Historical Investigation*, Wellington, 1989, pp 2–3; Frame; Ngata, *Te Tiriti*; Waitangi Tribunal, *Ngai Tahu Report*, pp 1016-19.

83   Frame, ch 9; Walker, *He Tipua*, pp 200, 212 and *Ka Whawhai*, p 191; Butterworth, 'Apirana Ngata: Politics of Adaptation', ch 12, pp 26–7; Ballara, *Iwi*, pp 313, 325 (for 'powerhouse' quote).

84   Hill, *Settlements*, p 3; Walker, *He Tipua*, pp 221, 228; Ballara, *Iwi*, pp 313–15 (includes 'parliament', 'primary', and 'alternative' quotes), 320–1, 324.

85   Report of Royal Commission on 'Confiscated Native Lands and Other Grievances', *AJHR*, 1928, G7 ['Sim Commission']; Marr, 'Crown Policy', pp iv, 3, 7–8, 27–8, 43, 82–3; King, 'Between Two Worlds', p 291; Hill, *Settlements*, *passim* and pp 3, 6 and *Enthroning 'Justice Above Might'? The Sim Commission, Tainui and the Crown*, Wellington, 1989; Hunn, p 62; Cody, pp 154, 157 (for 'Maoris were vindicated' quote); Bassett, Heather, Steel, Rachel and Williams, David, *The Maori Land Legislation Manual*, vol 2, Wellington, 1994; Walker, *He Tipua*, p 228; Burdon, p 279; Keenan, Danny, 'Ma Pango Ma Whero Ka Oti: Unities and Fragments in Maori History', in Dalley, Bronwyn and Labrum, Bronwyn (eds), *Fragments: New*

Zealand Social and Cultural History, Auckland, 2000, p 46; McCan, pp 181–3, 189; Sorrenson (ed), *Na To Hoa Aroha*, vol 1, pp 202–3 and vol 2, p 52; Marr, Cathy, 'An Overview History of the Taranaki Confiscation Claim: From the Sim Commission to the Submission of Taranaki Claims to the Waitangi Tribunal', a report for the Waitangi Tribunal, Wellington, 1991, ch 3.

86 Cox, pp 116, 127; Elsmore, Bronwyn, *Mana from Heaven: A Century of Maori Prophets in New Zealand*, Tauranga, 1989, pp 270–1; Henderson, J McLeod, *Ratana: The Man, the Church, the Political Movement*, Wellington, 1972 (2nd ed), pp 26, 57 (for 'shoemaker' quote); King, *Maori*, p 166; Belich, 'Myth, Race and Identity', p 15; Ballara, Angela, 'Ratana, Tahupotiki Wiremu', in *DNZB*, vol 3, pp 414–18; Raureti, Moana, 'The Origins of the Ratana Movement', in King, Michael (ed), *Tihe Mauri Ora: Aspects of Maoritanga*, Auckland, 1978, p 46; King, 'Between Two Worlds', p 292 (for 'unite' quote).

87 Henderson, *passim*, esp pp 26, 29, 33, 57ff (includes 'Pakeha friends' quote); King, 'Between Two Worlds', p 292; Love, pp 63, 113–14, 170, 214, 220, 223; Hill, Richard S, 'Worthington, Arthur Bently', in *DNZB*, vol 2, pp 588–9; Raureti, p 51.

88 Cox, pp 127, 157; Henderson, pp 10, 40, 55, 57 (includes Baucke and 'hands' quotes); Jones, 'Maori Kings', p 155; Love, pp 170, 179, 220, 230–44, 258; Butterworth, 'Apirana Ngata: Politics of Adaptation', ch 12, p 24; Raureti, p 46; Butterworth, G V, 'A Rural Maori Renaissance? Maori Society and Politics 1920 to 1951', *Journal of the Polynesian Society (JPS)*, 81(2), June 1972, p 166.

89 King, *Nga Iwi*, pp 59, 67; Love, pp i–ii (includes 'system of government' quote), 10–11, 64–5 (includes 'grass roots' quote), 244, 252–4 (for 'Secondly' quote); Butterworth, 'Health of the Body'; Ballara, 'Ratana, Tahupotiki Wiremu'.

90 Ngata, 'Maori Land Settlement', p 138 (for 'adjustment' quote); Belich, 'Myth, Race and Identity', p 22; Sissons, 'Post-Assimilationist Thought', esp p 50; Pere, Rangimarie Rose, 'Te Wheke: Whaia te Maramatanga me te Aroha', in Middleton, Sue (ed), *Women and Education in Aotearoa*, Wellington, 1998, p 205 (for 'divide and rule' quote); Webster, Steven, *Patrons of Maori Culture: Power, Theory and Ideology in the Maori Renaissance*, Dunedin, 1998, ch 3 (esp pp 74, 83, 90, 95) and p 254; Butterworth, 'Maori Renaissance', pp 166, 176; Walker, *He Tipua*, p 237; Belich, *Paradise Reforged*, p 201 (for 'Maoritanga' quote).

91 Farland, Bruce, *Coates' Tale: War Hero, Politician, Statesman, Joseph Gordon Coates, Prime Minister of New Zealand, 1925–1928*, Wellington, 1995, pp 34–5; Butterworth, 'Health of the Body', pp 11–12; King, *Te Puea*, pp 130–1; Bassett, *Coates*; Walker, *Ka Whawhai*, pp 189, 194 and *He Tipua*, pp 204ff, 216; Keesing, pp 180 (for 'spirit', 'hope' and 'aims' quotes), 189 (for 'superimposition' and 'basis' quotes); Love, p 61 (for 'corporate' quotes); Belich, *Paradise Reforged*, p 466 (for 'brilliant strategy' quote).

92 Dow, p 117, 132, 148–51, 158ff; Else (ed), pp 8, 31–3; Ritchie, James E, *The Making of a Maori: A Case Study of a Changing Community*, Wellington, 1963, p 25 (for 'proto-national' quote); Orange, 'Equality', p 148; Hunn, pp 84–5; Fleras, 'A Descriptive Analysis of Maori Wardens in the Historical and Contemporary Context of New Zealand Society', PhD thesis, Victoria University of Wellington,

1980, pp 190, 268–9, and *Village Runanga*, p 16; Lange, *May the People Live*, p 258; Bryder, Linda, *A Voice for Mothers: The Plunket Society and Infant Welfare 1907–2000*, Auckland, 2003, pp xv, 35; Butterworth, 'Maori Renaissance', p 169; Hill, *Iron Hand*, pp 128–9; Maclean, F S, *Challenge for Health: A History of Public Health in New Zealand*, Wellington, 1964, pp 202–3; Durie, *Whaiora*, p 44 (for 'likelihood' quote).

93   Walker, *He Tipua*, pp 236–7; King, *Te Puea*, pp 132, 140, 152–4; King, 'Between Two Worlds', pp 291–2; Keesing, pp vii, xv, 179–80, 189, 193, 196 (for 'steady' quote); Marr, 'Crown Policy', pp 24 (includes 'resentment' quote), 28, 32–61 (includes 'back seat' quote, p 35); Love, pp 61–3; Orange, 'Fraser', pp 91–2; Report of Royal Commission on 'Confiscated Native Lands and Other Grievances', *AJHR*, 1928, G7.

94   Bassett, Michael and King, Michael, *Tomorrow Comes the Song: A Life of Peter Fraser*, Auckland, 2000, p 107; Orange, 'Equality', pp 27–40 (for 'gathering' and Pomare quotes), 50–1, 211, Appendix 1; Love, p 285 (for 'Tohungaism' quote); Orange, *Treaty*, p 233 and 'Fraser', pp 92–3 (for 'revolutionary' quote); Burdon, pp 291–2.

95   Love, pp 65–6, 72, 272, 276–8, 283; Orange, 'Equality', pp 41–6, 48–51, 211; Brown, Bruce, *The Rise of New Zealand Labour*, Wellington, 1962, pp 176–7; King, *Nga Iwi*, p 67; Orange, *Treaty*, p 234; Burdon, p 292; Bassett and King, p 107.

96   Burdon, pp 292–3; King, *Nga Iwi*, p 67; Condliffe and Airey, p 138; Walker, *He Tipua*, p 328; Orange, *Treaty*, p 239, and 'Fraser'; Waitangi Tribunal, *Raupatu Document Bank*, vol 137, Wellington, nd; Marr, 'Taranaki Confiscation Claim', chs 3–4, and 'Crown Policy', p 54 (for 'settled' and 'settler' quotes).

97   Burdon, p 293 (for 'equality of status' quotes); Walker, *He Tipua*, pp 327–8; Marr, 'Crown Policy', pp 61ff; Orange, 'Fraser', pp 93–4, 105 and 'Equality', pp 50ff (includes 'administrative wing' quote, p 55), 101, 108, 117–19, 235–7; Gustafson, Barry, *From the Cradle to the Grave: A Biography of Michael Joseph Savage*, Auckland, 1986; Butterworth and Young, p 79; Butterworth, 'Aotearoa', ch 8, p 70 (for 'rural equivalent' quote); Metge, Joan and Kinloch, Patricia, *Talking Past Each Other: Problems of Cross-cultural Communication*, Wellington, 1978.

98   Gould, 'Land Development', pp 21, 34, 42, 54–7; King, 'Between Two Worlds', p 294; Orange, 'Equality', pp 69, 76, 83, 119 (for 'ultimate objective' quote), 123, 211–15 and 'Fraser', pp 94–5, 105; McClure, Margaret, *A Civilised Community: A History of Social Security in New Zealand, 1898–1998*, Auckland, 1998, ch 2; Burdon, p 293 (for 'party committees' quote); Wood, p 167; Walker, *He Tipua*, p 331; Walker, Ranginui J, 'Maori People Since 1950', in Rice (ed), p 500; Grace, Patricia, Ramsden, Irihapeti and Dennis, Jonathan (eds), *The Silent Migration: Ngati Poneke Young Maori Club 1937–1948*, Wellington, 2001; Meek, R L, *Maori Problems Today: A Short Survey*, Wellington, nd; Butterworth and Young, p 93.

99   Love, pp 75, 96–7, 299–307 (includes 'wrongly advised' quote); Burdon, p 294; Orange, 'Equality', pp 59–60, 91–2, 121, 123, 129; Walker, *He Tipua*, pp 328, 340–1; Ballara, 'Ratana, Tahupotiki Wiremu'; Ballara, Angela, 'Ratana, Haami Tokouru', in *DNZB*, vol 4, pp 422–3.

100   McCan, pp 191ff; Hill, *Enthroning 'Justice Above Might'?*, p 9; Bassett and King, p 251; Marr, 'Crown Policy', pp 55ff (includes 'initiative' quote, p 55, and 'water'

quote, p 60); Mahuta, Robert, 'Tainui, Kingitanga and Raupatu', in Wilson and Yeatman (eds), p 25; O'Malley, 'Paternalism', p 267; Hill, *Settlements*; McClure, pp 111–12; Ballara, *Iwi*, p 316.

101 Blythe, Martin, *Naming the Other: Images of the Maori in New Zealand Film and Television*, Metuchen, 1994, pp 15–16; Said, Edward W, *Orientalism*, New York, 1978.

102 Simon, Judith and Smith, Linda Tuhiwai (eds), *A Civilising Mission? Perceptions and Representations of the Native Schools System*, Auckland, 2001, pp 10, 174, 187, 191–2, 198, 255; Love, p 388; Walker, 'Maori People', p 499; Orange, 'Equality', pp 23, 113–17; King, *Maori*, p 201 (for 'good farmer' quote); Burdon, p 286; Orange, 'Fraser', pp 95–6 (for 'vital' quote); Walker, *Ka Whawhai*, p 196. For an overview of Maori education, see Barrington, J M and Beaglehole, T H, *Maori Schools in a Changing Society: An Historical Review*, Wellington, 1974. Chapters in Sutherland (ed) provide interesting contemporary engagements with issues of relevance to this book.

103 Orange, Claudia, 'The Price of Citizenship? The Maori War Effort', in Crawford, John (ed), *Kia Kaha: New Zealand in the Second World War*, Melbourne, 2000 (2002 ed), p 237; Soutar, Monty, 'Maori War Effort Overseas in the Second World War', in McGibbon (ed); Walker, *He Tipua*, pp 318, 344–5; Gardiner, esp pp 23–5, 30, 178; Orange, 'Equality', p 127 and 'Fraser', p 99; Belich, 'Colonization', p 190; Orange, Claudia, 'Maori War Effort Organisation', in McGibbon (ed), p 307; Milne, Jonathan, 'War Inquiry into Ratana Members', *Sunday Star-Times*, 26 January 2003; Orange, Claudia, 'An Exercise in Maori Autonomy: The Rise and Demise of the Maori War Effort Organisation', *NZJH*, 21(1), April 1987, p 161. For general discussion on 'Better Britishness' see Belich, *Paradise Reforged*, Part 1. Some of the text in this chapter reflects investigation of archival sources at Archives New Zealand, and work in progress on the Treaty of Waitangi Research Unit's 'Rangatiratanga Project', which is being undertaken with the assistance of the Marsden Fund; it is, more generally, informed by the works of Love and Orange.

104 Walker, *He Tipua*, pp 339–42, 348; Orange, *Treaty*, pp 237–8; Soutar, p 307; Ngata, Apirana, 'The Price of Citizenship', Wellington, 1943; Edwards, p 163 (for 'you were fine' quote); Kernot, Bernard, 'Maori Buildings for the Centennial', paper presented to *Celebrating the 1940 Centennial* conference, Stout Research Centre for the Study of History, Society and Culture, Wellington, 1999; Phillips, Jock, 'Reading the 1940 Centennial', paper presented to *Celebrating the 1940 Centennial* conference, Stout Research Centre, 1999 (includes 1940 quotes); Orange, 'Price'; Butterworth and Young, p 84; Taylor, Nancy M, *The New Zealand People at War: the Home Front*, Wellington, 1986, pp 1241, 1294; Harrison, Noel, *Graham Latimer: A Biography*, Wellington, 2002, pp 67–8; Orange, 'Exercise' (including 'recognition' quote, p 160) and 'Equality', p 215 (for 'asset' quote).

105 Butterworth and Young, pp 84–5; Wood, pp 178–9; Orange, 'Exercise', pp 158ff, 'War Effort' in McGibbon (ed), p 307, and 'Price', pp 238ff; Love, pp 342ff; Taylor, p 1241.

106 Baker, J V T, *The New Zealand People at War: War Economy*, Wellington, 1965, pp 452–3; Wood, pp 179–80; Orange, 'War Effort' in McGibbon (ed), p 307 and

'Price', p 238; 'Maoris Farewell Liaison Officer', *Northern Advocate*, 18 July 1944; 'Aid to Maoris', *New Zealand Herald*, 21 June 1944.

107 Orange, 'Price', p 240 and 'War Effort' in McGibbon (ed), p 307; Ballara, *Iwi*, pp 317–18; Baker, *War Economy*, p 453; Taylor, p 1241; Butterworth, 'Maori Renaissance', p 186; Gilling, Tui, 'Rangatiratanga and the Crown in the Twentieth Century: Case Study Three', draft paper, Treaty of Waitangi Research Unit, 2003, p 9 (for 'willingness' quote); 'Maori War Effort Unexcelled Anywhere: A Voluntary Organisation Achieves Grand Record', *Standard*, 28 September, 1944 (for 'total war effort' quote).

108 Love, pp 333–4, 356, 363ff (for 'unprecedented' and 'responsibility' quotes, p 356, and 'greatest thing' quote, p 368); King, *Te Puea*, esp pp 206–9, 290 and 'Between Two Worlds', pp 298–9 (includes 'degree of acceptance' quote); Orange, 'Equality', pp 132–3 (includes 'success' quote), 142 and 'Exercise', pp 102 (for 'first time' quote), 162–4; Baker, J V T, p 453; Gilling, Tui, pp 9 (for 'agar' quote), 14–18 (includes 'plight' quotes); Cox, pp 102–3, 192; Jones, Reimana R, 'Jones, Michael Rotohiko', in *DNZB*, vol 4, Wellington/Auckland, 1998, pp 257–8; Butterworth and Young, pp 85–6; MA1/364, 19/1/219, Pt 1 (for quotes from official documents); McClure, p 120; Orange, 'Price', pp 240–1 and 'War Effort' in McGibbon (ed), p 307; Ballara, *Iwi*, pp 317–18; Wood, pp 165–7 (includes 'fundamental problem' quote), 179–80 (includes 'adjustment' and 'renewed confidence' quotes); 'Maori War Effort Unexcelled Anywhere: A Voluntary Organisation Achieves Grand Record', *Standard*, 28 September, 1944; Meek, p 39 (for 'unity' quote).

109 Love, pp 368ff; Orange, 'Equality', p 144, 'Price', p 241, 'War Effort' in McGibbon (ed), and 'Exercise', p 164–5 (includes 'took away' quote); Butterworth and Young, p 86; Bassett and King, p 251; Wood, p 165 (for 'nationality' quote). The debates can be followed in the files in Archives New Zealand, esp MA 1, 19/1/219. That some supporters of Maori self-determination saw a revival of the Maori Councils as a viable way forward complicated the discussions; this view can be seen, eg, in Meek, p 41.

110 Orange, 'War Effort' in McGibbon (ed), p 308, 'Price', pp 243–4 and 'Exercise', pp 164–5 (for 'degree of autonomy' quote); Butterworth and Young, p 85; Butterworth, 'Aotearoa', ch 8, p 75 (for 'radical' quote); Ballara, *Iwi*, pp 317–18; Love, pp 377ff (includes 'vital matter' quote, p 381); 'Maori War Effort Unexcelled Anywhere: A Voluntary Organisation Achieves Grand Record', *Standard*, 28 September 1944.

111 Orange, 'Exercise', pp 163–6, 'War Effort' in McGibbon (ed) and 'Equality', pp 143ff; Love, pp 368–77, 381–5, 389; Cox, pp 102–3; Marr, 'Crown Policy', pp 74–5 (includes 'trappings' quote); Thomson, pp 139–40; Labrum, Bronwyn, '"Bringing families up to scratch": The Distinctive Workings of Maori State Welfare, 1944–1970', *NZJH*, 36(1), October 2002, pp 163–4; Else (ed), p 33; Royal, Te Ahukaramu Charles and Jamison, Tom, 'Royal, Te Rangiataahua Kiniwe', in *DNZB*, vol 4, pp 443–4.

112 Maori Social and Economic Advancement Act 1945 (No 43); Butterworth and Young, pp 87, 92; Orange, 'Price', p 245 and 'Exercise', pp 166–8; Love, pp 389–96

(includes 'self administration' and 'future authority' quotes); Orange, 'Equality', pp 184–5 and 'Fraser', p 100; Butterworth, 'Aotearoa', esp ch 8, p 76 (for 'policy initiative' quote) and ch 9, p 1 (for 'comprehensive' and 'perpetuating' quotes); Metge, Joan, *A New Maori Migration: Rural and Urban Relations in Northern New Zealand*, London, 1964, p 88 (for 'recognise' quote).

113 Maori Social and Economic Advancement Act 1945 (No 43); Metge, Joan, *The Maoris of New Zealand: Rautahi*, London, 1976 (rev ed), pp 88, 207; Orange, 'Equality', pp 156 (for 'unthinkable' quote), 220–2; Ormsby, p 14 (for 'fewer powers' and 'empowered' quotes); Love, pp 395–7 (includes 'acceptability' quote); Department of Maori Affairs, *The Maori Today, passim*; Butterworth and Butterworth, p 57; Walker, *He Tipua*, p 372 (for 'advantages' quote).

114 The preceding paragraphs in this section – together with some coverage of negotiations elsewhere in this book – are partly informed by access to departmental archives by the author when working on Treaty claims negotiations in the 1990s. See also Hill, *Settlements*, pp 5ff (for Maori summit resolution, p 6, and 'well discussed' quote, p 8); Marr, 'Crown Policy', pp 76ff (includes 'high spirited' and 'only country' quotes, pp 79–80, and 'recognition' and 'visioned' quotes, pp 85–6); Love, p 374 (for 'settlement' quote); Ballara, *Iwi*, pp 318–19; Bassett and King, pp 252, 304; Ngaitahu Claim Settlement Act 1944 (No 33); Ngaitahu Trust Board Act 1946 (No 33), s 14; Taranaki Maori Claims Settlement Act 1944 (No 32); Waymouth, Lyn, 'The Bureaucratisation of Genealogy', *Ethnologies Comparées*, 6, Printemps, 2003; Waitangi Tribunal, *Ngai Tahu Report*, chs 21–2.

115 Hill, *Enthroning 'Justice Above Might'?*; Butterworth and Young, pp 89–90; Mahuta, Robert, 'The Maori King Movement Today', in King (ed), *Tihe Mauri Ora*, pp 36–7; Hill, *Settlements*, pp 8–10; Walker, *He Tipua*, pp 103, 332; Marr, 'Crown Policy', pp 76–87; Love, p 374; King, *Te Puea*, pp 223, 225 (includes 'quality of life' quote); McCan, ch 8; Waikato–Maniapoto Maori Claims Settlement Act 1946 (No 19); *Koroki – My King*, [Ngaruawahia], 1999, p 224.

116 Hill, *Settlements*, pp 9ff; Mahuta, 'Tainui', pp 26–7; Marr, 'Crown Policy', pp 89ff (including 'historians' quote, pp 93–4); Belgrave, Michael, 'Something Borrowed, Something New: History and the Waitangi Tribunal', in Dalley, Bronwyn and Phillips, Jock (eds), *Going Public: The Changing Face of New Zealand History*, Auckland, 2001, p 94; Walker, *Ka Whawhai*.

117 Taylor, pp 805ff, 1239, 1244 (including 'Maori problem' quote); Orange, 'Price', pp 245ff, 'Fraser', pp 100, 102, 'Equality', pp 158–60 and 'Exercise', p 169 (for 'self-controlling' quote); Beaglehole, Ernest and Pearl, *Some Modern Maoris*, Wellington, 1946; Cox, pp 105–6; Meek, esp pp 37–9; Love, pp 409, 470 (for 'self government' quote); Butterworth and Young, pp 88ff.

118 Department of Maori Affairs, *The Maori Today*, p 40; Gardiner, p 181 (for 'who's who' quote); Jones, 'Jones, Michael Rotohiko'; Labrum, p 165; Love, pp 400–1 (for 'heat and spirit' quote), 410, 420, 453, 470; Orange, 'Equality', pp 158–64, 187–8 and 'Fraser', pp 100–4; Butterworth and Young, p 92; Henderson, p 95; Bassett and King, p 333; King, 'Between Two Worlds', p 295 (for 'governed with his heart' and 'dispossessed' quotes).

119 Butterworth and Young, p 92 (for Maori Welfare Organisation and 'pack horses'

quotes); Orange, 'Price', p 246 and 'Equality', pp 192–3 (includes Fraser quotes); Gardiner, p 181; Dalley, Bronwyn, *Family Matters: Child Welfare in Twentieth-Century New Zealand*, Auckland, 1998, p 154 (for 'assistance' and 'betterment' quotes).

120 Henderson, pp 66, 107; Love, pp 411–22 (includes 'Maori world' and 'crumbs' quotes); Orange, 'Fraser'.

121 McClure, p 122–3; Bassett and King, p 334; Orange, 'Equality', pp 189–96 (includes Fraser quotes), 'Exercise', pp 168–70 (includes 'proposals and plans' quote), 'Fraser', p 104 (for 'wide' and 'botch' quotes) and 'Price'; Love, pp 401, 411–25 (includes 'prime objective' quote, p 423); Cox, pp 103–6 (includes 'philosophical' quote); Butterworth and Young, pp 88ff; Durie, *Whaiora*, pp 47–8; Department of Maori Affairs Report for Year Ended 31 March 1950, *AJHR*, 1950, G9, p 10.

122 Belich, *Paradise Reforged*, pp 467–8 (includes 'mortality' quote); Department of Maori Affairs, *The Maori Today*, pp 8 (for 'widely promoted' quotes), 38ff; Orange, 'Equality', pp 193–6 and 'Exercise', p 169; Love, pp 401 (for 'shell' quote), 412ff (includes 'fusion' quote); Cox, pp 102ff; Orange, 'Fraser', pp 102–6; Butterworth and Young, pp 88ff (includes 'floundering' quote, p 92); Te Puni Kokiri, *Discussion Paper on the Review of the Maori Community Development Act 1962*, Wellington, 1998; Else (ed), pp 9–10 (includes 'prerogative' quote); McClure, p 124; Rogers, Anna and Simpson, Miria (eds), *Te Timatanga Tatau Tatau: Early Stories from Founding Members of the Maori Women's Welfare League as Told to Dame Mira Szaszy*, Wellington, 1993, p xvi; Wood, p 176 (for 'puzzlement' quote); Department of Maori Affairs Report for Year Ended 31 March 1950, *AJHR*, 1950, G9, p 11.

123 Dunstall, *Policeman's Paradise?*, pp 120, 203ff; Department of Maori Affairs, *The Maori Today*, p 39; King, *Te Puea*, pp 252–6 (includes 'sacred pact' and 'rangatiratanga' quotes); Mahuta, 'Maori King', p 37; Hutt, pp 72ff (including 'aroha' and 'treated the same' quotes); Bollinger, Conrad, *Grog's Own Country: The Story of Liquor Licensing in New Zealand*, Wellington, 1959 (1967 ed), pp 104–7; Fleras, Augie, 'Maori Wardens and the Control of Liquor Among the Maori of New Zealand', *JPS*, (90)4, December 1981 (including 'treated differently' quotes, p 499), and *Village Runanga*, pp 21, 24 (for 'social conscience' quote); Hill, *Iron Hand*, p 245 and *Introducing Policing*; Belich, *Paradise Reforged*, p 472; Taylor, p 1294 (for 'good enough' quote); Henderson, p 66 (for 'Chief of Police' quote).

124 Hutt, pp 72–6; Henderson, p 66; Fleras, 'Maori Wardens'; Walker, Ranginui J, 'The Politics of Voluntary Association: The Structure and Functioning of a Maori Welfare Committee in a City Suburb', in Kawharu, I Hugh (ed), *Conflict and Compromise*; Sissons, 'Post-Assimilationist Thought', pp 57–9 (includes 'Maoritanga' concept); Butterworth and Young, p 93; Bollinger, p 111 (for 'feet' quote); Belich, *Paradise Reforged*, p 467 (for 'explosion' quote).

125 New Zealand Government, *The New Zealand Official Yearbook, 1951–52*, Wellington, 1952, pp 23, 42; Poulsen, M F and Johnston, R J, 'Patterns of Maori Migration', in Johnston, R J (ed), *Urbanisation in New Zealand: Geographical Essays*, Wellington, 1973, p 150; Pool; Belich, *Paradise Reforged*, pp 471–2 (includes 'predominantly urban' quote); Butterworth and Young, p 95; Dunstall, Graeme, 'The Social Pattern', in Oliver and Williams (eds), pp 400, 403; Ausubel, David P, *Maori Youth: A Psychoethnological Study of Cultural Deprivation*, New York, 1961, p 110.

126 King, 'Between Two Worlds', p 299; Ausubel, *Maori Youth*, pp 114–15; Butterworth and Young, pp 92–3; Bollinger, p 111 (for 'Natives' quote); Pearson, *Dream*, p 193; Butterworth, 'Maori Renaissance', p 188 and 'Aotearoa', ch 8, p 70 (for 'well-being', 'understanding' and 'empowering' quotes); Tirikatene, E, 'Maori Purposes Bill', memo of 30 Nov 1945, AAMK 869, 692e, Archives New Zealand, Wellington (for 'heart and soul' quotes); Department of Maori Affairs Report for Year Ended 31 March 1950, *AJHR*, 1950, G9, p 10. Meek, writing during the Second World War, has some perceptive analyses of the socio-political situation of Maori, as well as interesting prescriptions that both take into account Maori self-determination and give primacy to class.

127 Belich, *Paradise Reforged*, p 191; Wharemaru, Heeni and Duffie, Mary Katharine, *Heeni: A Tainui Elder Remembers*, Auckland, 1997, p 130 (for Te Puea quotes).

128 Dunstall, *Policeman's Paradise?*, p 121 (for 'average European' quote). For an overview of state–Maori relations covering the period from 1950 onwards, see Hill, 'Autonomy and Authority', pp 164ff; see too Walker, *Ka Whawhai*, and Michael King's summary of, in effect, historiography on the issue in the 'Unsettlement' section of his *Penguin History of New Zealand*.

INDEX